Regulating Infrastructure

Regulating Infrastructure

Monopoly, Contracts, and Discretion

José A. Gómez-Ibáñez

Harvard University Press

Cambridge, Massachusetts, and London, England | 2003

Library of Congress Cataloging-in-Publication Data

Gómez-Ibáñez, José A., 1948–
    Regulating infrastructure : monopoly, contracts, and discretion /
José Gómez-Ibáñez.
        p.   cm.
    Includes bibliographical references and index.
    ISBN 0-674-01177-5 (alk. paper)
    1. Contracting out.   2. Privatization.   3. Public contracts.
    4. Government ownership.   I. Title.

    HD3860.G66 2003
    363.6—dc21   2003041745

To Nan

Contents

Acknowledgments

Many people have taught me about regulation, but I am especially indebted to John R. Meyer, Raymond Vernon, and the faculty and participants in the Infrastructure in a Market Economy executive program at Harvard's Kennedy School of Government. John Meyer has made many contributions to the study of regulation, including being one of the first to document the problems caused by U.S. railroad and airline regulation in the late 1950s. I was a member of the research teams he assembled to study the effects of airline and railroad deregulation in the 1980s, and we coauthored a book on the privatization of transport. Meyer taught me, among other things, to think of regulation as a last resort, given the inherent difficulties of the task. He was among the first to appreciate the potential importance of private contracts as a substitute for government regulation, an idea that plays a key role in this book.

Ray Vernon was more willing than most economists to entertain the idea that there might not be a lasting solution to problems, and that history might offer cautionary lessons for the present. This perspective was illustrated by his argument, first advanced in 1970, that the presence of multinational companies in developing countries was an "obsolescing bargain." The countries initially welcomed the foreigners for the capital, technical expertise, and access to overseas markets they offered. But these advantages declined over time as the locals gained experience. Eventually the natural desire of the countries to control their economic resources and destiny reasserted itself. When the movement to privatize infrastructure swept the developing world in the 1990s, Vernon was one of the first to worry that it would prove to be another example of an obsolescing bargain. He was no fan of public enterprises, having worked for many years to improve their performance without much success. But he encouraged me to read the histories of the firms that were being privatized to understand why they had once been nationalized, and to think about the risk that nationalization might happen again. Chapters 6 and 7 particularly are a product of this prodding.

My interest in regulation would not have grown into a book without the challenge of developing programs on infrastructure regulation for senior executives. This project grew out of concern among faculty at Harvard and staff at the World Bank and the Inter-American Development Bank (IDB) that countries were privatizing very fast, without adequate thought given to the regulatory institutions that were critical to long-term success. The programs brought together faculty interested in the topic and, equally important, senior officials from around the world who were involved in privatizing, regulating, financing, and managing infrastructure. The sessions were taught by the case method, and the discussions served as a laboratory to test whether the faculty's concepts and arguments were persuasive and helpful to men and women with practical responsibility in the field. Many of the examples presented in this book began as teaching cases in these executive programs.

At the Kennedy School I owe a particular debt to Henry Lee and Kathy Eckroad for being my partners in developing the Infrastructure in a Market Economy executive program, and to Ashley Brown, Jack Donahue, Alexander Dyck, Willis Emmons, Bill Hogan, David Luberoff, John Meyer, Ray Vernon, Jay Walder, Lou Wells, and the other members of the 1997–98 faculty seminar on infrastructure privatization and regulation for their stimulating discussions of the concepts and teaching cases we used in the program. Officers at the Inter-American Development Bank, particularly Terry Powers, Faith Wheeler, and Jim Wylde, provided critical early support by funding the development of cases and by sending some of the best IDB staff to attend and contribute. Later the IDB, led by Roberto Manrique, supported the creation of the Latin American University Regulation and Infrastructure Network (LAURIN), an association of eight universities (including Harvard) involved in research and executive training on private utilities. At the World Bank I owe a special debt to Antonio Estache, who designed the bank's executive program for transport regulators, invited me to teach in it, supported the development of cases used at both the bank and the Kennedy School, and has been a friend and advisor ever since.

The cases would not have been possible without assistance from many people. At the risk of some unfairness, I would like to single out Ian Byatt, who explained the pressures on him as Britain's water regulator; John Diandas, with whom I enjoyed spirited arguments about Sri Lanka's buses; Stephen Glaister, who guided me through the British railway industry; Jorge Kogan, the architect of transport reform in Argentina; and Martín Rodríguez-Pardina, who helped me understand electricity in Latin America. Alan Altshuler, my colleague at Harvard, was especially helpful in advising me on the relevant political science literature. Thanks also to the anonymous referees enlisted by Harvard University Press and to Michael Aronson and Elizabeth Gilbert of the Press for the many improvements they made to the manuscript. Doctoral students are the lifeblood of academia, and I learned a great deal from my conversations with Christoph Meier, Christopher Shugart, and Sashi Verma while they were working on their dissertations on regulation. I began this book in the fall of 1998 while on sabbatical at the University of California Transportation Center at Berkeley, where Martin Wachs and Melvin Webber were my gracious hosts. Thanks also to the Brookings Institution for permission to publish Chapter 8, which appeared in an earlier form (coauthored with John R. Meyer) as "Government and Markets in Transport: The U.S. Experience with Deregulation," in *Governance amidst Bigger, Better Markets,* edited by John D. Donahue and Joseph S. Nye, Jr. (Washington, D.C.: Brookings Institution, 2001). Obviously none of those named is responsible for the errors I have made.

Finally, I would like to thank my wife, Nanette Wilson, who has always supported this effort, even though I was often distracted by it. My mother-in-law, observing the painful process, concluded that it was much better to read books than to write them. I plan to take her advice, at least for a while.

Regulating Infrastructure

1

Monopoly as a Contracting Problem

The Search for Commitment

Interest in the regulation of private infrastructure increased during the last two decades of the twentieth century, when many countries turned to private companies to build and operate infrastructure and utility services. In the 1980s Britain was a leader, selling off its telephone, electricity, gas, water, and railway companies in the hopes that the private sector could provide better service at a lower cost. In the 1990s many other countries followed suit, particularly in Latin America but also in Southeast Asia, Austral-Asia, and Europe. For example, almost all of the new high-performance expressways and many of the new power plants opened in developing countries in the 1990s were built by private concessionaires. By the end of the century, most of the major railways and telephone companies and many of the electric companies in Latin America had been sold or offered as concessions to private operators as well.

One fear is that this latest round of privatization will not last. By the first years of the twenty-first century a backlash of sorts had already developed. Investors in many of the newly privatized utilities were voicing disappointment about the returns that they were earning. Meanwhile, consumers were increasingly skeptical that the tariffs they were being charged were fair and the service adequate. Several well-publicized failures—such as the collapse of California's private wholesale electricity market in 2000 and the bankruptcy of Britain's private rail infrastructure company in 2001—suggested to many that privatization had gone too far.

History cautions that this disenchantment may grow to the point where governments begin to take back the companies. Private provision of infrastructure was the norm throughout the world during the first half of the twentieth century, but this era ended with most private infrastructure companies being bought out or expropriated by government. Many of the utilities that Britain privatized in the 1980s had been nationalized only in the 1940s

1

and 1950s, for example, while many Latin American companies privatized in the 1990s had been nationalized as recently as the 1960s and 1970s.

The United States managed to retain a significant private presence in infrastructure throughout the twentieth century, which suggests that privatization can be a long-term solution in some circumstances. France also maintained private provision of certain municipal utilities, most notably water and solid waste, although it nationalized its electricity, telephone, and railway companies. But the U.S. and French experiences with private infrastructure have not been wholly satisfactory either. Concern about corruption in the award of private infrastructure concessions increased in France during the 1990s, for example, after French municipalities were granted more autonomy. And in the 1970s and 1980s, while other countries were beginning to shift to private but government-regulated utilities, the United States became so dissatisfied with that strategy that it deregulated its private railroads, airlines, long-distance telephone services, and natural gas pipelines.

Fifty years from now we may look back to view private provision of infrastructure as the norm, and public provision as a failed experiment of the mid-twentieth century. Indeed, the U.S. movement to deregulate suggests that the ultimate goal in infrastructure may be to dispense not just with public provision but, where possible, with public regulation as well. Nevertheless, it is striking that the United States was the only country that was able to maintain private ownership of most of its utilities throughout the twentieth century. In most other cases, the private providers were eventually taken over by government.

Many proponents of private infrastructure view the problem as one of establishing a commitment to a fair and stable set of rules governing the relationship between the government and private infrastructure providers. The usual concern is that the government will renege on commitments to private infrastructure rather than vice versa. Private companies are vulnerable because infrastructure requires expensive, durable, and immobile investments in roadways, power plants, local telephone or water lines, or other facilities that private investors can't withdraw if the government changes the rules.

In this view, the government usually feels compelled to regulate the prices and quality of infrastructure services because the services are essential to modern life and because infrastructure has elements of monopoly, so that consumers are at the mercy of a single provider. To induce private investment in infrastructure, the government also must commit to a schedule of tariffs and other terms that give the investors a reasonable return. Once the investments are in place, however, the government will be tempted to yield to popular pressures to lower tariffs or renege on other promises to the companies, knowing that they can't retaliate by withdrawing their investments. A government that engages in such opportunistic behavior is likely to have trouble convincing investors to renew or expand their facilities. If the facilities are long lived, however, the government may hope that some other solution will emerge in the interim, such as a crop of new investors naive enough to overlook a history of broken promises.

This account is one-sided, however, in that it focuses on the company's vulnerability to opportunism by government and downplays government and consumer vulnerability to opportunism by the company. The government and consumers are vulnerable because the incumbent local infrastructure company usually enjoys a monopoly, and that monopoly stems largely from the durability and immobility of both the company's and the consumers' investments. The company's durable and immobile investments discourage competitors from entering the market to challenge the incumbent. Potential challengers realize that an incumbent, fearful of losing the market, could rationally drop prices so that they just cover its short-run variable costs, leaving little chance for the challenger to recover its investments. And consumers also typically make durable and immobile investments in their local communities that make it difficult for them to move elsewhere in search of cheaper infrastructure services. In these circumstances, the customers of the infrastructure company, or the government acting on the customers' behalf, will want some commitment that the local infrastructure company will not take advantage of its position by raising prices well above costs. In short, the expensive, durable and immobile investments help make all parties—the company, its customers, and the government—vulnerable to opportunism and desirous of stability and commitment.

The prospects for commitment are complicated, however, by the long lives of most infrastructure investments. In the case of a highway, for example, the paving may last ten or twenty years, the bridges and the sub-base for forty years or more, and the basic grading and right of way indefinitely. How realistic is the desire for commitments that last as long as infrastructure assets, particularly in a world where the infrastructure companies, their customers, and governments have complex needs that may change in ways that are difficult to anticipate? What are the basic forms that commitment can take? And how can one design schemes that balance the desire for commitment with the need for flexibility to accommodate unexpected developments?

The basic perspective of this book is that the problem of infrastructure monopoly is similar to any other long-term contracting problem, and particularly analogous to contracting in private sector procurement. Infrastructure is not the only sector of the economy that employs assets so durable and specialized that their suppliers and users are vulnerable to each other. The developer of a shopping center and the lead tenant are often vulnerable to each other, for example, as are the power plant and the coal mine that supplies it. The usual remedy in other sectors is to sign a long-term contract before such specialized investments are made. One hundred percent of a new shopping center need not be preleased, but a significant portion is usually required before financing is forthcoming. And most lead tenants would never move in without the protection of a multiyear lease.

From this perspective, monopoly does not necessarily require government intervention. Just as private long-term contracts can protect suppliers and users of other durable assets, they may be able to protect utility companies and their customers as well. Whether government regulation is necessary and the form it should take will depend fundamentally on how difficult it is to negotiate and enforce an explicit long-term contract. Before we explore these issues, it is helpful to define infrastructure and review the various reasons, including monopoly, why government is so often involved in its provision.

Motives for Government Involvement in Infrastructure

Infrastructure has special characteristics that have traditionally justified or encouraged government involvement. Infrastructure means beneath *(infra)* the building *(structure),* and thus usually encompasses services or facilities that are underground, such as piped water and sewerage, or that lie on the surface, such as roads and railways. Electric power and telecommunications are often included as well, even though they are frequently provided by lines strung on poles or towers rather than in underground conduits. All of these industries involve networks that distribute products or services over geographic space, and in most cases the networks are capital extensive and the investments are durable and immobile. Infrastructure industries are often called public utilities, and the two terms will be used interchangeably here.

One motivation for government involvement, and the primary focus of this book, is the tendency toward monopoly in infrastructure industries. This tendency arises because many infrastructure networks have the characteristics of a so-called natural monopoly, which are a combination of durable and immobile investments and strong economies of scale or traffic density. The economies of scale mean that the cheapest way to serve a community is with a single company, particularly if the local network has a relatively low density of traffic. And the durability and immobility of the investments increase the risk for new entrants who seek to challenge the incumbent. Concern over monopoly often leads the government either to provide infrastructure services itself or to regulate the prices and quality of service of private infrastructure companies.

A second motive for government involvement—and one that often predates and enhances concerns about monopoly—is the difficulty of assembling the right of way required for an infrastructure network. Railroads, highways, and power, water, and telephone lines all require long, linear, and contiguous rights-of-way that would be difficult to assemble without the government's power to expropriate private property through the process of eminent domain. Absent the threat of eminent domain, private landowners along the alignment could extort high prices for key or missing parcels. The government often exercises the power of eminent domain on behalf of infrastructure companies, or allows the companies to place their pipes or lines in local streets or other publicly owned rights of way. Governments are hesitant to delegate eminent domain powers to private companies or to grant companies unrestricted access to local streets, however, for fear these privileges will be abused. Moreover, the understandable reluctance of the government to expropriate property for new infrastructure rights of way can contribute to monopoly by making it harder for a new company to enter the business and challenge the incumbent.

A third rationale for government involvement is that some types of infrastructure generate benefits beyond those that accrue to its immediate users or subscribers. For example, clean drinking water and sanitary waste disposal protect the general public from the spread of disease and the contamination of the environment. Similarly, a lamp outside a private residence or business reduces the risk of accidents and crime for neighboring properties and passersby. If important benefits of infrastructure services accrue to nonsubscribers, then it may be difficult to persuade subscribers to pay voluntarily for the level of service that is socially desirable. Nonuser benefits have stimulated governments to promote infrastructure provision in a variety of ways. Most city governments contract directly with electricity companies for street lighting, for example, and compel all households and businesses to subscribe to piped water and sewerage services.

Economic development and equity considerations are two additional and related motives for government intervention, and they also often enhance monopoly concerns. Infrastructure is viewed as an important ingredient to local economic development, and thus governments are often concerned about the infrastructure endowments of lagging or underdeveloped regions of their countries. Similarly, ensuring universal access to a basic level of infrastructure services is often thought to be important to the protection of equal opportunity for individual citizens, much as universal access to basic education and basic health care is. Infrastructure may not be deemed as essential to development and equal opportunity as education or health, but it is often just behind.[1]

These developmental and equity considerations have led governments to encourage the development of more extensive infrastructure networks than can be financed with the tariffs that users are willing to pay. Many governments have created special programs to support rural electrification, telephones, and roads, for example, in the belief that such important services ought to be available throughout the country. Similarly, many countries try to keep the tariffs for basic levels of service low so that even poor households can afford piped water, electricity, and a telephone. Developmental and equity considerations also have led some governments to promote monopoly and limit competition, so as to allow the infrastructure company to charge some customers prices in excess of costs and use the proceeds to cross-subsidize low tariffs in rural areas or for poor households.

A final motivation for government involvement in infrastructure is to reduce safety and environmental problems. Railroads, highways, and power lines present safety hazards to both users and nonusers, for example, while power plants, locomotives, and motor vehicles pollute the environment. To the extent that these risks fall on nonusers, the government often feels justified in regulating the harms on the public's behalf. And even if the safety and health risks fall on users, government intervention may be warranted if users are not well enough informed to judge the hazards that they are being exposed to. In most countries, the regulators in charge of safety and environmental concerns are separate from those responsible for controlling monopoly. The separation is designed to avoid any potential conflict of interest between setting tariffs and setting health and safety standards.

The Nature of Monopoly

Sources of Market Power

When one is assessing the degree of competition that a firm faces, the concept of market power is more helpful than that of monopoly. Monopoly is defined as a single seller serving a market. Market power is usually defined as the degree to which a company can raise the prices for its products above its costs without losing too many sales. Monopoly can be misleading, because the presence of only a single seller is neither a necessary nor a sufficient condition for effective market power. Even if there is only one seller in a market, for example, that firm may not be able to charge prices above costs if it believes that doing so will simply invite many other firms to enter the market and compete with it. Similarly, even if there are several sellers in a market, they may find ways to collude so as to effectively inhibit competition.

Two conditions are necessary for a firm to have market power. The first is the presence of some type of barrier that prevents other firms from entering the market to provide competing services. Barriers to entry can be either created by governments or firms or inherent in the technology of the industry. Examples of created barriers are the patent protections that governments award to inventors and the brand loyalty that some firms attempt to develop through extensive advertising. The primary example of an inherent barrier is the combination of large economies of scale and durable and immobile investments commonly referred to as a natural monopoly.

The second condition is that there must be few close substitutes to the good or service in question. Even if there are barriers to entry, the firm serving the market will not have much power over its customers if they can find close substitutes to the services it provides. These substitutes might be similar goods or services or alternative locations where the identical good is produced or sold. The idea is to avoid defining the market too narrowly by overlooking the competition provided by alternative products and sources of supply.

To illustrate these two conditions, consider local buses, which provide an example of a service that is likely to be highly competitive. Buses are mobile and not very durable, and studies show that economies of scale in local bus services are exhausted with fleets of twenty-five to fifty buses. Thus it is usually possible to have several firms serve a single city, or a single corridor within a city. Moreover, the private automobile usually competes with the bus in high-income countries, while walking, bicycles, and motorcycles often provide competition in low-income countries and where climates are mild.

At the other extreme, the distribution of piped water to residential neighborhoods is usually a classic natural monopoly. Underground pipes last fifty years or more, and there are strong economies of scale because it is more economical to serve all the households on a street from a single pipe than from two or three competing parallel pipes. One pipe is cheaper because the cost of digging and back-filling the trench for the pipe and the cost of the pipe itself do not increase proportionately with the pipe's capacity. Moreover, the alternatives to piped water—such as private wells, tanker trucks, or bottled water—are usually more expensive and less convenient. As a result, a local piped water company often faces little effective competition and could price its services well above costs.

Within any given infrastructure industry, market power often varies according to the types of customers involved or the specific circumstances of the firm. Freight railroads typically have less market power over shippers of high-value, manufactured commodities than they do over shippers of low-value, bulk commodities, for example, since trucks are a more viable alternative for manufactured than for bulk commodities, especially over short distances. Similarly, a railroad may have limited market power even over shippers of bulk commodities if it competes with a navigable waterway.

The degree of market power can also vary among the different stages or components of an infrastructure service. Many countries recently have broken up or unbundled their electric utilities into separate companies for generation, long-distance transmission, and local distribution, because electricity generation is potentially competitive while transmission and distribution are not. Similarly, wireless, long-distance, and local telephone services are now often provided by separate companies, because competition is possible in long-distance and wireless services but more difficult in local hard-wire services.

In addition, market power varies over time as markets and technologies evolve. The potential for competition in electricity generation increased in the last several decades after technological advances reduced the minimum size of a cost-efficient power plant. Competition in long-distance telephony was made possible by the development of microwave, satellite, and fiber optic transmission technologies. Competition in local telephony may become more effective in the future if wireless technologies become more cost-competitive with the hard-wire local telephone line.

Natural Monopoly and Long-Term Contracts

Natural monopoly is the most important form of barrier to entry in infrastructure. Created or artificial barriers are common as well, particularly those established by governments reluctant to exercise powers of eminent domain to create new infrastructure rights of way or desirous of protecting cross-subsidies that support low tariffs for poor customers or remote sections of the network. But natural monopoly is the most common barrier, and harder to avoid since it is inherent in the technology.

Most descriptions of natural monopoly stress the importance of large economies of scale and underplay the role of durable and immobile investments in establishing the barrier to entry. Economies of scale occur when average or unit costs of a firm fall as volume increases. If the economies extend over volumes sufficient to serve the entire market, then it will be cheaper for a single firm to serve the market rather than two or more. And since a larger firm always has a cost advantage over a smaller one, only one firm is likely to serve the market at any given time.

In telecommunications and transportation industries, economies of scale are sometimes confused with network economies. In network economies, an infrastructure network is more valuable to each of its subscribers the more other subscribers it allows them to connect with. This implies that larger networks will have an advantage over smaller networks in recruiting new subscribers, and that the most valuable network of all is one that allows the entire universe of subscribers to communicate with one another. Network economies mean that a universal interconnected network is likely to emerge because of the advantages it offers subscribers, but it does not mean that the network inevitably will be operated by a single firm. That occurs only if there are economies of scale in the supply of networks such that it is cheaper for one firm to provide a universal network than for several independent or interconnected firms to do so.[2]

Despite the emphasis traditionally placed on them, economies of scale are arguably less important than durable and immobile investments in establishing the barrier to entry in natural monopoly. Economies of scale mean that only one firm will serve the market at any given time, but they don't prevent "hit and run" competition. If investments are short-lived or mobile, then the threat of entry by a challenger is still credible, because both the incumbent and the challenger have the option of exiting the market and taking their investments with them. If investments are durable and immobile, by contrast, then neither firm can exit the market without losing its investments. The most likely result of entry is a punishing price war that ends with either the challenger or the incumbent losing its investments. And if capital costs account for a large portion of total costs and the facilities are long-lived, an incumbent is likely to drop prices sharply and keep them low for a long time until the challenger is driven off.[3] Indeed, some economists argue that durable and immobile investments, not economies of scale, are *the* defining characteristic of infrastructure monopolies.[4]

An effective monopoly in local infrastructure depends on the customers, as well as the company, making durable and immobile investments. The customers make their durable and immobile investments when they establish their residences and businesses in the territory served by the infrastructure company. These investments include the time a family must spend to find a suitable local home, job, and schools for the children, for example, or the resources a business devotes to developing a local workforce or customer base. The households and businesses could conceivably move to another community if their local infrastructure company increased prices. The costs of replacing their local and immobile investments are so high, however, that relocation is seldom a realistic option.

Seen in this way, the problem of an infrastructure monopoly is a variant of a larger and more common problem of relationship-specific investments in procurement.[5] Often a supplier and a customer can reduce their costs by making investments specific to their relationship. A parts manufacturer and an automobile company it supplies might be able to cut costs by, for example, investing in specialized machinery or training or by moving their plants closer together. If the investments are durable and specific to the relationship, however, then the party that makes them becomes vulnerable to opportunistic behavior by the other. Once the parts manufacturer invests in specialized machinery, the auto company can demand lower prices, knowing that the parts manufacturer has no other use for the machines. There are a variety of methods to allow suppliers and customers to make relationship-specific investments by protecting them from opportunism, but one of the most common is the long-term contract. In our auto parts example, neither the parts manufacturer nor the automobile company is likely to invest in specialized machinery without a contract guaranteeing certain prices and quantities.

The infrastructure natural monopoly is a variant of the procurement problem in which relationship-specific investments are not optional but are an inevitable consequence of the technology. It is hard for an infrastructure company to avoid investments in durable and immobile facilities or for its customers to avoid investments specific to their communities. The company's facilities cannot be transported to other locations if the local customers, or the government representing those customers, insist on price reductions. And the customers can't easily relocate if the infrastructure company decides to raise prices.

As in the more general procurement problem, one way to protect against opportunism is to sign a long-term contract before making the relationship-specific investments. And as in the general procurement problem, these contracts need not involve the government: they can be private contracts between the infrastructure company and individual customers. Private contracts are not far-fetched, particularly for customers that purchase such large quantities of infrastructure services that it is worthwhile to spend the time and resources needed to negotiate a contract. A manufacturer might find it worthwhile to negotiate long-term rates with the local railroad, power, or water company, for example, before it invested in a plant in their community. Similarly, a local railroad or water company might insist on a long-term contract before it built a special spur or a major water main to the manufacturer's plant.

Government regulation can be viewed as a substitute for private contracts, used when it is too costly or difficult for the companies and customers to reach individual agreements. In effect, the government contracts with the infrastructure company on the customers' behalf. In some cases the agreement between the government and the companies takes the form of an explicit contract, as in the franchise or concession contracts that governments often grant infrastructure companies. In other cases the understanding is less detailed and more flexible.

The Range of Solutions to Monopoly

The solutions to monopoly can be arrayed along a continuum according to the relative roles that markets and politics play in determining infrastructure prices and service quality, as shown in Figure 1.1. At one extreme prices and quality are determined largely or entirely by markets, at the other extreme largely by politics, and in between by a mixture of the two. Along the continuum from markets to politics the basis for commitment gradually shifts from commercial contracts and courts, to specialized regulatory institutions, and finally to the broader social and political institutions and interests that shape public policy.

There are many variants and hybrids along the continuum, but most can be assigned to one of four main groups or categories. *Private contracts* between

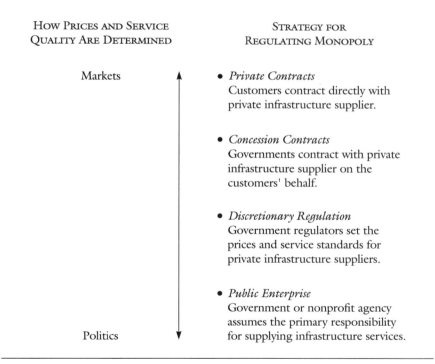

Figure 1.1 The range of solutions to monopoly.

infrastructure companies and customers is the category in which the market plays the largest role and politics the smallest. Politics is involved because the legislature and the courts enact and enforce the laws that govern private commercial contracts. But within that general legal framework, infrastructure suppliers and their customers negotiate voluntary agreements about the prices to be paid and the quantities and qualities of services to be provided.

The next alternative is *concession contracts,* which were popular in many parts of the world in the nineteenth century and were rediscovered and improved in the late twentieth century. Under this scheme the government awards a private firm a concession or franchise to provide a specific infrastructure service for a limited period of time, typically ten or twenty years. The services the concessionaire must provide and the maximum tariffs it can charge are specified in the concession contract. The contract is usually awarded competitively, often to the bidder proposing the lowest tariff for a specified level of service. The government monitors the concessionaire's performance to make sure it is in compliance with the contract, but neither it nor the concessionaire is supposed to unilaterally change the contract after it is awarded.

Concession contracts increase the role of politics by substituting contracts between the private suppliers and governments for contracts between the suppliers and individual customers. In effect the government represents consumers in deciding what combination of price and service quality would be best. Market forces still play a major role, however, because the concessionaire signs the contract voluntarily and the contract is not supposed to be changed subsequently without his agreement. If the contract is awarded competitively, moreover, consumers have some assurance that the concessionaire's expected profits will not be excessive relative to those of firms in competitive markets.

The third alternative is *discretionary regulation,* which is used extensively in the United States and Britain and has been applied selectively in many developing countries. The discretionary approach involves creating a government regulatory agency with the power to unilaterally establish the infrastructure firm's tariffs and service standards. The legislation establishing the regulatory agency usually sets out the principles the agency must consider when making its decisions. And the agency's decisions can usually be appealed to the courts or some other tribunal on the grounds that it has not followed its statutory guidance. The principles and guidelines are stated in fairly broad terms, however, in contrast to the highly specific language of a concession contract. The broad language gives the regulator substantial discretion and flexibility to respond to novel or unforeseen circumstances.

The discretionary approach increases the role of politics further by abandoning the effort to describe all the commitments between the government and the infrastructure company in an explicit contract. The market is still importantly involved, however, because the regulated firm depends entirely or in part on private capital markets to finance its investments. If the regulatory agency's decisions are too harsh, the company will not be able to raise capital to replace worn-out facilities or to accommodate growth in demand. But to the extent that the assets are durable and provide adequate capacity, the consequences of harsh decisions may not be apparent for many years.

The final option is to give the responsibility for providing the infrastructure services to a *public or nonprofit enterprise*. Private firms might still be involved as contractors to the public agency, but the contracts would be more limited in scope or duration than a concession. And markets are still influential, since the public agency's revenues are affected by the prices consumers are willing to pay for its services while the agency's costs are affected by the prices it has to pay in the labor, equipment, materials, and other input markets. The main difference is that the enterprise responsible for the service is not owned and controlled by private investors, so that it may have less incentive to take advantage of its monopoly position by charging prices above costs.

The Plan of This Book

This volume explores the advantages and disadvantages of these regulatory options and various hybrids in different industries and countries. Almost all the attention is devoted to the first three options: private contracts, concession contracts, and discretionary regulation. While the choice between private and public provision overshadows the entire discussion, it is a complex topic that has been studied by many others.[6] This volume assumes that private provision of infrastructure is generally desirable, particularly if the problems of regulating monopoly can be solved in a politically acceptable and economically sensible way. The main question is what those acceptable and sensible solutions might be.

The book draws on the existing literature on regulatory economics and politics to set out the basic regulatory options and then explores how these options work in the real world by examining specific cases in which they have been applied. The case approach is critical, because the key questions are empirical. Each regulatory strategy has its strengths and limitations in theory, but how powerful are these strengths and limitations in practice? Cases are also valuable because they allow one to examine how the interplay of economics, politics, and institutions affects regulatory commitment and performance. Some researchers have tried to examine this interplay using large data sets, and their results are reported here. Few such data sets exist, however, and they capture only a portion of the many variables that might be involved. To appreciate how regulation works in practice, there is simply no substitute for examining the evolution of a specific concession contract or the history of a particular regulatory agency.

The undeniable danger of using cases is that the selection may be so unrepresentative that the generalizations developed from it are misleading. The cases used here are drawn from a wide variety of infrastructure industries, including electricity, railways, telecommunications, and water. The cases also cross a considerable time span: from the middle of the nineteenth century to the beginning of the twenty-first century. The selection of countries is considerably narrower, however: most cases are based in the United States, Britain, or Latin America. The United States is of special interest because many of its private utilities were never bought out or expropriated by the public sector. U.S. cases provide the opportunity to consider why this country was an exception and how regulatory systems evolve over long periods of time. Britain and Latin America are heavily represented because they were pioneers in the latest wave of privatization, and the sources of many innovations in regulation.

The book is divided into three parts. It begins with two introductory chapters, this one and the next, which set out the principal regulatory options and their pros and cons, drawing on the literature on transaction costs and institutional economics to provide a basic framework. The next three parts are designed to be read together but can be read selectively as well, according to the reader's interests.

Part I, Chapters 3–6, focuses on the politics and dynamics of regulation. The options and framework introduced in this chapter and Chapter 2 are basically static, but regulatory systems change over time and some may be inherently unstable. Chapter 3 examines the behavior of regulatory agencies, focusing particularly on the economic, political, and institutional factors thought to influence the risk that a regulatory agency will be "captured" by special interests. Chapter 4 examines how capture can undermine a discretionary regulatory system. Two common forms of unstable capture are illustrated: one with the case of bus regulation in Sri Lanka and the second with telephone regulation in the United States. Chapter 5 examines the dynamics of concession contracts, using Argentina's railways as the case. Finally, Chapter 6 considers the circumstances that discourage government expropriation of private utilities by examining the history of the electricity industry in North and South America. The obvious question is why almost all of the private electric companies in South America and two-thirds of those in Canada were expropriated or bought out by 1970, while very few private electric companies in the United States suffered the same fate.

Part II examines the pros and cons of the three main regulatory options in more detail. Chapter 7 considers the strengths and limitations of concession contracts by considering the rise, fall, and revival of municipal franchises in the United States and Canada in the nineteenth and twentieth centuries. Chapter 8 considers the potential for private contracts to substitute for public regulation by examining the deregulation of the U.S. railroad and airline industries. Private contracts were a deliberate and central part of the plan to deregulate the railroads and an unplanned but surprisingly important development in the deregulation of the airlines. Chapter 9 examines price-cap regulation, the modern form of discretionary regulation pioneered in Britain in the 1980s and adopted by many other countries since. The advantages of price cap over older forms of discretionary regulation are explored through the experience of Britain's water industry.

Part III focuses on the important experiments with the vertical unbundling or restructuring of utilities. The idea of unbundling is to separate the activities that are potentially competitive from those that are not, so that regulation can be confined to those activities where it is absolutely necessary. Vertical unbundling threatens to reduce the coordination between the formerly integrated activities, however, since this coordination now must be achieved through contracts between separate firms. The coordination is further complicated because these contracts may have to be supervised by a regulator, if one of the parties enjoys a monopoly. Chapter 10 considers the options for achieving this coordination, including the possibility of private contracts negotiated without the supervision of a regulator. Chapter 11 examines the problems regulators face in setting tariffs for the remaining monopoly suppliers in the industry, using Britain's railroads as the case study. Chapter 12 explores the possibility that markets for infrastructure capacity could be developed to alleviate coordination problems by considering the experience of Argentina's electricity industry. The part concludes with Chapter 13, which compares the potential for vertical unbundling across the main infrastructure industries.

The book's concluding chapter speculates about the future of regulation, including the ways in which the private contract, concession contract, and discretionary approaches might evolve.

Commitment and Flexibility

Three main themes emerge from this survey. The first is that the market-oriented and contractual solutions to monopoly are preferable where they are practical. All things being equal (which they seldom are), private contracts are better than concession contracts and concession contracts are better than discretionary regulation. One reason for this ranking is that the stronger the exposure to market forces, the greater the incentives to improve services and reduce costs. Private contracts are better than concession contracts, for example, because the private contract directly involves the consumer in the design of her service while the concession contract requires that the government design the service offerings on the consumer's behalf. Another reason for the ranking is that contracts enforced through the normal commercial courts usually provide a clearer and stronger form of commitment than specialized regulatory institutions. Our understanding of how to design specialized regulatory institutions is limited, and experience strongly suggests that they eventually fall prey to tendencies and forces inimical to the long-term interests of the regulated industry and its customers.

It is striking how often the market-oriented or contractual solutions can be applied. The potential for private contracts to alleviate monopoly is suggested by how common relationship-specific investments seem to be throughout private industry. Private contracts may be more practical where the quantities purchased are large enough to make the negotiation and enforcement of a contract worthwhile. But the experience of the American airline industry recounted in Chapter 8 suggests that private contracts sometimes can be developed for customers purchasing relatively small quantities.

The second theme, which qualifies the first, is the importance of being realistic about the level of commitment that is possible, even through contracts. The world often changes in unexpected ways to undermine commitments. And commitments that impose large and unforeseen costs on either party are hard to sustain, no matter how sincere the parties were at the outset. Less specific and more flexible arrangements pose their own problems, of course, by exposing the firm, its customers, and the government to the risk of opportunistic behavior. But if it is impossible to draft a commitment that has a reasonable chance of surviving, then the parties will be exposed to opportunism anyway when the agreement collapses.

The degree of commitment possible varies from one type of industry and situation to another. It is easier to write a complete and workable contract, for example, where the investments are not very durable and somewhat mobile, or where the technological, economic, and political environments are relatively stable. The limitations of commitment also make hybrid strategies—combining some of the specificity of a contract with some of the flexibility of discretion—more interesting. It may be desirable to build some elements of discretionary regulation into a contract, for example, so as to limit the scope for opportunism if the contract has to be renegotiated. The limitations of commitment also make extra-contractual strategies more attractive, such as promoting widespread stock ownership to increase popular support for the firm.

The final theme, which is a corollary of the second, is that regulatory schemes are bound to change, especially in the long run. Very specific commitments, such as contracts, are vulnerable to unanticipated changes. More flexible commitments, as in discretionary regulation, may be inherently unstable because of the tendency of discretionary regulators to be captured by special interests or to ossify and lose their flexibility over time. Many utility policy reforms, like vertical unbundling, are experimental in the sense that they are adopted before their implications are fully understood. And the choice among private contracts, concessions, and discretionary regulation may change as technology changes and legal, social, and political institutions evolve.

The inevitability of change means that it may be reasonable to adopt a scheme that is unlikely to last—if it is still the best of those currently feasible. In the space of 150 years, the American railroad industry was regulated first through a regime of private contracts, then through concession systems, later discretionary regulation, and finally private contracts again. During any particular regime, moreover, the rules of the game typically changed in relatively important ways every decade or so. Each scheme was arguably the most appropriate at the time it was adopted. The changes had their costs as well as their benefits, but if there was an error it was probably a tendency to change too slowly, the most obvious example being the maintenance of discretionary regulation for several decades after it had ceased to be useful.

Nevertheless, it is important to choose the regulatory scheme carefully if private infrastructure is to survive. This means relying on private and contractual solutions where practical, since they generally increase the level of commitment and the chances that consumers will get the infrastructure services they value. But it also means being realistic about when private or contractual solutions will work, adopting discretionary schemes where necessary, or not privatizing at all where no regulatory scheme seems workable.

2

The Choice of Regulatory Strategy

Markets, Politics, and Values

The choice of whether and how the government should regulate monopoly depends in part, if not fundamentally, on the values or goals one considers important. What criteria should one use for judging the performance of alternative remedies to monopoly?

One obvious response is to use the values embodied in the competitive market as the standard. Monopoly is defined as a lack of competition, and the corrective implied is to make the market behave as if it were competitive. The values at the heart of the market are individualistic and utilitarian. Free markets allow individuals to engage in voluntary exchanges of goods and services. Subject to certain conditions to be discussed later, the voluntary nature of the exchange ensures that the parties regard themselves as better off than they were before. Otherwise, the parties would not agree to the exchange. From that perspective, the role of society is to encourage individual happiness by facilitating voluntary transactions, and smoothly functioning, competitive markets are a primary vehicle for doing so.

The individualistic values embodied in the market enjoy wide popular support in most developed and market-oriented societies, but there are other values that are widely shared as well. In particular, support for individualism is often combined with a concern that the inequities in society should not be too large. People disagree about the definition of equity and the best ways to protect it, but many believe that society should ensure that individuals start out on a relatively equal footing by providing them universal access to basic education and health care. Such equity concerns are particularly salient for infrastructure, moreover, since, as noted in the previous chapter, many people would add water, electricity, and a telephone for emergencies to the list of basic services that should be universally available.

Moving from strategies that rely primarily on markets, such as private contracts, to those that rely more heavily on politics, such as concession contracts or discretionary regulation, changes values in two ways. First, the involvement of government and politics almost inevitably opens the door to a wider set of values than the individualism of the market. If the government becomes involved in regulating telephone companies, for example, then it is very likely to insist on low "lifeline" tariffs for basic service to poor households, or on similar tariffs for basic services in rural and urban areas. The government might have adopted a scheme to improve access to telephones by poor households or in rural areas even if it were not regulating telephone service as a monopoly. Once the government takes responsibility for regulating telephone tariffs, however, then the pressure to include regulations that respond to other popular concerns, such as equity, is often overwhelming.

Whether one regards the introduction of other values as desirable depends upon one's sympathy for them. A long-standing concern of regulatory scholars is that government agencies may be vulnerable to "capture" by "special interests," including the regulated firms, their employees, customers, and others. The adjective "special" is used to indicate that they do not have the interests of the general public at heart, and thus that their influence over the regulatory agency should be seen as undesirable. Interests that seem special to one person may seem public to another, of course. It's all in the eye of the beholder. Nevertheless, experience demonstrates there is a significant risk, discussed at greater length in Chapters 3 and 4, that a regulatory agency will be captured by interests that conflict with widely shared values or goals, such as the promotion of efficient and affordable services.

A second way that the shift from more market- to more government-based strategies affects values is by increasing the concern with procedural fairness, both perceived and real. Procedural concerns arise because the government has a power that markets do not: the power to coerce individuals to do things that, from their own selfish perspectives, make them worse off. The most fundamental reason for using government to help solve a problem like monopoly is because coercion is thought to be needed. Problems that can be solved by voluntary agreement among self-interested individuals will be solved automatically by markets, without the government.

If the government's unique coercive powers are to be used against members of society, then the public is understandably anxious that coercion will be used fairly and only for important public purposes. The well-warranted price of using coercion in a democracy is usually elaborate procedural safeguards to prevent its abuse. These procedures are educational in the broadest sense, both in alerting policymakers to unanticipated problems and opposition and in building popular understanding and support for the actions ultimately taken. And for that reason the perception of fairness is often as impor- tant as the reality of fairness. In the public sector, the process of reaching decisions is often as important as the decisions themselves.[1]

The understandable concern with procedures and perceptions may conflict with other goals, including the promotion of efficient markets. Elaborate procedural safeguards may delay important decisions, for example, and are often thought to give regulatory processes a strong bias in favor of the status quo. If regulatory powers can only be adopted after lengthy and careful pro- cedures, then regulatory change is likely to be slow. Similarly, the concern over perceptions of fairness may result in broad classes of consumers or firms being treated the same way despite substantial differences among them.

Much of the analysis in this book assumes that the primary goal of public policy toward monopoly is to encourage efficient markets. But it recognizes that other values and goals are also relevant and widely supported, particu- larly the desire to promote equity through universal access to certain basic services. And it recognizes, further, that the understandable consequence of invoking government powers to solve monopoly is both the introduction of wider values and an enhanced concern over procedures and perceptions.

Transaction Costs and Government Intervention

Given the perspective adopted, the choice of whether and how to regulate monopoly can be understood by using the concept of transaction costs to an- alyze the performance of markets and contracts. The concept of transaction costs was developed by Ronald Coase, Oliver Williamson, Douglass North, and the many researchers they inspired.[2] The central idea is that all economic activities can be broken down into a series of transactions, such as buying a good or service, and that executing these transactions imposes costs on the parties involved.

Transaction costs occur for two fundamental reasons. First, it is impossible for the parties to a transaction to know every relevant fact or anticipate every relevant contingency. Gathering information is time consuming and costly, and there are limits to our cognitive abilities to process information and fore- cast the future. Second, a party will behave opportunistically by withholding relevant information if it can gain advantages by doing so. In a world with perfect information and foresight and where parties were completely honest with each other, even complicated transactions could be arranged easily. But in the real world, the parties usually must spend time and money gathering and interpreting information and drafting and enforcing complex contracts to protect themselves against contingencies and the opportunistic behavior of the others.

Different institutional arrangements can affect the costs of a transaction, and some institutional arrangements may be more efficient for a given type of transaction than others. In an influential book, for example, Douglass North and Robert Thomas argued that the development of a legal system to enforce contracts was critical to Western economic development, because it dramatically reduced the costs of the many commercial transactions essential to a modern specialized economy.[3] It was easier for the government, rather than private individuals, to organize an effective legal system, because only the government has the power to coerce individuals to comply.

As the example of the legal system suggests, economists increasingly use transaction costs as a framework to help decide when and how government should intervene in an economy.[4] Ronald Coase demonstrated many years ago that there would be far less reason for government to intervene in markets in a world with no transaction costs, including fully defined property rights.[5] Coase singled out property rights as a special source of transaction costs because ambiguous rights made it easier for one party to harm others without gaining their consent. Zero transaction costs would make it possible for individuals to engage in a variety of different voluntary transactions, and fully defined property rights would protect third parties not participating directly in the transaction. Government might intervene for equity reasons, for example, to help ensure that all individuals start out on a relatively equal footing by guaranteeing access to basic education and health care. The market would be efficient, however, in the sense that (1) all the transactions that could make at least one person better off and no one else worse off would be completed and (2) no transaction that failed this test would occur.

In this framework, government intervention is justified if it either clarifies ambiguous property rights or otherwise reduces transaction costs. Government regulation of pollution, for example, can be seen as a response to problems of property rights and other sources of transaction costs. If other transaction costs are low, pollution can be resolved by simply clarifying property rights. Imagine that a stream forms the boundary between two neighbors and that the rights to use the stream for various purposes are not clearly defined. Imagine further that one neighbor finds it convenient to dump his trash in the stream, harming the second neighbor, who uses the stream for fishing and as a source of drinking water. In the absence of clearly defined rights for the use of the stream, the two neighbors may find it difficult to reach an agreement as to whether the trash can be dumped. If the government establishes either a clear right to dump trash in a stream or a clear right to a fishable and drinkable stream, however, then the two neighbors should be able to negotiate an efficient use of the stream.

One of Coase's famous contributions was to argue that the solution would be efficient no matter how the property right was defined. Either way, the first neighbor would dump his trash only if the benefit he received was greater than the harm to his neighbor. If trash dumping was a right, then the second neighbor would pay the first not to dump only if the loss of fishing and drinking from the stream exceeded the convenience of dumping. If a fishable and drinkable stream was a right, then the first neighbor would pay the second for permission to dump only if the convenience of dumping exceeded the value of fishing and drinking.

The clarification of property rights alone may not solve the pollution problem if there are other sources of serious transaction costs. Suppose that our stream is now a river that is hundreds of miles long and passes by thousands of households and businesses that want to use it for trash disposal, fishing, and drinking. Suppose further that the issue is no longer whether to dump a fixed amount of trash at one site but rather what quantities of a dozen different pollutants should be dumped at hundreds of different locations. Even in the presence of clearly defined property rights, the transaction costs of negotiating, monitoring, and enforcing a voluntary agreement among the thousands of river users are likely to be enormous.

In the presence of such high transaction costs, it may be more practical for the government to regulate the quality of the water and the amount of dumping permitted. In effect, the government tries to estimate the agreement that the thousands of parties would have reached voluntarily if the transaction costs were zero, and then uses its unique power of coercion to enforce compliance. The government is likely to make errors in its estimate, however, and may introduce other problems by its involvement. Even in the presence of high transaction costs, government intervention is desirable only if it moves society closer to the solution that the parties would have agreed to in a world free of transaction costs. In other words, the cure must be better than the disease.[6]

The case for government intervention in infrastructure monopolies is similar to that for intervention in pollution. The main difference with monopoly is that ambiguous property rights are not a major source of high transaction costs. As explained in Chapter 1, both the infrastructure company and its customers make durable and immobile investments that leave them vulnerable to opportunism. The logical solution is for the parties to sign contracts to protect themselves before they make their investments. As in the case of pollution, however, the transaction costs of negotiating and enforcing these contracts may be high, particularly if many small customers are involved or if their infrastructure requirements are complex and hard to predict. And as in the case of pollution, there are a variety of ways the government might intervene. The appropriate intervention depends on how high the transaction costs are and how effective the government is at reducing them without introducing new problems.

In the case of monopoly, the scope of government intervention increases gradually as one moves from private contracts to concession contracts, discretionary regulation, and public enterprise. Government intervention can only approximate the results of voluntary agreements in a world with zero transaction costs, since the government can never know as much about the potential costs and benefits of the transaction as the individual parties do. The greater the range of issues the government must decide, the cruder the overall approximation is likely to be.

From this perspective, the most intrusive forms of government involvement are justified only when transaction costs are relatively high, so that even a crude approximation is an improvement. Private contracts are appropriate if transaction costs are relatively low, concession contracts might be justified if transaction costs are moderate, and discretionary regulation or public enterprise could be justified only if transaction costs are extremely high and less intrusive remedies impractical.

Contractual Completeness and Contract Types

Options in Procurement

Many solutions to monopoly rely on a contract of one form or another, the most obvious being private and concession contracts. Some of the practical issues that arise in the contractual approach to monopoly are analogous to those found in a firm's decision about how vertically integrated it should be. Indeed, Oliver Williamson's analysis of procurement and vertical integration was one of the seminal studies of transaction costs, and Williamson would later apply many of these same insights to the analysis of concession contract regulation.[7]

Imagine a firm that produces a final product to sell to consumers by assembling various intermediate products or parts. The firm could produce the parts itself or buy them from independent suppliers. The more inputs the firm produces itself and the farther back those inputs reach into the chain of potential suppliers, the more vertically integrated the firm is said to be. In deciding whether to make or buy a particular part, the firm faces a range of possibilities, as shown in Figure 2.1. At one extreme the firm could produce the part itself, and at the other extreme it could buy the part on the spot market, where goods are offered for immediate delivery. In between are a variety of other options that involve long-term contracting between the firm and an independent parts manufacturer.

Buying on the spot market is often the preferred solution, since competition in spot markets provides built-in incentives for the suppliers to keep the costs of the part low. If the part is produced internally, by contrast, the firm must develop an internal management system to monitor the performance of the employees producing the part and to motivate them to produce it efficiently. The spot market is also typically more reliable, because there are many alternative suppliers instead of just one. The spot market has limitations, however, among the most important being that it may discourage the buyer or its suppliers from taking advantage of the potential economies of tailoring their facilities, employees, and processes to one another's capabilities or needs. As with monopoly, the parties making such durable, relationship-specific investments become vulnerable to opportunistic behavior unless they can protect themselves with some form of long-term contract.

A central limitation of long-term contracts is the possibility that the contract may prove to be incomplete or become obsolete if circumstances change. To protect against opportunism, the contract must last as long as the lives of the relationship-specific investments that it is designed to protect. The longer the contract, however, the more the circumstances of the parties are likely to change over the contract's life. One can include contingencies in the contract, of course. But identifying all the relevant risks and negotiating appropriate contingencies is time consuming, costly, and impractical, however, especially if the contract is to last for a long time and the needs of either party are highly uncertain and complex. And if the contract proves to be incomplete before it is scheduled to expire, then the parties will face the choice of either living with unsatisfactory terms for the remaining life of the contract or exposing themselves to opportunism by renegotiating the contract.

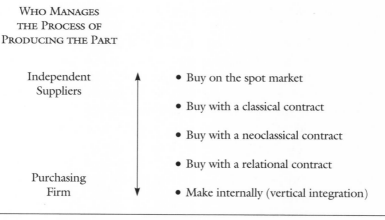

Figure 2.1 The continuum of strategies for procurement by a firm.

The problem of contractual completeness has spawned a variety of contract types, of which Williamson distinguishes three.[8] The first is the classical contract, which presumes to describe, in advance, all relevant future contingencies and to provide specific remedies for them. This is likely to be an unrealistic ideal for all but the simplest and shortest relationships.

The second type is the neoclassical contract, which acknowledges the possibility of incompleteness and includes provisions for a third party, usually an arbitrator of some sort, to resolve certain classes of disputes. Arbitration is often called for because it can be more efficient at discovering information and resolving disagreements about facts or states of the world than normal litigation. However, the circumstances under which arbitration is allowed, the factors the arbitrator can consider, and the scope of the remedies that he can order are often carefully prescribed.

The third and most flexible type is the relational contract. The relational contract anticipates that the relationship between the parties will have to adapt over time in unforeseeable ways. It relies on renegotiation between the parties as the remedy, and provides a general framework for those negotiations rather than specific remedies for identified contingencies. Relational contracts leave the parties vulnerable to holdups over specialized investments, because the guidelines for renegotiations are general. As a result, relational contracts are likely to be used only where there are additional protections outside the contract against opportunism. One form of extra-contractual protection is when reputation matters because the parties expect to engage in repeat contracts with the same or similar firms. The prospect of repeat contracts is important because the parties' willingness to behave opportunistically in any one situation is reduced by threat of retaliation in the future.

Empirical research confirms that long-term contracts are common in industries where relationship-specific investments are important.[9] Classical or neoclassical contracts are by far the most common contract types. Relational contracts are used only if the requirements of the parties are difficult to specify in advance *and* there are extra-contractual protections against opportunism. Finally, the firm is likely to produce the part internally rather than buy it from others if relationship-specific investments and flexibility are important but extra-contractual protections are not available.

The Implications for Monopoly

The range of solutions in procurement is similar to the range of solutions for infrastructure monopoly presented in the previous chapter (compare Figure 2.1 with Figure 1.1).[10] The firm trying to buy parts plays the same role as the consumers trying to buy infrastructure services, except that in some cases the government acts on the infrastructure consumers' behalf. At the two extremes, buying on the spot market is analogous to buying from a private and unregulated infrastructure supplier; producing the part internally is analogous to having a public or nonprofit enterprise provide the infrastructure service. In between the extremes are a variety of types of contract, some more classical and some more relational. In particular, most private and concession contracts could be classified as classical or neoclassical contracts. Similarly, discretionary regulation can be understood as a form of relational contracting, because the regulatory statute sets out the obligations between the government and the enterprise in only general terms. In discretionary regulation, as in relational contracts, both parties usually rely on other sources of protection against opportunism besides the statute.

There are two important differences between the problem of infrastructure monopoly and the more general problem of procurement. The first is that relationship-specific investments—in the form of durable and immobile investments—are the hallmarks of an infrastructure monopoly, whereas they are not found in every procurement situation. This means that buying on the spot market is a much less common and attractive option in monopoly than it is in procurement generally. In cases of monopoly, some form of contract is usually superior to the spot market.

The second difference is that the monopoly problem often involves many consumers buying from a single infrastructure supplier, whereas the typical procurement problem involves a single firm buying from one or more suppliers. The presence of many buyers can complicate the use of contracts, particularly if each buyer is purchasing a relatively small amount so that the transaction costs of negotiating and enforcing individual contracts are large relative to the total value of each transaction. The high transaction costs of contracting with many small buyers may make it desirable for the government to act on the consumers' behalf through a concession contract or discretionary regulation.

These differences aside, the procurement analogy offers two important lessons for the use of contracts as a solution to monopoly. One lesson is the potential vulnerability of contracts to incompleteness or obsolescence. The contract protects against opportunism best if it anticipates all the important events and provides appropriate contingencies for them. This means that an approach based on a classical contract (whether a private contract or a government concession) is less attractive in situations where it is difficult to anticipate what might happen and how to respond. Classical contracts tend to be difficult for infrastructure monopolies because the lives of the investments tend to be long, and the longer the contract the harder it is to anticipate what will happen.

The second important lesson from procurement is that there are a variety of contract types, ranging from the classical contract to the relational contract, with hybrids in between. The relational contract acknowledges that drafting a complete contract is an impossible goal in some situations; the protection against opportunism rests partly on the specific provisions of the contract and partly on extra-contractual circumstances and institutions. In the case of procurement between private firms, the extra-contractual protections are often the prospect of repeat business and the social ties and trust that have developed between the purchasing agent and the supplier over time. Repeat business and reputation can be important in the case of discretionary regulation as well. The government's incentives to be opportunistic are more limited, for example, if it knows the infrastructure company must return regularly to the private capital market to replace worn-out assets or to expand capacity to accommodate growing demand. Similarly, the infrastructure company is less likely to behave opportunistically if it hopes to win permission to provide other infrastructure services from the same or similar governments.

Reputation and repeat business do not seem to provide as effective protection in discretionary regulation as they do in procurement between private firms. One sign that reputational concerns are not enough is that governments and infrastructure companies often take deliberate steps to develop extra sources of protection. As we shall see in later chapters, governments often attempt to protect themselves by threatening to franchise another private firm or establish a publicly owned competitor, for example. Similarly, the infrastructure suppliers try to protect themselves by buying control of key assets or by selling stock to the general public to broaden the popular support for their cause. The extra-contractual protections are not confined to the specific defenses that the government and the regulated firm erect. The broader legal, social, or political institutions limit the behavior of governments and companies in important ways as well. As discussed in Chapter 6, for example, constitutional restrictions on the government's taking private property without compensation have significantly limited opportunism by U.S. regulatory agencies.

The Pros and Cons of the Principal Options

Private Contracts

In assessing the basic advantages and disadvantages of the different regulatory strategies, it is helpful to think of private contracts, concession contracts, and discretionary regulation as three distinct types. In practice many schemes mix elements of the approaches, but the strengths and weaknesses of the hybrids can be understood as products of their components. The strengths and weaknesses of the three principal regulatory strategies are summarized in Table 2.1.

One key strength of private contracts is that they can establish clear commitments. The commitments depend on the completeness of the contract and on the integrity of the courts that enforce commercial or contract law. Assuming one has a reasonably complete contract and a fair legal system, however, the contract describes all the obligations of the two parties in advance.

The second strength of private contracts is that they allow the greatest scope for competitive market forces to shape the infrastructure services. Market forces have a strong influence because the infrastructure suppliers and their customers draft the private contracts without interference from government. This means that the parties are free to search for opportunities to redesign or tailor the services in ways that add value for the consumer or reduce costs for the infrastructure company. Under both concession contracts and discretionary regulation, by contrast, the government regulatory agency typically requires that the firm offer customers only a limited menu of service offerings. A limited menu makes it easier for the regulator to monitor the firm's

Table 2.1 Principal options for regulating a private infrastructure monopoly: Advantages and disadvantages

Option	Advantages	Disadvantages
Private contract	• Clear and specific commitment of a commercial contract • Greatest scope for competitive market forces to shape service offerings and control costs	• Risk of an incomplete contract • Depends on integrity of commercial law courts • Small customers may make it costly to negotiate and enforce private contracts
Concession contract	• Clear and specific commitment of a commercial contract • Competitive market can be used to determine supplier costs	• Risk of an incomplete contract • Depends on integrity of commercial law courts • Regulator must second-guess consumer preferences
Discretionary regulation	• Flexibility to respond to changing and unforeseen circumstances	• Regulatory agency must second-guess both consumer preferences and supplier costs • Greater risk of capture of regulatory agency by special interests

compliance with the tariff rules set out in the concession contract or by the regulator. A limited menu is often politically more acceptable as well, because to the general public it often seems fairer to offer broad classes of consumers similar services and prices than to vary price and service offerings from one consumer to the next. But the limited menu may suppress important differences among customers and reduce opportunities for market-driven tailoring and innovation. The more heterogeneous the customers, the more advantageous the private contractual approach.

The main disadvantages of private contracts are the risk of an incomplete contract and the potentially high costs of negotiating contracts with many small customers. In many cases, the needs and circumstances of the two parties are predictable enough to draft a complete contract. If they are not so predictable, however, then the parties must either find extra-contractual forms of protection or reconcile themselves to the risk that the contract will fail and leave them vulnerable to opportunism. Similarly, not all infrastructure systems have many small customers, and sometimes strategies can be developed for reducing the costs of negotiating with small customers (as explained in Chapter 8). Nevertheless, the costs of negotiating and enforcing a contract usually do not decrease proportionately with the value of the transaction, so that it may not be worthwhile to negotiate individual contracts for small customers.

Concession Contracts

Concession contracts maintain the clear commitment of a commercial contract and some significant influence for market forces while eliminating the difficulty of negotiating with many small customers. The concession contract is no different than a private contract in its aspiration to describe obligations completely in advance. Usually a government regulatory agency monitors the company's compliance with a concession contract, but that agency cannot unilaterally change the terms once the contract is awarded. Contractual disputes are normally adjudicated by the same commercial law courts that enforce private contracts rather than by the regulatory agency. The presence of the government as a party to the contract may influence the courts, but the fact that the entire economy depends on the integrity of the contract law system provides a potentially powerful countervailing pressure.

The influence of market forces is not as strong as in the case of the private contract, because consumers are represented by the government instead of participating directly. Often the government specifies the minimum quality of services to be provided and then awards the concession to the bidder proposing the lowest tariff. Another common variant is for the government to specify both the minimum service and the maximum tariff and then award the concession to the bidder offering the largest concession fee or requesting the lowest subsidy. Either way, the government must estimate what consumers want when it drafts the basic concession framework.

Nevertheless, market forces are involved, because the concession is usually awarded through competitive bidding. A competitive award should ensure that the infrastructure supplier is driven to offer terms that reflect his costs, and no more. And if the concession expires and is rebid periodically, then the terms should reflect reasonably up-to-date market conditions. Equally important, open and competitive bidding can enhance popular perceptions of fairness and help maintain political support for the regulatory process.

Concession contracts share with private contracts the limitation of contractual completeness. Again, some situations are predictable enough to make a complete contract a realistic goal. And there are ways to build some flexibility in contracts through such schemes as arbitration and buyout clauses. But foreseeing the future and drafting appropriate contingencies is often difficult.

Discretionary Regulation

The best-known examples of discretionary regulation are cost-of-service regulation as developed in the United States and price-cap regulation as developed in the United Kingdom.[11] Discretionary regulation is often called commission regulation in the scholarly literature, since, until recently, the primary examples were in the United States, where it is customary to appoint a commission of three to seven members who decide regulatory issues by majority vote. The British gave individual regulators the authority to make decisions in the original price-cap schemes of the 1980s, but they began to replace individual regulators with commissions in 1998. The term *discretionary regulation* better reflects the distinctive characteristic of this approach.

The basic advantage of discretionary regulation is its flexibility, enabling it to adapt to changing and unforeseen circumstances. Unlike contract regulation, the discretionary approach does not attempt to anticipate all the developments that may happen during the life of the investments that need protection. Instead, a regulatory commission or an individual regulator is granted substantial discretion to set the prices and service standards for the regulated firm. The authorizing statute usually constrains the regulatory body to some degree by, for example, setting out the factors that it must consider. And there is usually some provision for appeal to the courts or a similar body if the firms or consumers feel the regulator's rulings are inconsistent with the statute. But the statutory guidance is seldom formulaic, so the regulatory body enjoys substantial freedom in interpreting it.

A major disadvantage of the discretionary approach is that the influence of market forces is drastically reduced. In essence, the regulatory agency must predict almost all of the decisions that the infrastructure supplier and its customers would have made in a market with no transaction costs. Markets are still involved, in that the private capital market will not finance new investments if the regulator treats the infrastructure company too harshly. But the constraints of the capital market are obvious only in the long term or when capacity is limited, and even within those constraints the regulator has plenty of latitude to influence the services provided. As in the concession contract, the regulator must represent consumers in deciding what combination of quality and service they prefer. But unlike the concession contract, the regulator can no longer rely on competitive bidding to ensure that the infrastructure supplier is providing those services at the lowest cost and without earning excess profits.

The need to estimate what the efficient market solution would have been in the absence of transaction costs makes discretionary regulation technically challenging. Under cost-of-service regulation as developed in the United States, for example, the regulator is supposed to set tariffs high enough to cover the costs of an efficient firm, including operating expenses, depreciation, and a reasonable return on invested capital. But to make this calculation, the regulator needs to know what the operating expenses for an efficiently run firm are, how rapidly investments depreciate, whether the investments being made are prudent and well managed, and the minimum rate of return that the private capital market requires to finance investments of comparable risk. Many of these questions are hard for the firm itself to answer, let alone the regulator.

The tariff-setting task is complicated by the fact that the regulator inevitably has less information and analytic staff than the firm has. Although the firm is obligated to provide actual cost data and other information that the regulator asks for, the data seldom tell the regulator all he needs to know. A regulator can ask the firm to supply figures on actual and projected operating expenses and output, for example, but the regulator will have to determine independently whether the costs can be reduced further or not. The British price-cap system was developed in part to reduce the regulator's need for information but, as explained in Chapter 9, it has not been totally successful in this regard.

The second major drawback of discretionary regulation is the risk that the agency will be captured by special interests and therefore will not exercise its discretion in ways that are in the long-term interests of the infrastructure supplier and its customers. The agency needs discretion because tariff setting is too complicated to be reduced to a contract or a formula that can be specified in advance. But the fact that the agency has so much discretion makes it a more inviting target for capture. Moreover, a regulatory agency that is specialized in a particular industry does not have the same built-in defenses against capture found in the commercial law courts. While all industries and consumers have a stake in the integrity of the courts, only the regulated firms and their customers have a stake in the integrity of the specialized regulatory agency.

Usually the regulatory agency is designed to provide some insulation from day-to-day political pressures. The commissioners or individual regulators are typically appointed to fixed terms, for example, and cannot be removed except for specific and limited causes. In the case of commissions, the terms of the members are usually staggered so that it takes years before the president, prime minister, or governor has appointed a majority of its members. Commissions are sometimes required to take evidence or deliberate in public, and to provide written justifications for their decisions. Nevertheless, political pressures inevitably affect regulators. Many regulators hope for reappointment at the end of their terms, for example, while those that don't usually still want the regulatory system to be regarded as successful, or at least to maintain enough popular support to survive. The fact that the risk of capture cannot be eliminated entirely by the design of the regulatory statute or agency often leads regulated firms and consumers to rely on other sources of protection against opportunism.

Variants and Hybrids

In practice, regulatory schemes are often mixtures or hybrids of the private contract, concession contract, and discretionary regulation approaches. The scheme to regulate U.S. freight railroads relies primarily on private contracts, for example, but it includes the opportunity to appeal to a discretionary regulatory agency. The appeals process is designed primarily as a safety valve for small shippers, and appeals are permitted only under limited circumstances. Similarly, British price-cap regulation relies primarily on a discretionary approach but with an important contractual component.

Figure 2.2 provides a sense of the variation by arraying a number of schemes along the continuum from markets to politics. There is substantial variation even among schemes that would be classified as predominantly using a single approach. Concession contracts that are awarded through competitive bidding are subject to more direct market forces, for example, than concession contracts awarded without bidding. The variation among discretionary schemes is perhaps even broader. In some schemes politics enters directly and the scope of discretion is virtually unlimited. An example is the bus industry in Sri Lanka where, as described in Chapter 4, ministers and the Parliament set tariffs. In other schemes the scope of discretion and the potential influence of politics are substantial but limited by various statutory and institutional constraints. Most modern forms of discretionary regulation fit this description, including the U.S. cost-of-service and the British price-cap approaches.

Some schemes include such a strong mixture of the contractual and discretionary approaches that they can only be classified as hybrids. One example is the French system of municipal concession contracts with a special adminis-

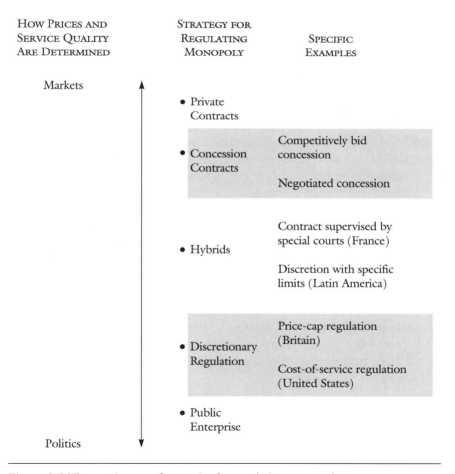

HOW PRICES AND SERVICE QUALITY ARE DETERMINED	STRATEGY FOR REGULATING MONOPOLY	SPECIFIC EXAMPLES
Markets	• Private Contracts	
	• Concession Contracts	Competitively bid concession
		Negotiated concession
	• Hybrids	Contract supervised by special courts (France)
		Discretion with specific limits (Latin America)
	• Discretionary Regulation	Price-cap regulation (Britain)
		Cost-of-service regulation (United States)
	• Public Enterprise	
Politics		

Figure 2.2 The continuum of strategies for regulating monopoly.

trative court to supervise renegotiations. This system, which has been developed over many years, is used by municipal governments in France and in some of the former French colonies in Africa to regulate private water, sewage, solid waste, and bus and streetcar companies.[12] As in conventional contract regulation, the government awards a concession for a fixed term and the concession contract specifies the prices to be charged and services to be provided. Unlike the conventional contract, however, the French contract anticipates that the municipality and the concessionaire may need to renegotiate price or service terms during the life of the contract. The contract sets out the circumstances under which either party can request renegotiations and the general criteria the parties must consider in negotiating changes, but the language is not as specific or formulaic as in the adjustment clauses found in conventional contracts. Equally important, disputes over renegotiations can be appealed to specialized administrative courts that apply broad principles for adjusting municipal contracts that are set out in French administrative law. In essence, the specialized administrative courts play the role of a discretionary regulator in that they are empowered to change a contract, not just interpret its terms. But these courts are used only in the event that the two parties cannot reach agreement on their own.

Similarly, some discretionary systems attempt to establish explicit commitments that are more characteristic of a contract. The most common method of doing so is by legislating a few very specific constraints on the conduct of the discretionary regulatory agency. For example, the law might specify the minimum rate of return that the regulator must provide private investors. Mexico adopted this approach in the 1930s, when it passed a law requiring regulators to allow private electric companies to earn a return at least as large as the rate of interest paid on government debt. Similarly, in the 1930s and again in the 1980s Chilean law required regulators to allow a return of at least 10 percent per year.[13] These constraints were not sufficient to prevent the gradual impoverishment and nationalization of many private electricity companies in Latin America between the 1930s and the 1970s, as described in Chapter 6. But more modern versions may prove successful in combining the flexibility of discretion with some of the specific commitments found in contracts.

Finally, it is worth remembering that the performance of any regulatory scheme can be deeply influenced by its broader social and political environment, sometimes enough that it has the effect of changing the basic regulatory approach. The most obvious example is a concession contract scheme in a country without an independent judiciary. If the courts do the bidding of the executive or the legislative branches of government, then concession contracts amount to discretionary regulation in disguise.

Conclusion

The more market-oriented solutions to monopoly have two basic advantages. First, the more market-oriented the remedy, the more closely it is likely to approximate the agreements that infrastructure companies and their customers would reach voluntarily in a world with no transaction costs. Any intervention will only approximate the results desired, and the broader the scope of the intervention the more prescient the regulator must be to come close. No intervention is the best course of action if intervention cannot improve on the protections against opportunism that the companies and customers could develop for themselves, despite the transaction costs involved. And the more extensive forms of government regulation are likely to be justified only where the transaction costs of private long-term contracts are high, so that the uncorrected market performs poorly relative to the ideal.

The second advantage of the more market-oriented approaches is that they have the potential to provide stronger protection against opportunism. One reason is that the market-oriented approaches typically rely on some form of explicit contract, either private or concession. These contracts work only if they are reasonably complete and if the legal system that enforces them is reasonably fair and efficient. If these two conditions are met, however, contracts provide a clearer and stronger commitment than discretionary regulation.

Market-oriented solutions are also more stable because they raise fewer concerns about the use of government powers and the fairness of regulatory proceedings, and thus are less likely to generate the kinds of political controversies that lead to intervention and broken commitments. Private contracts will be politically controversial if some customers remain vulnerable to opportunism because the transaction costs of negotiating satisfactory long-term contracts are prohibitively high for them. These political objections may be fatal if the remaining problems of opportunism are too broadly or intensely felt.

With the shift from private contracts to concession contracts or discretionary regulation, however, the focus shifts from whether the market is fair to whether the government is fair. And as one moves from concession contracts to discretionary regulation, the difficulty of demonstrating fairness increases. The concession contract has the important advantage that it can be awarded through an open and competitive bidding process, which the public is likely to accept as fair. Critics may object that the government should have set a different minimum service standard or maximum tariff when it drafted the concession contract, but if the contract is then awarded competitively it is harder to argue that the firm is making unreasonably high profits. With discretionary regulation, by contrast, the government has no analogous procedure that it can use to win the instant credibility of competitive bidding. As a result, the task of demonstrating fairness and maintaining public acceptance becomes much harder in discretionary regulation than it is with concessions.

Nevertheless, market-oriented solutions have important limitations. Private contracts are potentially vulnerable to the problems posed by large numbers of small customers, and both private and concession contracts are vulnerable to courts that lack integrity and to the difficulties of drafting a complete contract. If the contract proves to be incomplete, moreover, all its advantages of procedural fairness and protection against opportunism disappear quickly. Any political advantages of awarding a concession contract competitively are lost, for example, if the contract has to be renegotiated.

Given these limitations, discretionary regulation may be the best solution where the circumstances are too complex or unstable to draft a complete contract. Discretionary regulation should not be entered into lightly, however, because the difficulty of approximating what the market might have done is great and the risk of capture and difficulties of maintaining public support are high.

I

Regulatory Politics
and Dynamics

3

The Behavior of Regulatory Agencies

The Public Interest

To the extent that regulatory agencies have the discretion to set tariffs and service standards, how will they use that discretion? Three theories are often advanced to explain why government regulation is established and how regulatory agencies behave once they are created. The first views the agency as a tool for discovering and advancing the broad public interest in the performance of the regulated industry. The second presumes that special interests will capture the agency in order to use the agency's powers for their own parochial ends. A final theory suggests that the mix of public and special interests that the agency will pursue depends on the design of the agency and the institutional environment in which the agency operates. These theories have been explored most intensively in the United States, because of its longer continuous experience with regulated private utilities. But they are increasingly the topics of research in other countries as well.

The concept of the public interest assumes that members of society have common or widely shared goals, and that the best means to identify and advance these goals is through rational and expert analysis. In the case of infrastructure regulation, the primary goal is usually the promotion of economic efficiency that is threatened by the presence of natural monopoly. Often there are secondary goals as well, such as a desire to promote universal access to basic infrastructure services for the poor or for those in remote or lagging areas.

Regulatory agencies are almost always created in the name of the public interest. In the United States, for example, the pursuit of the public interest was the avowed reason why many states replaced regulation by municipal concession contracts with regulation by state public utility commissions (PUCs) between 1907 and 1914. As explained in Chapter 7, the PUCs were the product of a debate within the Progressive political movement in the United States and Canada about whether public ownership, municipal regulation, or state regulation would best protect the public from private monopolies. The PUCs triumphed in part because they embodied the rationalist, public interest perspective. PUC commissioners were appointed to fixed terms and were removable only for specific causes, for example, so that they could make decisions that might be unpopular in the short term without fear of political interference. Similarly, by shifting regulation from the municipal to the state level, advocates of PUCs hoped to create regulatory agencies that had enough responsibilities and resources to justify and support an expert staff.

The public interest was also the rationale for the creation of federal regulatory commissions in the United States. Congress established the Interstate Commerce Commission (ICC) to regulate railroads in 1887, but federal regulatory agencies did not proliferate until the 1930s, when the Depression undermined popular confidence in private enterprise. President Franklin D. Roosevelt, as part of his New Deal, argued that government coordination was needed to ensure that industries performed in the public interest, and new regulatory agencies were created to supervise the securities, telecommunications, energy, airline, and other industries.[1] A similar faith in the pursuit of the public interest was professed by the designers of the regulatory agencies for the utilities privatized in Britain during the 1980s and in many other countries during the 1990s. (See, for example, the description of the origins of the British price-cap system in Chapter 9.)

Critics of this perspective often argue that the public interest is an illusion or that it cannot be discovered through rational analysis. There may be widespread agreement when goals are stated at a very general and abstract level, but the consensus often dissolves when the goals are translated into specific policies. We may all agree that some basic level of electricity or telephone service should be widely available and affordable, for example, but then disagree about what constitutes basic service, how to define affordability, and whether taxpayers or other utility customers should finance any losses on basic service.

Even if there is a public interest, moreover, it may not be discoverable through the rational deliberations of an expert regulatory agency. Some critical information simply may not be available with reasonable time or effort, or so much information may be required that even a large and expert staff cannot comprehend and analyze it all. Given that we don't and can't know everything necessary to make completely informed and rational decisions, some critics argue that relying on experts is actually risky. There is virtue in developing policy incrementally, through political competition among parochial interests.

To proponents of the public interest, these criticisms seem overblown. Just because there is controversy or uncertainty about the nature of the public interest doesn't mean that it doesn't exist. Since all citizens rely on infrastructure services, they have a common interest in seeing that infrastructure is provided reasonably efficiently and priced not too much above cost. The promotion of universal access is more controversial, but often enjoys widespread support. The general public has an interest in promoting universal piped water and sewerage, for example, inasmuch as they help protect everyone against the spread of disease. Similarly, rural roads, electricity, and telephones may be important to the general public because they promote social integration and political stability, particularly in developing countries.

In addition, many proponents have faith that the public interest will emerge from the give and take of different interest groups in a democracy. This belief was particularly strong among political scientists in the United States in the 1950s, perhaps because the principal alternative at the time seemed to be some form of fascism. The belief became popular once again toward the end of the twentieth century after the fall of many communist states. The presumption is that society is "pluralist," in that power is widely distributed rather than concentrated. As a result, public policies are adopted only after debate, compromise, and the formation of broad and heterogeneous coalitions.

Finally, public interest proponents do not put their faith in democracy alone, but also seek to perfect regulatory institutions that will encourage the development of the public interest. The issue of institutional design is discussed later in this chapter, but the state PUCs established in the first third of the twentieth century are examples of regulatory institutions crafted to encourage the rational discovery of the public interest.

Capture by Special Interests

Whether or not there is a real and knowable public interest, many scholars argue that in practice it has proved difficult to prevent regulatory agencies from being captured by special interests.[2] The concern about capture is as old as regulation, although our understanding of who might capture the agency, how, and with what degree of influence has evolved over the years.

During the late nineteenth and early twentieth centuries there were many allegations in the United States, Latin America, and elsewhere that municipal and state officials had been bribed by the companies they were supposed to regulate. Just how extensive the problem was and who had corrupted whom were not always obvious. Nevertheless, outrage over corruption was a major factor in the regulatory reforms put in place in the United States during the first decades of the twentieth century.[3]

During the 1950s, some U.S. scholars began to point out that the reforms had not prevented the regulated firms from exercising substantial influence over regulatory decisions.[4] In an influential 1955 book about federal regulatory agencies, Marver Bernstein proposed that agencies go through a life cycle, beginning as aggressive advocates of consumer interests but then declining into protectors of the status quo or, worse, servants of the firms they regulate.[5]

Bernstein and others noted that firms could capture the regulators with much more subtle and legal methods of influence than bribes. It was common at the time, for example, for the commissioners and senior staff of U.S. regulatory agencies to take well-paid jobs with the firms they were regulating when they retired. This practice was eventually restricted, but typically by requiring retirees to wait only a year or two, so that the prospect of a comfortable job presumably still made at least some regulators more sympathetic to the industry's perspective. Moreover, it has always been perfectly legal for a regulated firm to lobby and provide campaign contributions to the legislators who oversee a regulatory agency. Indeed, the industry representatives might capture the regulators intellectually simply because they spent so much time in each other's company.

The heart of the argument by Bernstein and his successors was not just that there were legal ways for the firms to influence regulators, but that the firms also typically had stronger incentives and more resources to press their cases than consumers did. Soon after Bernstein's book appeared, Anthony Downs and Mancur Olson described more formally the difficulties of organizing a group to pursue policies of collective benefit.[6] Among the obstacles were the time and resources it took for the members of a group to become informed and to influence policy. In addition, if all members of the group stood to benefit once favorable policies were enacted, then members had an incentive not to contribute resources to the common campaign but to "free ride" on the efforts of their peers instead. The larger the membership of the group, the harder it was to detect and discourage free riding. In a regulated industry the producers were more easily mobilized than their customers, because they were fewer and had more at stake. Regulatory decisions were critical to the financial health of the firms, while they affected only a small part of the budget of a typical customer.

During the 1960s, other researchers advanced the proposition that regulatory agencies were actually established at the behest of producers rather than being captured by them later. Producers might lobby to be regulated, for example, because the industry had elements of competition as well as monopoly, and regulation could be used to suppress those competitive sectors or elements. The historian Gabriel Kolko was among the first to make this argument in two books on the origins of railroad and economic regulation in the

United States.[7] Kolko claimed, for example, that the railroads were the single most important advocates for the ICC in the 1870s and 1880s, because the ICC could protect them from aggressive state regulators and provide the means for suppressing rate wars between railroads with parallel trunk lines. Historians soon found that firms had been active in lobbying for regulation in other industries. These revisionist histories coincided with the publication of several influential studies by political scientists that argued that pluralism was an illusion in the United States. Although not specifically focused on regulation, these studies contended that business and economic groups held disproportionate political power and that the public interest was usually a disguise for policies that served their private interests.[8]

Some economists, led by faculty at the University of Chicago, began to think along the same lines as the historians and political scientists. In an influential 1971 article, George Stigler offered an extreme version of Kolko's argument by proposing that the creation and operation of regulatory agencies could be understood entirely as a device to transfer economic resources to various private interests in return for those interests providing votes or campaign contributions to politicians.[9] Stigler hypothesized that every industry or occupation that had enough political power would seek to establish regulations that limited competition by controlling entry and fixing prices. Public interest goals, such as monopoly protection or promoting universal access, simply provided a plausible cloak to hide the real purposes of regulation.

The Chicago law professor Richard Posner soon advanced an alternative: that regulatory agencies were more likely to be captured by subsets of their consumers rather than by producers.[10] Because the regulated firm is a monopoly, it can charge some customers tariffs well above costs and use the profits to cross-subsidize low tariffs for other customers. Customer groups therefore have incentives to try to influence the regulator to give them favored treatment at the expense of others. In the United States, for example, it was often alleged that pressure from farmers had led railroad regulators to set very low rates for shipments of agricultural products that were cross-subsidized by very high rates on shipments of manufactured products. Posner labeled this strategy "taxation by regulation" and argued that the high prevalence of cross-subsidies in regulated industries strongly suggested that this was the dominant form of capture.

A third Chicago professor, the economist Sam Peltzman, attempted to combine Stigler's and Posner's theories by viewing the regulators (or the legislators who oversee regulatory agencies) as politicians in search of support from competing interest groups.[11] Producers may be more motivated and influential in some circumstances and consumers in others. The regulator will favor the interest group that can most readily deliver the votes or other support the agency needs. If no one group can supply the support the agency needs, moreover, Peltzman hypothesized that regulatory policy would be a compromise that left all the agency's supporters optimally dissatisfied. At its heart, however, Peltzman's approach still viewed regulatory agencies primarily as devices to transfer resources among interest groups in return for votes or other sources of support.

The work of Bernstein, Kolko, and the University of Chicago faculty stimulated several decades of research into the origins and behavior of regulatory agencies. In the midst of this effort, U.S. regulatory policy underwent two dramatic changes that seemed to undermine Kolko and Stigler's views that regulation is created to serve the interests of the regulated. First, the traditional pricing and entry regulations that Kolko and Stigler thought served corporate interests were either wholly or partially abandoned in the U.S. railroad, trucking, airline, telephone, and financial service industries during the late 1970s and early 1980s. Second, environmental and occupational safety regulations expanded dramatically and over the strenuous objections of business during the 1970s. Had U.S. researchers thought foreign experience relevant, they might have been equally intrigued by a third change: the expropriation of many private utilities in Europe and in developing countries between World War II and 1970. In any event, all three of these developments suggested that regulation might not always serve the regulated industry's interests, and that regulatory regimes were not necessarily stable.

Scholars made several attempts to reconcile these developments with the idea that regulation was usually initiated or captured by special interests. One was to argue that industry costs or demand could change over time in ways that made regulation more or less attractive to special interests.[12] Railroad regulation had been desirable for the railroads and their more politically influential shippers in the nineteenth century, for example, because railroads were the dominant mode of transportation and regulators could protect profits and cross-subsidies by limiting entry and preventing rate wars among railroads. The regulators' ability to protect railroad profits and cross-subsidies was undermined in the twentieth century, however, by the development of highway and air competition. As the demand for railroad services weakened, the benefits to special interests from regulation declined, those interests withdrew their support, and railroad regulation was abandoned.

The argument that changes in industry costs or demand could make regulation less attractive to special interests could not be the whole explanation, however, since it seemed to fit developments better in some industries than in others. In the U.S. trucking, airline, and telecommunications industries, for example, regulation was abandoned before the returns to the special interests thought to benefit from regulation had been dissipated.[13] And in the case of the U.S. railroads, the returns to regulation had been dissipated decades before deregulation. If the railroads had been earning little or no profits since the early 1950s, why was deregulation delayed until the end of the 1970s?

A second response to the deregulation movement was to acknowledge that competition among special interests could encourage policies that favored broader public interests. Gary Becker, another Chicago economist, pointed out that the introduction of regulation to favor special interests in markets that were otherwise efficient would be discouraged by the fact that the regulations created inefficiencies.[14] The inefficiencies meant that the benefits received by the favored interests would be less than the costs imposed on the other interests. The excess of costs over benefits gave the opponents of regulation a stronger incentive to mobilize than the proponents, all else being equal, thereby limiting the extent to which regulation was likely to be introduced solely as a means to redistribute wealth from one interest group to another. Theodore Keeler extended Becker's argument to markets that were not efficient in the absence of regulation, such as those characterized by natural monopoly.[15] In such markets the introduction of properly designed regulation could correct the inefficiency, which meant that the regulation's benefits would be greater than its costs. The excess of benefits over costs made it easier to form coalitions that favored the efficient corrective regulation of monopoly, again all else being equal.

Unfortunately, Becker and Keeler's models provided little guidance regarding the circumstances under which competition among special interests would lead to the public interest. Although economically efficient regulatory policies produced benefits in excess of costs, that advantage might not be enough to overcome other factors, such as the tendency for the regulated companies to be smaller in number and to have larger stakes in the outcome of regulatory policy than their consumers. It might be easier to organize coalitions that favored efficient regulatory policy all else being equal, but all else was seldom equal.

The most significant response to the deregulation movement was to recognize that the models of interest group competition advanced by the Chicago economists were probably too simplistic. In the first place, they assumed that the principal actors—the interest groups—could effectively control the behavior of the agents acting on their behalf—the voters, the regulators, and the regulated firms. Social scientists had become intrigued with the difficulties that principals face in controlling their agents if the principals' and agents' interests don't coincide and the principals have trouble monitoring and second-guessing the agents' actions. Regulation seemed to be a classic "principal-agent" problem. As the political scientist James Q. Wilson explained:

> To say that firms prefer higher profits, politicians more votes, and bureaucrats larger incomes is to make an important but incomplete assertion. If we wish to explain public policy by reference to such preferences, we must be able to say more—to show that policies are made so that profit-seeking firms can affect the votes won by vote-hungry politicians who will in turn constrain the behavior of money-hungry (or power-hungry, or status hungry) bureaucrats, whose behavior will in turn affect the profitability of firms. It is a long and complex causal chain.[16]

Moreover, the Chicago economists generally assumed that the regulatory agency (or the regulated industry) was ultimately supervised by a single political master: the politician who won the most votes. In fact, regulatory agencies were typically subject to supervision from a variety of different political bodies, including the elected executive, the different chambers of the legislative branch, and often several different committees within each chamber. This diffusion of oversight responsibility provided opportunities for a wider variety of politicians or interest groups to try to affect the behavior of the agency, but probably made it harder for any one group to exercise decisive influence. Politicians might be attentive when the agency was initially established or during crises, but the difficulties of exercising oversight and the diffusion of responsibility meant that the agency's activities were often largely unsupervised.[17]

These observations helped to stimulate a group of economists, led by Jean-Jacques Laffont and Jean Tirole of the University of Toulouse, to develop mathematical models of the relationships between the principals and their agents in the regulatory process. The central feature of these models is that the principals have imperfect information about the capabilities or performance of their agents. Some models incorporate several layers of principals and agents (for example, voters, politicians, regulators, and regulated firms), while others recognize that an agent might be supervised by more than one principal. Although the models have generated interesting suggestions for reducing principal-agent problems, the yield in new insights about how regulatory agencies behave has been modest so far.[18]

More generally, however, recent scholarship tends to support Peltzman's argument that regulators often draw support from a variety of sources instead of being captured by a single interest, and that these patterns of support change over time.[19] In a series of studies of the railroad industry, for example, later scholars argued that Kolko had understated the roles of agricultural and mercantile interest groups in the establishment of the ICC and state regulatory agencies.[20] Railroad regulation seems to have originated with a broad base of support, including consumers as well as producers. Once an agency is established, however, the political forces that continue to focus on it may be narrower than those that created it. And the political bargain may have to change over time as, for example, changes in technology alter interests or events shape popular perceptions. Regulatory systems seem to have enormous inertia, so that pressures may have to build for a while before significant changes occur. Ultimately, however, the agency's performance has to be reasonably consistent with what a preponderance of interests will support or its statute will be revised.

Another idea that has survived is that whether the costs and benefits of regulation are narrowly concentrated or widely distributed helps determine which interests will influence regulatory policy and whether broader public interests are pursued. James Q. Wilson distinguishes four different patterns. When both the costs and the benefits of a regulatory issue are widely distributed, then interest groups will have little incentive to form around the issue, and what Wilson calls "majoritarian" politics will result. When both costs and benefits are highly concentrated, however, the result is "interest group politics." In this case, the affected interest groups have strong incentives to mobilize and battle for influence, and the general public is not likely to be heard from. Concentrated benefits and widely dispersed costs generate "client" politics, in which the group that benefits will dominate policy, since it has a strong incentive to mobilize while the general public does not. Finally, concentrated costs and widely distributed benefits generate what Wilson calls "entrepreneurial" politics. In such cases, Wilson hypothesizes that the regulatory policy will be adopted only if a skilled political entrepreneur can mobilize latent public sentiment and put the opponents on the defensive.[21]

As Wilson's "entrepreneurial" category indicates, recent research also suggests that interest group pressures alone do not shape regulatory policy, and that individuals and ideas can play an important role. If a regulatory agency is subject to pressures from a variety of interest groups with roughly similar strength and conflicting positions, for example, then regulators and their staff may have room to advance their own ideas about what might be best. And some of their ideas may be of the public interest variety. The need to explain government policy to the public also can constrain interest group influence and increase the role of ideas and ideology.[22] Some researchers argue, for example, that individual political or bureaucratic entrepreneurs, armed with the scholarship critical of regulation that had developed since the 1950s, played an important role in stimulating the deregulation of various transportation and telecommunications industries in the United States in the late 1970s and early 1980s.[23]

Institutional Protections

The Institutional Perspective

Yet another perspective is that the risk of capture by special interests depends on the design of both the regulatory agency and the other broader institutions that shape the interactions between private citizens and government. The study of institutions was fashionable among political scientists and economists in the first half of the twentieth century and has come into favor again. Many of the more recent studies are rooted in economics, and particularly in the work on transaction costs by Ronald Coase, Oliver Williamson, and Douglass North and others mentioned in the previous chapter.[24] From this perspective, institutions are defined as the formal and informal rules that govern the ways in which individuals and organizations interact with each other. Thus institutions include a nation's constitution, laws, and political system as well as its more informal customs or social conventions. Institutions affect the transaction costs of various types of activities by influencing, among other things, the exposure of parties to opportunism and the defenses they can use against it.

The proponents of this perspective argue that institutions change in the long run but tend to be stable in the short run. Institutions evolve in response to political, economic, and other forces. In the long run they are a product of their larger environment, and cannot be too much at odds with it. But institutions are slow to change in part because their stability is advantageous to society. Stable institutions make the behavior of individuals and organizations more predictable, and thus make it easier for individuals and organizations to engage in cooperative activity. And because institutions evolve only gradually, they shape and constrain the behavior of individuals and organizations.

The Design of Regulatory Agencies

During the first half of the twentieth century, U.S. reformers devoted a great deal of effort to the design of regulatory institutions that would resist capture by special interests. These schemes typically tried to balance independence from elected politicians in the executive and legislative branches of government with some form of direct accountability to the larger public and to the regulated companies and their customers. In effect these schemes replaced the normal process for political decision making in a democracy with alternative forms of accountability.

The primary measure for promoting independence was to appoint regulatory commissioners to long terms and make them removable only for specific and limited causes, such as corruption. In many cases commissioners were also appointed to staggered terms so that it would take many years before the elected officials who appointed them could name a majority on the commission. In some cases the regulatory agency's budget was removed from the normal process of legislative and executive review so as to make it harder for elected officials to retaliate against the commission by cutting its funding.

A variety of measures were used to promote public accountability. Most PUCs had five to seven commissioners instead of one, for example, in order to make it harder to keep corrupt agreements secret. Many of the commissions were also required to hold public hearings and to deliberate on the record in an effort to further limit the risk of secret influence.[25] Similarly, the U.S. Congress imposed a variety of institutional constraints on the federal regulatory agencies created in the New Deal in response to complaints that the agencies were abusing their powers over the firms and individuals they regulated. Under the Administrative Procedure Act of 1946, Congress specified that a federal regulatory agency could issue a rule only if it (1) gave adequate public notice of its intention to issue the rule, (2) provided interested parties an opportunity to participate through the written or oral submission of arguments and data, and (3) provided a written explanation of the basis for the final rule adopted. If an individual case was being considered rather than an industrywide rule, the procedural protections were even stricter. The idea was that regulatory agencies had a quasi-judicial function, and thus their procedures ought to embody the principles of fairness that had developed in common law and were enshrined in the Constitution.[26] Many states subsequently adopted similar constraints.

The effectiveness of these institutional strategies came into doubt in the second half of the twentieth century, as scholarly criticism of the regulatory agencies grew. The very idea that a politically independent regulator could best discover the public interest was challenged by Sam Huntington in a 1952 study of the ICC. Huntington argued that the independence designed to allow the ICC to discover the public interest had instead made its capture by special interests possible.[27] The railroads had captured the ICC after World War I and then used the agency to suppress competition among railroads, trucks, and barges. Huntington viewed the results as so contrary to the public interest that he proposed that the ICC be abolished as an independent commission and replaced by a government agency that would be directly accountable to Congress and the president and, through them, to the broader electorate. While most scholars were reluctant to recommend such a radical step, Huntington's study made it clear that a regulator's political independence had costs as well as benefits.

In the 1960s and 1970s, scholars began to argue that some of the specific regulatory procedures adopted to promote accountability also made it easier for the regulated firm to capture the regulator.[28] Requirements for public hearings, oral testimony, written testimony, and rebuttal made arguing a case before a regulator a long and elaborate process, which gave an advantage to interest groups that could mobilize the resources needed to participate on a sustained basis. And even if the regulator was not captured, the lengthy procedures contributed to the impression that the regulatory agencies were lethargic and out of touch. These criticisms encouraged efforts to streamline the regulatory process and to provide assistance to help the general public and small firms participate.

A less pessimistic view emerged during the 1980s, in which administrative procedures were seen as a device to help politicians maintain control over the regulatory agencies they created.[29] Politicians faced a classic principal-agent problem, because the regulatory bureaucrats might not share their preferences or priorities. The politicians could not rely on the enabling statute to control the regulators' behavior, since it was difficult to draft a statute that anticipated all the problems that might develop. And effective oversight was difficult, because it was costly for the politicians to find out what the agency was doing and the sanctions they could apply were limited. The Administrative Procedure Act aided in control because the requirements for notice, comment, and hearings all generated, at no cost to the politicians, much of the information they needed for oversight. Moreover, the politicians could design procedures that favored certain interest groups over others by specifying who bore the burden of proof, who had standing to intervene, and who could initiate a regulatory change. The intent, these scholars argued, was to mandate a set of procedures that reproduced the balance of power among interests when the regulatory agency was established, so that the agency's subsequent decisions would be consistent with the political intent of its creators.

The Broader Institutional Environment

More recent scholarship has focused on the broader institutional environments in which regulatory agencies operate rather than on regulatory agencies or their procedures. A major theme of this research is that governments are less likely to be able to behave opportunistically toward private individuals in political systems where power is divided and there are checks and balances among government institutions. In a famous article, for example, Douglass North and Barry Weingast argued that England's economic development was facilitated by the Glorious Revolution of 1688 because the rebellion led to the establishment of Parliament as a counterweight to the monarchy.[30]

Parliament limited the discretion of the king to expropriate private property through taxation and other means, and the security of property in turn led to an expanded private capital market that was better able to finance both the wars of the state and the coming industrial revolution. North and Weingast suggested that the lack of a similar check against royal power in France retarded the development of French capital markets and contributed to the relative decline of French power in the eighteenth century.

A related theme is that legal systems are critical for modern economic development, because they reduce the costs of enforcing contracts and protect private property against theft or expropriation. Legal scholars classify the legal systems of countries into different traditions or families. These classifications do not depend on the specific rules in the country's laws but rather on the methods "through which the rules to be applied are discovered, interpreted and evaluated."[31] The two dominant legal families in the modern world are English common law and the European civil law.[32] Britain and its former colonies, including the United States and Canada, have common law systems; the European countries and their former colonies, including Latin America, generally have civil law systems.[33]

Recent research suggests that common law systems provide more protection for individual property rights than civil law systems. In a series of papers, Rafael La Porta, Florencio Lopez-de-Silanas, Andrei Shleifer, and Robert Vishny compared, across a large sample of countries, the size of the markets for private corporate debt and equity and the extent to which major companies are owned by small stockholders or are closely held by families or large institutions.[34] They classified the countries according to whether they belonged to the civil or common law traditions. In addition, they looked for the presence of specific legal rules designed to protect shareholders against management, such as provisions that give investors one vote for each share they own or that allow a small minority of shareholders to force a special shareholder meeting. Their statistical analyses demonstrate that the specific legal rules matter: countries that have rules to protect shareholders tend to have larger debt and equity markets and more widespread stock ownership. But these investigators also found that the legal traditions have an independent effect. Even with the same specific rules, common law countries tend to have deeper capital markets and more small shareholders than civil law countries.

Civil law systems may provide less protection for private property and individual liberties, because civil law judges are supposed to only interpret the letter of the law and not go beyond it. A judge can intervene only if she finds a violation of a specific statute, which gives the executive and legislative branches of government, who write the statutes, more control over the scope of the judiciary's activities. In common law systems, by contrast, judges are not restricted to the statutes but can base decisions on the "common law" of case precedents and past decisions as well. The ability to appeal to a common law that has evolved over centuries provides an independent check on the powers of the executive and the legislature. It is no accident that the common law system evolved out of popular opposition to the English monarchy while civil law assumes that the state is the ultimate arbiter in society.

One implication of this research is that contractual and discretionary regulation may be more viable in some types of political and legal systems than in others. Political institutions that have checks and balances should provide stronger regulatory commitment, for example, because they make it harder for government to change the rules of the regulatory game. Checks and balances that limit the arbitrary use of government powers should also help discourage special interests from abusing the powers of a discretionary regulatory agency. And legal institutions that provide strong protection for private property should protect private contracts and concession contracts as well.

Very little research has been done to confirm whether or how these broader political and legal institutions affect the performance of regulatory agencies. One exception is a study by Brian Levy and Pablo Spiller of the history of private telephone companies in Argentina, Britain, Chile, Jamaica, and the Philippines.[35] Telephone systems are usually too complex to be regulated through a concession contract system, so all five of the countries used some form of discretionary regulation during the periods when the telephone companies were privately owned. In most countries and during most years, however, the regulatory scheme also included contractual elements that constrained the regulator. For example, regulators were obligated by statute to provide a specific minimum rate of return to telephone companies in Chile from 1958 to 1970 and in Jamaica before 1966 and after 1987. Similarly, Britain after 1984 and Chile after 1987 used a price-cap scheme, in which the regulator is allowed to adjust the tariff formula only every five years.

According to Levy and Spiller, the experience of the private telephone companies suggests that private investment is more likely with a discretionary regulatory scheme that has contractual elements and in countries that have an independent judiciary and a presidential rather than a parliamentary system of government. The authors' reasoning is that private investment is more likely if investors believe the government is committed to reasonably clear rules. Statutory provisions that limit the regulator's discretion help make the regulator's decisions more predictable. An independent judiciary is needed to enforce the statutory constraints on the regulator. And a presidential system makes it harder to change the statute, since the executive and the legislature are often controlled by different political parties.

Levy and Spiller's results offer some support for the advantage of an independent judiciary but less for the advantages of statutory constraints on discretion or a presidential system. Three of the five countries studied have enjoyed sustained periods of private investment, and they are the three that Levy and Spiller classify as having independent judiciaries (Britain, Chile, and Jamaica). But only one of the three countries with sustained investment has a presidential system; the other two have parliamentary governments (Britain and Jamaica).[36] Moreover, the three countries with presidential systems (Argentina, Chile, and the Philippines) seemed to change regulatory regimes roughly as often as the two countries with parliamentary systems. All five of the countries imposed fairly specific statutory constraints on the regulators, the only exception being Jamaica between 1966 and 1987. Although the Jamaican telephone investment suffered during the 1966 to 1987 period, it would be difficult to conclude from that one case that detailed statutory constraints on the regulator are highly beneficial.[37]

Levy and Spiller's study has inspired efforts by other researchers to examine the relationship between regulatory performance and the broader institutional environment using larger samples of countries and regulatory systems. Assembling data sets has been difficult, because most countries outside the United States have only a decade or so of recent experience with private utilities and because a large number of variables are needed to make cross-country comparisons.[38] But this approach is likely to yield some interesting results.

The Chances of Capture

In sum, the chances that a regulatory agency will be captured seem to depend on a variety of factors, not all of which are well understood. One factor is the pattern and visibility of the costs and benefits of the actions the agency might take. The traditional fear is that the agency will be captured by the companies it regulates, since the benefits of tariff increases are concentrated in the companies while the costs are often spread thinly over many customers. But utilities often have large customers as well as small ones, and those large customers may mobilize to protect their investments. Moreover, many utility tariffs are highly visible, which may make it easier to mobilize many small consumers against tariff increases even though each customer bears only a small share of the costs.

Institutions also appear to be important, but our understanding of when and why is fairly limited. Institutional differences probably explain why regulatory agencies seem more likely to pursue the public interest soon after their creation or after major restructuring. The creation or restructuring of an agency usually requires a change in legislation, which brings the issue into a more open forum where a broader coalition may be needed to effect change.

The routine business of a regulatory agency does not require legislation, however, which increases the possibility for the agency to be captured by special interests over time, or possibly to escape effective supervision altogether.

The design of the regulatory agency also matters, although here we have learned that the choices are not always easy. Measures that insulate regulatory agencies from day-to-day political pressures make it easier to make decisions that are unpopular in the short run, including decisions that are not in the public interest. And procedures designed to make regulatory agencies accountable to particular coalitions or to the general public may have unintended and undesired effects as well. Provisions to ensure that affected parties have opportunities to be heard and participate, for example, may impart such a strong bias toward the status quo that the regulatory system cannot cope with change.

Finally, the broader institutional environment of the regulatory agency is probably influential as well. Legal systems and other institutions that protect private property may also help protect utility investors from abuse by regulatory agencies. And political systems with checks and balances may make it harder to change regulatory regimes. How strong these influences are is far from clear, however. Moreover, our understanding of the effects of the broader institutional environment is still too primitive to help us choose among regulatory strategies. The institutional environments that seem helpful to private contracts or concession contracts seem to help discretionary regulation as well.

4

Capture and Instability: Sri Lanka's Buses and U.S. Telephones

Capture as a Source of Instability

Regulatory regimes can change, as the nationalization of regulated utilities in many countries after World War II and the deregulation of some U.S. industries in the 1970s and 1980s demonstrate. Many of the explanations for change recounted in the previous chapter credit technological and other forces exogenous to the regulated industry. The development of highway and air transportation during the twentieth century weakened the monopoly power of U.S. railroads, for example, and made continued regulation either less necessary (from the public interest perspective) or less lucrative (from the special interest perspective). But there is also a tradition, dating back at least to Marver Bernstein's 1955 book on the life cycle of a regulatory agency, that the forces for change may be partly endogenous; in other words, that regulation contains the seeds of its own decay or destruction.[1]

With discretionary regulatory regimes, the accounts of endogenous change and instability all involve the capture of the regulatory agency by special interests. The simplest but most compelling versions are based on the observation that the special interests that capture the regulatory agency benefit at the expense of others. Gary Becker noted that the benefits to the agency's captors are inevitably less than the costs imposed on others, since the policies pursued by the captured agency create market inefficiencies.[2] Becker reasoned that this pattern of costs and benefits made it risky for a regulatory agency to pander too much to special interests. Becker had in mind that excessive pandering might mobilize the losers to overthrow the agency's policies. But the losers might also have the option of exiting the regulatory system, so as to avoid bearing its costs. Moreover, the losers' ability to exit increases over time as any durable investments that are specific to the regulatory regime wear out and have to be replaced. In the long run, the losing interests may be able to withdraw enough to undermine the benefits received by the regulator's captors, so that the regulatory regime collapses.

This chapter examines two common forms of capture in which the losing interests eventually exit. The first involves capture by short-sighted consumers at the expense of investors. The consumers are concerned with keeping tariffs affordable, and fail to appreciate their long-term interest in supporting the investments needed to maintain the capacity and quality of the services they enjoy. Often the problems begin during a period of strong inflation, when consumers petition the regulatory agency to provide some relief by not raising utility tariffs. Eventually the real value of the tariff erodes so much that the companies no longer earn an adequate return on their investments, and they respond by not replacing assets as they wear out and not expanding capacity when needed. Usually the resulting deterioration in the quality of service reaches a point where the regulatory agency defies popular pressure and grants a tariff increase. Once the crisis has passed, however, the process of capture and the erosion of the real value of the tariff often repeat, so that the industry and its customers are condemned to periodic crises of poor service followed by enormous tariff increases. In some cases, however, the crisis of poor service—or a history of repeated crises—so undermines popular support that the private companies are expropriated, and service is provided by public agencies instead.

Capture by short-sighted consumers is fairly common in developing countries, although examples can be found almost everywhere. One might think this form of capture rare, since consumers are often numerous and the benefit each stands to gain is relatively modest. But utility tariffs are often highly visible and politically sensitive. Commuters pay their bus and subway fares every day and households receive their gas, electricity, and telephone bills every month, so that even a small tariff increase may be quickly noted and resented by many. In developing countries, moreover, there is the perception, not always justified, that utilities absorb a large share of household incomes. Developing economies also tend to suffer from more frequent and severe bouts of inflation, and utility tariffs are among the few prices governments can readily control to provide the public with inflationary relief. Regulatory systems that are poorly insulated from immediate political pressures and political systems with limited checks and balances may also encourage this form of capture.

The second common form involves capture by a subset of the consumers at the expense of the rest. The subset of customers presses the regulator for low tariffs on the services it uses. Eventually a system of cross-subsidies develops, in which the profits on services used by other customers support losses on services used by the favored group. The other customers are often referred to as the industry's "cream," because of the high markups they are charged. But the overcharged customers have strong incentives to find some way to bypass the regulated industry by buying from unregulated sources. And the prospect of "skimming off" some of the cream encourages alternative suppliers to help customers find their way around the regulated providers. If enough bypassing or cream skimming develops, the regulators must find a means to suppress the alternative suppliers or face the collapse of the regulated industry.

Capture for cross-subsidies seems to be common in both the developing and the industrialized world, in part because cross-subsidies are often easy to hide. Many infrastructure industries have such complex networks and cost structures that it is hard to know which customers are paying their way. Usually the controversy revolves around the allocation of the costs of facilities used by several different groups of customers. Both local and long-distance callers use local telephone lines and switchboards to complete their calls, for example, while both freight shippers and passengers often use the same railroad track and signal systems for transportation. The difficulties of cost allocation may be exaggerated by customers who try to argue that their share should be lower, but sometimes the uncertainties are real.[3] In extreme cases, it may be impossible to determine who is cross-subsidizing whom—the most one can say is that some customers pay a higher markup over direct costs than others. In any event, such controversies make it easier to hide cross-subsidies, at least until they are exposed by cream skimming.

Cross-subsidies are also encouraged by popular support for universal access to basic service at affordable prices. The goal of universal access is often alleged to require some form of subsidy for basic services to households that are poor or that live in remote or otherwise costly-to-serve areas.[4] Cross-subsidies among customers are an attractive source of financial support for basic or lifeline tariffs, especially since the main alternative source—government tax revenues—is often in short supply. Even when the regulator is not captured by a subset of the consumers, the combination of support for universal access and uncertainties about cost allocation often encourages the regulator to engage in a fair amount of "averaging" when setting prices. Charging the same price for a broad range of customers may seem fair to the public, especially if the cost differences are obscure and hard to explain.

Finally, the regulated firms usually find it in their interests to join the coalition supporting cross-subsidies. By so doing, the firms ingratiate themselves with the regulatory agency, since the firms' support makes it easier for the agency to accommodate the pressures for cross-subsidies from proponents of universal access or from subsets of consumers that may have captured it. Equally important, cross-subsidies provide the firms with a rationale for discouraging the development of competition either within or outside the industry. Cross-subsidies can be sustained only if the industry remains a monopoly; the cream will disappear as soon as the firms must compete for customers. Thus a regulatory agency that is committed to cross-subsidies must be committed to suppressing competition as well, which is a happy thought for the incumbent firms.

This chapter illustrates the dynamics of capture by short-sighted consumers and capture for cross-subsidies using the cases of buses in Sri Lanka and telephones in the United States. These cases are particularly vivid, but it would be easy to find many comparable examples.

Capture by Short-Sighted Consumers

Sri Lanka's Bus Industry

Buses account for 60 to 80 percent of all passenger trips in many developing countries, which forces most countries to use private bus companies or a combination of private and public companies. Public bus companies tend to be less efficient and to require subsidies, so that governments simply can't afford to rely on public companies entirely.[5] But the dependence of so many citizens on buses also makes bus fares and the quality of bus service politically sensitive issues. Sri Lanka experimented with many different methods of providing and regulating bus service over the course of the twentieth century, and its experience, summarized in Table 4.1, is fairly typical.[6]

Sri Lanka, formerly known as Ceylon, is an island nation of 18 million people located off the southeast tip of India. Sri Lanka's gross national product of US$700 per capita in 1995 places it in the upper quartile of the group of countries the United Nations classifies as low income. Its economy is based on exports of tea, rubber, and rice and, more recently, clothing and light manufacturing. Soon after gaining its independence in 1948, Sri Lanka de-

Table 4.1 Chronology of bus regulation and reform in Sri Lanka

1916	Introduction of licensing for motor vehicles.
1942	Consolidation of bus industry into eighty-five companies, each with exclusive service territories and with regulated fares.
1958	Nationalization of bus companies and the creation of the Ceylon Transport Board as the public bus company.
1979	Public bus company reorganized and private operators allowed to return, but without exclusive franchises or regulated fares. Fares increased but regulation introduced surreptitiously soon after.
1990	Overcrowding forces first bus fare increase in seven years and yet another reorganization of the public bus companies.
1997–2001	Fares increase and public bus companies reorganized again.

clared itself a socialist republic and nationalized the large tea plantations and many other industries. In 1977, after decades of slow growth, a new government shifted policies and began to open the economy to the private sector and competition. In the mid-1990s, Sri Lanka initiated a program to privatize some of the nationalized industries, starting with the tea plantations, a steel mill, and the compressed gas company. The annual rate of real economic growth increased to 4 percent in the years immediately after liberalization, a significant gain but less than hoped for. A key reason for the slow economic growth has been an insurgency since 1983 by the Tamil minority, whose guerrilla army controls parts of the northeast of the island.

As in most countries, urban and intercity buses appeared in Sri Lanka in the second decade of the twentieth century, and the services were initially operated by private companies. The British colonial government established its authority to license buses and other motor vehicles in 1916, but regulation of the bus industry was otherwise minimal until 1942. In that year, the government consolidated the industry into eighty-five companies in response to complaints that competition among bus operators had become so intense that it was destructive for the firms and unsafe for passengers. Each company was given an exclusive franchise to provide service over a particular route or in a particular territory and, in return, had to accept government control over fares.

This private but regulated system survived the first decade of independence until 1956, when a new government was elected on a platform of nationalizing key industries, including transport. At the time there were reportedly widespread complaints about overcrowding and poor service by the monopoly bus operators, which may have been due in part to the failure of regulators to increase fares with inflation. Whatever the cause, in 1958 the private bus companies were nationalized and consolidated into a single public company, the Ceylon Transport Board (CTB).

For at least its first decade, the CTB was generally regarded as a success. The civil servants brought in to manage the new company were competent and dedicated, and the government bought two thousand new and reconditioned buses to allow the CTB to retire its oldest vehicles, relieve overcrowding, and extend routes into underserved areas. Over the years, however, the government pressed the CTB to take on large numbers of staff, raise wages, and further expand services in rural areas where traffic was unprofitably light. The government also was slow to allow fares to keep pace with inflation, which created serious problems after the oil crisis of 1973–1974 stimulated strong inflation in many countries. By the mid-1970s the CTB was grossly overstaffed and incurring substantial losses. The government, suffering from a stagnating economy and budgetary deficits, did not have the funds to buy the CTB new buses; complaints about poor service and overcrowding were again widespread.

The situation deteriorated further after a new government came to power in 1977 with a mandate to revive economic growth by reversing the protectionist policies of the past and opening up the economy to competition. The new government's efforts were successful, but the CTB found itself completely unable to cope with the sharp increases in bus ridership stimulated by the economic revival. At first, the government attempted to solve the problem by raising bus fares and pressing the World Bank for a large loan to buy the CTB additional buses. The bank was reluctant to finance new vehicles without some effort to reform the system, however, and proposed that private operators be permitted to provide service once again. The government was ideologically sympathetic to the idea and agreed to allow private bus services to resume in 1979.

The new private bus scheme differed from the 1942–1958 scheme in two important ways. One was that both public and private companies were allowed to provide service. The CTB was divided into nine regional transport boards (RTBs) on the theory that nine smaller public companies would be easier to manage and more responsive to local problems. The RTBs were also provided with a fleet of new buses. The second key difference was that the private firms were not granted the territorial or route monopolies they had enjoyed from 1942 to 1958 and, in return, were not subject to fare regulation. A private bus company had to obtain government permission to serve a particular route, but this was intended only to protect against excessive congestion or safety problems. Fare regulation would be unnecessary, the reformers reasoned, since private operators would be disciplined by competition among themselves and with the RTBs. RTB bus fares were increased significantly, however, to give the reorganized public bus companies a better chance of becoming financially self-sufficient.

The reforms succeeded in more than doubling the capacity of the bus system, but competition among the new private bus operators was so intense that it created coordination and safety problems. Between 1979 and 1983, the private sector put approximately 13,300 buses on the road while the public sector's operating fleet held steady at approximately 5,500 buses, as shown in Table 4.2.[7] Most of the private bus operators owned only one or two buses, however, and the private operators serving a route seldom maintained a regular or coordinated schedule or offered much service after 6 P.M., when passenger traffic thinned. In addition, bus drivers often raced each other to stops or engaged in other unsafe behavior to capture passengers. Some large companies reportedly attempted to enter the market in the early 1980s but were driven off by the intensity of the competition. The government tried to improve coordination by requiring that all the private operators join a route

Table 4.2 Public and private bus fleets and fares (in constant rupees) in Sri Lanka, 1971–1995

Year	Average number of buses operated per day		Fares indexed constant rupees (1990 = 100.0)
	Public	Private	
1971	N.A.	0	72.9[a]
1972	N.A.	0	68.6
1973	N.A.	0	62.7
1974	4,302	0	94.8[a]
1975	4,469	0	89.0
1976	4,425	0	87.7
1977	4,583	0	86.8
1978	5,097	0	89.2[a]
1979	5,376	809	81.2
1980	5,670	1,103	84.4 and 136.3[a]
1981	5,496	5,075	115.8
1982	5,614	9,500	104.6
1983	5,541	13,300	113.8 and 134.4[a]
1984	5,062	13,700	115.2
1985	4,880	14,060	113.5
1986	4,750	13,970	105.0
1987	4,676	13,434	97.6
1988	4,407	12,423	85.5
1989	3,888	11,564	76.7
1990	3,428	12,567	100.0 [a]
1991	3,370	13,454	89.1
1992	3,654	12,720	80.0
1993	3,709	11,453	71.6
1994	4,207	10,600	66.1
1995	3,867	12,815	61.3

Sources: Fleet data from John Diandas, "The Future of Government Owned Bus Transport in Sri Lanka," in *Aspects of Privatization in Sri Lanka* (Colombo: Friedrich-Ebert-Stiftung, 1988), pp. 111–112 and updated from the National Transport Commission, Sri Lanka. Fare data from Halcrow Fox Ltd., *Appraisal of the Bus Industry,* working paper no. 9 of the Colombo Urban Transport Study, London and Colombo, December 1993, p. 4. Fares were deflated with the consumer price index for Sri Lanka as reported in International Monetary Fund, *International Financial Statistics Yearbook 1995,* pp. 702–703.

Note: The fare increase in 1971 was only 18 percent in nominal terms. Fares were increased by 15 percent in 1996 and remained at that level through 1998. *N.A.*–Not available.

a. Year of fare increase. Two fare figures are shown in years when there were two fare increases (1980 and 1983).

association to agree on and enforce a common timetable. The government eventually disbanded the associations, however, because many came to be dominated by small cliques of operators who ran the route for their own benefit and maintained control through physical intimidation of other members and bribery of local officials.

Despite the reformers' intentions, the private bus operators gradually became subject to fare regulation, which soon threatened their profitability and ability to replace their vehicles. When private operators applied for a license to serve a route, they had to specify the fare that they would charge. Although the fare was not a legal grounds for denying a route license, private operators were told informally that their license applications would be denied if they proposed fares higher than those charged by the public bus companies.

By the late 1980s, the limitation on fares had become a serious problem. The public bus companies had not had a fare increase since 1983, and inflation had reduced the real value of bus fares by almost 50 percent (see Table 4.2). The private bus fleet began to shrink, and the public bus companies were in no position to fill the gap. The breakup of the CTB into nine RTBs had done little to improve the efficiency of the public companies, who also suffered from the erosion in fares. The RTBs remained heavily dependent on central government support, particularly for the purchase of buses, but the government could not afford to be generous enough to prevent the RTBs' decline.

The deterioration in service provoked another round of reforms in 1990. During negotiations over a further loan for new RTB buses, the World Bank pressed the Sri Lankan government to raise fares and privatize the RTBs. The government increased fares by 40 percent, which restored part, but not all, of the value they had lost since 1983. The government was reluctant to eliminate its public bus companies completely, however, and decided to "peoplise" the companies instead. Under the peoplisation program, the RTBs were broken up into 93 separate companies, each organized around an existing bus depot. The government retained title to the immobile assets, primarily bus depots and stations. Those employed at the depot were given, free of charge, shares worth 50 percent of the mobile assets, with the Treasury retaining the rest of the shares for later disposal.

Like the 1979 reforms, the 1990 reforms provided only temporary relief. The fare increase stimulated a modest increase in the size of the private bus fleet, but by 1993 inflation had already eroded the real value of fares below the previous low reached in 1989. The peoplised depots increased service by about 30 percent in the first years, largely because the government bought them approximately 2,700 new buses. But peoplisation proved to be a disastrous compromise, effectively creating companies that were neither fully public nor fully private. The peoplised services soon deteriorated as most depots failed to earn enough to repay the government for the new buses they received, much less to buy new ones themselves. The private and public bus fleets declined fairly steadily during the 1990s, creating a crisis severe enough to provoke another round of substantial fare increases and another reorganization of the public bus companies again at the end of the decade.[8]

By the end of the twentieth century, Sri Lanka's bus industry seemed doomed to poor performance whether in the private or the public sector. The experience had convinced the former chairman of Sri Lanka's National Transport Commission, John Diandas, that both private and public bus systems inevitably deteriorated over time, and that the industry was condemned to a privatization-regulation-nationalization cycle, which he illustrated in Figure 4.1. According to his count, the industry had been around the cycle one and one-half times already, beginning as private and unregulated before World War I, imposing fare and route regulation in 1942, nationalizing in 1958,

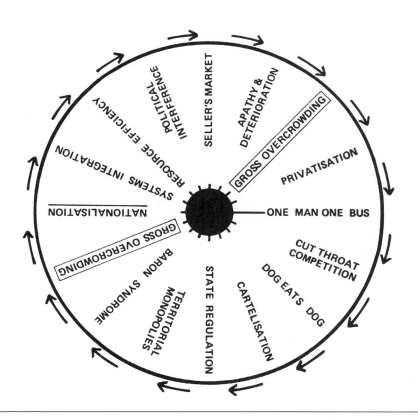

Figure 4.1 John Diandas's bus history cycle. (John Diandas, "Notes for Benefit Comparison of Government Sector and Private Sector Supplied Bus Services" in *Aspects of Privatization in Sri Lanka,* Colombo: Friedrich-Ebert-Stiftung, 1988, p. 75.)

privatizing (at least partially) in 1979, and reimposing fare regulation soon thereafter.

Sri Lanka seemed unlikely to take the next step in Diandas's cycle, however, simply because the government knew it could not afford to take over the private bus companies again and operate all bus service in the public sector. A public takeover had been more attractive in 1958, when the bus industry was smaller and the country more optimistic about the performance of public enterprises. Despite repeated efforts to reform the public bus companies, however, the government estimated that their costs per passenger kilometer remained roughly 20 percent higher than those of the private bus companies.[9] But if Sri Lanka was unwilling to take over the private companies, it was also unable to increase fares gradually with inflation. Instead it seemed condemned to raise fares in large increments roughly every ten years, suffering through periodic crises of overcrowded buses and unhappy passengers.

Regulation's Creation and Capture

Sri Lanka's bus industry illustrates how changing combinations of producer and consumer interests can motivate and influence regulation. The regulation of Sri Lanka's bus fares is probably not in the broad public interest except under special and limited circumstances. Buses have few of the characteristics of a natural monopoly. Only a small percentage of the industry's investments are immobile and durable, primarily those in downtown bus stations or terminals. The problems these investments might create are usually avoided by having the government own the key terminals so that it can ensure that the bus bays are available to competing private bus companies on a nondiscriminatory basis. There is also little evidence of economies of scale for firms with more than fifty buses in industrialized countries, and the economies are probably exhausted with even smaller fleets in developing countries.[10] Indeed, the fact that Sri Lanka's private bus industry consists mostly of firms with only one or two buses is powerful evidence of the absence of natural monopoly.

If there is a problem with competition, it is that there is too much rather than too little. The small bus companies, uncoordinated schedules, and aggressive driving found in Sri Lanka are typical of private bus industries in many developing countries. Daniel Klein and his colleagues argue that the problems stem from the failure to establish clear property rights for curbside bus stops.[11] If one bus company creates a service that stops at defined points along a street according to a reliable schedule, for example, then passengers will begin to assemble at those stops to catch its buses. If the company does not have the exclusive right to pick up the passengers assembling at the designated stops, however, another bus operator can put a bus on the route just ahead of one of the first company's buses and collect the passengers assembled. The interloping bus company doesn't assume the responsibility or cost of providing a reasonably regular and reliable service, but it captures many of the benefits in the form of the assembled passengers. These circumstances weaken the incentives of bus companies to establish regular and reliable schedules and encourage the bus companies sharing a route to race each other to stops. Interlopers were probably to blame when one or two large tour bus operators in Sri Lanka entered regular route service in the early 1980s and were quickly forced to withdraw. And the ambiguity about curb rights probably encouraged violence by Sri Lanka's route associations, since there was no other way to discipline the behavior of members and interlopers.

Fare regulation alone does nothing to solve the problems of curb rights and interlopers, but assigning curb rights may create a monopoly that makes fare regulation necessary. The most common solution to the curb rights problem is for the government to award exclusive franchises for each route, as Sri Lanka did in 1942. The exclusive franchise serves as a barrier to entry against interlopers, increasing the returns from offering a reliable schedule and reducing the incentives for aggressive driving. The franchise may give the holder market power, however, particularly in developing countries where there is only limited competition from private motor vehicles. And the market power may in turn justify fare regulation.

Sri Lanka first imposed fare regulation in 1942, as part of a package of reforms that included exclusive franchises. The reform package appears to have been supported by a broad coalition of consumers and producers and was arguably in the public interest. In the years leading up to the reforms, several commissions of British colonial officials investigated the problems of the bus industry, consulting with representatives of both the passengers and the bus operators. Passengers supported exclusive franchises in the hopes of reducing the chaos that seems to have characterized private bus service before 1942. Passengers presumably also supported fare regulation both because of the pressures of wartime inflation and because exclusive route franchises left the passengers vulnerable to the companies. But at least some of the bus operators seem to have supported the reforms as well, presumably the bigger companies who would have suffered most from interlopers and stood the best chance of winning one of the eighty-five exclusive route franchises.[12]

Once the regulatory scheme was in place, however, the influence of consumers seems to have grown rapidly. The overcrowding that stimulated nationalization in 1958 was almost surely caused by the regulators holding bus fares below levels that could support fleet renewals. Although data are not readily available, the decline of the bus fleet probably began or accelerated after independence in 1948, assuming the new government was more sensitive to popular pressure than the colonial regime.

The circumstances surrounding the reintroduction of fare regulation after 1979 were completely different, and the base of support for this policy seems to have been much narrower. Fare regulation was reintroduced surreptitiously by bus licensing authorities, without the benefit of the special investigative commissions and public debate that characterized both the 1942 reforms and the 1979 legislation. Indeed, the laws debated and passed by Parliament in 1979 assumed that fare regulation was unnecessary, because there would be few restrictions on the numbers of companies serving a route. The licensing authorities decided to regulate fares on their own, presumably because they thought regulation was in the consumers' interests. In a sense the 1979 reforms, as implemented, combined the worst features of the regulated and unregulated worlds. Sri Lanka embarked on the difficult task of regulating fares as if the bus firms were monopolies, but without gaining the more reliable and orderly service that monopoly route franchises would have brought.

The Politics of Tariff Regulation

Bus fares and service are politically sensitive because Sri Lanka, like most developing countries, is so heavily dependent on its bus system. In 1995, buses accounted for roughly 76 percent of the passenger travel in Sri Lanka, while the railroad accounted for only 5 percent and motorcycles, vans, and cars the remaining 19 percent.[13] Because incomes are low, moreover, Sri Lankans don't travel much for social or recreational reasons. Almost all of the bus passengers are either workers commuting to their jobs or children traveling to and from school.

Sri Lanka's transport ministers find it hard to raise bus fares largely because the public does not seem to understand how strong the link is between fares and the quality of bus service. The lack of understanding is surprising, because fares affect investment and service quality much more quickly in buses than in other infrastructure industries. Buses have useful lives of only 10 or 15 years, so a significant portion of the fleet is ready for retirement in any given year. Moreover, Sri Lanka's private bus industry relies heavily on importing used buses and vans from Japan and elsewhere, which presumably have shorter useful lives than new vehicles. As a result, the active private bus fleet in Sri Lanka can shrink by 20 percent in just a few years once fares fall below the levels needed to support vehicle replacement. The average passenger load per bus increases as the fleet declines, and the decline in the fleet stops only when the buses are so crowded that the operators can earn enough to replace their vehicles despite the low bus fares. Severe overcrowding makes bus travel very unreliable, because passengers don't know how long they will have to wait for a bus that has room to carry them. The overcrowded buses are also uncomfortable and unsafe, and increase fears among parents that school girls will be molested.

Raising fares is also difficult because fare increases are usually most needed when they are most unpopular. In this sense, the political pressures run counter to the economic realities. The trouble usually starts when inflation increases, eroding the real value of the bus tariffs. But when inflation is strong, governments are loath to appear to be adding to the problem by raising bus fares. Once quality starts to deteriorate, moreover, raising fares becomes more difficult because it seems to reward companies that are providing terrible service. Poor service makes raising fares less popular, which in turn leads to poorer service that only strengthens public opposition to fare increases. Given this political vicious circle, it is perhaps not surprising that Sri Lanka and many other developing countries raise their bus fares only every decade or so, and only after bus service has deteriorated severely.

These political pressures are hard to resist even though the ministers often understand that unrealistically low fares probably are not in their constituents' best interests. During the mid-1990s, for example, the Sri Lankan government established a series of expert committees that evaluated the situation of the bus industry and recommended substantial fare increases and other reforms. One committee pointed out that Sri Lankans could afford a fare increase, since even the poorest families spent only 2 to 5 percent of their income on bus fares.[14] Transport planners understood, moreover, that it was the poor who suffered most from bus overcrowding, because higher-income families could afford alternatives. As bus services deteriorated during the 1990s, vans offering subscription service to popular workplaces and schools proliferated. The monthly subscription often cost ten times more than the equivalent bus fares, so the vans were not an option available to many. But the wealthier workers and their children were assured of a ride to work or school while poor families had to depend on the increasingly unreliable and overcrowded bus services.

Capture for Cross-Subsidy

The Origins of U.S. Telephone Regulation

The U.S. telephone industry offers a well-known example of the ways in which capture for cross-subsidies can be a source of instability.[15] From the late nineteenth century through 1982, the U.S. telephone system was dominated by the Bell System and its holding company, American Telephone and Telegraph (AT&T). One AT&T department (Long Lines) provided virtually all of the long-distance telephone services in the country, twenty-two subsidiaries (popularly known as the local Bells) provided local telephone services through much of the country, a manufacturing company (Western Electric) supplied all of the equipment used by AT&T affiliates, and an in-house laboratory (Bell Labs) developed new communications technologies. AT&T was broken up in 1982 largely because an elaborate system of cross-subsidies among different classes of telephone users eventually stimulated enough competition to undermine the company. A chronology of the developments is provided in Table 4.3.

The Bell System had its beginnings in Alexander Bell's 1876 patents for the invention of the telephone. The Bell business interests initially leased equipment of their design to local companies that had franchises to provide telephone service in their communities. The Bell interests soon began to buy up local telephone companies, however, because local investors could not raise enough capital to meet the rapidly increasing demands for telephone service.

When the key Bell patents expired in 1893 and 1894, many new companies entered the telephone business and the Bell System had to develop new tactics to protect itself from competition. Telephone service had the characteristics of a natural monopoly in that it required durable and immobile investments and there were economies of scale that made it efficient to serve all the customers on a street with a single set of telephone poles or conduit. These barriers to entry were not always enough to prevent competition, however, especially in cities where the density of customers was high.

To compensate, the Bell System developed a new type of barrier to entry based on the economies of interconnected networks. From the customer's perspective, the value of a telephone system depends on how many other customers one can connect with. For example, two independent telephone systems are worth more to their customers when the systems are interconnected than if they remain isolated. AT&T had a key advantage in interconnections because it had begun to build a national long-distance network that could connect large numbers of local companies as early as 1885. Moreover, AT&T also owned more local telephone companies than any other group in the industry. Recognizing its advantages, AT&T adopted a policy of refusing to interconnect independent telephone companies with its local subsidiaries or its long-distance network.[16]

In 1907 Theodore Vail became chairman of AT&T and, with the backing of Morgan financial interests, began aggressively buying up independent operators and merging them into the Bell System. The combination of AT&T's

Table 4.3 Chronology of U.S. telephone regulation

1876	Alexander Bell patents telephone.
1893–1894	Bell patents expire and AT&T adopts policy of not interconnecting with competitors.
1907	Theodore Vail becomes chairman of AT&T as the states begin to establish public utility commissions (PUCs) to regulate intrastate telephone tariffs.
1910	Congress gives the Interstate Commerce Commission (ICC) the authority to regulate interstate telephone tariffs.
1913	AT&T agrees to stop acquiring its competitors and to interconnect with them to settle a Department of Justice antitrust suit.
1920s	State regulators encourage "value-of-service" pricing.
1930	Supreme Court rules in *Smith v. Illinois Bell* that state regulators can question AT&T practice of not allocating local costs to interstate long-distance service.
1934	Congress creates the Federal Communications Commission (FCC) to regulate interstate telephone and radio.
1942	FCC allows some local costs to be recovered from interstate long-distance revenues for the first time.
1951	FCC proposes "Charleston plan" to increase local costs recovered from interstate long-distance revenues.
1956	U.S. Court of Appeals overturns the FCC's ruling against Hush-A-Phone.
1959	FCC approves licenses for private microwave services.
1969	FCC approves Carterphone and AT&T requires a "protective device" for foreign terminal equipment. FCC approves MCI application for shared private line service, which provokes a wave of similar applications.
1971	FCC decides to license shared private line services, and AT&T responds with differential rates for calls in high- and low-density areas.
1973	John deButts becomes AT&T chairman and fights liberalized regulations.
1974	Department of Justice files antitrust suit against AT&T.
1975	FCC approves MCI application for Execunet shared foreign exchange service, then tries to reverse its decision and is stopped by the courts.
1980	FCC adopts technical certification program for foreign terminal equipment.
1982	AT&T and Department of Justice settle antitrust suit by agreeing to the breakup of AT&T.

refusal to interconnect and its acquisitions helped to stimulate complaints about monopoly and a movement for government regulation. In the same year Vail became chairman, the states began to establish public utility commissions to regulate telephones and other utilities. Between 1907 and 1913, twenty-six states also enacted laws requiring compulsory interconnection.[17] Federal regulation was also deemed necessary, since the states had no authority to regulate interstate calls. In 1910 the U.S. Congress gave the Interstate Commerce Commission, which had been established in 1887 to regulate railroads, the responsibility for regulating interstate telephone service as well.

Matters came to a head in 1913, when the U.S. Department of Justice filed an antitrust suit against a local Bell operating company on the grounds that its acquisitions were monopolizing the telephone industry. By this time Vail had decided that AT&T's best strategy was to embrace government regulation. Telephones were a natural monopoly, Vail argued, and it was in the public interest to have a single, interconnected system. AT&T resolved the antitrust suit by agreeing not to acquire any more competing independent companies and to allow independents to interconnect with the Bell System for long-distance and inter-exchange calls. A 1921 law left the Bell System free to buy noncompeting companies, however, eventually allowing it to increase its share of stations (the industry's jargon for telephones) from 58 percent in 1913 to 79 percent in 1930.[18] AT&T deflected political criticism by adopting a cooperative policy with the independents that remained and by slowing its acquisitions after 1930. In 1982, the year of AT&T's breakup, 1,432 independent companies still served 19 percent of the nation's telephone lines, mainly in rural areas, while the Bell operating companies served the remaining 81 percent.[19]

In 1934 Congress created the Federal Communications Commission (FCC) to regulate "every common carrier engaged in interstate or foreign communication by wire or radio." The new agency replaced the Federal Radio Commission and assumed the ICC's powers to regulate telephones. The FCC was governed by seven commissioners (five after 1983) appointed by the president and confirmed by the Senate. The commissioners' terms were fixed and staggered, so that it took four years for a president to appoint a majority of the commission.[20] The FCC was established in part because the ICC had been so preoccupied with its responsibility to regulate railroads that it had paid little attention to telephones. The FCC commissioners spent less time on telephone issues than on the politically sensitive task of awarding radio and television broadcast licenses, however, at least until telephone issues became highly controversial beginning in the late 1960s.

By the mid-1930s, the basic structure that would last for almost fifty years was in place: AT&T dominated the telephone industry with roughly 80 percent of the subscribers and virtually all of the long-distance service, while regulatory responsibilities were divided between the state PUCs for local and intrastate calls and the FCC for interstate calls.

The Development of Cross-Subsidies

Cross-subsidies emerged and spread in the industry soon after regulation was imposed. Beginning in the 1920s, state regulators imposed tariff systems that kept the basic monthly rates for local telephone service low and relatively uniform within each state. To make this possible, state regulators encouraged "value of service" pricing, under which the tariffs for different services were based on what the regulators thought customers were willing to pay rather than on what the service cost to provide. In practice, this meant high mark-ups on intrastate long-distance calls, since those were more likely to be made by businesses or by more affluent residential customers. In addition, businesses were commonly charged a higher basic monthly charge for a line and a telephone than residential customers, and often their local calls were metered while residential customers enjoyed unlimited local service.

Until 1930, however, all the revenue from interstate long-distance toll calls was kept by AT&T's Long Lines Department, and none went to the local operating companies to defray the costs of the local exchanges and lines. This practice had developed in part because the local exchanges and lines had been built first and the long-distance lines later. Thus it was natural that the local company should be responsible for the costs of the local lines and switchboards, while the long-distance company was responsible only for the costs of the lines between local switchboards, or, in the industry's parlance, from "board to board." Moreover, many local company costs, such as those for building and maintaining the lines between the customer's station and the local switchboard, were not sensitive to the number of calls the customer made.[21] It seemed logical, therefore, to recoup those traffic-insensitive costs from the basic monthly charge rather than from the toll charges for long-distance calls.

In 1930 the U.S. Supreme Court ruled in *Smith v. Illinois Bell* that state regulators had the right to question the local Bell operating companies' practice of not charging AT&T Long Lines for some of the local costs of completing long-distance calls. The Court did not say how costs should be allocated, only that it seemed unreasonable to allow long-distance callers to escape any responsibility for the costs of equipment used jointly by local and long-distance services. This decision began a decades-long debate between state and federal regulators about "separations," the industry's term for the allocation of expenses and investment between intrastate and interstate calling.[22]

During the 1930s state regulators became increasingly restive as the FCC announced a series of tariff reductions for interstate long-distance calls. The cost of a long-distance call was falling more rapidly than the cost of basic monthly service, as long-distance costs benefited from improvements in transmission and switching technology and from economies of scale. In 1941 the FCC, at AT&T's urging, began to meet with state regulators and their association, the National Association of Railroad and Utility Commissioners (NARUC), over the separations issue.[23] In 1942, for the first time, the FCC allowed some of a proposed reduction in long-distance tariffs to be used to defray local company costs. The FCC agreed, however, only because AT&T argued that another sharp reduction in long-distance tariffs would complicate wartime efforts to discourage private calls and leave long-distance lines free for war-related uses.

The separations issue came to a head soon after World War II, as interstate long-distance costs continued to fall while the local Bells, citing postwar inflation, were applying to state regulators for substantial local tariff increases. State regulators pursued every opportunity to keep basic monthly residential rates low by raising other intrastate charges. By the late 1940s, however, they had pushed this strategy to the point where charges for intrastate long-distance calls were often much higher than the charges for interstate calls over comparable distances. Clearly the possibilities for cross-subsidies within states were reaching their limits.[24]

In 1947 the first separations manual prepared by a joint committee of federal and state regulators went into effect. Although the manual abandoned the old board-to-board costing in favor of a station-to-station approach, the share of local costs allocated to interstate long-distance service was very modest. In 1950, however, state regulators meeting at the annual NARUC convention in Phoenix approved a more radical separations scheme. The so-called Phoenix plan essentially treated the intrastate and interstate long-distance facilities located within each state as a unified system, so that the lower costs per circuit-mile of the interstate plant could be averaged in with the higher-cost intrastate plant.[25]

The primary source of opposition to the Phoenix plan was the FCC. Even before 1950, AT&T had become convinced that the old board-to-board approach had to be abandoned because of the difficulties its local operating companies were having in persuading state regulators to approve tariff increases. The Phoenix plan was arbitrary, however, in that it benefited most the states that, by accident of geography, had a disproportionate share of interstate facilities. For the FCC, some more intellectually defensible system of allocating costs needed be developed.

Congress reacted angrily to the FCC's position. Senator Ernest W. McFarland—a longtime member of the Senate committee that supervised the FCC and the newly elected Senate majority leader—wrote a scathing letter explaining the virtues of cross-subsidy to the obtuse agency:

> The trouble is that the general public does not realize that every move that is made to reduce long-distance toll rates results directly or indirectly in an eventual increase in local exchange telephone rates and in intrastate toll telephone rates. But very plainly and simply, this merely

shifts the load from the big user to the little user; from the large national corporations that are heavy users of long distance to the average housewife and business or professional man who do not indulge in a great deal of long distance but are the life blood of the telephone business in this country.[26]

By the 1951 NARUC convention that met in Charleston, South Carolina, the FCC had seen the light and presented a new plan for separations that it had developed in collaboration with AT&T. The Charleston plan took a more direct approach to the problem of basic local rates by allocating the traffic-insensitive portion of the local subscriber plant between local and long-distance service on the basis of the relative number of minutes of local and long-distance calls.[27] The Charleston plan was just as arbitrary as the Phoenix plan in that there could be no cost-based rationale for allocating traffic-insensitive plant between call types. But allocating costs by relative use was more appealing than allocating costs by accidents of geography.

Over the next thirty years, NARUC successfully pressed the FCC to adopt a series of obscure technical modifications to the Charleston formula that gradually increased the average share of the traffic-insensitive local plant allocated to interstate calls from around 5 percent in the 1950s to 26 percent by 1982.[28] The separations formula was particularly advantageous for small rural telephone companies, which often had a high ratio of long-distance to local calls and could recover as much as 85 percent of the cost of their traffic-insensitive plant from interstate toll revenues.[29]

Cream Skimming in Terminal Equipment

Cream skimming did not appear until the 1950s, but once established it proved hard for AT&T or the regulators to contain. Cream skimming began in two areas: terminal equipment and long-distance calling. Under the old Bell System, all telephones and other terminal equipment on the customers' premises were owned by AT&T and leased to the customers. AT&T's tariffs specifically prohibited customers from attaching "foreign equipment" to its lines.[30] The only reason emphasized publicly was the technical integrity and quality of the system. AT&T had legitimate concerns that foreign equipment might damage the lines or switches, for example, or interfere with the network switching signals used to initiate, route, and terminate calls.

Behind the scenes, however, there was a sense within the company and among its regulators that AT&T's stockholders had spent billions developing the network, and that they should be the ones to reap any benefits from providing attachments to it. In addition, terminal equipment had become an important part of the cross-subsidy scheme that had developed over time. State regulators often encouraged the local Bells to mark up the leases for phones with multiple lines and other business equipment in order to keep the leases for the basic residential telephone affordable. Terminal equipment also accounted for roughly 40 percent of the traffic-insensitive local plant on which interstate revenue separations were based.

The first crack in the dike was caused by the Hush-A-Phone, a simple rubber cup designed to snap over a telephone mouthpiece and provide the user more privacy in a busy office environment. The manufacturer appealed to the FCC in 1948, after AT&T warned stores selling the device that subscribers caught using it would be disconnected. In hearings in 1950, AT&T argued that the device distorted the caller's voice and that if the caller wanted privacy he could cup his hand over the mouthpiece and have the same effect. The FCC upheld AT&T's position in a preliminary ruling in 1951 and in a final decision issued in 1955. Privately, the FCC staff did not believe the Hush-A-Phone posed a serious technical threat, but they were fearful of setting a precedent.

Hush-A-Phone's manufacturer appealed to the courts, however, which overturned the FCC, ridiculing its position that distortions produced by a cupped hand were acceptable while those by a rubber mouthpiece were not. The agency's decision, the court concluded, "was an unwarranted interference with the telephone subscriber's right reasonably to use his telephone in ways which were privately beneficial without being publicly detrimental."[31] AT&T made minor modifications to its foreign attachments rule to comply, but continued to prohibit electrical connections and connections to other communications devices.

The opening initiated by the Hush-A-Phone was soon widened by the Carterfone, a device invented by a Texas entrepreneur to help oil workers equipped with mobile radios to receive telephone calls when in the field. The Carterfone was merely an acoustical coupler that could connect a telephone in the office to a mobile radio transmitter. But even though the connection was not electrical, the device violated AT&T's foreign attachments rule by connecting the telephone system with another communications device. In 1969, after an investigation that lasted several years, the FCC finally ruled in favor of Carterfone on the grounds that the device was privately beneficial without being publicly detrimental.

AT&T responded to the Carterfone ruling with a more imaginative amendment to its foreign attachment rules. Both the company and the FCC had been concerned about how the advent of computers might affect the telephone business, especially since time-sharing of computers using telephone lines was such an attractive possibility. A strict interpretation of the attachment rule would require that AT&T manufacture every computer that was connected to the telephone system. AT&T wanted to encourage the new use of its lines for data transmission, but it was impractical for the company to make all the specialized equipment that customers might want to attach. AT&T proposed instead that subscribers be allowed to attach their own equipment provided they leased a protective connecting device from AT&T.

AT&T's protective device only generated more controversy, however, as current and would-be manufacturers of telephone equipment argued that it was unnecessary and wasteful. AT&T's lease rates for its protective device were higher than those for an extension phone, for example, so that manufacturing the phone to Bell specifications would be cheaper. The controversy caused the FCC to initiate an inquiry over how best to protect the network, including the possibility of establishing technical standards and an equipment certification program.

At this point, AT&T appointed a new chairman, John deButts, who decided the company had to stop the drift toward liberalized regulation. So far, both AT&T and the FCC had framed the terminal equipment issue in terms of technical protection for the network. In a speech to the 1973 NARUC convention, however, deButts pointed out that the separations formula gave state regulators an economic stake in preventing customer provision of terminal equipment. If the telephone companies lost only 10 percent of the terminal equipment market, deButts told the attendees, then state revenue requirements would increase by $220 million a year. The North Carolina PUC quickly moved to preempt the FCC by prohibiting the use of customer-supplied terminal equipment for intrastate calls, with or without protective devices. The FCC issued a declaratory ruling against North Carolina, since the equipment was used for both interstate and intrastate calls. The dispute was soon in the courts, with AT&T and NARUC supporting North Carolina and equipment manufacturers and many other large corporations supporting the FCC.

The case was finally resolved in the FCC's favor in 1977, and by that time the agency had decided that a system of equipment standards and certification was the only sensible and sustainable policy in the long run. The growing use of the telephone system for data transmission made it impossible and undesirable to distinguish between telephone and other terminal equipment. Moreover, there was no technical reason why the terminal equipment market could not be competitive, provided appropriate standards were enforced. In 1980 the FCC issued a ruling deregulating tariffs for all new customer-premises equipment installed after January 1, 1983, and prohibiting AT&T from providing customer equipment unless through a fully separate subsidiary.

Cream Skimming in Long Distance

Cream skimming in long-distance calling developed at the same time as cream skimming in terminal equipment, and eventually posed an even greater threat to the established system of cross-subsidies. The U.S. Army Signal Corps had developed microwave transmission as an alternative to wire or co-axial cable during World War II, and AT&T began to build microwave links in its network after the war. During the 1950s a Texas railroad and a Florida orange juice producer applied separately to the FCC for licenses to build private microwave systems to link their far-flung operations.

The FCC responded to the two applications by opening hearings on the allocation of the radio spectrum above 890 megahertz for microwave communication. In the proceedings, AT&T opposed the licensing of private microwave systems on the grounds that there was not enough available spectrum and that private systems would be an uneconomic duplication of the common carrier facilities. The electronic equipment manufacturers association, whose members were interested in selling equipment for private systems, presented convincing evidence that AT&T had exaggerated the spectrum capacity problem, however, and in 1959 the FCC decided to license private systems.

The FCC expected that the economic effects of its 1959 decision would be modest, since few private corporations had operations large and far flung enough to justify private microwave systems. The costs of building a microwave link were much lower than the costs of stringing a cable, however, and made private systems more of a threat to AT&T than they had been before. AT&T had long offered businesses special rates for a private long-distance line, which was leased for a fixed monthly rental, regardless of how many minutes it was used. In 1961, however, AT&T responded to the microwave threat by introducing new "telpak" rates that provided deep discounts for lessors of twelve or more private lines. The telpak rates effectively undercut private microwave in most applications, but they also encouraged many large U.S. corporations to become heavy users of private line services and created pressures to allow these corporations to "share" their private lines with one another.

Although it was not obvious at the time, a key turning point came in the mid-1960s, when a startup company called Microwave Communications, Inc. (later MCI) applied to the FCC for a license to offer a shared private microwave service between Chicago and St. Louis. AT&T opposed the application on the grounds that it would undermine the long-established practice of nationwide averaging of long-distance rates. AT&T argued that it would no longer be able to charge the same low national long-distance rates in rural areas if competitors were allowed to pick off the high-volume corridors. The FCC staff believed the threat was low, because MCI was so small and the services it was proposing were of lower technical quality than AT&T's. Nevertheless, the staff thought that MCI might fill some valuable niche, possibly in data transmission. In 1969 the commission approved the MCI request on the grounds that it was a safe and prudent experiment in new services.[32]

Others were less blind to the implications of the decision, and by mid-1970 the FCC had over 1,500 applications for shared private microwave stations.[33] Unable to hear each application individually, the FCC instead began a new rulemaking on what the agency called "specialized common carriers." The FCC staff still believed the economic threat of specialized carriers was small, in part because they thought the primary target of the new carriers would be private line services, which accounted for only 3 percent of AT&T's revenues. Moreover, the intellectual climate was changing, as academics and others were increasingly critical of regulatory agencies for being overly protective of the industries they supervised and for thwarting innovation.

In 1971 the FCC ruled that it would license specialized common carriers. The FCC required local Bell companies to connect the specialized carriers' lines with their subscribers and to negotiate "reasonable terms and conditions" for these connections. Needless to say, AT&T and MCI had different ideas about what those terms and conditions should be, and AT&T's position hardened after deButts became its chairman in 1973. AT&T also sought to discourage new specialized carriers by abandoning its nationwide uniform long-distance tariff schedule. Under AT&T's new "hi-lo" tariff, the calling charge per minute was lower in high-density than in low-density areas.

As the negotiations over connection charges dragged on, MCI came up with a new scheme that allowed it to compete directly with AT&T's conventional switched long-distance service. AT&T had long offered a variant of its private line service called foreign exchange, or FX, service. Under FX service, a private line could be connected with a distant local exchange so that the subscriber could receive a local number in that exchange and could make and receive calls there. FX allowed a business to list a local telephone number in cities where it had no offices. In 1975 MCI proposed a "shared FX" service which it called Execunet. Under Execunet, a subscriber would call the local MCI office, dial his identification code and the number to be called, and be patched into the shared FX lines to complete the call. Execunet was less convenient than AT&T's conventional switched services, since it required the caller to dial more numbers. MCI might significantly undercut AT&T tariffs, however, especially if the local Bells charged MCI the same price for accessing the foreign exchange that they were charging AT&T's private lines unit. Under FCC procedures, tariffs that were not opposed went into effect after 90 days. MCI had drafted its Execunet proposal so that its implications were unclear; the tariff was unopposed, and it went into effect.

Once the FCC realized what had happened, it quickly disallowed Execunet as beyond the scope of MCI's authorized services. But by this time it was too late. MCI appealed to the courts, which overturned the FCC on procedural grounds. The court ruled that the FCC had authorized MCI to provide FX among other private line services. In addition, the court reasoned that the FCC could not disallow Execunet as a threat to AT&T's monopoly on conventional long-distance service, because it had never had a proceeding to establish that AT&T's monopoly was in the public interest.

The court's Execunet ruling seemed to change attitudes at the FCC, and the agency began to support liberalization in earnest. Under the FCC's supervision, AT&T and MCI negotiated an interim agreement on connection charges in 1978 that allowed MCI to begin to offer its new service. MCI and another company offering similar services (Sprint) expanded rapidly in the early 1980s. But further debates at the FCC were soon superseded by an antitrust case against AT&T.

Divestiture and Its Aftermath

The Antitrust Division of the U.S. Department of Justice had been monitoring the developments in the telephone industry, and had become convinced that both terminal equipment and long-distance service were potentially competitive markets and that only local service was a natural monopoly that needed regulation. The department finally filed an antitrust suit in late 1974, after AT&T's tactics toward its competitors became more aggressive under Chairman deButts.[34] The suit charged AT&T with attempting to suppress competition in terminal equipment and long-distance service by two methods. The first was to price its services so as to deter entry rather than on the basis of costs. The department alleged, for example, that the telpak and hi-lo tariffs were designed to underprice microwave rather than to reflect AT&T's cost structure. The second method was to use the regulatory system to tie up competitors in lengthy and costly regulatory proceedings, even when AT&T believed it might ultimately lose. AT&T responded that telephone services as a whole were a natural monopoly, since there were important cost and technical advantages to having a single integrated company provide equipment, local, and long-distance services. Regulation by the states and the FCC would protect the public from abuse.

The suit was finally resolved in 1982 by a consent decree in which AT&T agreed to divest itself of its local operating companies within two years and keep only its long-distance, equipment manufacturing, and research subsidiaries. AT&T agreed to settle only after it became clear that the judge was likely to rule against it and that Congress was not going to rescue the company by passing legislation that would have reaffirmed its monopoly position.

On the whole, most observers regard divestiture as a success. Some economists argue that consumers have not benefited greatly, because the reduction in long-distance rates in the first decade after the breakup of AT&T was roughly offset by increases in the basic monthly rates and in charges for local calls.[35] But most researchers believe that this financial calculus undervalues the dramatic innovations in services, such as the Internet and the spread of wireless telephones, and that these innovations probably would have occurred more slowly without divestiture.[36]

Divestiture did not eliminate the need for regulation or the resulting political pressures for cross-subsidies. The local operating companies are still monopolies, so the states still regulate the rates they charge for local calls and the access charges they can collect from long-distance companies to complete intrastate calls. The FCC still regulates the access charges that local operating companies can charge long-distance carriers to complete interstate calls. In addition, Congress and federal and state regulators have all been debating the issue of the circumstances under which local operating companies should be allowed to enter long-distance service and vice versa.

The problems of regulating industries where competitive and monopoly activities have been divided into separate firms are discussed in more detail in Part III below. It is worth noting here, however, that the continuing pressure for cross-subsidies is still creating problems of cream skimming or bypass in telephones. State regulators have continued to press the local operating companies to keep basic residential monthly telephone rates low and geographically uniform by charging higher monthly rates for business subscribers.[37] In addition, most states have allowed the local operating companies to recover some of their traffic-insensitive costs by charging access fees for intrastate long-distance calls that are much higher than the incremental costs of connection. Rural states generally have imposed higher access charges than urban states, but in 1996 the average intrastate caller paid connection fees of 6 cents per minute when the incremental local costs were only ½ cent per minute.[38] The FCC had planned to base the access charge for interstate calls after divestiture on incremental local costs, but then to continue interstate support for local traffic-insensitive costs through an interstate subscriber line charge of $6 per month. The political uproar caused the FCC to introduce the subscriber line fee gradually and cap it at $3.50 per month and to continue to set interstate access charges above local incremental costs.[39]

Regulators have been careful to ensure that a local operating company charges all long-distance carriers the same access fees so that they compete on a level footing. But the fact that the access charges and monthly line charges are still not based on costs has created new opportunities for bypass. Long-distance companies and others have incentives to build local telephone networks in major downtown and suburban business centers, for example, because the local businesses are being charged monthly subscription fees and long-distance access charges that are well above costs. If new local telephone services are allowed to skim off this cream, then the current system of markups and cross-subsidies might collapse.

The Appeal of Cross-Subsidies

The U.S. telephone system illustrates the powerful appeal of cross-subsidies to customers, the industry, and regulators alike. Business subscribers have generally paid higher markups over costs than residential subscribers, which might seem surprising if one expects businesses to be better organized to lobby regulators, all else being equal. But all else has not been equal. Telephone charges were a modest portion of the total expenses for most businesses in the first half of the twentieth century, except for a minority that had many far-flung operations. And the businesses with the most dispersed operations, most notably railroads, sometimes had private telephone or telegraph systems. Telephone charges probably didn't account for a much higher proportion of household than business budgets, but almost every household in the country soon became a subscriber and the telephone bill was one of a few that arrived every month to every home.

The development of cross-subsidies was also encouraged by a plausible rationale. Low basic monthly residential rates ensured that most households would have a telephone available for emergency purposes. Long-distance toll rates that varied only by time and distance called prevented the social and political isolation of farming and other low-density areas. Moreover, it wasn't always clear that cost-based tariffs would be so different, given the complexity and confusion surrounding cost allocation. Economists might argue that long-distance callers are not responsible for much of the costs of the local telephone system, for example, since the local costs depend mainly on the number of subscribers rather than on the number of minutes they talk. To the courts and the public, however, it seemed only logical that long-distance callers should help pay for the local lines and switchboards they used.

The appeal of cross-subsidies is suggested by the speed with which they were adopted. State regulators recognized their merits by the end of the 1920s or the beginning of the 1930s, and the local Bell operating companies seemed not to resist. The FCC didn't allow significant cross-subsidies from interstate long-distance to local service until the early 1950s, and even then only after considerable pressure from NARUC and Congress. The FCC may have resisted only because it was not directly responsible for setting the monthly rates for basic residential service, and thus not subject to as immediate popular pressure on this score as the state PUCs. Indeed, the FCC had earlier shown its willingness to go along with cross-subsidies in the tariffs that it reviewed, the most obvious example being the cross-subsidy from high- to low-density regions embodied in AT&T's uniform national toll rates for interstate long-distance calls.

The Incentives to Bypass

The other lesson of the U.S. telephone experience is the seeming inevitability of efforts by customers and alternative providers to bypass the regulated companies and skim off the cream. It is hard to prevent bypass from starting. The beginnings may seem too small to matter, as the FCC staff thought in the case of private microwave and MCI's shared private lines. Even where the danger seems clear, it is difficult to keep the door closed completely. The FCC was worried about the precedent that Hush-A-Phone might establish, but the device itself seemed so innocuous that the courts ridiculed the agency for trying to suppress it.

Once bypass begins, it is hard to contain. Often the industry and the regulators hesitate to publicly acknowledge the real stakes involved. The FCC and AT&T undermined their long-term positions in both the Hush-A-Phone and the private microwave cases, for example, by framing their initial objections as technical. Attachments might damage AT&T equipment, and the radio spectrum was too crowded to permit private microwave systems. Presumably the industry and the regulators emphasized technical objections because they were concerned that an explicit discussion of cross-subsidies might generate enormous political controversy and pressures for change. If the proposals could be defeated on technical grounds, then there was no need to start a battle between business and residential subscribers. The industry lost credibility, however, by trying to change the terms of the debate once opponents had demonstrated that its technical objections were unfounded.

The early openings for bypass also built a constituency for further change by demonstrating the possibilities to both customers and alternative service providers. Each successive step in liberalization seems small, but each expands the constituency for change. Increasing numbers of equipment manufacturers and big business users began to support liberalization as the potential savings from customer-provided terminal equipment and private microwave services became more apparent. And these new constituencies eventually grew strong enough to check the powerful supporters of the system of cross-subsidies. In the late 1970s, for example, AT&T could not convince Congress to pass legislation that would have barred customer-supplied terminal equipment, and in the early 1980s the company failed again to get legislation to bar further competition in long-distance calling. In both cases the bills were strongly supported by the states, NARUC, and the telephone unions as well as AT&T, one of the largest corporations in the world. By that time, however, the potential benefits of liberalization to other big business interests were so obvious that it was much harder to protect the status quo.

The development of bypass was aided by exogenous technological changes. Microwave technology developed by the military helped to undermine the cross-subsidies from long-distance calls, while the advent of the computers increased the pressure on the FCC and AT&T to relax attachment rules. But while technological change was undoubtedly helpful in expanding the possibilities for bypass, the incentives to bypass were established by the cross-subsidies. Many of the key new products in the telephone story—such as Hush-A-Phone, Carterfone, and Execunet—didn't exploit innovations in technology, suggesting that bypass would have emerged even if technology had been stagnant.

Capture and Instability

In sum, both capture by short-sighted consumers and capture for cross-subsidies are powerfully attractive but hard to sustain. The example of Sri Lanka's buses is especially striking in that the government seemed unable to resist popular pressures to hold down fares even though the consequences for service quality were fairly immediate and reasonably well understood by public officials, if not by bus passengers. If short-sighted pressures are hard to resist for bus regulators, then imagine how much more tempting they must be for regulators of industries where the assets are much longer lived, such as toll roads or power plants. Similarly, the experience of the U.S. telephone industry suggests how tempting cross-subsidies are. Not only did cross-subsidies develop early in the industry's history, but state regulators have been trying hard to retain cross-subsidies in some form even after bypass forced AT&T's breakup and the expansion of competition.

Some might argue that these regulators weren't captured in that the policies they pursued were in the public interest. This argument is less plausible in the case of capture by short-sighted consumers than in the case of capture for cross-subsidies. With capture by short-sighted consumers, the putative beneficiaries eventually suffer from the policies pursued. In cases like Sri Lanka, moreover, the poorest customers—in whose name tariffs are being held down—often are harmed the most while the wealthier customers escape to costlier but better-quality alternatives. With capture for cross-subsidies, the argument assumes that the favored customers deserve the support they receive. Many telephone subscribers probably supported lifeline rates for basic telephone service and the maintenance of similar tariffs in urban and rural areas. It is unlikely that subscribers understood how extensive the system of differential markups had become, however, and at least some would have objected had they known. The initial reluctance of the FCC and AT&T to make explicit the stakes in bypass suggests that they were not confident that the policies would survive wider public scrutiny and debate.

The bus and telephone examples also illustrate that capture occurs in a wide variety of institutional settings. Capture might be expected in Sri Lanka, where the bus regulator reported to the minister of transport and fare increases were subject to parliamentary approval. There was nothing to insulate the regulators from political forces, and the executive and legislature were always in the control of the same party. But the state PUCs and the FCC eventually were captured as well, even though they were regulatory commissions designed by Progressive reformers to resist short-term political pressures.

Finally, although instability seems inevitable given the incentives for exit these forms of capture create, it is surprising how long the day of reckoning can be delayed. The roughly ten-year intervals between significant bus fare increases in Sri Lanka seem long when one considers how rapidly bus investment can respond to fare levels and how much the passengers suffer from overcrowded and unreliable service. And cross-subsidies in U.S. telephones survived for approximately fifty years at the state level and thirty years at the federal level before the 1982 divestiture of AT&T. Cream skimming did not appear until the late 1950s, and the industry and regulators were able to resist its implications for more than two additional decades. Nevertheless, in the long run capture by short-sighted consumers or for cross-subsidy is very hard to sustain.

5

Incompleteness and Its Consequences: Argentina's Railroads

Incomplete Contracts and Instability

If capture is an important source of instability in discretionary regulation, incompleteness is the key source of instability in the contractual approach. Private contracts and concession contracts promise stability because they purport to describe all the obligations of the parties in advance. In so doing, contracts eliminate the need for discretion and thus the temptation for capture. If a contract does not anticipate all the important developments that occur during its life, however, the parties involved face an unhappy choice. They can live with a contract that no longer serves their interests, or they can renegotiate the contract despite having made investments that leave them vulnerable to opportunism.

The dilemmas created by incompleteness are even more acute for concession contracts than for private contracts. With private contracts the utility and its customers negotiate directly, but with concession contracts the interests of the customers are represented by government, which raises the issue of trust. Modern concession contracts are usually awarded through open and competitive bidding to reassure citizens that their government is securing a fair agreement. But if that concession contract proves to be obsolete, then any renegotiations take place without the safeguard of competitive bidding. And renegotiation can also raise popular doubts as to whether the bidding in the original, or any subsequent, competition was really sincere. Governments usually opt to renegotiate incomplete contracts, because the prospect of living with inadequate services under the old contract seems too painful. But the government that renegotiates puts its credibility at risk with citizens as well as with investors, and ultimately jeopardizes popular support for private infrastructure.

Concession contracts were widely used in the nineteenth century and were revived in the twentieth century, particularly in developing countries. Many of the concession contracts proved to be incomplete. The experience of Argentina's railway concessions at the end of the twentieth century is a typical and cautionary example.

The Revival of Concession Contracts

During the nineteenth century, private providers of infrastructure—such as plank roads, canals, railroads, or waterworks—typically had to secure a special charter, franchise, or concession from the government. In many cases a concession was required because the private company wanted to lay pipes or tracks on public streets or needed the government's assistance in expropriating private lands for the right of way. In return, the government would sometimes specify the maximum prices the company could charge and the minimum services it had to provide during the life of the concession.

The practice of concession contract regulation died out in most countries during the first half of the twentieth century. In the United States, state public utility commissions and federal regulatory commissions had largely replaced municipal or state concession contracts by the 1930s. These new agencies were not bound by an explicit contract and had discretion to change the prices the companies were allowed to charge. In most other countries, private utilities were nationalized in the decades immediately after World War II. Many of these countries had adopted discretionary regulatory agencies a few decades before nationalization, but others stuck with concession contracts to the end.[1]

Interest in concession contracts revived in the last third of the twentieth century, thanks in part to an influential 1968 article by Harold Demsetz provocatively titled "Why Regulate Public Utilities?"[2] Demsetz was among the growing group of economists that were critical of the performance of U.S. regulatory agencies, and he saw a return to concession contracts as the answer to many of their problems. Demsetz's key idea was that competition for the right to serve a market could substitute for competition within a market. Natural monopoly made competition within a market impractical for many utilities. But the government could introduce competition for the market by competitively awarding a concession of limited duration to the bidder who offered the lowest prices and best service. The fact that the concession was competitively awarded would ensure that the prices and service standards were fair to both consumers and investors. And the concession would be rebid at regular intervals to ensure that prices and services reflected up-to-date and competitive terms.

Oliver Williamson and Victor Goldberg independently published influential critiques of Demsetz's proposal in 1976.[3] Their key objection was that even carefully drawn contracts are unlikely to anticipate every contingency, especially if uncertainty is great or the duration of the contract is long. If the contract had to be renegotiated the results would depend on the relative bargaining positions of the two parties at the time, and there would be no guarantee that it would be fair to either consumers or investors.

Williamson and Goldberg also argued that Demsetz's proposal that the concession could be frequently and competitively rebid was unrealistic. Frequent rebidding might be suitable for a contract to manage an existing facility. A contract that anticipated substantial investment would have to last for the expected economic life of the new facilities, however, if the concessionaire was to recoup his investment through reasonable charges to consumers. Short contracts that required large investments would mean either very high tariffs or a large payment to the concessionaire at the end of the term. Short contracts would also require substantial safeguards regarding the quality of the investments made and their condition at the time they were transferred to the new concessionaire. Any rebidding was unlikely to be fully competitive, moreover, since the incumbent concessionaire would inevitably know more than its challengers about the economics of the concession.

These criticisms may have helped slow the revival of contract regulation in the United States. Contracts did not replace the state PUCs and federal regulatory agencies for most of the established regulated industries, such as electricity and telephones. Where new private infrastructure industries developed, however, contracts were often used. U.S. municipalities turned to contracts when the cable television industry emerged in the 1960s and 1970s, and again when private solid waste disposal and water and sewage treatment providers expanded their operations beginning in the 1980s. In addition, private contracts were used as a partial substitute for federal regulation of railroads and natural gas pipelines in the 1980s. The U.S. experiences with municipal concession contracts and with private contracts are recounted later, in Chapters 7 and 8.

Concession contracts proved very popular, however, in the wave of infrastructure privatizations that swept the developing countries beginning at the end of the 1980s. Concession contracts were the norm for the private-toll expressways, railways, electric power–generating stations, and water and sewage treatment plants that many countries established at the time. Concession contracts were a little less common for privatized telephone and electricity distribution companies, probably because those services seemed so complex that governments had little faith that they could specify the needed service standards or investment programs in advance. The concessions were usually awarded and monitored by the national government, although municipal or provincial governments occasionally awarded concessions for local services.

Concession contracts were appealing in developing countries precisely because they promised greater commitment. The fear of regulatory capture and opportunism was often strong, particularly among foreign investors who were often being courted for their money and expertise. The courts seemed less vulnerable to political influence than the specialized government agencies that supervised the infrastructure and utility sectors. And when the integrity of the local courts was in doubt, foreign investors often insisted that the concession contracts be enforceable in a foreign court or that disputes be submitted to an international arbitration panel.

One important difference between the recent concession contracts and their nineteenth-century predecessors is that the recent contracts are much more likely to be awarded through competitive bidding, as Demsetz suggested. In the nineteenth century, governments often awarded concession contracts that were not exclusive, so that they could award additional concessions if they were dissatisfied with the performance of the incumbent. Nonexclusive concessions proved to be an ineffective strategy for regulating natural monopolies, however, and organized competitions for the initial award or renewal of a concession were rare. During the 1980s and 1990s, by contrast, governments usually held a formal competition for each franchise, and were careful to organize the bidding and selection process in as open and transparent a manner as possible.

The efforts to increase competition in the award of concessions did not solve the problem of contractual completeness, however, and many concession contracts drafted in the 1980s and the 1990s had to be renegotiated long before their terms expired. One study by José Luis Guasch examined a sample of approximately one thousand concessions awarded between 1982 and 2000 by countries in Latin America and the Caribbean. Guasch does not distinguish between contract and discretionary regulation, so one must guess at the approach used from knowledge of the sector. In telecommunications and electricity, where discretionary regulation is more common, he found that only 1 and 5 percent, respectively, of the concessions had been renegotiated. In transport and water and sewerage, where contracts predominate, 55 and 75 percent, respectively, of all concessions had been renegotiated. The average time between award and renegotiation was only 3.1 years in transport and 1.7 years in water and sewage.[4]

The high rates of contractual incompleteness and renegotiation are due partly to the pioneering nature of many of these concessions, but they also reflect pressures that are likely to endure. The early experiences made government officials and investors more wary of the contractual approach, but usually not enough to make discretionary regulation seem less risky. And while the economic and political situations in many developing countries seemed to stabilize somewhat, it was seldom enough to make drafting a complete contract easy. It would be an exaggeration to say that incompleteness was inevitable, so that concession contracts were inherently unstable. But there were strong pressures to use contracts in situations where the risk of incompleteness was high.

The statistics on renegotiation also give little sense of the dilemmas that the governments and concessionaires usually faced once it became clear that their contract was incomplete. A public takeover of the service was usually out of the question, because the private concessionaire had improved performance considerably and because the government still faced the same budgetary constraints that had forced it to privatize in the first place. Putting the concession out to bid again was often unattractive, because service might be disrupted during the transition and there were difficult questions about the compensation owed the incumbent concessionaire either under the contract or out of some notion of fairness. Renegotiation with the incumbent was difficult, because there was no assurance that the results would be fair to consumers or investors. In the end, many governments chose to renegotiate as the lesser of several evils, but renegotiation often undermined both public and investor confidence in the integrity of the concession program, threatening its long-term future.

These dilemmas are illustrated by the experience of Argentina's railway concessions. Argentina was one of the pioneers of infrastructure privatization among the developing countries in the late 1980s and early 1990s. In just five years, Argentina sold its national telephone, electricity, and airline companies and granted concessions for its major ports, over 12,000 kilometers of intercity highways, four new toll expressways in the Buenos Aires metropolitan area, the country's main waterway, and its passenger and freight railways.[5] In the case of the railways and many of the other concessions, performance improved greatly, but events unfolded in ways not anticipated by the concession contracts, placing all the parties in a difficult position.

The Origins of the Argentine Railway Contracts

The Political and Economic Context

Argentina's privatization program was a response to decades of economic decline, political chaos, and government irresponsibility.[6] As late as the 1920s, Argentina was considered one of the most successful countries in the world, with a stable, democratic government and an average per capita income comparable to that of Europe. Argentina's wealth was based on exports of grain and beef, however, which made the country vulnerable to fluctuations in world commodity prices, especially as the United States, Canada, and other countries began to develop large exportable surpluses of grain and meat.

When successive governments seemed unable to reverse the decline, in 1946 the Argentines elected Juan Domingo Perón as their president. Perón, a colonel who had participated in an earlier coup, was the head of a populist and nationalistic movement. He and his party sought to restore prosperity by increasing workers' wages and benefits and by protecting domestic industry from imports. As part of that strategy, many foreign-owned banks and utilities, including the railroads, were nationalized, and the government became deeply involved in regulating the economy. Perón's program proved unsustainable because it depended on taxing grain and beef exports to finance the new social services and public enterprises, and in 1955 he was ousted in a coup.

The next thirty years were marked by increasing conflict between the conservatives and the military on the one hand and the unions and working classes on the other. The military would take over from civilian governments to restore "order," only to resign after their efforts to improve the economy failed. The last military government discredited itself not just by mismanaging the economy but by murdering many left-wing activists and involving the country in an ill-fated invasion of the Malvinas (or Falkland) Islands. When elections were held in 1983, the voters, tired of polarized politics, rejected the presidential candidate of the Peronist Party in favor of the candidate from the middle-class Radical Party.[7] The new administration failed to control the public sector deficit, however, and confidence collapsed with the onset of a hyperinflation of nearly 5,000 percent per year as the 1989 presidential elections approached.

The Peronist candidate, Carlos Menem, won the 1989 elections but soon surprised the country by announcing a program of reforms to drastically reduce the size of the public sector, deregulate the economy, and open Argentina to world markets. Menem understood that his victory reflected not a popular desire to return to the traditional statist policies of the Peronists but rather a complete collapse in confidence in the Radical Party's ability to manage the economy. When, after a lull, hyperinflation reemerged, President Menem appointed a new minister of finance, Domingo Cavallo, who in March 1991 took the further step of establishing a new currency, the new peso, and fixing its value to the U.S. dollar. Every peso in circulation was backed by a dollar in the government's vaults, and anyone could go to a branch of the national bank and exchange his pesos for dollars, one for one. Pegging the peso to the dollar made it more difficult for the government to finance public deficits in the customary way, by simply printing more currency.

The Menem administration's policies finally stopped inflation, restored international and domestic confidence in the economy, and led to an influx of investment and real growth rates averaging 6 percent per year through 1999.

Unemployment remained stubbornly high despite the growth in output, however, a testament to how inefficient Argentina's economy had become after decades of protectionism. Menem was elected to a second term in 1995, despite growing controversy about the unequal sharing of the benefits of economic reform.

Matters came to a head at the end of the 1990s, as economic growth first slowed and then stopped altogether. Argentines debate the reasons, but several factors were involved. First, the public sector continued to run structural deficits. These were disguised by the revenue from the sales of state-owned enterprises in the early 1990s and then financed by issuing debt when international confidence in Argentina recovered in the mid-1990s. But they helped drive up domestic interest rates, slowing investment and the economy. Second, the dollar strengthened against foreign currencies, making Argentine exports less competitive in world markets. Finally, the interest on government debt rose as international capital markets began to worry about the weak economy and the chances of default. Higher interest rates meant larger budget deficits, which undermined confidence further in a vicious circle.

The economic decline helped an alliance of opposition parties win the November 1999 elections, but the new president, Fernando de la Rua of the Radical Party, was unable to restore confidence and stop the decline. In December 2001, rumors of default and devaluation provoked a run on the banks and required the government to freeze deposits. The outraged public rioted and forced de la Rua and one successor to resign. The legislature finally appointed Eduardo Duhalde, who had been the Peronist candidate in the 1999 presidential election, to serve out the rest of de la Rua's term. In 2002, President Duhalde defaulted on Argentina's debts and devalued the peso and was struggling to restore domestic and international confidence in the economy.

Concession Contract Design and Award

Argentina's railway network was built by a combination of private investors and the national and provincial governments. By 1940 eleven private companies, mostly financed by British capital, owned 33,113 kilometers of line while public companies owned another 12,532 kilometers. During the 1930s and 1940s the private railways suffered from growing competition from trucks and buses and from government policy discouraging tariff increases. When one private railway went bankrupt in 1948, the Perón government took the opportunity to nationalize the entire system.[8]

The performance of the new national railway, Ferrocarriles Argentinos (FA), gradually deteriorated as competition from highway modes intensified and the company was pressed to take on additional staff, hold down tariffs, and maintain lightly used and unprofitable services. By the 1980s FA was losing enormous sums of money, which made it a major source of budgetary and inflationary pressures and an obvious target for President Menem's reformers.[9]

The Menem government divided FA into three separate lines of business—freight, intercity passenger, and urban commuter—and privatized them in that order. The government was prepared to continue some subsidies for the urban commuter services on the grounds that affordable rail service was important to prevent traffic congestion from getting worse in Buenos Aires. However, it thought that the intercity freight and passenger concessions should be financially self-supporting from shipper or passenger revenues alone. The national government identified approximately 34,000 kilometers of the rail network as suitable for concessions and offered the remaining 8,000 kilometers to the provincial governments for them to operate or abandon.

The freight concessions accounted for 32,000 kilometers of the network, divided into six separate concessions for thirty years each, with the possibility of one ten-year extension. The six freight concessions re-created the route networks of some of the major independent railroad companies that had existed prior to nationalization. Five operated in separate corridors radiating to the north, west, and south out of Buenos Aires; the sixth ran north-south between the ports of Rosario and Bahía Blanca crossing the other concessions at right angles. The first concessions were offered in early 1990, and by October 1993 five were in private operation (see Table 5.1). The remaining concession, the former Belgrano line, did not attract any bids and remained in public hands until the government gave it to the railroad unions.

Most of FA's intercity passenger services had deteriorated to the point where large investments would have been needed to improve service. Only the busy Buenos Aires–Mar del Plata line was thought to be commercially viable, and it was offered for concession in 1992 and attracted four bids. The government of Buenos Aires Province was skeptical about privatizing the Mar del Plata line, however, and when it raised concerns about the two best bids the national government decided to give the province the line instead. In theory, the province was to operate the line only temporarily and then offer it as a concession again. The remaining intercity passenger services were offered to the provinces that wanted to run the service or to select a private concessionaire to do so. Most of these services were ultimately abandoned.

FA's urban commuter railroad service was centered on Buenos Aires and included a network of 899 kilometers, 267 stations, and 1,800 trains carrying over 1 million passengers each weekday. In addition, a municipally owned subway system, the Subte, carried over 500,000 passengers per day on five

Table 5.1 Argentina's railroad and subway concessions

Concession	Length (km)	Years	Private concessionaire	Date of takeover
Freight				
Rosario-Bahía Blanca (north-south)	5,163	30	Ferroexpresso Pampeano (FEPSA)	1 Nov. 91
Mitre (northwest from Buenos Aires)	4,520	30	Nuevo Central Argentino (NCA)	23 Dec. 92
Roca (south from Buenos Aires)	4,791	30	Ferrosur Roca	12 Mar. 93
San Martín (west from Buenos Aires)	5,493	30	Buenos Aires al Pacífico (BAP)	26 Aug. 93
Urquiza (north from Buenos Aires)	2,751	30	Ferrocarril Mesopotámico	22 Oct. 93
Belgrano (north from Buenos Aires)	10,451		Not awarded (eventually given to unions)[a]	
Freight subtotal, excluding Belgrano	22,781			
Intercity passenger				
Buenos Aires–Mar del Plata			Not awarded (given to Province of Buenos Aires)	
Urban commuter				
Urquiza and Subte	25.6 and 44.1	20	Metrovías	1 Jan. 94
Belgrano Norte	51.9	10	Ferrovías	1 Apr. 94
San Martín	55.4	10	Trenes Metropolitano	1 Apr. 94
Belgrano Sur	58.4	10	Trenes Metropolitano	1 May 94
Roca	252.4	10	Trenes Metropolitano	1 Jan. 95
Mitre	182.1	10	Trenes de Buenos Aires	27 May 95
Sarmiento	166.6	10	Trenes de Buenos Aires	27 May 95
Commuter subtotal	836.5			

a. The Belgrano line was turned over to the unions with a five-year commitment by the government to provide US$50 million in subsidies.

subway and one streetcar line.[10] The FA commuter and municipal subway lines were divided into seven separate concessions. Six consisted of commuter rail lines only, and were offered for ten years with the possibility of a second ten-year renewal. The seventh combined a commuter rail line and the subway, and was offered for twenty years because of the greater investments needed in the subway. These urban rail concessions attracted a large number of bids. Private operations began on the first concession in January 1994, and by May 1995 all seven lines had been transferred to private firms.

As in most countries in the 1990s, Argentina's concessions were offered through a two-stage bidding process. In the first stage, the government reviewed the technical qualifications of the prospective concessionaires and selected those qualified to bid. In the second stage, the qualified bidders submitted their final business proposals and the government selected the winner. The government announced clear selection criteria in advance for both stages so as to increase the transparency of the process and reduce opportunities for favoritism and corruption.

As it gained experience, Argentina simplified the selection criteria used in the second and final stage of the award process. The government had established seven criteria for the award of the freight concessions, including the quality and experience of the organization, the size and quality of the investment plan, the annual fees to be paid to the government, the amount the freight concessionaire would charge passenger train operators to use its tracks, and the number of former FA employees to be hired. Each criterion was given a specific weight, and the bidder with the highest total score won. The system created difficulties, however, because some of the criteria were subjective and the government had little confidence that it had set the appropriate weights. As a result, the government used a single criterion for all its later concession programs. In the case of commuter rail, for example, the government set out in great detail the minimum levels of service required, the minimum investment program needed, the maximum tariffs that the concessionaire could charge, and the sanctions for poor performance. The concessions were awarded to the bidder who requested the lowest total subsidy over the life of the concession, calculated as a present value by using a discount rate of 12 percent per year.[11]

The railroad concessions were won by consortia headed by Argentine investors.[12] The five freight concessions were awarded to five separate consortia, while the seven urban passenger concessions were awarded to four different consortia (see Table 5.1). Most consortia were controlled by businesses with some interest in railways. Several urban railway concessions were won by consortia headed by a bus company, for example, while several freight railway concessions were won by consortia headed by the major shippers along the line and another was won by a major construction company with an interest in railway projects.[13]

The government initially established separate regulatory agencies to monitor the performance of the freight and commuter rail concessionaires, but in 1996 these activities were consolidated in a single transportation regulatory agency, the Comisión Nacional de Regulación del Transporte (CNRT), which was also responsible for regulating trucks and buses. The CNRT reported directly to the secretary of transportation and did not have the discretion to modify the terms of the railroad concession contracts.[14]

Early Improvements in Railway Performance

The concession program stimulated a significant improvement in railway performance, particularly from the perspective of government taxpayers and many railway users. Taxpayers gained, because privatization cut the government's subsidy commitments substantially. Before privatization, FA and the municipal subway absorbed approximately US$1.5 billion per year in government subsidies.[15] After privatization, the intercity freight concessions received no subsidies and even promised to pay modest concession fees to the government.[16] The commuter railway and subway concessionaires received subsidies for both operating losses and capital investments, although these declined over time.[17] In addition, several provinces (mainly Buenos Aires) provided some modest subsidies for intercity passenger services, while the national government continued to subsidize the Belgrano freight concession that had not attracted any private bids. An exact accounting would be difficult to provide, but altogether the government had managed to cut its subsidy payments by two-thirds to around US$500 million per year in the early years of the concessions. The promised savings gradually increased so that subsidy payments were less than US$100 million by year 10.

Most railway customers benefited despite the government's subsidy cuts. The only large group of railway users that may have suffered is intercity passengers, since most intercity services except the Mar del Plata line were abandoned. In many cases these passengers probably lost little, however, because intercity buses offered an attractive alternative to rail. Indeed, intense bus competition was a major reason why rail ridership and investment had fallen to such low levels on most intercity lines before privatization.

Freight shippers gained significantly from better service and lower tariffs. Some shippers complained that freight concessionaires were not maintaining service on the most lightly traveled branches, in violation of the terms of their concessions. The vast majority of shippers were located on operating lines, however, and most saw the reliability of their rail service increase while tariffs fell by roughly one-third in real terms between 1992 and 1997.[18] The service improvements and tariff reductions helped to reverse the decline in FA's freight traffic, as shown in Table 5.2. The early 1990s were transition years, when railroad service and traffic deteriorated as the government reorganized FA in anticipation of privatization.[19] Between 1989 (two years before the transition began) and 1997 (four years after most freight lines were in private hands), the tonnage carried by the railroads increased by 33 percent while ton kilometers increased by 19 percent. Part of the turnaround in rail freight traffic was due to the revival of the Argentine economy, but much seemed to be due to significantly better service and lower tariffs.[20]

Table 5.2 Trends in railroad and subway traffic, 1930–1997

Year	Railroad freight traffic		Public transit passengers carried in the Buenos Aires metropolitan area (millions)		
	Tons (millions)	Ton kilometers (billions)	Railroad	Subway	Bus
1930	42.5	11,249	*N.A.*	*N.A.*	*N.A.*
1940	30.8	12,880	*N.A.*	*N.A.*	*N.A.*
1950	32.5	17,309	*N.A.*	*N.A.*	*N.A.*
1960	25.9	15,180	604.1	280.9	2000.6
1970	22.1	13,640	413.1	275.5	2393.4
1980	16.3	9,788	383.1	201.1	2135.3
1989	14.2	8,277	270.3	149.0	1972.3
1990	14.2	7,574	273.7	141.1	2085.5
1991[a]	9.7	5,458	209.0	143.5	2071.4
1992[a]	8.6	4,343	209.4	146.2	2107.4
1993[a]	9.5	5,023	212.1	145.3	2036.5
1994	13.2	6,613	246.0	171.2	1865.0
1995	15.2	7,620	346.7	187.2	1727.0
1996	17.0	8,309	413.7	198.0	1686.4
1997	18.9	9,835	456.1	221.9	1589.8
Percentage change from first private takeovers					
1991–1997	+95%	+80%			
1993–1997			+115%	+53%	−22%
Percentage change from before transition					
1989–1997	+33%	+19%	+69%	+49%	−19%

Source: CNRT data as reported Fundación de Investigaciones Económicas Latinoamericanas (FIEL), *La Regulación de la Competencia y de los Servicios Públicos: Teoría y Experiencia Argentina Reciente* (Buenos Aires: FIEL, 1999), pp. 180, 229–230.
Note: N.A.–Not available.
a. Transition years.

Passengers on the commuter rail lines and the subway also gained significantly from the railway privatization. The concession contracts called for large improvements in the reliability and frequency of commuter services and prohibited fare increases for the first three years. The combination of improved service and stable tariffs together with a crackdown on fare theft by railroad employees contributed to dramatic increases in reported ridership, as shown in Table 5.2. Commuter rail ridership increased by 115 percent between 1993, the year before the private concessionaires began to take over the lines, and 1997. On the subway, where fare theft had not been a problem, ridership increased by 53 percent in the same period. The commuter lines were affected by the same transitional disruptions as the freight lines, however, and if 1989 is used as the prereform baseline, ridership increased by 69 percent on the commuter rail lines and 49 percent on the subway. Much of the ridership gain appears to have been captured from buses, which began to lose passengers after decades of relatively stable patronage (again see Table 5.2).[21]

The primary loser from railroad privatization was railroad labor. Employment dropped dramatically both because the government abandoned lightly used intercity passenger services and because the concessionaires greatly increased labor productivity on the services that remained. FA and the Subte had employed 98,443 workers in the years immediately before privatization, but by December 1997 only 17,064 workers remained on the job (Table 5.3). Of those still working, only 12,944 were employed by the private freight and urban passenger concessionaires; the balance were employed by the government agencies or cooperatives that supervised the sector or operated the Mar del Plata passenger and the Belgrano freight lines. The laid-off workers received approximately US$1 billion in severance payments and services, financed in part with a US$300 million loan from the World Bank. The

Table 5.3 Railroad and subway employees before and after privatization

Period	Employer	Employees
Preprivatization (1989 or 1991)		
	Ferrocarriles Argentinos (June 1989)	94,800
	Subte (December 1991)	3,643
	Total preprivatization	98,443
Postprivatization (December 1997)		
	Private freight concessions	4,747
	Private urban passenger concessions	8,197
	Subtotal, private concessions	12,944
	Intercity passenger services (government)	1,820
	National government supervisory agencies[a]	1,650
	Cooperatives for maintenance	650
	Subtotal, other	4,120
	Total, postprivatization	17,064

Source: Jorge H. Kogan, "Experiencias Ferroviarias: Una Revisión del Caso de Buenos Aires," presentation made to the World Bank Seminar on Transport Regulation, April 8, 1999, Las Palmas, Spain.

a. Includes 920 employees remaining in Ferrocarriles Metropolitanos S.A. (FEMESA), the company created to take over commuter operations during the transition period, and approximately 700 employees remaining in Ferrocarriles Argentinos.

average payment was US$12,000 per worker, the equivalent to only about two years of salary. The laid-off workers averaged nineteen years of experience, so many may have retired. Most of the younger workers probably were unable to get new jobs for several years, however, because the national unemployment rate remained stubbornly high throughout the 1990s.[22]

Problems with the Concession Contracts

Although services and traffic were increasing dramatically, the trends were not consistent with those assumed in the concession contracts. In the case of the freight concessions, the main problem was that the growth in freight traffic, though impressive, was less than the concessionaires had been counting on. Competition from trucks was much fiercer than expected, in part because the government had relaxed regulations controlling truck tariffs and entry into the trucking business in 1991 as part of its program to liberalize the economy.[23] In addition, some of the laid-off railway workers reportedly used their severance payments to buy trucks and enter into competition with their former employers. The railroad concessionaires also may have competed against one another to some extent, since the lines of the concessionaires were often close enough to give shippers an effective choice of railroads. In any event, the railroad concessionaires were forced to reduce the average rail tariff 23 percent below the levels they had forecast for the 1992–1997 period. Even with the tariff reductions, rail traffic was 26 percent below the concessionaires' forecasts; in all, total freight revenues were 43 percent less than had been expected.[24]

The concessionaires compensated for the lost revenue in part by not paying the concession fees or making the investments they had promised in their concession contracts. Between 1992 and 1997, the freight concessionaires paid fees of only US$12 million instead of the US$38 million they had promised. In the same period, they invested only US$199 million in improved infrastructure and rolling stock instead of the promised US$526 million.[25] Although none of the five concessionaires was meeting its obligations, their profitability varied significantly. Two of the concessions were thought to be fairly profitable, although not necessarily profitable enough to afford their promised fees and investments. Two others were surviving mainly because they were skimping on their fees and investments, and almost surely would be forced into bankruptcy if they were made to live up to their commitments. The fifth was thought to be losing money even though it had paid almost none of its concession fees and had made the smallest contribution toward its promised investments.[26]

The urban passenger concessionaires had the opposite problem: more traffic than expected, not less. By 1997, only three years after the subway had been turned over to the private sector, subway ridership was already 33 percent higher than the concessionaire had projected. Ridership on the commuter rail lines was up only 4 percent above projections overall, but the pattern varied significantly. Two lines (San Martín and Belgrano Sur) had 22 and 27 percent fewer riders than expected, for example, while two others (Belgrano Norte and Mitre) had 25 and 29 percent more riders than projected.[27]

The traffic bonanza was a mixed blessing for the concessionaires. On the one hand, it meant that their passenger revenues exceeded expectations. On the other hand, the lines with the largest ridership increases were already becoming overcrowded. The government and the concessionaires were worried that the lines would not have the capacity to accommodate demand if the trend continued. The fact that urban passenger service was unprofitable limited the concessionaires' incentives and abilities to expand service without receiving additional capital or operating subsidies. A concessionaire might be able to profitably accommodate some unexpected traffic by adding coaches to existing trains or increasing train frequency. Eventually, however, further increases in service would require investments in rolling stock, signals, and other facilities that were not anticipated in the government's subsidy and investment program.

The Choices with Incomplete Contracts

Renegotiate, Enforce, or Rebid?

Between 1995 and 1997, the Argentine government faced a growing dilemma. Should it renegotiate the railway concession contracts, enforce them as written, or cancel and rebid them? The arguments against renegotiation were clear: renegotiation threatened to undermine both public support for the current concession contracts and the incentives for future concession bidding. Since the renegotiation would not be competitive, what trust could the public have that the terms agreed to were fair? And if the government set the precedent of renegotiating concession contracts when concessionaires were in trouble, what incentive would competitors for future concession contracts have to bid honestly?

There were grounds to be concerned about both trust and precedent. Rumors about possible corruption in the administration of President Menem had slowly grown over the years, and many of the rumors centered on the privatization program. In 1995, for example, there had been intense controversy over the proposed privatization of the Argentine Post Office. The expected bidders included the operators of domestic courier services, but most of those had been recently taken over through violence and intimidation by a businessman who was rumored to be both a criminal kingpin and a large contributor to the Peronist Party. When the Senate passed a law prohibiting foreign companies from bidding for the Post Office concession, the fix seemed to be in. Finance Minister Cavallo, who wanted to protect the reputation of privatization, responded by denouncing corrupt influences in the sale of the Post Office during seven hours of nationally televised testimony before Congress. President Menem fired Cavallo six months later over a different issue, but many suspected that the real reason was Cavallo's earlier accusations of corruption. There had been no rumors of corruption surrounding the award of the railway concessions, but the public was bound to be suspicious of any contract renegotiations in the prevailing climate.

Similarly, precedent was a concern, because there already were signs of insincere bidding for concession contracts in Argentina. Minor problems had arisen, for example, in the bidding for both the freight and the commuter railway concessions. Some consortia bidding for the freight concessions had promised to hire large numbers of FA employees, since that was one of the criteria for the final award. Once the consortia won their concessions, however, some argued that they could not meet their commitments because most FA employees were not qualified for the new jobs. In another instance, immediately after the award of the urban commuter concessions, some of the winners argued that there were ambiguities in the contracts that had to be resolved before they could take over the lines. Government officials thought the concessionaires were exaggerating the ambiguities and had not mentioned them earlier to provide a pretext for negotiations after the bidding. The resulting disputes had delayed the takeover of some lines by as much a year. The extent of any insincerity in actual bidding had been limited so far. Once renegotiation was established as a precedent, however, the problems would presumably escalate.

The arguments for renegotiation were as strong as the arguments against. If one set aside the issue of precedent, it was clear that the existing contracts no longer served the best interests of the railway users or the general public. In the case of the freight railways, strictly enforcing the contracts would force at least three of the five concessions into bankruptcy. Shippers on the three bankrupt concessions would probably suffer serious service disruptions while the government rebid the concessions. Investments in these three lines would not necessarily increase, moreover, since the new concessionaires, now armed with experience, would bid less generously. Shippers on the two concessions likely to survive might not be better off either. Investment levels would increase, but the improvements might be of limited value to shippers or the nation since they were designed to accommodate traffic patterns and levels that had not materialized. Forcing these investments might even prevent the concessionaires from making improvements needed by the current traffic.

In the case of the commuter railways, the argument that the existing contracts no longer served the public interest was even more obvious. Transportation officials had been delighted by the unexpectedly rapid increase in railway ridership, because they viewed the subway and railway systems as key tools for combating traffic congestion. Sustaining that ridership growth was becoming more important, moreover, because the economic recovery was stimulating auto ownership and use in Buenos Aires. At the same time, crowding was becoming so bad on the subway and several other lines that officials were worried that it was discouraging prospective riders.[28] The concession contract for the subway and the Urquiza line would not expire for another sixteen years, and the other six commuter rail concessions still had six to seven years to go. It would be difficult for the government to wait that long before taking steps to protect the system's quality of service and its ability to attract new riders.

The concessionaires faced the same unhappy choice between enforcement and renegotiation as the government. For the freight concessionaires, renegotiation was clearly preferable to enforcement, since the existing contracts could drive them into bankruptcy. The best option was probably the status quo, however, since the government was allowing them to ignore their current obligations without attempting to impose new ones.[29] For the commuter railway concessionaires, enforcement was a reasonably attractive possibility, since their contracts were not as unworkable. But the crowded services might eventually threaten the concessionaires' ability to meet the quality standards set out in the concession agreements. Moreover, the commuter railway concessionaires would be less vulnerable to government opportunism in negotiations because they had made few fixed investments themselves; the bulk of the investments were being directly subsidized by the government. Finally, the government's negotiating position was further weakened because it seemed so committed to solving the crowding problems.

In the summer of 1997, the government issued two executive orders authorizing the secretary of transportation to renegotiate the freight and the commuter railway concessions.[30] The secretary got the job rather than CNRT (the regulator) presumably because the negotiations would be politically sensitive and raise issues of basic transportation and budgetary policy that CNRT was poorly equipped to deal with. Despite all the risks involved, the government preferred to renegotiate rather than to continue to live with freight contracts that the concessionaires were openly violating and commuter contracts that provided the public with inadequate service. As one senior public official explained privately: "I would rather see the government do something wrong every five years than do something wrong every day."[31]

The Realities of Renegotiation

A variety of factors soon intensified the political pressures surrounding the negotiations. First, the renegotiated agreements had to be approved by a legislative commission called the Bicameral Commission for the Reform of the State. The commission had been created in 1989, the year that President Menem was first elected. The economy had been close to collapse, and faith in the government was so low that the rival Radical Party asked the president-elect to take office early. Menem agreed to do so on the condition that the Radical Party support two laws, one allowing him to restructure Argentina's debt and the second giving him the power to reform the state through privatization. The second law established the bicameral commission to review and approve privatization programs proposed by the executive. Normally the commission would review only the broad design of a concession program, leaving the appropriate ministry to develop the details of the concession contracts and supervise the competition for them. Because the railway contracts were being renegotiated rather than competitively tendered, however, the commission would have to approve each one.

Second, the presidential elections of November 1999 were approaching and the outcome was highly uncertain. It was unclear who the Peronist candidate would be until early 1999, when President Menem, no longer popular, finally abandoned efforts to persuade Congress to amend the constitution to allow him to run for a third term. The Peronists eventually nominated Duhalde, a party leader who had been openly critical of privatization, while the two major opposition parties united as the "Alliance" in support of Fernando de la Rua, the Radical Party mayor of Buenos Aires, as their presidential candidate. The Alliance campaigned on promises to clean up the corruption in government and to ensure that the benefits of economic reform were more widely shared. The race was extremely close and would be in doubt until election day.

Third, in January 1998, just as the renegotiations were beginning, the CNRT announced fare increases averaging 30 percent on the commuter railway and subway lines. The concession contracts allowed fare increases averaging a little over 3 percent per year over ten years if the concessionaire improved service quality to certain levels, but it held any increases in abeyance for the first three years. Most concessionaires had met the targets they were expected to achieve over ten years in three, so they were entitled to the full ten-year increase when the freeze expired. The increases shocked user groups, who complained that the quality targets in the contracts had been too easy to achieve.

Finally, the Argentine economy went into a recession that began with the Asian financial crisis of 1997–1998, continued after Brazil, Argentina's major trading partner, devalued its currency in January 1999, and deepened when the U.S. dollar appreciated in 2000. The recession heightened tensions over whether the poor and the middle class had benefited much from the economic reforms and reduced the chances that the government could subsidize new commuter railway investments.

In this context, little progress was made on renegotiating the freight railway concessions. The task was difficult. Each concessionaire faced a very different financial situation, and the government was unsure what it could—or should—ask for in return for waiving past investment commitments. The government didn't feel much urgency, moreover, since neither the shippers nor the concessionaires were pressing strongly for a resolution. Matters were further complicated in 1998 when a Brazilian private railway bought two of the weaker concessions with the idea of eventually operating a rail network that would extend from southern Brazil through Argentina to Chile.[32] Two freight agreements were finally submitted to the commission in late 1998, but the commission never approved them. The legislators may have sensed that there was no need to act quickly, but there were rumors that some commission members were holding out for large campaign contributions from the concessionaires.

More progress was made on the commuter railway concessions, although it would prove only temporary. Since the government had no additional money for subsidies, the concessionaires proposed major new investments that would be financed by approximately doubling fares over five years and by extending the length of the concessions to thirty years (twenty-four years in the case of the subway). When the mayor of Buenos Aires objected to the prospect of another subway fare increase, the president reportedly told him that the city should either take a place at the negotiating table for that concession or he would return responsibility for the subway back to the city. The city joined in the summer of 1998, and by that fall the government submitted to the bicameral commission new agreements with three of the four commuter concessionaires.[33] The fourth agreement would not be submitted to the commission until July 1999.[34]

In March 1999 the commission approved two of the agreements it had received, including the one for the subway, but by that time the opposition had decided to make the commuter concessions a campaign issue.[35] Lawyers from the Alliance sued to stop the government on the grounds that a public hearing was needed, and when the hearing was held they complained, with some justification, that it had been poorly organized and perfunctory.[36] A report by congressional staff estimated that five of the concessionaires were earning returns of 20 to 67 percent per year.[37] An Alliance think tank issued a report critical of the new agreements, charging, among other things, that the concessionaires had inflated the costs of the investments they had proposed. Groups of railway passengers formed to protest, and the Buenos Aires newspapers published critical stories.

The government would have been hard pressed to persuade the public of the need to double fares even in a less highly charged environment. Most riders were unaware that the existing investment program was subsidized by the government and not financed by fares. As a result, it was difficult for riders to understand why the new investment program required such large fare increases. The proposed fare hikes also seemed outrageous coming so soon after the 30 percent increase of January 1998. There was also suspicion that the government negotiators had been corrupted by the companies, and these fears grew when the bicameral commission approved the last two commuter concession agreements just days before the election. The public was glad that railway service had improved, but now the incumbent politicians and the concessionaires seemed to be taking advantage of their positions.

The opposition won the elections only to find that it faced the same dilemmas. In January 2000, just a month after taking office, the new secretary of transportation suspended three of the four commuter rail contracts that had been renegotiated. The only contract that would be honored was the one involving the subway, which de la Rua had helped to renegotiate when he was mayor of Buenos Aires. The new administration was compelled to suspend the other three contracts given the charges it had made during the campaign. Moreover, the administration felt that because it had campaigned against corruption and was not tainted by scandal, it had a better chance of negotiating an agreement that the public would accept.

The basic financial calculus had not changed, however: a fare increase was needed because the government lacked the budgetary resources to subsidize additional investments. The government could reduce the fare increase by paring the investment program to its essentials and by challenging the cost of every new facility and piece of equipment. In the end, however, fares would rise and the public would have to trust that the government had bargained hard on its behalf. The new secretary of transportation met repeatedly with user groups to explain the situation, but much of the hostility and suspicion they had expressed toward the old government was soon transferred to him.

The deteriorating fiscal situation quickly undermined the last chances for agreement by forcing the government to default on the original commuter concessions. By the summer of 2000, the government and the commuter rail concessionaires had negotiated draft agreements for new investments. The agreements still relied on fare increases, but the new investment programs were scaled back 30 percent so that fares would increase by only around 75 percent over five years instead of doubling.[38] Before the last details could be resolved, however, the growing fiscal crisis forced the government to cut the transportation budget for fiscal year 2001, including the US$212 million the government owed the commuter railways that year under the original concession contracts.[39] To compensate, late in 2000 the transportation secretary authorized the concessionaires to increase fares by 10 cents.[40] The concessionaires objected, disputing the secretary's claims that the increase would generate enough revenue to make up for the government's shortfall. The user groups were furious that the government was breaking its original funding commitments and increasing fares at a time when household incomes were falling. The secretary had become so controversial that the president fired him the following spring, although it was unclear what his successor could do differently.

The collapse of the Argentine economy at the end of 2001 put an end to renegotiations for the moment. If and when the economy improved, however, the same issues would reappear. The commuter rail concessions were scheduled to expire in 2004 and 2005 and therefore might be rebid again fairly soon, although the government or the courts would have to resolve the legacy of claims and counterclaims about the contract extensions that were canceled in 2000. The subway and freight concessions had many years still to go, with little prospect of finding solutions that would be widely regarded as fair.

The Limitations of Foresight

The designers of the railway privatization program must have understood that the concession contracts were potentially vulnerable to a variety of uncertainties. Economies have their ups and downs, especially in developing countries, so it would have been foolish not to consider the risk of a serious recession during the lives of the contracts. Argentina was in the midst of a program of radical economic reforms when the railway contracts were being drafted in the early 1990s, which added further to the macroeconomic uncertainties. Moreover, few other countries had privatized their railways at the time, which meant there was little experience to draw on. Drafting complete concession contracts for a pioneering railway program in a rapidly changing economy was clearly a daunting task.

Nevertheless, it is not obvious that the government or the concessionaires could have anticipated the specific events that undermined the contracts or drafted appropriate contingencies to deal with those events. In the case of the freight concessions, the key problem was the shortfall in revenue caused by stronger-than-expected truck competition. In retrospect it seems foolish for the government to have drafted contracts that committed the concessionaires to specific investment programs, regardless of traffic volumes and profitability. The competition for the contracts may have encouraged prospective concessionaires to assume overly optimistic traffic forecasts, or perhaps even to bid insincerely. But the alternatives were not that attractive either. A contract that made investment contingent on traffic levels might have made it more difficult to compare bids, for example, and would have done nothing to reduce the incentives for overly optimistic or insincere bidding.

Moreover, the freight concessionaires' traffic and revenue forecasts may have seemed perfectly reasonable at the time. The government had required that each bidding consortium include an operating railroad, and most had chosen a U.S. freight railroad because there were few other private railways in the world at the time. Rail freight had been growing phenomenally in the United States since the U.S. government deregulated its railroad industry in 1980.[41] The U.S. rail freight revival was occurring despite the simultaneous deregulation of the U.S. trucking industry, moreover, which may have made the railroads less concerned about truck competition. Given the appalling condition of FA's freight equipment and services, the U.S. railroads might well have predicted that it would be easy to recapture a significant share of traffic with only a modicum of effort. And the Argentine companies leading the bidding consortia probably would have deferred to the views of their railroad partners in these matters.

In the case of the commuter rail concessions, the key problems were the underestimates of traffic and the fiscal crisis that made it hard for the government to increase subsidies for investments. The government officials who planned the original concessions had wanted to require more investments, but had scaled back their ambitions because of the government's budget constraints. Nonetheless, they seemed surprised by the speed with which ridership increased and overwhelmed the investment program. Unlike the case of freight, there was no dramatic revival of commuter services in the United States or elsewhere that might have cautioned Argentine policymakers. The commuter services also had not been as starved for capital as the freight services, although they were still in very bad shape. Indeed, much of the ridership growth occurred in the first two years, well before the concessionaires had the chance to spend much money on investments. The government had anticipated that there were important opportunities to increase service reliability, punctuality, and cleanliness even with the existing track and rolling stock, but they had little reason to expect the ridership to respond so quickly.

It is also unclear that the government should have anticipated a fiscal crisis so severe that it would prevent it from meeting its contractual obligations. The government knew it could not sustain the levels of subsidy FA and Subte were absorbing before privatization, but it would have been harder to anticipate that the government would be unable to afford the much reduced subsidies that the new concessions required. By the time the government defaulted on its payments to the concessionaires, the annual payments were only about one-eighth of the subsidies before privatization.

Concession Contracts and Instability

One reason so many concession programs initiated in the late twentieth century suffered from incomplete contracts was the dearth of recent experience with concessions. Pioneers like Argentina taught policymakers important lessons about the risks of an incomplete contract, and started them thinking about the possibilities for reducing those risks by, for example, writing contracts for shorter durations, drafting appropriate contingencies, and inserting workable arbitration or buy-out clauses.

But the prevalence of incomplete contracts also reflects the inherent limitations of the contractual approach and the pressures to use it even in difficult situations. Contracts are intended to increase rather than reduce stability, and in many applications they do. But if it is difficult to align all the incentives and describe all the obligations of the parties in advance, then a formal contract provides little protection.

Moreover, the temptations to use contracts are often strongest in situations where they are most likely to fail. Contracts may seem more attractive than discretionary regulation where the political and economic environments are unstable, but those are also the situations where it is difficult to draft a complete contract. Argentina used concession contracts, or discretionary regulation with strong contractual elements, for all the utilities that it privatized in the 1990s, for example, because the appearance of strong commitment was essential given the country's history of economic and political turmoil. But the turmoil helped undo the contracts.

Once a concession contact proves to be incomplete, it becomes extremely difficult to restore stability and commitment. An incomplete or obsolete contract presents the government and the concessionaire with an impossible choice between enforcement and renegotiation. On the one hand, it seems absurd for the government to enforce a contract that no longer serves the public interest, or that will only force a bankruptcy and a painful transition that may leave customers no better off in the end. On the other hand, renegotiation risks undermining public confidence in the fairness of the new contract and threatens the integrity of future contract bidding. Most governments choose renegotiation, as in the case of Argentina. The immediate pain of inadequate service, or of a contract's being flagrantly violated, usually trumps more distant considerations of precedent.

After a contract has been renegotiated once, however, inhibitions over subsequent negotiations seem to be reduced. The principle that the contract is complete and binding has been violated, and the bad precedent is already set. Future renegotiations will strengthen that precedent, but most of the harm is already done. Thus when additional problems develop, the government is quicker to tear up the agreement than it was the first time. By 2002 many of Argentina's freight railway concessions had been renegotiated once and its commuter concessions twice. Six of the original commuter concessions would have expired in 2004 or 2005, but those concessions had been extended in subsequent renegotiations—so there would be no opportunity for a clean break and rebidding soon. The system of regulation by contract had been transformed into regulation by periodic negotiation, and the commitments that contracts were meant to establish were largely gone.

Periodic negotiations also encourage instability by eroding popular support for the private provision of infrastructure. The issues in the negotiations are almost always complex, which makes it harder for the government or the concessionaire to stimulate an informed public debate. And if the public begins with suspicions about the government's competence or honesty or about the concessionaire's motives, the task is even harder. It would have been difficult for the Menem administration to win popular acceptance for the renegotiated contracts given its reputation for corruption. But even the reformist de la Rua administration did not have the political trust or skills to overcome popular suspicions.

In the case of the freight railways, Argentina could have most likely avoided the problems of concession contracts by relying on private contracts between the railroads and their customers to control monopoly power instead. Both the freight and the commuter railways were probably natural monopolies, inasmuch as the railroads and their customers make durable and immobile investments that leave them potentially vulnerable to opportunism. In the case of freight, however, Argentina's railways face much stronger competition from alternative modes and locations, which limits the railroads' leverage over their customers. In addition, much of the rail freight is shipped by large corporations, such as grain exporters or building materials suppliers, which makes the costs of negotiating private contracts more reasonable. Private contracts are not an option for the commuter railways, however, both because traffic congestion limits competition from buses and cars and because the millions of daily users make contracting more complex.

Argentina was almost certainly better off with concession contracts than it had been under the old regime of public railways, even if there might have been better solutions for freight. The younger railway workers who were laid off suffered, but their future was questionable in any case, since it would have been impossible for the government to sustain the old levels of subsidy and employment in the public railway. In the meantime, railway users and taxpayers gained significantly from the improved service and lower costs that the concession schemes brought. In short, as vulnerable and unstable as concession regimes seem to be, they still may be superior to the alternative of public enterprise.

6

Forestalling Expropriation: Electricity in the Americas

Expropriation's Price

Regulation may include seeds of instability, but regulatory disputes do not inevitably lead to government buyouts or expropriation. Many infrastructure companies survived in private hands for a hundred years or more, particularly in the United States, while others were expropriated relatively quickly. Why did private infrastructure companies survive in some places and not in others? What does past experience suggest about the prospects for the infrastructure companies that were privatized at the end of the twentieth century?

The history of the electricity industry in North and South America suggests some of the factors that affect expropriation, because a common technology was applied in a variety of circumstances and with different results. Private companies began to sell electricity throughout the region beginning in the late nineteenth century. From the outset the technology was international, spread by electrical engineers and equipment manufacturers from Europe, Canada, and the United States. Electricity quickly came to be considered a basic necessity of modern life, and everywhere governments soon regulated private utility rates.

Although the technology was common, the companies operated in a variety of environments. In some countries regulation was a responsibility of municipal or provincial authorities, for example, while in others it was the responsibility of national governments. Some countries enjoyed more stable and democratic governments than others. Some had legal systems based on Anglo-Saxon common law; others relied on the European civil law tradition. The extent of foreign ownership also varied. Many of the larger utilities in Latin America and several in Canada were foreign owned, but at least one major Latin American utility and many Canadian and U.S. firms were domestically owned.

Not surprisingly, the longevity of these private electricity companies varied as well. In broad terms, the pattern was simple: most private companies survived in the United States while most were eventually nationalized in Latin America and Canada. But there were some fascinating variations and exceptions. In Latin America, for example, three large private companies survived the waves of nationalization. Similarly, in Canada, four provinces began the process of nationalization as early as 1906 and 1919 while four provinces waited until after World War II, and three allowed large private electricity companies to survive throughout the twentieth century.

Although the histories of many private electricity companies are reasonably well documented,[1] it is impossible to know for certain why some companies survived and others did not. There are simply too many possible explanations relative to the number of well-documented cases. Some explanatory factors tend to be correlated, moreover, which makes them hard to disentangle. Latin America had a higher concentration of foreign-owned utilities, for example, but it also had less stable governments and a civil law tradition that also may have encouraged nationalization. Given these limitations, the most one can hope for is to identify some of the factors that seem to have been involved.

What emerges from these histories is a very simple idea: that private utilities are more likely to survive where the political or financial cost of expropriation is high. High expropriation costs encourage governments to try to resolve disputes by means short of expropriation. Four factors seem to affect expropriation costs, broadly understood: specific legal constraints on expropriation, the presence of foreign owners, whether the firm is regulated by municipal or national authorities, and the extent to which the firm's stock is widely held. Before describing these factors and their possible influence, it is helpful to review briefly the industry's history.

The History in Overview

The first electricity companies appeared in the United States and Canada in the 1880s and in most Latin American countries in the 1890s.[2] The initial application was usually to replace gas or kerosene as a source of public lighting. In the larger cities, major increases in generating capacity were soon sought to electrify street railway systems. In some cases providing power for large mining or industrial enterprises was a key early goal. Almost all of the early electric companies were privately owned and financed by local or domestic investors. Typically the municipal government awarded local citizens or companies concessions to develop and provide electric service for a period of twenty to fifty years. Sometimes permission from provincial or national governments was also needed, particularly to obtain the water rights required for hydroelectric projects.

The industry experienced a wave of consolidation that began in the last decade of the nineteenth century in Canada and the United States and lasted into the third decade of the twentieth century in Latin America. At its end, most cities had only one electricity supplier, and often there was consolidation across industries. It was common for the electric company to own the street railway, since the railway was usually its largest customer. And in many cities the electric company bought up the competing gas company as well. Most economists believe that consolidation within the electric industry was inevitable, because improvements in generating and transmission technologies made it cheaper to serve a city from a few large generating stations coordinated on a single grid. However, the aggressive efforts of companies to buy up or drive out their competitors often left the popular impression that the resulting monopolies were the creatures of a deliberate business strategy rather than the inevitable consequence of technology.[3]

In Latin America, consolidation was often accompanied by foreign ownership, because foreign investors had superior access to technology and capital. In the decade before World War I, many key concessions were acquired by investors from Britain, Germany, Switzerland, and Canada. A second wave of foreign investment occurred between World War I and the onset of the Great Depression, when U.S. and Canadian investors bought up concessions from British, German, French, and domestic owners.

Initially, there seems to have been little controversy over whether the electric industry should be privately owned or not. Private ownership may have been acceptable at first because of the industry's modest origins and prospects. Often a local mechanic or merchant bought the first small generator and began to supply electricity to his neighborhood.[4] But private ownership also fit with the liberal political ideology that dominated the region. The United States and most Latin American countries had rebelled against their colonial masters in the late eighteenth or early nineteenth centuries in the name of individual liberty and a more limited role for the state. Given this heritage, it was more consistent to grant private entrepreneurs concessions than to have the public sector supply electricity.

Controversy over private ownership began to surface during the 1890s in the United States and Canada and in the following decade in Latin America. By that time, electricity had proved its utility as a clean and relatively inexpensive source of illumination and power. Electricity was transforming lighting, urban transportation, and manufacturing to the extent that it was difficult to imagine life without it. Moreover, the industry was beginning to consolidate, generating fears that customers would become dependent on a single supplier for this valuable service. The same political liberals who had supported private over state enterprises often opposed the private monopolies that were emerging.

Controversy intensified significantly during the Depression of the 1930s.

Table 6.1 Electric power generation in the United States by sector, 1902–1970

Year	Private utility	Cooperative	Municipal	Federal	State and other	Total public	Self-generated	All sectors
				Public agency				
Millions of kilowatt-hours								
1902	2,311	N.A.	196	N.A.	N.A.	196	3,462	5,969
1920	37,716	N.A.	1,373	59	257	1,689	17,154	56,559
1930	86,109	N.A.	3,604	465	934	5,003	23,525	114,637
1940	125,411	37	6,188	8,584	1,617	16,389	38,070	179,907
1950	266,860	1,010	15,244	40,388	5,639	61,271	59,533	388,674
1960	580,286	5,006	37,029	112,509	20,545	170,082	88,814	844,188
1970	1,183,190	23,459	71,394	185,753	67,813	324,960	108,162	1,639,771
Percentage of kilowatt-hours								
1902	38.7	N.A.	3.3	N.A.	N.A.	3.3	58.0	100.0
1920	66.7	N.A.	2.4	0.1	0.5	3.0	30.3	100.0
1930	75.1	N.A.	3.1	0.4	0.8	4.4	20.5	100.0
1940	69.7	0.0	3.4	4.8	0.9	9.1	21.2	100.0
1950	68.7	0.3	3.9	10.4	1.5	15.8	15.3	100.0
1960	68.7	0.6	4.4	13.3	2.4	20.1	10.5	100.0
1970	72.2	1.4	4.4	11.3	4.1	19.8	6.6	100.0

Source: U.S. Bureau of the Census, *Historical Statistics of the United States: Colonial Times to 1970* (Washington, D.C.: U.S. Government Printing Office, 1975; reprinted by Kraus Publications, 1989), pt. 2, p. 821.

Note: N.A.–Not available.

Private electric utilities often refused to reduce their rates, despite the fact that household incomes and the prices for many other goods had declined. The utilities resisted rate cuts because electricity generation and distribution were capital-intensive businesses, and many of their expenses were fixed. With electricity consumption declining, moreover, it may have been harder to recover capital costs even with the old tariffs. But many utility customers could not pay their bills, and the reluctance of the utilities to reduce rates in such difficult times further eroded their base of popular support.

In the United States, these controversies were resolved primarily by shifting the responsibility for regulating private utilities from municipal governments to new state public utility commissions. The new PUCs were designed to professionalize regulation and avoid the complaints of corruption and political influence that had plagued municipal regulation. Wisconsin and New York are widely credited with establishing the first modern PUCs in 1907, and by 1939 all but one state used PUCs to regulate their private electric companies.[5]

This solution worked well enough that private utilities' share of the electricity generated in the United States increased from 38.7 percent in 1902 to 75.1 percent in 1930 and remained at roughly 70 percent through 1970 (see Table 6.1). As the capacity and reliability of private utilities improved, self-generation—that is, electricity generated by manufacturers or others for their own use—declined from 58.0 percent of electricity generated in 1902 to 20.5 percent in 1930 and to 6.6 percent in 1970. Public agencies generated less than 5 percent of electricity until 1930, but increased their share to around 20 percent over the next thirty years.

The modest increase in public power between 1930 and 1960 was due largely to the federal government's creation of the Tennessee Valley Authority (TVA) and to federal and state construction of enormous multipurpose dams to provide power, irrigation, and flood control in the West. President Roosevelt argued in the 1930s that these public projects would provide a benchmark against which the efficiency of private power could be measured.[6] But the TVA and the Western dams were primarily designed to put people to work during the Depression and to stimulate the economic development of lagging areas of the country rather than to supplant existing private utilities. Some proponents of these dams may have hoped that they would stimulate a wider movement for public power, but they did not.

In Latin America most private electric companies survived the Depression and World War II, only to be nationalized between 1943 and 1979. As late as 1950, public agencies were generating only 10 percent of Latin America's electricity while private utilities accounted for 66.9 percent and self-generation for 23.1 percent (see Table 6.2). Many of the first large public compa-

Table 6.2 Electric power generation in Latin America by sector, 1950–1975

	Millions of kilowatt-hours				Percentage of kilowatt-hours			
Country and year	Private utility	Public agency	Self-generation	Total	Private utility	Public agency	Self-generation	Total
All Latin America								
1950	18,470	2,754	6,379	27,603	66.9	10.0	23.1	100.0
1960	24,735	25,755	17,189	67,677	36.5	38.1	25.4	100.0
1975	22,609	179,615	27,041	229,265	9.9	78.3	11.8	100.0
Argentina								
1950	3,920	603	780	5,303	73.9	11.4	14.7	100.0
1960	4,242	3,621	2,595	10,458	40.6	34.6	24.8	100.0
1975	2,293	22,621	4,915	29,829	7.7	75.8	16.5	100.0
Brazil								
1950	7,500	0	708	8,208	91.4	0.0	8.6	100.0
1960	14,898	3,616	4,351	22,865	65.2	15.8	19.0	100.0
1975	9,142	66,804	4,447	80,393	11.4	83.1	5.5	100.0
Chile								
1950	780	379	1,784	2,943	26.5	12.9	60.6	100.0
1960	751	1,591	2,250	4,592	16.4	34.6	49.0	100.0
1975	0	6,203	2,259	8,462	0.0	73.3	26.7	100.0
Colombia								
1950	800	250	220	1,270	63.0	19.7	17.3	100.0
1960	455	2,340	525	3,320	13.7	70.5	15.8	100.0
1975	0	12,693	1,906	14,599	0.0	86.9	13.1	100.0
Mexico								
1950	3,050	500	874	4,424	68.9	11.3	19.8	100.0
1960	200	8,389	2,139	10,728	1.9	78.2	19.9	100.0
1975	0	39,400	4,106	43,506	0.0	90.5	9.5	100.0
Peru								
1950	380	60	380	820	46.3	7.3	46.4	100.0
1960	800	378	1,470	2,648	30.2	14.3	55.5	100.0
1975	0	4,565	3,131	7,696	0.0	59.3	40.7	100.0
Venezuela								
1950	430	123	600	1,153	37.3	10.7	52.0	100.0
1960	1,851	1,040	1,679	4,570	40.5	22.8	36.7	100.0
1975	7,121	11,558	2,500	21,179	33.6	54.6	11.8	100.0
Rest of Latin America								
1950	1,610	839	1,033	3,482	46.2	24.1	29.7	100.0
1960	1,538	4,780	2,180	8,496	18.1	56.3	25.6	100.0
1975	4,053	16,231	3,507	23,791	17.0	68.2	14.8	100.0

Source: Joseph W. Mullen, *Energy in Latin America: The Historical Record* (Santiago, Chile: United Nations, CEPAL, 1978), p. 65.

Note: In the original source the total power generated is not always equal to the sum of the power generated by private utilities, public agencies, and self-generation. The differences are not large, but in five cases where they are too large to be explained by rounding error we changed the total to equal the sum of the reported components.

nies established in the 1930s and 1940s were modeled explicitly on the TVA, and intended to develop hydro power in order to stimulate the economies of remote and lagging regions. Major expropriations did not begin until the 1940s, and were confined largely to Argentina at first. At the end of the 1950s and the beginning of the 1960s, however, a wave of expropriations swept through most of Latin America.

By 1975 private utilities were generating only 9.9 percent of Latin America's electricity while the public sector generated 78.3 percent. The remaining few private utilities were generating about as much electricity in 1975 as all the private utilities had in 1950. But total electricity production increased almost tenfold between 1950 and 1975, and all of the growth was in the public sector. In 1979 two of the last remaining large private utilities in Brazil and Argentina were finally nationalized. On the eve of the privatization movement that would sweep Latin America in the 1980s and 1990s, private electric utilities had all but disappeared, with the only notable exceptions being three distribution companies serving Caracas, La Paz, and Guayaquil.

In Canada, public power supplanted private power in two distinct phases. The first phase occurred during the first two decades of the twentieth century, before nationalization had begun in Latin America. At the turn of the century there were no significant public power companies in Canada, but by 1920 the public sector was generating 24.4 percent of Canada's power (Table 6.3). The leader in this phase was the province of Ontario, which established Ontario Hydro to build generating plants near Niagara Falls in 1906. Ontario Hydro was a response in part to the fears of small businesses in southern Ontario that all the concessions for cheap hydro power had been

Table 6.3 Electric power generation in Canada by sector, 1920–1975

	Millions of kilowatt-hours				Percentage of kilowatt-hours			
Year	Private utility	Public agency	Self-generation	Total	Private utility	Public agency	Self-generation	Total
1920	4,456	1,438	N.A.	5,894	75.6	24.4	N.A.	100.0
1930	12,937	5,157	1,374	19,468	66.5	26.5	7.1	100.0
1940	22,287	7,822	2,953	33,062	67.4	23.7	8.9	100.0
1950	28,432	20,061	6,544	55,037	51.7	36.5	11.9	100.0
1960	31,306	57,850	25,301	114,457	27.4	50.5	22.1	100.0
1970	20,504	151,407	32,793	204,704	10.0	74.0	16.0	100.0
1975	50,805	187,543	35,044	273,392	18.6	68.6	12.8	100.0

Source: Statistics Canada, *Historical Statistics of Canada* (2000), table Q75, available at www.statcan.ca/english/Freepub/11-516-XIE/section q.

Note: N.A.–Not available.

given to a private firm that supplied Toronto and to two U.S. companies that exported power to New York State. In 1908 the city of Toronto also established a municipal lighting company to distribute power supplied by Ontario Hydro. By 1923 these public companies had absorbed their private counterparts, so that all the power in Ontario was supplied by the public sector.[7] Three other provinces—Manitoba, Nova Scotia, and New Brunswick—also established provincial power companies modeled on Ontario Hydro between 1919 and 1920. In addition, Winnipeg, Manitoba's capital, established a municipal light company as early as 1906 to compete with the private utility that also served the city. Although these public companies grew steadily in strength, private companies continued to play a significant role in these three provinces for the time being.[8]

In the remaining Canadian provinces, private power reigned almost unchallenged until after World War II.[9] Private companies were the only electricity providers in Quebec and British Columbia,[10] for example, and faced competition from only one or two small municipal companies in Alberta.[11] Many provinces established PUCs modeled after those in the United States to regulate the tariffs of their private companies.[12] Quebec and Nova Scotia led the way in 1909, although the electric companies serving Montreal and Halifax managed to remain exempt from PUC control until the 1930s. New Brunswick and Manitoba created PUCs in 1910 and 1912 while British Columbia established a PUC in 1917, although the company serving Vancouver was exempt from its control until 1938.

The Canadian PUCs were not successful in forestalling the pressure for public power, and the second round of government takeovers began after World War II. British Columbia, Quebec, and Saskatchewan all created provincial power companies between 1944 and 1949. The last private power companies were taken over in Manitoba in 1953, British Columbia in 1962, Quebec in 1963, and Nova Scotia in 1972. By the mid-1970s, only 18 percent of Canada's power was being generated by private utilities, and major investor-owned companies survived in only three provinces: Alberta, Newfoundland, and tiny Prince Edward Island.[13]

Legal Systems and Constraints: The United States and Canada

One factor that appears to explain some of the variation in the survival of private electricity companies is the degree to which the legal system constrains the government from expropriating private property without compensation. If the government must compensate investors when it expropriates their property, nationalization is a more costly policy for the government. It is important that this protection extend to more gradual and subtle forms of expropriation, such as holding down tariffs below the levels that would allow the utility's owners to recover their investment. If the government can hold down tariffs without compensation, then it can gradually extract the value of the company to the point where formal expropriation, even with compensation, is far less expensive.

The degree of protection against expropriation is thought to be a function of many aspects of the legal system. Recent research, described in Chapter 3, suggests that legal systems based on Anglo-Saxon common law provide stronger protection for private property than those based on European civil law. Many scholars believe that an independent judiciary is also important; independence is often defined as a combination of informal traditions and formal systems of appointment and tenure that allows judges to rule against the government on controversial matters without fear of retribution. Some have argued that a presidential system of government might make it harder to change the laws affecting investors, since the executive and legislative branches of government are often controlled by different parties.[14]

While common law systems, independent judiciaries, and presidential governments may have helped private electric utilities survive in certain parts of the Americas, their influence does not appear to have been decisive. If one ignores Canada, the case for common law systems and an independent judiciary seems strong. Most private utilities survived in the United States, which has a common law tradition and an independent judiciary, but not in Latin America, which has a civil law tradition and a less independent judiciary. Canada is a sticking point, however, since it is a common law country with an independent judiciary that nationalized most of its private electric utilities by the 1970s, much like Latin America. If civil law was critical in encouraging nationalization in Latin America, then one must find some other explanation for the nationalization of electricity in Canada. And common law cannot have been the key protector of private utilities in the United States, since it failed to play the same role in Canada. Indeed, the most interesting question is why the United States and Canada, both common law countries with traditions of judicial independence, took such different paths.

An important part of the answer appears to lie in explicit protections against the expropriation of private property found in the Fifth and Fourteenth amendments to the U.S. Constitution. The Fifth Amendment is one of ten approved by Congress in 1789 that are known collectively as the Bill of Rights. The Fifth Amendment states that:

No person shall . . . be deprived of life, liberty, or property, without the due process of law; nor shall private property be taken for public use, without just compensation.

The Fourteenth Amendment is one of three approved in 1868, after the end of the Civil War, and makes it clear that the provisions of the Fifth Amendment apply to the states:

> No State shall . . . deprive any person of life, liberty, or property, without due process of law; nor deny any person within its jurisdiction the equal protection of the laws.

The Fourteenth Amendment would prove particularly important in protecting private utilities, since the states would become the main locus of utility regulation.

When the states began to experiment with commissions to regulate railroad tariffs after the Civil War, some railroads sued on the grounds that the states had no right to control tariffs. The right of the government to regulate certain trades or "callings" that were "imbued with the public interest" had been a part of the common law that the United States had inherited from England. These callings included, for example, those of a ferryman or a carter, and persons who entered these occupations could be subject to more rigorous obligations than those in other businesses.[15] Most such regulations had apparently disappeared in the United States by the 1800s, however, and the courts had to decide how the precedent applied to railroads.

In 1877 the U.S. Supreme Court in *Munn v. Illinois* affirmed the right of a state legislature to regulate railroad tariffs, basing its decision in part on the public interest doctrine of common law.[16] The Court also decided that the legislature could delegate the right to regulate to a regulatory commission. The Court refused to rule on the reasonableness of the tariffs, however, which left the investors potentially subject to gradual expropriation through low rates. The Court argued that the legislature, or its delegate the commission, should determine reasonableness, although it acknowledged the risks involved: "In countries where the common law prevails, it is customary from time immemorial for the legislature to declare what reasonable compensation must be in such circumstances. . . . We know that this is a power which may be abused; but that is no argument against its existence. For protection against abuses by legislatures the people must resort to the polls, not the courts."[17]

By 1890, however, the Court reversed itself and decided that the reasonableness of tariffs should be subject to judicial review. In 1898, in the landmark case of *Smyth v. Ames,* the Court established the standard that regulated rates must provide a "fair return" on "fair value" of the property being used. The Court confused matters, however, by mandating that regulators consider the original or historical cost, the modern reproduction cost, and the market value of the company in determining the fair value of the company's assets.[18] These three different standards usually led to very different values, and the Court offered no guidance as to how they should be weighed. Historical cost was often higher than replacement cost in periods when relevant technologies were improving, for example, and lower than replacement cost in periods of general price inflation. The market value of the company suffered from circularity, moreover, inasmuch as it depended in large part on the market's expectations about the tariffs that the regulators would set.

The several standards for fair value established by *Smyth v. Ames* stimulated nearly fifty years of unproductive litigation that was not resolved until 1944 in *Federal Power Commission v. Hope Natural Gas*. In the *Hope* decision, the Supreme Court recognized that market value was circular and therefore should not be considered. The Court also ruled that it would no longer compel regulators to consider replacement cost in calculating fair value, although they could do so if they wished. But perhaps most important, the decision acknowledged that the reasonableness of the tariffs was a product of the fair rate of return as well as of the fair value, and established a practical test that the tariffs should be sufficient to allow the company to attract capital.[19]

This series of cases on regulation made it more difficult for state or federal governments to expropriate or nationalize private utilities without compensation. Outright expropriation would clearly invoke the requirements for compensation in the Fifth and Fourteenth amendments to the Constitution. And gradual expropriation by means of unreasonably low tariffs was also recognized by the courts as confiscatory, and thus also in violation of the Constitution. There were still ambiguities in determining what fair compensation should be, occasionally made worse by confusing decisions of the courts. But the general requirement to compensate was at least clear, and the courts would intervene if the compensation was too unreasonable.

Scholars of Canadian regulation, including Christopher Armstrong, Vivian Nelles, and John Baldwin, argue that the absence of similar legal constraints on expropriation contributed importantly to the nationalization of private utilities in Canada.[20] The Canadian constitution includes no specific protections for private property, unlike its U.S. counterpart. Moreover, the constitution gives jurisdiction over property and individual rights to the provinces instead of to the federal government. In the same year, 1898, that the U.S. Supreme Court was declaring in *Smyth v. Ames* that the reasonableness of rates was subject to judicial review, its Canadian equivalent, the British Privy Council, came to the opposite conclusion in a key case. In language reminiscent of the U.S. Supreme Court's 1877 *Munn v. Illinois* decision, the Privy Council declared that the provinces could confiscate private property without judicial review: "The supreme legislative power in relation to any subject-matter is always capable of abuse, but it is not assumed that it will be abused; if it is the only remedy is an appeal to those by whom the legislature is elected."[21]

The Canadian courts did not back away from this position, unlike their U.S. counterparts. Indeed, some years later in a similar case, another Canadian judge would make the point more bluntly: "The Legislature within its jurisdiction can do anything which is not naturally impossible and is restrained by no rule, human or divine. If it be that the plaintiffs acquired any rights—which I am far from finding—the Legislature has the power to take them away. The prohibition 'Thou shall not steal' has no legal force on a sovereign body, and there would be no necessity for compensation to be given."[22]

Gradually the law evolved to require compensation in certain situations. In a 1904 decision the Canadian courts held that municipalities that expropriated a utility had to compensate the owners at the cost of reproduction less depreciation. The courts also decided that a provincial government could avoid compensation only if its legislature had specifically authorized expropriation without it. But provincial legislatures determined not to compensate could avoid doing so, and they could also absolve municipalities from their obligation to compensate. Perhaps more important, Canada did not develop a large body of court decisions constraining more subtle or gradual forms of expropriation, such as through unrealistic tariffs, as emerged in the United States.[23]

There are some reasons to believe that Canada's weaker constraints on government expropriation were not that important in practice. It is notable, for example, that when the provinces finally got around to taking over their private utilities they seem to have always paid the owners compensation. Moreover, Canada's PUCs apparently were reasonably sympathetic to private investors even without the same threat of appeals to the court that existed in the United States. Unlike the general public, PUC commissioners often understood that maintaining a financially healthy company was in the long-term interests of consumers as well as investors. When the private electric and street railway company that served Vancouver was concerned about proposals to establish a PUC in British Colombia, for example, it surveyed utilities in other provinces about their experiences. The reports it received often noted that the PUC could be a haven in times of conflict, and was generally much more understanding than municipal officials.[24]

Nevertheless, the requirement to compensate clearly did constrain the efforts of Canadian municipalities to take over local private utilities. In every major Canadian city, popular resentment against the local private street railway or electric monopoly led to a movement for municipal operation at some point during the first two decades of the twentieth century. But the city usually didn't have the sums to purchase the private company outright. Often the private company had protected itself by securing an exclusive franchise, so that the city could not establish a municipal company without buying the private company out. The city would sometimes appeal to the province to authorize it to establish a municipal system without compensating the private company, but the legislature was usually reluctant to act on the city's behalf.

Moreover, the provinces occasionally exercised their power to expropriate without compensation, and often by gradually eroding the private company's value before condemning it outright. In 1899, for example, the Ontario legislature included in the Ontario Municipal Act a clause requiring cities to buy out any private utility if they established a municipal electric, water, or gas company. This clause encouraged private investors to found Toronto Electric to provide electricity for the city. In 1906, however, when the legislature decided to establish Ontario Hydro to develop public power, it exempted any municipality that bought electricity from Ontario Hydro from the buyout requirements of the Municipal Act. This exemption, which the private utilities bitterly protested, allowed Toronto to establish a new municipal electricity distribution company, thereby providing Ontario Hydro a ready market for its power. The municipal company, supplied by Ontario Hydro with power on favorable terms, steadily stole Toronto Electric's customers, increasing its share of the market from 18 percent in 1911 to 75 percent in 1921. By then Toronto Electric's owners were happy to sell out for any reasonable price, and in 1923 the province finally bought out the company and merged it into Ontario Hydro.[25]

The strongest evidence that Canada's inferior legal protections for private property posed a serious threat to private utilities is that Canada's business leaders believed them to be so. In 1909 and 1910, once the views of the Canadian courts had become clear, representatives of investors pressed leaders in the federal government to help start a movement to amend the constitution to include property protections based on the U.S. model. The federal politicians expressed sympathy in private, but they argued that amendment was impossible. It would be difficult to take away powers that the provinces had become accustomed to exercising, they argued, especially when there was little popular support for the view that the provinces were abusing these powers.[26]

It is worth noting that a constitutional protection against the taking of private property may not be enough to force compensation in the event of expropriation. The constitutions of many Latin American countries include clauses affirming the rights of private property, for example, but there is less of a tradition in the region that constitutional rights can be enforced by an appeal to the courts. Even if the courts accepted such a lawsuit, moreover, the outcome might be in doubt, because these constitutions usually include potentially conflicting rights, such as to a job or a home, or statements that property also has "social" functions and responsibilities.[27]

The stronger legal protections in the United States may reflect deeper differences in the underlying political and social cultures. Although both the United States and Canada are primarily capitalist in orientation, for example, Canadians are generally thought to be slightly more sympathetic to the public sector and to collective action.[28] But the Fifth and Fourteenth amendments were also the product of very unusual historical circumstances: the Fifth was passed after a revolution against a colonial government accused of, among other things, taking citizens' property, and the Fourteenth after a civil war that had eroded the traditional deference accorded to the states. Even in the United States these amendments might not pass if proposed today.

Foreign Ownership: Latin America and Canada

Foreign ownership also encouraged expropriation, although the experience with electricity suggests that it may not have been as influential as commonly thought. The argument is that it is politically easier for the government to expropriate the assets of a foreigner than those of its own citizens.[29] There are limitations, of course, particularly for weak nations that feel dependent on strong ones. But nations that feel dependent and vulnerable may resent foreigners all the more. And if the foreign investors are also monopolists, the potential for popular resentment is even greater.

The Extent of Foreign Ownership

Foreign ownership was much more common in Latin America than in the United States or Canada. In the United States, foreign investors undoubtedly owned some stocks and bonds of electric utilities, but foreign-controlled utilities seem to have been extremely rare. In Canada, there were important examples, although only a few. British investors controlled the major utility serving Vancouver, and Anglophone (although not foreign) investors owned the major companies serving Montreal and the rest of Quebec. U.S.-owned companies generated power in southern Ontario near Niagara Falls, although they exported their power to U.S. factories across the border.

In Latin America, by contrast, many important electricity concessions were acquired by foreign investors in the decade before World War I. Foreign investment was generally welcomed at the time for many of the same reasons it would be welcomed again during the infrastructure privatizations of the 1980s and 1990s. One motive was that domestic capital markets simply could not supply the large investments needed to develop the electricity business. British and Canadian investors took over the concession for Mexico City, for example, in order to finance a large hydroelectric project that would provide low-cost power to meet the growing demand for electricity in the capital and in nearby mines.[30]

Foreign investors were also welcomed because they brought needed technical expertise. For example, the skill and experience of the Canadian railway promoter William MacKenzie and the American electrical engineer Fred Stark Pearson helped convince the cities of São Paulo and Rio de Janiero to award concessions for streetcar and electricity service to their Brazilian Traction, Light and Power company, more popularly known in Brazil as "Light." Light, headquartered in Toronto and backed by British and Canadian investors, developed electric streetcar systems that were the envy of Latin America in the first decade of the twentieth century. And Light's engineers were widely admired when, to meet the growing power needs of São Paulo in the 1920s, they created a waterfall of 720 meters by reversing the course of a river so that it flowed into a different basin. The abundant power from this ingenious scheme helped to develop São Paulo as Latin America's leading industrial region.[31]

A second wave of foreign investment occurred in the period between World War I and the Great Depression, in this case dominated by investors from the United States and Canada. Particularly notable was American and Foreign Power, a U.S. holding company owned by Electric Bond and Share. The General Electric Corporation (GE) had formed Electric Bond and Share in 1905 as a subsidiary to manage the stocks and bonds of many early U.S. utilities that GE had acquired as partial payment for equipment it had sold to the utilities.[32] Most of these securities were not marketable because of the small size and weakness of the companies, and Electric Bond and Share's strategy was to increase their value by providing management and financial services to the companies it had interests in.

Electric Bond and Share's first involvement overseas came during World War I, when the U.S. government asked it to take over a German-owned concession that supplied electricity in Panama, including to the strategically important Panama Canal.[33] In 1923, deciding that the investment opportunities in foreign countries were more promising than those left in the United States, Electric Bond and Share created American and Foreign Power as its subsidiary to acquire foreign utilities. By 1930 the new subsidiary owned utilities in eleven Latin American countries that provided electric power and light to 696 communities with a combined population of 9.6 million people.[34] A similar but smaller Canadian holding company, the Canadian International Power Company, was formed in 1926 by investors who had been active in developing and managing Canadian electric utilities. At the end of the 1920s, Canadian International Power controlled electric utilities in five Latin American countries plus the U.S. territory of Puerto Rico.[35]

By the 1930s foreign-owned electric utilities served most of the major cities and industrial areas of Latin America (see Table 6.4). In some countries, such as Argentina, virtually the entire industry was in foreign hands. Over 90

Table 6.4 Major foreign-owned electric utilities in selected Latin American countries during the 1930s

Country	Company (in order of size within country)	Nationalities of principal investors	Service area	Year nationalized[a]
Argentina	CADE (Cia. Argentina de Electricidad)	Belgian (Sofina subsidiary)	Greater Buenos Aires	1958[b]
	CIADE (Cia. Italo-Argentina de Electricidad)	Swiss (Motor Colombus subsidiary)	Parts of Buenos Aires	1979
	ANSEC[c]	U.S. (American and Foreign Power subsidiary)	Central, southern, and western provinces	1943-1945, 1949
	Cia. Suizo-Argentina de Electricidad	Swiss (Motor Colombus subsidiary)	Northern provinces	1943?[d]
Bolivia	Bolivian Power Company[e]	Canadian (Canadian International Power subsidiary)[f]	La Paz and Oruro	Never nationalized
Brazil	Light (Brazilian Traction, Light and Power)	Canadian, British and European	São Paulo and Rio de Janeiro	1979
	Empresas Electricas Braziliaras	U.S. (American and Foreign Power subsidiary)	Recife, Belo Horizonte, Pôrto Alegre, and others	1959 (Pôrto Alegre and Vitória), 1962 (rest)
Chile	CCE (Cia. Chilena de Electricidad)	U.S. (American and Foreign Power subsidiary)	Santiago and Valparaiso	1970
Colombia	CCE (Cia. Colombiano de Electricidad)	U.S. (American and Foreign Power subsidiary)	Calí and other areas	1945 (Calí), 1961 (rest)
Cuba	Cia. Cubana de Electricidad	U.S. (American and Foreign Power subsidiary)	Havana	1960
Ecuador	Emelec (Empresa Eléctrica de Ecuador)	U.S. (American and Foreign Power subsidiary)	Guayaquil, Riobamba	Never nationalized
Mexico	Mexlight (Cia. Mexicana de Luz y Fuerza Motriz)	Belgian (Sofina subsidiary)	Mexico City	1960

	CEE (Cia Impulsora de Empresas Eléctricas)	U.S. (American and Foreign Power subsidiary)	Veracruz, Tampico, Puebla, Potosí, and many other cities	1960
	Monterrey Railway, Light and Power	Canadian (Canadian International Power subsidiary)[f]	Monterrey	1962
Peru	Lima Light and Power (Empresas Eléctricas Asociados)	Swiss (Motor Colombus subsidiary)	Lima	1972
Venezuela	CALEV (Cia. Anónima Luz Eléctrica de Venezuela)	U.S. (American and Foreign Power subsidiary)	Parts of Caracas	(1964)[g]
	Venezuelan Power Company	Canadian (Canadian International Power subsidiary)[f]	Maracaibo and Barquisimeto	1976

Sources: See particularly Henry Leslie Robinson, "American and Foreign Power in Latin America," Ph.D. dissertation, Stanford University, 1967; British Electrical and Allied Manufacturers' Association, *Combines and Trusts in the Electrical Industry: The Position in 1927* (London: Statistical Department, British Electrical and Allied Manufacturers' Association, 1927); Herbert Bratter, "Latin American Utilities' Nationalization Proceeds Inexorably," *Public Utilities Fortnightly* 66, no. 1 (July 7, 1960): 4; United Nations, *Estudios sobre la Electricidad en América Latina*, vol. 1: *Informe y Documentos* (Mexico, DF: United Nations, 1962); and Jorge del Río, *Electricidad y Liberación Nacional: El Caso de SEGBA* (Buenos Aires: Colección la Siringa, 1960).

a. The year nationalized is the year the government assumed effective control of the company. In some cases the actual sale or compensation did not occur until many years later.

b. Between 1958 and 1960 the company was operated as a joint government-private company.

c. The initials ANSEC came from the five main companies included: *A*–Cia. de Electricidad de Los Andes, *N*–Cia. de Electricidad del Norte Argentino, *S*–Cia. de Electricidad del Sud Argentino, *E*–Cia. de Electricidad del Este Argentino, and *C*–Cia. Central Argentina de Electricidad. Four other companies were part of ANSEC as well. See Jorge del Río, *Política Argentina y los Monopolios Eléctricos* (Buenos Aires: Editorial Cátedra Lisandro de la Torre, 1957), p. 22.

d. Both Bratter and del Río mention that there were four Argentine groups, but there is no account of the demise of Compañía Suizo-Argentina de Electricidad. It may be that that company was bought out by ANSEC before ANSEC was nationalized.

e. Bolivian Power's name was changed to Cia. Boliviana de Energía Eléctrica (COBEE) in 1968.

f. Canadian International Power's name was changed to International Power around 1955.

g. CALEV was not nationalized but was sold to La Electricidad de Caracas, the domestically owned private company that served the rest of Caracas.

percent of Argentina's electricity was provided by four foreign groups.[36] The largest of the four (in terms of power generated) was a company serving Greater Buenos Aires that was owned by Sofina, a holding company headquartered in Brussels that owned electricity and streetcar companies and manufacturers of related equipment in Belgium, Luxembourg, Spain, Germany, Mexico, the United States, and the Belgian Congo as well as in Argentina.[37] The third-largest group in Argentina was a collection of companies owned by American and Foreign Power, while the second and fourth largest were apparently controlled by a Swiss investment company called Motor Colombus.[38]

Most other Latin countries were not far behind Argentina. In Brazil, for example, two foreign groups generated approximately two-thirds of the electric power; the largest was the Toronto-based Light company, which alone accounted for more than half of the electricity generated in the country, and the other was a group of ten companies controlled by American and Foreign Power.[39] Similarly in Mexico, Brussels-based Sofina owned Mexlight, which served Mexico City; Canadian International Power owned Monterry Railway, Light, and Power; while the local American and Foreign Power subsidiary, CEE, owned the concessions in most of the other major cities.

In a few countries, such as Colombia and Venezuela, foreign-owned companies were important but not nearly as dominant. Many Colombian electricity companies were municipally owned, including those serving Bogotá and Medellín, although an American and Foreign Power subsidiary had purchased approximately a dozen domestically owned private concessions beginning in 1927, including the one for Calí.[40] In Venezuela, most utilities were owned by domestic investors, including the company that generated all and distributed most of the power for the Caracas metropolitan area. The principal exceptions were a company owned by American and Foreign Power that distributed power in approximately one-third of Caracas and a subsidiary of Canadian International Power that served Maracaibo and Barquisimeto.

Early Acceptance of Foreign Investors

Foreign ownership did not become highly controversial in Latin America until the 1930s. Even when the industry was consolidating during the 1910s and 1920s, the focus of popular complaints was monopoly and not foreign ownership, even though the company doing the consolidating was usually foreign owned. Nationalistic feelings were often tempered because the foreign company had much more technical and financial credibility than its competitors. In São Paulo, for example, there were few complaints when Light bought up competing street railway companies that were powered by mules instead of electricity, or when it took over a small, under-financed Brazilian-owned electric company and a British-owned gas company that gave indifferent service. There was a fight later, when Light asked the city council to grant it consolidated and exclusive streetcar and public lighting concessions, but the issue was monopoly, not foreign ownership.[41]

Only in those rarer cases where the foreign company faced a determined and credible domestic rival were nationalistic feelings mobilized. In Rio de Janiero, for example, Light had to fight off an attempt by a wealthy Brazilian family, the Guinles, to establish an electric company in Rio, where Light had an exclusive franchise. Light argued that the Guinle proposal violated Light's concession contract and made little sense given the economies of scale in the electricity business. The Guinle family raised Light's foreign provenance as an issue, however, and although Light won in the courts, the battle tarnished the company's public image and earned it the nickname of the "Canadian octopus."[42]

The intensity of the battles about monopoly increased as electricity's importance became more apparent. In his history of the Mexican electricity industry, for example, Miguel Wionczek reports that opposition to private utilities was confined to a few intellectuals before the Revolution began in 1910.[43] The Revolution put matters on hold for fifteen years, but by the 1920s the electricity issue was raised again, this time championed by small industrialists and merchants, particularly in Puebla and San Luis Potosí, two centers of Mexico's emerging entrepreneurial class. These entrepreneurs complained that electricity was essential to modern businesses, and that small customers often paid fifteen to twenty-five times the rates charged the big industrial customers. Wionczek suspects that these entrepreneurs exaggerated the economic damage they suffered, since electricity accounted for only a small portion of total costs in the Mexican textile industry, a center of opposition to high electricity tariffs. But by the 1920s, the belief that cheap and abundant electricity was critical for economic development was widely held throughout the world. Electrification was a centerpiece of Soviet development plans, for example, and would soon play a major role in President Roosevelt's recovery program in the United States.

Nevertheless, foreign investors were bullish about Latin American utilities through the 1920s. Mexico was emerging from its Revolution and other key countries seemed to be politically stable and poised for economic growth. American and Foreign Power embarked on an aggressive program for acquiring new companies, and all of the major private utilities were investing heavily to meet the growing demand for electricity by households, commerce, and industry. The complaints about monopoly and high prices made for occasional bad press, but usually little more. The foreign-owned utilities were acting no differently, and receiving no more criticism, than they did in their home countries. A certain amount of controversy seemed inherent in the utility business, whether at home or abroad.[44]

The Rise of Economic Nationalism

The turning points were first the Great Depression of the 1930s and later the movements for political and economic independence after World War II. The Depression intensified economic conflict and complaints about monopoly tariffs, and it also seemed to demonstrate the perils of relying on foreigners and the benefits of economic nationalism and self-sufficiency. Latin America was crippled for a decade by a depression that started in, and presumably was the fault of, the United States and other developed countries. That foreign electricity companies should insist on maintaining high tariffs during a depression caused by foreigners must have added insult to injury.

Latin American suspicions of foreign private utilities were strengthened by the criticisms being levied at them in their home countries during the 1930s. President Roosevelt had devoted a chapter of his 1933 book *Looking Forward* to the scandals in the U.S. public utility industry and the need for a stronger public role in it, and his views were cited widely in Latin America.[45] The passage of the Public Utility Holding Company Act of 1935 lent weight to the charges that utility holding companies—such as American and Foreign Power, Sofina, and International Power—were devices to defraud the small shareholders of the companies they acquired and to hide profits from the public.[46] Roosevelt's TVA was seen as a model of how public power could serve as a catalyst for coordinated economic development and was visited frequently by foreign delegations.[47]

Nationalism took on a stronger edge among developing countries after World War II. Latin America had won its independence from Spain and Portugal in the early nineteenth century, but nationalistic feelings in the region were stimulated by watching the European colonies in Africa and Asia begin their final push for independence after the war. In the field of development economics, the strategy of import substitution was ascendant, with its implied endorsement of self-sufficiency. The idea was to stimulate economic growth by replacing foreign imports with domestic products. As part of the effort, tariff or trade barriers were often erected to protect infant domestic manufacturing industries against foreigners.

By the time the private electricity companies were expropriated, the resentment that they were foreign owned seemed as intense as the resentment that they were monopolies. Nationalistic feelings played particularly important roles in the takeovers of the foreign power companies in Cuba and Mexico in

1960. In April 1959, only three months after it took power, the new Cuban government led by Fidel Castro established a commission to look into electricity and gas prices. In August 1959 the government unilaterally reduced the rates of the American and Foreign Power subsidiary that served Cuba by 22 percent and blocked the subsidiary's remittances to its parent in dollars.[48] Exactly a year later, after the relationship between the United States and Cuba had deteriorated further, Cuba expropriated the subsidiary without compensation.

The Cuban developments were the last straw for American and Foreign Power, which was already involved in fairly serious disputes with governments in three other Latin countries.[49] Early in 1960 the company decided to withdraw from the electricity business in Latin America gradually and without fanfare, so that it could get the best prices for its assets. In March, American and Foreign Power quietly sent a team to Mexico, the location of one of its largest subsidiaries, to discuss possible terms of a sellout with the government. The team arrived when the conflict between Cuba and the United States was threatening to polarize politics in Mexico. The business community generally supported the United States, but many in labor and on the left thought Mexico should demonstrate its solidarity with Cuba. In this context, the Mexican government decided that buying out the foreign power companies would help restore national unity. All Mexicans would be proud that this important industry had finally been taken out of foreign hands. And the business community would be reassured because the government would negotiate a price that the foreigners would not complain about, at least publicly. The company eventually agreed to sell out for the low value the government had set for tariff-setting purposes and to invest the proceeds in Mexico. Sofina, which had not wanted to sell out its Mexican subsidiary, was quickly pressed to leave on similar terms.[50] It took over a decade for American and Foreign Power to sell off its other Latin American subsidiaries.

Latin America's Few Survivors

The only major foreign-owned utilities to escape expropriation in Latin America were those serving La Paz and Guayaquil, both apparently protected by the unusually chaotic politics in Bolivia and Ecuador at the time. In the case of La Paz, for example, Bolivian Light and Power was formed in 1925 when Canadian investors bought out a French company that served the city and a German company that served the rapidly growing tin-mining district in Oruro Province.[51] Bolivian Power moved quickly to develop the hydroelectric potential of the Zongo River valley to serve La Paz and the Miguillas River to supply Oruro. These engineering feats may have helped the company survive the growing political violence that began in the 1930s and culminated in a popular revolution in 1952.

In the 1952 revolution, a coalition of the urban middle class, miners, and landless peasants organized as the Movimiento Nacionalista Revolucionario (MNR) and overthrew the small landed elite that dominated Bolivia. The MNR quickly moved to nationalize most of the tin mines, which were largely foreign owned, and to break up the haciendas and distribute the land to the peasants. At the beginning of the revolution, the mayor of Oruro expropriated a small telephone system that Bolivian Power operated in the city, but in the twelve years of MNR rule that followed, the government never got around to nationalizing Bolivian Power's electricity business.[52] At first the MNR may have been too preoccupied with its mine and land expropriations. Later the movement was distracted by growing conflicts between its miner and peasant members, who wanted a socialist economy, and its middle-class members, who wanted a state-dominated but capitalistic society. In addition, the combination of low world tin prices and increased government spending soon led to deficits and inflation that increased Bolivia's dependence on aid from the United States and the International Monetary Fund, who undoubtedly were hostile to further expropriations.

The Bolivian government did establish a public electricity company, ENDE, to promote rural electrification in the 1950s, and by 1962 it was embroiled in a serious dispute with Bolivian Power about brownouts and the company's reluctance to invest in new generating capacity without substantial tariff increases.[53] But in 1964, before matters got worse, the conflicts within the MNR and the deteriorating economy provoked a military coup. Over the next eighteen years, Bolivia was ruled by two right-wing dictators sympathetic to private enterprise and foreign investment, each followed by periods of chaos in which left-wing governments never lasted long enough to expropriate the company.[54]

The last serious threat to Bolivian Power came after democratic government was restored in 1982 and Hernán Siles Suazo of the left wing of the MNR was elected president. The company had been burnishing its image since the late 1960s by promoting Bolivian managers to senior positions, using the Spanish version of the company's name,[55] flying the Bolivian flag outside its headquarters, and taking community groups on tours of its facilities. The company's efforts and three decades of chaotic government had raised popular doubts about the wisdom of nationalizing Bolivian Power. What saved the company in the end, however, was a rivalry between President Siles and the mayor of La Paz. In 1982, just after the Siles government submitted an expropriation law to Congress, Bolivian Power proposed to the mayor a limited partnership in which the city would buy out the company's shareholders over twenty years. This compromise assuaged Bolivia's socialists while leaving the company, at least temporarily, in the hands of proven management.[56] The Siles administration's mismanagement of the economy led to widespread calls for early elections in 1985, and the next three elected presidents reversed economic policy, promoting private markets over public ownership. In 1990 the national government granted Bolivian Power a new forty-year concession, and a few years later it restructured the electric sector and privatized ENDE.[57]

Economic Nationalism in Canada

In Canada, nationalism played a role in the demise of private power in Quebec but not in British Columbia. British Columbia was the only Canadian province with a major foreign-owned power company: the British Columbia Electric Railway Company (BCER), which served Vancouver but was controlled from London. British Columbians apparently felt more nostalgia than hostility toward England, however, and BCER was careful to cultivate its ties with provincial politicians. BCER was frequently criticized as a monopolist that charged excessive rates, and its franchise negotiations with the cities it served were often acrimonious. But the company beat back two attempts to impose PUC-style regulation before World War II, and the fact that it was foreign owned never became a major issue.[58] When BCER was finally taken over in 1961, the justification was that rates would decline because a provincial company was not liable for federal income taxes, which BCER had to pay as a private corporation. But the timing was dictated by the fact that the Canadian and U.S. governments were negotiating an agreement to govern the development of the Columbia River. The provincial premier wanted to strengthen his role in the negotiations by making the province the sole significant producer and consumer of hydroelectric power in British Columbia.[59]

In Quebec, the major private utilities were owned by English-speaking Canadians, who eventually came to be regarded as the equivalent of foreigners by the French-speaking majority of the population. As in Latin America, however, the issue of foreign ownership was a relatively late development. There were two successful campaigns for public power in Quebec. The first began in the 1930s and culminated in 1944 with the creation of Hydro-Quebec and its absorption of the private utility that served Montreal. The second campaign began in 1960 and ended in 1963 with the takeover of the remaining private utilities in the province.

The first Quebec campaign focused on the corrupting influence of private monopoly on government, but not on foreign ownership. By the second campaign, however, the focus had shifted to charges that French Canada was underdeveloped because its economy, controlled by U.S. and English Canadian investors, was based primarily on the export of raw materials and had little manufacturing. Cheap hydroelectric power could be used to attract industry, the nationalists argued, but only if French Canadians took control of the electricity industry. One of the leaders of the campaign in the 1960s compared his position to that of Dr. Phillipe Hamel, the dentist and citizen-activist who had led the earlier campaign for public power in the 1930s: "Through the nationalization of industry, Dr. Hamel's main aim was to break the monopoly or trust which dominated and paralyzed our economic and political life. In our day, the most important argument is that public ownership of electric power is essential to our economic independence and to the planned development of our industry."[60]

In sum, foreign ownership probably was not essential to provoke the nationalization of electricity in either Latin America or Canada. In both places, the foreign provenance of the companies emerged as an issue only later, after the issue of monopoly. Moreover, Canada demonstrates that domestic ownership was not sufficient protection against nationalization, since most of Canada's utilities were domestically owned and most were eventually nationalized. But foreign ownership seemed to intensify the resentment of monopolies. Fear of monopoly may have been the principal motive for nationalization, but foreign ownership and monopoly were an especially lethal combination.

Municipal versus National Regulation: Latin America

A third factor that apparently affected expropriation is whether a company was regulated by municipal government rather than by provincial or national governments. Nationalization was generally slower or less likely where the responsibility for regulation was at the national or provincial level. National and provincial officials have broader perspectives and responsibilities, and thus may be more sensitive to the risk that expropriation might put a chill on other private investments or foreign relations. National officials also have more resources than local officials, and thus more ways to resolve disputes between utility companies and their customers short of expropriation.

Evidence that municipal officials are more likely to expropriate comes from a variety of sources. Private electric companies may have survived in the United States not just because of superior legal protections but also because the locus of regulation shifted from the municipal to the state level with the creation of the PUCs. In Canada, the creation of provincial PUCs did not prevent expropriation of private companies in most provinces, but it did seem to slow the tide for two or three decades.[61] Latin America provides interesting evidence as well, particularly in the contrast between the countries that maintained municipal regulation, most notably Argentina, and the countries that shifted to national regulation, such as Brazil, Colombia, and Mexico. Argentina led the wave of public takeovers in Latin America in the 1940s, while Brazil, Colombia, and Mexico expropriated more slowly and with stealth.

The Origins of National Regulation in Latin America

With the exception of Argentina and Venezuela, most major Latin American countries shifted the authority to regulate electricity tariffs from the municipal or provincial government to the national government during the 1930s. One reason Argentina and Venezuela did not make regulation a national responsibility may be that their political systems repressed the populist and nationalistic reaction to the Depression.[62] In Venezuela, one dictator, Juan Vincente Gómez, ruled from 1908 to 1935, and his two successors were only slightly less repressive. Not until the revolution of 1945 did Venezuela experience democracy and freer expression, and then only briefly. In Argentina the conservative oligarchy, fearful of the social unrest brought on by the Depression, staged a coup in 1930 to oust the elected president Hipólito Yrigoyen, whose middle-class Radical Party had been in power since 1916. Civilian rule was restored in 1932, but the oligarchy kept tight control of the national electoral process to ensure a series of conservative presidents over the next decade. The conservatives handled the economy poorly and the military, losing faith, staged a second coup in 1943. But it was not until 1946 that Colonel Juan Perón won the presidential election at the head of an openly populist and nationalistic political party, ending a three-year power struggle among the coup leaders.

In Brazil, Colombia, and Mexico, by contrast, the Depression brought leftist and nationalistic governments into power rapidly. Mexico's Revolution had barely finished before the Depression began, and the Depression supported the nationalistic and left-wing elements already powerful in the new Mexican government. In Colombia, the Depression helped the Liberal Party to defeat the Conservative Party in the elections of 1930, and encouraged the Liberals to try to implement programs of social reform in the following decade that so polarized society that a civil war broke out in 1946.[63] Similarly, in Brazil the Depression helped to precipitate the 1930 coup by Getúlio Vargas that ended the Old Republic, dominated by the traditional coffee and cattle elites of the states of São Paulo and Minas Gerias. Vargas ruled as provisional president and then as dictator from 1930 to 1946, and as elected president from 1950 until his suicide in 1954. In the process, he built a wider and more popular political base for the national government and emphasized the need for Brazil to take charge of its own economic destiny.

An even more important reason why Argentina and Venezuela did not shift regulation to the national level is that neither country developed important regional hydroelectric projects during the 1930s. As late as 1950, hydro accounted for only 3 percent of the electricity generated by Argentine utilities and 33 percent by Venezuelan utilities, compared with 89 percent of the electricity generated by Brazilian utilities, 77 percent by Colombian utilities, and 52 percent by Mexican utilities.[64] Argentina's hydro resources are in the foothills of the Andes, hundreds of miles from the major consumption centers along the coast. Given the high costs of long-distance transmission in the early twentieth century, Argentina relied on thermal plants located in the cities or provinces they served. Venezuela had more hydro resources close to its major population centers, but the largest resources were in remote regions and the country was extremely well endowed with oil, so thermal plants were economical.

In Brazil, Colombia, and Mexico, by contrast, hydro resources were often located close enough to the major consumption sources that transmission was economical. Moreover, the hydro projects were often big enough to serve other cities and industries besides their primary market, so that the utilities that operated them were often more regional rather than local in nature. In addition, the rivers and dams were usually located outside the principal municipality they would serve, raising the troubling question of whether one local government should have the authority to develop the natural resources of another. Consolidating regulation at the federal level may have seemed more sensible compared with the welter of municipal, provincial, and national controls that were developing around hydroelectric power.[65]

The combination of hydro power and populist governments encouraged Brazil, Colombia, and Mexico to enact national regulatory statutes by the end of the 1930s. In Mexico, the national government had reserved for itself the power to award concessions for hydro projects as early as 1888, and this included a veto over the prices the concessionaire could charge. The government never exercised that right before the Revolution, and probably didn't attempt to do so during the country's revolutionary chaos.[66] In 1926, in response to growing criticism of private utilities, Mexico passed a law authorizing federal control over all electricity prices, whether from thermal or hydro plants. Initially, the law was mainly a symbolic gesture, not enforced by the government and largely ignored by the utilities. It would not become effective until 1938, after the constitution was amended to permit federal regulation, a regulatory agency was created, and the law clarified.[67] In Brazil, the government amended the constitution in 1934 to state that all mines and waterfalls were the property of the national government and required a federal concession. That same year it passed the Water Code that detailed the conditions the new concessions would have to meet, including the procedures for setting tariffs. This meant that all the old municipal and provincial concessions had to be renegotiated as federal concessions, a process that took many years.[68] Colombia's law, passed in 1936, maintained municipal franchises but gave the national government the authority to review rates set by municipal regulators.[69]

The new national regulatory systems of the 1930s were modeled after U.S. PUCs, since many of the Latin American utility experts and public officials drafting the laws were foreign-trained engineers who followed the debates about utility regulation taking place in the United States and elsewhere.[70] The Latin American regulatory systems departed from the U.S. model, however, in that the regulatory agencies were less politically independent and were guided by more detailed regulatory statutes.[71] The Latin regulatory agency usually was not an independent commission but rather a bureau within a ministry. The head of the agency served at the pleasure of the minister, and his decisions were subject to the minister's review and approval. In Brazil, for example, the regulatory function was placed within the Water Division of the Ministry of Agriculture until 1961, when it was transferred to the newly created Ministry of Mines and Energy. The Mexican regulatory agency, the Comisión de Tarifas, was a dependency of the Ministry of Planning and its decisions were subject to broad veto power by that minister.[72] In Colombia, the regulatory authority was lodged in the Ministry of Development and no separate regulatory staff was appointed until the early 1950s.[73] To compensate for the lack of independence, the statutes defined tariff-setting formulas in greater detail. The Brazilian law specified, for example, that rates be sufficient so that a company could earn a 10 percent return on its investment valued at their historical cost. The Mexican and Colombian laws also specified that investments be valued at historical cost, although they didn't mandate a specific rate of return.[74]

The private utilities did not welcome national regulation as a replacement for municipal regulation. In Brazil, for example, the historian of Light, Duncan McDowall, documents the company's long fight against the implementation of the Water Code.[75] Light worked behind the scenes for the most part, recognizing that a vigorous public defense might inflame the more nationalistic elements of the Vargas government. But the basic terms of the code were so inimical to Light's interests—particularly its reliance on historical cost—that the company did whatever it could to influence or delay the drafting of the regulations that were needed to implement it. Similarly, in Mexico the foreign utilities initially discouraged the government from implementing the 1926 regulatory law by suing on the grounds that the constitution did not list electricity regulation as a permissible activity for the federal government.[76] The foreign utilities lobbied for favorable terms when the law was revised in 1938, but by then they recognized that national regulation was inevitable. The Depression and the growing conflict between Mexico and the foreign-owned oil companies had pushed the country farther to the left. The government had just passed a new expropriation law in 1937, and applied it to nationalize the oil industry a year later. The oil industry had helped provoke the takeover by miscalculating that a developing country would never expropriate U.S. businesses. The Mexican government probably stopped at taking over the electricity industry as well because it did not want to risk a complete rupture with the United States. In this climate, national regulation of their tariffs was the least that the private electric companies could have expected.

Municipal Revolts in Argentina

Although the private utilities may not have welcomed national regulation in Brazil, Colombia, and Mexico, the first expropriations occurred in Argentina from 1943 to 1945, when the provincial and municipal governments took over utilities belonging to ANSEC, American and Foreign Power's Argentine subsidiary, in more than a half-dozen secondary cities.[77] Even earlier, in the 1930s, the city of Buenos Aires almost took over its two foreign-owned electric companies: CADE (Compañía Argentina de Electricidad), a Sofina subsidiary that served most of the Buenos Aires metropolitan area, and CIADE (Compañía Italo-Argentina de Electricidad), a much smaller Swiss-controlled company that served some of the outskirts.[78]

CADE and CIADE had survived several disputes with municipal government before the 1930s. CADE began as a German-owned company in 1898 and operated without a concession until 1907, when it convinced the city council to reject the mayor's proposal to start a municipal electric company and to give it a fifty-year concession instead.[79] The length of the concession was controversial, but in return CADE promised to provide adequate supplies, keep residential rates below certain levels, and reduce the rates if technological improvements reduced its costs.[80] In addition, CADE was to return its facilities to the city at the end of the concession in perfect repair and for the price of only the historical investment cost less depreciation. In 1912 the city granted CIADE a similar fifty-year concession.

CADE and CIADE expanded greatly during the 1920s by building new generating plants and distribution networks and buying up small companies in the rest of the province of Buenos Aires. Any hope that CIADE might compete with CADE was disappointed as the two firms appeared to reach some understanding delimiting their service territories. CADE, by far the larger of the two, became the main focus of public complaints and got into several disputes with the city council during the 1920s over the interpretation of its concession contract. These were generally resolved in CADE's favor, to the consternation of the left-wing minority on the city council.

The disputes with the city intensified in 1932, when the military finally permitted the resumption of municipal elections two years after the coup of 1930. The left-wing parties did not win a majority on the new city council, but councilors from center and right-wing parties had also become critical of the utilities. The council appointed a special investigative commission to hear complaints that CADE and CIADE had been violating their concession contracts in numerous ways. Witnesses argued that the companies refused to acknowledge their obligation to reduce rates despite enormous technological advances in the twenty years since the contracts were signed. CADE was slow to connect customers or areas that it thought were less profitable and sometimes insisted that customers pay the cost of the connecting cables and other charges not sanctioned in the concession contract. There was surprisingly little mention of the companies' foreign ownership at this stage.[81] The critics complained that the companies were arrogant, but they generally blamed the companies' behavior on the fact that they were monopolies rather than that they were foreign owned.

The companies may have felt justified in exploiting any ambiguities in their contracts to offset the effects of inflation and currency devaluation. The 1907 and 1912 contracts had fixed the residential tariffs in the national currency rather than in gold, so that their real value had declined in the intervening years. Nevertheless, the improvements in technology had brought about enormous reductions in costs that offset, at least in part, the effects of inflation or currency devaluation.[82] And the fact that CADE and CIADE were still investing in new plants in the late 1920s and early 1930s strongly suggests that electric rates were still compensatory.[83]

Just when CADE seemed destined to be expropriated, however, it was saved under suspicious circumstances. The Radical Party won control of the city council in the 1936 municipal elections, after boycotting the 1932 elections to protest the fact that the military had ousted an elected Radical Party president in the 1930 coup. Notwithstanding its name, the Radical Party was a middle-class party, sympathetic to free enterprise although not necessarily to monopolies or foreign-owned businesses.

The new Radical majority on the council argued that CADE and CIADE's concession contracts should be revised to make them clearer. But the new contracts the council approved seemed much more favorable to the companies than the old. The companies agreed to reduce some residential rates, but in return, the council extended CADE's concession by twenty-five years and CIADE's by twenty years so that both expired in 1972. The provision that the companies would pass on part of their savings from technological advances to consumers was eliminated and replaced by a clause that provided for automatic tariff increases when fuel or salary costs increased. When the concessions expired, moreover, the city would have to pay the companies for the replacement rather than the historical cost of investments.[84]

Meanwhile, several ANSEC subsidiaries were engaged in similar disputes with local officials in other provinces. The governor of Córdoba began an investigation of the two ANSEC companies serving his province that lasted from 1932 to 1936, and the Chamber of Deputies of Tucumán conducted an inquiry into the two ANSEC companies serving that province from 1938 to 1942. The fact that these companies were subsidiaries of a large foreign holding company played a more prominent role in these investigations than in the earlier Buenos Aires inquiry. The Tucumán study commission accused the ANSEC companies of hiding profits by paying its U.S. owners high fees for management and other services, paying inflated costs for imported equipment, and giving preferential electricity rates to manufacturers in which the U.S. owners had a financial interest. The Córdoba commission concluded that ANSEC had established a monopoly that made foreigners rich and the nation poor. Neither of these studies resulted in the immediate expropriation of the ANSEC properties, apparently because of pressure from the national government.

The situation deteriorated rapidly after the military coup of 1943, which was motivated by frustration over the slow recovery of the economy. Soon after the coup, the new national government authorized two commissions to investigate electric utilities: one focusing on ANSEC and the other on the controversial extension of the Buenos Aires concessions in 1936. The ANSEC commission repeated many of the accusations of the earlier Córdoba and Tucumán reports, and led to the expropriation of the most important ANSEC companies from 1943 to 1945. The Argentine government dragged out the negotiations for compensation, and it wasn't until 1959, several years after Perón was overthrown, that American and Foreign Power got a modest payment for its properties.

The Buenos Aires investigation was more explosive but was suppressed, again under suspicious circumstances. On the basis of copies of cables between CADE and Sofina's headquarters in Brussels and the testimony of disaffected officials, the commission claimed that the revised concession contract had been written in Brussels and passed by the city council in return for secret contributions to the Radical Party's 1937 presidential election campaign. When the commission recommended that the government revoke CADE and CIADE's concessions and expropriate their property, however, the national government decided not to publish the commission's report and to forward it instead to a judge who eventually dismissed its findings.[85]

The difference in the results of the ANSEC and Buenos Aires commissions aroused deep suspicions, especially since the contents of the Buenos Aires report were leaked widely. The report was finally released after Perón was overthrown in 1955, amid allegations that CADE had bribed Perón himself to suppress the findings.[86] A new commission reaffirmed the earlier findings and, in 1958, the government passed a law placing the Buenos Aires electricity system under national control and transferring CADE's assets to a new public company, SEGBA (Servico Público de la Electricidad del Gran Buenos Aires). CADE's investors received a minority interest in SEGBA as compensation, but were finally bought out by the government in 1961.[87]

The formation of SEGBA largely completed the government takeover of electricity in Argentina. In the 1940s, as the provinces were expropriating the ANSEC companies, the federal government created AEE (Agua y Energía Eléctrica), an agency charged with building hydroelectric projects and selling the power to the provincial electricity companies.[88] In the following decades, the federal government would establish four other special agencies to develop hydro facilities in Northern Patagonia, to build hydro facilities cooperatively with Uruguay and Paraguay, and to develop nuclear power plants.[89] CIADE continued as a small private company and was finally bought out and incorporated into SEGBA in 1979.

The initiative to expropriate the private companies clearly came from the local rather than from the national governments in Argentina. The Buenos Aires, Córdoba, and Tucumán investigative commissions of the 1930s were municipal and provincial, and probably would have resulted in expropriations in that decade had not the national interests stepped in to prevent them. What role corruption played and who corrupted whom will probably never be known. But the popular pressure for expropriation was intense at the local level, and could not be denied for long.

Gradual Displacement: Brazil, Colombia, and Mexico

Municipal revolts similar to those in Argentina flared up occasionally in Brazil, Colombia, and Mexico. In 1945 the municipality of Calí took over the American and Foreign Power subsidiary serving the city. The electric company had convinced city officials that higher tariffs were needed to finance increased generating capacity, but the tariff increases had provoked a general strike. The American and Foreign Power subsidiaries serving Pôrto

Alegre and Vitória in Brazil and Veracruz in Mexico were also taken over by their respective provincial or local governments during the late 1950s.[90]

But the fact that the national governments were in charge of regulating electricity tariffs seemed to slow the transition from private to public power in Brazil, Colombia, and Mexico. National officials granted the private companies rate increases just sufficient to allow them to survive and maintain their systems, but not large enough to allow them to build the additional generating capacity they needed to meet the postwar surge in demand for electricity. At the same time, the governments created new public companies, usually subsidized by government revenues, to distribute electricity in rural areas and to build new generating capacity for the country as a whole. These public companies were established well before nationalization might have created the need for them, unlike in Argentina. After two or three decades of low tariffs, the private utilities had declined in importance and profitability and seemed to welcome nationalization as a relief.

The national regulatory authorities treated the utilities harshly in many respects. The most serious problem was the authorities' unwillingness to revalue company assets at current or replacement cost. In Brazil, Colombia, and Mexico the law constrained the regulators to use historical cost. The governments never tried to change the regulatory statutes, however, even after the rapid wartime and postwar inflation made it obvious that it would be very difficult to attract further private investment under such terms.[91] Proponents of using historical cost had argued that the regulators could adjust the allowed rate of return upward to compensate for inflation or currency devaluation, but in practice this was not done. Brazil's law restricted the rate of return to no more than 10 percent, for example. Mexico's law was more flexible on the rate of return, requiring only that the company be allowed to earn at least the rate paid on government bonds. The Mexican regulators usually picked a rate close to that minimum, however, failing to recognize that the company's equity had to earn more than its debt.[92] Allowances for depreciation or replacement reserves were often unrealistic as well, thus reducing the possibility that the companies could maintain or renew investments through retained cash flow. By the mid-1950s, for example, Mexlight had persuaded its regulators to raise its target rate of return to 14.7 percent, but the company was earning only 10.1 percent and was receiving almost no allowance for depreciation. The average return on capital invested in Mexican private industry was around 19 percent at the time, making it impossible for Mexlight to attract additional private financing.[93]

Everyone understood that raising electricity tariffs was politically difficult for the government. In Brazil, the basic electricity tariff Light could charge remained frozen for thirty years: from the enactment of the Water Code of

1934 until a military coup in 1964 finally brought in a government more sympathetic to free enterprise and foreign investors.[94] In Mexico, the electric industry soon learned that tariff increases would be decided on political grounds. The companies petitioned for increases as soon as the electricity law was passed in 1938, hoping at least to restore tariffs to the levels of the early 1930s (when they had been pressed by the government to make "voluntary" reductions). The deputy minister of agriculture responsible for regulation ordered tariff increases in 1939, but the minister suspended them on orders from the president. According to Wionczek, the minister wrote to Mexlight explaining that the suspension was needed to study the complaints that had been received when the new rates were announced:

> This attitude is moreover perfectly justified; whereas the Ministry concedes that the regulation of public service enterprises is primarily a technical function, it must not fail to recognize that government action in this area is directly connected with the public weal since the effects of the regulation are felt throughout every part of the community served by the power companies.[95]

After an additional six-month delay, the minister granted a smaller increase than originally ordered, and then only in return for the companies' promises to make certain investments.[96]

The authorities recognized, privately at least, the financial difficulties their tariff policies created for the companies, and they searched for politically acceptable means to grant the companies some relief. One method used by Brazil was simply to delay the implementation of the most onerous features of the regulatory statute. The Water Code of 1934 applied retroactively, which meant that the concessions of Light and of American and Foreign Power all had to be rewritten as federal contracts and their assets revalued at actual historical cost. The revaluation would have meant a disastrous reduction in electric rates, since the value of the historical costs of many of the key assets had been eroded by a decade or two of domestic inflation and currency devaluation. But repudiating the principle of historical cost would have alienated the more radical elements of Getúlio Vargas's government. The solution was to freeze rates at 1934 levels for years while various commissions studied the detailed regulations needed to implement the law. The 1934 tariffs may have been unrealistic, but not as unrealistic as the tariffs that would have resulted had the law been strictly enforced.[97]

A second strategy was to leave the basic tariff unchanged but to add surcharges for politically popular or palatable causes. In Brazil, the practice started during World War II, as wartime inflation drove up the cost of living and made it hard for Light to recruit workers at its old wage rates. The deal eventually negotiated was that the government would allow Light to add an additional charge to its electric tariffs sufficient to pay for the wage increase.[98] The principle was extended during the 1950s to include "additionals" for fuel price increases at Light's thermal plants, for foreign exchange transactions after currency devaluations, and for increases in the rates for power Light purchased wholesale from government-owned generating stations.[99] Between 1954 and 1964, revenues from the additionals increased from 5 percent to 94 percent of Light's electricity receipts, while the revenue from the basic tariff declined from 95 percent to 6 percent.[100] The additionals were acceptable because they did not challenge the popular resistance to increasing the basic tariff. The government could explain that the added revenue was not going to the private company, but rather to more popular causes, such as workers' wages or the public power companies.

A third strategy was to subsidize the cost of inputs used by the company. This was the approach favored by Mexico, which gave both Mexlight (the Sofina subsidiary) and CEE (the American and Foreign Power subsidiary) unrestricted access to wholesale power from government generating plants at favorable prices, persuaded the electrical unions to moderate their wage demands for the two companies, and granted domestic credits at below market rates from government-owned banks.[101] Both Mexico and Brazil also guaranteed loans made by international agencies to the private utilities for the construction of new generating plants. But perhaps the most important subsidy granted by Mexico and Brazil was preferential rates for the exchange of foreign currency. These various subsidies had the benefit of not appearing on the consumer's electricity bill, unlike the additionals. But they also had the disadvantage of imposing a budgetary cost on the government that was hard to sustain.

Surprisingly, the foreign-owned utilities continued to invest in new generating capacity in the postwar period. Issuing conventional corporate debt or equity was out of the question, and retained earnings were nowhere near adequate to meet the growing demand for power. Instead, the companies turned to the emerging international lending agencies or to government guarantees. In Brazil, Light financed new generating capacity through loans either from the World Bank or guaranteed by the government of Brazil. American and Foreign Power relied heavily on loans guaranteed by the U.S. Export-Import Bank or provided by banks owned by the Mexican government. The international agencies and governments were willing to lend because the capacity shortfalls were leading to blackouts and rationing that were harmful to economic development. From the companies' perspective, the loans must have been welcomed to help protect their reputation for adequate service. But even though a number of American and Foreign Power subsidiaries approximately doubled their capacity between 1945 and 1960 and Light approximately trebled its capacity during the same period,[102] demand grew even faster and shortages and rationing were chronic problems.

In the meantime, the governments were establishing the publicly owned electric companies that would gradually displace the private utilities. Many of the advocates for these new companies believed that electric power should be provided by the public rather than by the private sector. But the government usually took pains to establish a distinct role for the new public ventures so as not to challenge the existing private enterprises directly. The first national agency established was often charged with planning and coordinating the development of the nation's electric system rather than with generating or distributing electricity directly. This was the case with Mexico's CFE (Comisión Federal de Electricidad) when it was created in 1937 and Colombia's Electraguas when it was established in 1946.

When the public sector first expanded into electricity generation and distribution, it usually restricted its role to serving remote rural areas or to developing multipurpose hydroelectric projects, sometimes citing the TVA in the United States as an inspiration. In the early 1940s Mexico's CFE took on the tasks of building small plants in unserved rural areas and of developing the largest remaining undeveloped hydro resource in central Mexico. In Colombia, the national government had been giving aid to municipally owned electric companies since 1940, but in 1954 it created an autonomous regional agency to develop the Cauca Valley that was modeled explicitly on the TVA.[103] In the 1950s the state and federal governments in Brazil created several hydroelectric power companies whose primary mission was to develop and distribute energy in underserved and remote areas, although in a couple of cases the potential to sell excess power to São Paulo or Rio was an important part of the justification.[104]

The public companies didn't confine their activities to electrifying remote areas or rural development for long, however. They usually did not invade the distribution areas of the large private utilities, but developed instead into major generators of wholesale power for the private utilities. The fact that the private companies were not expanding their generating capacity in pace with demand gave the public companies their opening. As power shortages appeared, providing more wholesale power for the private utilities became the primary rationale for capacity expansions in the public sector. The investments by the public companies were financed through a combination of grants and loans from their governments and loans from the World Bank and the Inter-American Development Bank. One or the other of the two international lending agencies was involved in financing almost every major public power project in Latin America during the 1950s.[105]

The private companies had mixed feelings about the expansion of public power companies. In public, they usually welcomed the public companies as complementary rather than competing. In private, they may also have been grateful for the added generating capacity that the public companies were creating. The electricity shortages and rationing were a public relations embarrassment for the private companies that might lead to expropriation, but it was too risky for the private companies to invest heavily in new generating capacity themselves given the hostile regulatory environment.

In her study of the rise of public power in Brazil, Judith Tendler argues that the specialization of the public companies in generation and the private companies in distribution played to the needs and strengths of each sector.[106] Distribution technology was more susceptible to overloading, so that investments in added distribution capacity could be more easily postponed. When funds became available, moreover, distribution investments often could be made quickly and incrementally, and usually by the same employees that maintained the system, avoiding the need to recruit a new workforce. Moreover, major customers could often be persuaded to help finance the increments in distribution capacity needed to improve their service. By contrast, major generating stations were extremely expensive and usually required many years of construction before they could be put into service, particularly if they were hydroelectric plants. The engineering challenges and monumental nature of the projects—all of which increased the financial risks for the private companies—increased their attractiveness to the public sector. The pioneering nature of the projects helped attract skilled engineers and managers, who otherwise might have been leery of public service, while the technological complexity helped keep political patronage and corruption at bay.

Nevertheless, the private companies must have resented the public sector's expansion. In the first place, the division of labor between generation and distribution was not always clear enough to prevent conflict. In Mexico, for example, the public company, CFE, extended its distribution system into territory in central Mexico that the private companies considered their own. To add insult to injury, CFE's expansion was financed in part with a new 10 percent tax on all electricity sales, private and public.[107] But at a more fundamental level, the private companies undoubtedly would have preferred tariffs that were sufficient to allow them to expand capacity too, instead of seeing their share of power generation steadily decline.

The private companies and international agencies pressed Latin American governments to reform electricity tariffs throughout the 1950s, but to little avail. The international agencies feared that low tariffs would ultimately cause the collapse of the private companies and impose intolerable burdens on public budgets. For example, the United Nations funded studies that argued that raising electricity rates was preferable to allowing continued underinvestment. Raising rates need not cause social problems, the UN studies contended, because electricity typically accounted for a modest share of household budgets and industry costs. Rates could be kept low for the poorest households without unduly burdening other consumers, moreover, because poor households accounted for a very small portion of total electricity consumption.[108] In Mexico a special government commission on the electricity tariffs reached similar conclusions, arguing that the regulatory system was endangering the future of the power industry and that the assumption that the state could underwrite the financing of the electricity industry was simply unrealistic.[109] These studies all were ignored, and the policy of piecemeal and inadequate rate increases continued. According to Wionczek, the frustrated companies viewed the postwar period from 1946 to 1960 as the era of the "great deception."[110]

The end for most of the private power companies in Brazil, Colombia, and Mexico came in the late 1950s and early 1960s. Mexican electricity policy had reached an impasse because the government was still unwilling to raise tariffs to more realistic levels while international and U.S. aid agencies were now insisting on tariff increases as a condition for further credits to the sector. The conflict between Cuba and the United States in 1959 and 1960 broke the deadlock by making nationalization politically more attractive. Shortly after it bought out CCE and Mexlight, the Mexican government raised electricity tariffs to satisfy international lenders, much to the irritation of the American and Foreign Power and Sofina.[111] In Colombia, the final act came after the government devalued the local currency by 94 percent in 1957. The local American and Foreign Power subsidiary petitioned for a 73 percent rate increase, and the government finally agreed to a 40 percent increase in mid-1960. When popular protests forced the government to rescind the rate increase, American and Foreign Power offered to sell out on terms similar to those agreed to in Mexico.[112] In Brazil, state governments took over several local American and Foreign Power companies beginning in 1959, and in 1962, to preserve good relations with the United States, the federal government bought out all the holding company's assets in the country.[113]

Light survived as a private company until 1979. Light may have been protected by its policy, accelerated during the 1950s, of promoting Brazilian nationals to senior positions.[114] But Light had been considering selling out in the early 1960s too, and stopped only after the populist policies of the Brazilian government provoked a right-wing military coup in 1964. The new military government was much more sympathetic to private enterprise and foreign investors. In 1964 the government revised the Water Code to require the valuation of investments at current rather than historical cost, a change that resulted in the first increase in Light's basic tariff since 1934. Light prospered under the military government, but the situation deteriorated after 1973 as a result of both the economic strains created by the world energy crisis and the return to civilian government. In 1978 Brazilian Traction, Light and Power, which had by then changed its name to Brascan, announced that it was willing to sell Light, and in 1979 it agreed to a sale price that was half of Light's book value.[115]

The more gradual transition from private to public in Brazil, Colombia, and Mexico is probably due largely to the fact that their national governments seized control of electricity regulation and policy in the 1930s. The national governments were more sensitive to the implications of expropriations, and they had the resources to establish public power companies in the late 1930s and early 1940s, which reduced the pressures for takeovers by appeasing the advocates of public power and by providing subsidized wholesale power to alleviate shortages in the areas served by private companies. The fact that the major private utilities in Brazil and Mexico operated large and complex hydroelectric facilities may have played a role as well, by making the public sector more reluctant to take them over until it had gained more experience and confidence. Eventually the private companies gave up and sold out, tired of struggling to survive on minimal tariff increases while they watched their new public counterparts thrive.

Widespread Stock Ownership: Caracas

A final lesson from the electricity industry is the potential of widespread stock ownership to forestall expropriation. The more widely held the stock, the more politically difficult it is for the government to expropriate the company without compensation. Prime Minister Margaret Thatcher used this strategy in the 1980s when she privatized many of Britain's state-owned companies by selling their stock to the general public. But the same strategy had been employed two decades earlier by La Electricidad de Caracas, the only major domestically owned private utility to survive through the twentieth century in Latin America.[116]

La Electricidad de Caracas was the larger of two companies that emerged to serve Caracas. It was founded in 1895 by Ricardo Zuloaga, whose descendants would dominate the company for the next seventy years. Zuloaga had secured permission to supply electricity from both the municipality of Caracas and the governor of the Federal District, but these permissions apparently did not set maximum tariffs, perhaps because electricity was not considered essential or a monopoly at the time.[117] The second electric company serving Caracas, CALEV, began in 1912 when a Venezuelan entrepreneur managed to secure a concession from the governor of the Federal District to provide service to the center of Caracas. The concession contract gave the company exclusive rights for twenty-five years to provide public streetlights for the city and specified the price per lamp that the city would pay, but not the prices that private consumers would be charged.[118] The Venezuelan sold his concession to Canadian investors in 1913 and that company and several others were bought up by American and Foreign Power in 1930 and 1931 and consolidated into CALEV (Compañía Anónima Luz Eléctrica de Venezuela).[119] CALEV and La Electricidad de Caracas developed an understanding that CALEV would serve the traditional center of Caracas and the cities of Los Teques and San Felipe while La Electricidad de Caracas would serve all the rest of the metropolitan area.

The two companies seemed to do best in the years when Venezuela was a dictatorship, which, fortunately for them, were many. There was little public controversy about either company until 1938, probably because of the political repression under the long reign of the dictator Juan Vincente Gómez. CALEV's contract for public lighting was amended twice to reflect improvements in streetlamp technology.[120] The municipality apparently did not regulate the rates charged the general public for electricity, however, even though it gained the right to do so under Venezuela's basic municipal law.

Gómez died in his sleep in 1935, and his personal style of rule proved difficult to replicate.[121] The development of the oil industry beginning in the early 1920s was transforming Venezuela from one of Latin America's poorest nations to one of its richest, with a growing urban and middle-class population. Bowing to popular pressures, Gómez's two successors allowed some limited experimentation with democracy, including restoring popular elections for the city council of Caracas in 1937. The final say on most issues concerning Caracas was still reserved for the governor of the Federal District, however, who was a presidential appointee. In 1938, as the streetlighting contract was about to expire, the city council petitioned the governor, saying that electricity was too important to leave in the hands of CALEV. The council asked the governor to either help the city purchase the private companies or negotiate a lower tariff that would reduce the need for expropriation. Instead, the governor renewed the lighting contracts under the same terms as before.[122]

When greater democracy finally arrived at the national level in the late 1940s, electricity was one of the first targets for reform. Dissatisfaction with dictatorial rule among the middle class and young army officers led to a coup in early 1945, to elections for a national assembly later that year, and to presidential elections in 1947. In 1945 the revolutionary junta ordered reductions in electricity rates ranging from 25 percent for the customers with the smallest monthly bills to 5 percent for the largest customers.[123] The following year, the junta expanded the public sector's role in electricity. An electric energy office was established within the Ministry of Development to do technical studies and long-range planning for the industry. Municipalities were offered grants to help finance electrification in small cities and rural areas. A new national development corporation, the CVF (Corporación Venezolana de Fomento), was created to help the government invest its oil profits in modernizing and diversifying the economy, including the construction of major public hydroelectric projects. Finally, the government created the first national electric company to help develop sources of power and an interconnected network in the north-central spine of the country.[124] In the following year, 1947, the government drafted a law to allow the national government to regulate the tariffs of all electric companies, public or private.

Venezuela's experiment with democracy was interrupted in 1948, however, when the military overthrew the elected president out of concern over his proposed military cutbacks and populist policies. For the next ten years the Venezuelan government was run by the military, with Marcos Pérez Jiménez as president.[125] The country prospered as the oil industry grew and the government used its oil royalties to build Venezuela's infrastructure and industry. According to their critics, the private electric companies—and particularly La Electricidad de Caracas—used their influence with the Pérez Jiménez regime to loosen some of the constraints the democratic government had begun to impose on them. The CVF's program of investments in large public hydroelectric projects continued to provide power for areas not served by La Electricidad de Caracas, but La Electricidad de Caracas was given loans from CVF to expand its own generating capacity so that it did not become dependent on public power. The draft electricity regulatory law was scrapped, although in return for the CVF loans La Electricidad de Caracas agreed to a one-time review of its rates.[126]

The fall of Pérez Jiménez and the restoration of democracy in 1958 changed La Electricidad de Caracas's world. The Pérez Jiménez regime's reputation for corruption and its blatant disregard for democratic procedures and electoral results had provoked widespread unrest and eventually embarrassed even its military supporters. Moreover, a broad cross-section of Venezuelan society came to resent the close relationship between the regime and foreign companies, which seemed to be underlined by the strong support of the U.S. government for the dictator.[127] In the first years of democracy, Venezuela was beset by political tensions and the left was very active, inspired by the example of the Cuban revolution. Private companies that had prospered under the old regime were nervous, and foreign companies especially so.

La Electricidad de Caracas soon became the object of a campaign to either regulate or expropriate the company. The most outspoken critic of the company was Juan Pablo Pérez Alfonso, a former minister of development during the democratic interlude of the late 1940s and one of the founders of the Organization of Petroleum Exporting Countries (OPEC). Pérez Alfonso pointed out that electric companies were either publicly regulated or publicly owned in every other major country in the world. The municipal government of Caracas published reports by Pérez Alfonso and others arguing that La Electricidad de Caracas's tariffs were excessive and that the company had never secured the proper permits to provide electric service in the city or to place its poles and lines in public rights of way.[128]

La Electricidad de Caracas responded in part by stressing the high quality of the service it offered and the fact that it was Venezuelan owned. The company argued that its critics had made basic arithmetic errors in their tariff calculations which, when corrected, showed that La Electricidad de Caracas charged much less than most other electric utilities.[129] It acknowledged that it had been required to ration electricity in the late 1940s, when the postwar surge in demand caught the company short of generating capacity. But the company argued that the rationing had been more limited than in other Latin American and European cities, and that there had been ample supplies of electricity since.[130] The company also pointed with pride to the fact that it had resisted American and Foreign Power's efforts to take it over in the 1930s, even though the sums offered were very "flattering."[131] Venezuela could be proud of a domestic company with such a long record of distinguished service.

But La Electricidad de Caracas went further by deliberately shifting from a company whose stock was largely controlled by the Zuloaga family to a widely held corporation. By offering stock in denominations of only 20 or 25 shares, the company encouraged the general public to become stockholders. Employees were also made stockholders through the investments of their pension funds. The company's most ingenious and effective step, however, was to waive or refund the deposit of 500 bolivars normally required to obtain electric service for those households that bought 5 or more shares of the company's stock.[132] The company's reputation and the offering prices were so attractive that by 1963 the head of the company, Dr. Oscar Machado Zuloaga, reported that he now owned only 5 percent of the stock.[133]

The strategy of broad stock ownership was not without risks, however. The company walked a fine line in issuing dividends that were generous enough to maintain the support of its numerous stockholders but not so generous as to call attention to the fairness of its electricity tariffs. Pérez Alfonso attacked the company's dividends as excessive in the early 1960s, and the controversy forced the company to reduce tariffs in the middle of that decade.[134]

Competent service and broad-based Venezuelan ownership were enough to save La Electricidad de Caracas as an independent private company. American and Foreign Power sold CALEV to La Electricidad de Caracas in 1964 and the Canadian International Power subsidiaries serving Maracaibo and Barquisimeto were nationalized in the 1970s, at about the same time that Venezuela nationalized its petroleum industry. By the 1990s only La Electricidad de Caracas and a small company serving the Valencia area remained in private hands.[135] Venezuela's public power companies continued to multiply and to expand their capacity, but they stayed out of the distribution territory of La Electricidad de Caracas.[136]

National regulation of electricity rates was imposed gradually, in part at the behest of La Electricidad de Caracas. Beginning in 1977 the national government negotiated with the electric companies over rate increases, but without the authority of a specific law regulating electricity. This system seemed to work reasonably well until the late 1980s, when inflation, which had been suppressed by foreign exchange controls, increased significantly. La Electricidad de Caracas and the other electric companies sought the creation of some more formal and dependable method of tariff adjustment, and in 1989 the government issued a decree establishing U.S.-style cost-of-service regulation for both the public and the private companies.[137] In 1992, a regulatory commission and agency were created.[138] By the mid-1990s the government still had not passed a law establishing the primacy of national regulation over municipal regulation, however, so there were occasional conflicts in which some mayors would tell their citizens not to pay rate increases ordered by the national government.[139]

The strategy of selling most of its stock to small investors, customers, and employees is not the only factor that saved La Electricidad de Caracas. The company probably benefited from the creation of the large public companies, since they took on politically important tasks that the private company might have shirked as too risky, particularly rural electrification and the development of the vast hydro resources of the remote Guayana region. La Electricidad de Caracas also gained from Venezuela's stable foreign exchange rates, which meant that it did not need to constantly seek rate increases to pay for imported generating equipment. Widespread stock ownership had its own risks, moreover, since it could make the trade-offs between tariffs and dividends very obvious.

In addition, Canada's experience demonstrates that widespread stock ownership is not a decisive bar against expropriation. Utility stocks were probably much more widely held in Canada than in Latin America, for example, but that did not protect most Canadian utilities from eventual expropriation. Canadian governments may have been wealthier than their Latin counterparts, and thus more able to compensate the stockholders during expropriation. But the widespread stock ownership must have increased the political pressures to compensate at a fair price in Canada too.

Nevertheless, it is striking that La Electricidad de Caracas appears to be the only major private utility in Latin America that pursued a strategy of broad ownership. Both Light and American and Foreign Power also tried to encourage local investors to buy the stocks and bonds of their subsidiaries during the 1950s, but their efforts were half-hearted. In Light's case the motive was largely political; in American and Foreign Power's case the motives seemed to be a desire to raise additional capital and reduce foreign exchange requirements. Neither company courted small local shareholders in anything like the systematic way that La Electricidad de Caracas did, however, and in the end their efforts were neither financially nor politically very significant.[140]

It is also striking that La Electricidad de Caracas seemed in great peril until it deliberately broadened its stock ownership. The company thrived for many years while politics was suppressed, but once democracy arrived briefly in the 1940s and more permanently in 1958, it felt very vulnerable. The fact that it had supplied good service and was domestically owned did not protect it from attack or the fear of expropriation. In the end, the company felt that it had to take the further step of distributing its shares at bargain prices to customers, employees, and the general public.

Implications for the Future

It is dangerous to use the experience of the electricity industry to develop prescriptions about how to avoid expropriation in the future. Our understanding of why private utilities survived in some places and not in others is too tentative and incomplete. History suggests that no single factor was decisive in determining whether a company would be nationalized or not. The basic root of controversy, not surprisingly, was that the electric companies were monopolies providing a service on which the public had come to depend. But which other factors were essential is far from clear.

In addition, one of the factors that appears to have been important—the strong protections against the taking of private property in the U.S. Constitution—would probably be hard to replicate. The Fifth and Fourteenth amendments to the Constitution were the products of unusual circumstances: a revolution for national independence and a bloody civil war. Canada was unwilling to enact similar constraints simply to protect its private utilities.

Two other factors that might help forestall expropriation—reduced foreign involvement and more widespread local stock ownership—probably could be replicated, but at a cost of limiting access to capital and expertise and weakening corporate governance. Foreigners are often solicited precisely because they have money and technical expertise not available locally, and limiting their ownership to a minority or noncontrolling share might dampen their interest in investment considerably. And small shareholders often are not very effective in exercising control over management, particularly in developing countries and transition economies where small shareholders usually enjoy less legal protection. One would want to be more confident that the benefits to be gained in protecting private utilities were worth the potential costs in investment, expertise, and management control.

The last potentially influential measure—locating regulation at the national rather than at the local level—might, if history is a guide, provide only temporary relief. Indeed, the most chilling story in the history of the electricity industry is how stealthfully public power replaced private power in countries like Brazil, Colombia, and Mexico, where electricity was regulated by the national government. The process proceeded in steps so small that their implications were not fully understood at the time. When public power companies were first established, they often had a mandate to serve only remote and rural areas. When rate increases were denied, the private companies were usually offered enough "additionals" or other forms of compensation to sustain their hopes of survival. It took several decades for the positions of the private companies to deteriorate to the point where a public takeover seemed inevitable. Only in retrospect does the incremental process seem irresistible.

Putting aside the possibility of prescription, are the factors that encouraged nationalization in the past present in the wave of privatizations that began in the 1980s? At first glance, the answer to this question is depressing. Many of the factors that seem to have encouraged expropriation in the past are present today. The legal systems and constraints seem little changed, for example, although the quality and the independence of the judiciary has probably improved in many developing countries. Many of the newly privatized companies are owned or controlled by foreign investors, just as most of the private electricity companies were after the 1920s.

Nevertheless, there are reasons for optimism. Although foreign ownership of private utilities is common in developing countries, it is less common than it was in the 1920s. Domestic capital markets and technical skills are stronger in developing countries than they were in the 1920s, so there is less need to rely on foreigners except in limited areas, such as telecommunications. And where foreigners are involved they sometimes have domestic investors as highly visible and important partners. Politicians and the public are unlikely to treat such partnerships with the same favor that they would show a wholly domestic company. But if foreign involvement is lower, the tensions and complications may be reduced as well.

Another reason for optimism is that some countries have made an effort to ensure that the shares of the private infrastructure companies are widely held. Britain sold its state-owned utilities in public stock offerings, with provisions to favor buyers of small numbers of shares. Among the developing countries, pension funds have been the main vehicle for spreading share ownership for infrastructure companies. For example, Chile requires that all workers invest a portion of their wages in a pension, and private pension funds compete to attract the workers' investments. Chile's private pension funds have been major investors in the shares of Chile's private infrastructure companies. Bolivia auctioned off half of the shares of many of its infrastructure companies to strategic investors, usually foreigners. The buyers were required to invest the sale price in the company, however, so that services would be modernized and improved. More important, the remaining half of the company shares was reserved to start a pension system to cover all Bolivian families. It is hoped that the investments of these pension funds will provide increased popular understanding of the financial needs of the private companies.

In addition, the poor performance of many state-owned enterprises in the 1970s and 1980s has made many countries considerably more skeptical of the potential for publicly owned utilities than they were in the 1940s, 1950s, and 1960s. Nationalization may have prevented monopoly abuse, if that indeed was a problem, but it created a host of inefficiencies and shortcomings of its own. It proved politically difficult to raise electric rates in pace with inflation even after the utilities were nationalized, for example, and the combination of low rates and increasing inefficiency often led to large deficits and deteriorating services. And the collapse of the Soviet Union and Eastern Europe in 1989–1991 dramatically underscored the shortcomings of public ownership. Although the memories of the poor performance of government-owned utilities are likely to fade, most countries will be skeptical of nationalization for some time to come.

The degree of monopoly or market power also has declined for some types of infrastructure, and with it the need for regulation and its attendant problems. In some cases changes in technology have reduced monopoly power. Railroads enjoy far less market power since the development of competition from modern highways, trucks, and buses. The development of microwave, satellite, and fiber optic technologies has eliminated the market power in long-distance telephony and may soon do the same for local calling. In other cases the industries have been restructured to introduce competition wherever possible. Many countries are separating long-distance from local telephony and the generation of electricity from its distribution, for example, since competition is possible in long-distance calls and electricity generation.

Another reason for optimism is that democracy is more widespread now than it was when many private utilities were nationalized. The possibility that democracy might protect private utilities seems to run counter to the history of the electricity industry in the Americas. Democracy didn't prevent most Canadian provinces from taking over their private electric utilities, for example, and elected governments proved more ready to expropriate utilities than military dictators in Bolivia, Brazil, Venezuela, and other Latin American countries. But while democracy provides more potential avenues for the expression of popular resentment against monopoly, it also may increase the popular faith that the basic regulatory bargain is fair. Where the problem of private monopoly can be publicly debated and not suppressed, the possibility of reaching a solution that has widespread and sustained public support may be greater.

Finally, we have become more sophisticated about the design of regulatory systems for controlling private monopolies. This is not to say that the task has become easy. The basic dilemmas involved in developing a regulatory system that can balance infrastructure supplier and user interests over many years are still very hard to resolve. But we now have over a century of experience in regulation. And we have been learning how to regulate better, as we explore in the next two parts of this volume.

II

Contract versus Discretionary Regulation

7

The Evolution of Concession Contracts: Municipal Franchises in North America

Three Stages of Development

The last four chapters explored the politics and dynamics of regulation, focusing both on regulatory capture and contractual incompleteness as sources of instability and on various defenses against expropriation. The next three chapters examine more closely the circumstances under which three principal regulatory strategies—private contracts, concession contracts, and discretionary regulation—are likely to be successful. This chapter begins that examination by considering the strengths and weaknesses of the concession contract approach as illustrated by the experiences of municipal franchises in the United States and Canada over the nineteenth and twentieth centuries. The initial enthusiasm, eventual collapse, and selective revival of municipal franchises may point the way to the more sustainable use of contracts in the future.

Municipal franchises in the United States and Canada went through three stages of development. The first stage, which coincided more or less with the nineteenth century, was one of broad application and experimentation. Private entrepreneurs led in the construction of modern water- and gasworks in the first half of the nineteenth century, in the introduction of horse-drawn street railways in the middle of the century, and in the development of electricity systems and electric street railways at the end of the century. The speeds with which these new technologies were adopted were often breathtaking. And the needed investments would not have been made without the franchise system, since they far outstripped the abilities of the cities to raise capital at the time.

The strains of writing workable contracts were apparent from the beginning, however, and the cities responded by experimenting with different types of contracts. In the beginning, municipal officials underestimated the importance of these services or the limitations of competition. As a result, the earliest contracts were often for long terms and vague about the obligations of the company to provide specific services or to charge reasonable prices. Later contracts tended to be more specific, but the rapid pace of economic and technical change in the nineteenth century quickly made such highly specific contracts obsolete as well. As the century wore on, cities began to shift to contracts that sought to control profits directly, instead of indirectly through prices and quality, and to establish independent committees or arbitrators with the discretion to adjust prices and conditions of service.[1] By the late nineteenth century, the franchise system was migrating from a purely contractual approach to one with more discretionary elements. In that respect, the municipal franchises were pioneering many of the features of the twentieth-century state public utility commissions that would replace them.

In the second stage, the states and provinces assumed a dominant role in the regulation of those utilities that remained in private hands. The beginnings of this stage overlapped with the end of the first, as the state and provincial role expanded gradually. Municipal powers are delegated from state and provincial governments in the United States and Canada, so the states and provinces determine the types of utilities their cities can franchise and the aspects of company performance the cities can regulate. Early-nineteenth-century North America had a strong tradition of decentralized government, however, and state and provincial legislatures were generally reluctant to get embroiled in the details of awarding local franchises. States and provinces took the lead in chartering and regulating the infrastructure that crossed municipal boundaries or provided intercity service, such as canals and steam railways. They let their cities take the lead in regulating utilities whose services were largely local and involved the occupation of city streets.

From the beginning, however, state government remained available as a court of appeal or mediator if either a city or a private franchise holder felt it was being treated too unfairly. In essence, the option of appealing to the state introduced an element of discretion in the otherwise contractual approach. And although that appeal was cumbersome to exercise, it was called on increasingly as the nineteenth century wore on and disputes between cities and franchise holders became more common. The spread of some formerly local utilities across city boundaries at the end of the nineteenth and the beginning of the twentieth centuries added pressure for state intervention. But the final straw, especially in the United States, was the assessment of many turn-of-the-century reformers that municipalities could not be trusted to regulate private utilities wisely or without corruption. By the mid-twentieth century municipal franchises had all but disappeared, with most of the remaining private utilities now subject to state regulation. Gas and electric companies were more likely to remain private and state regulated, while most of the water and street railway franchises were eventually taken over by the cities they served.

The third stage saw the revival of municipal franchises for private utilities, beginning in the 1970s. The revival involved fewer industries and shorter contracts than its nineteenth-century predecessor. Cable TV franchising lasted only two or three decades, ending because technological change had reduced cable TV's monopoly power and thus the need for regulation. The other industries—solid waste disposal, water, and sewerage—are ones where large private firms seem to have important advantages in technology and experience over municipal operators. Contracts for a period longer than ten or fifteen years are still relatively rare, and the longer contracts are generally restricted to the construction and operation of a single facility rather than applying to the entire systems. Although it is too early to tell, this selective approach and shorter-term contracts may reduce conflicts and make the revival more sustainable than the original.

Early Applications and Experiments

The Gas and Water Industries

The water and gas industries appeared in the first half of the nineteenth century, before street railways or electricity, and thus were the subjects of some of the earliest applications and experiments with concession contracts. In the United States, the number of cities with private water systems increased in two waves, as shown in Table 7.1. The first wave occurred in the decades immediately before and after 1800, when roughly 30 large cities built water systems, most of them private. By 1825 private companies accounted for 84.4 percent of all systems. Over the next fifty years another 390 smaller and medium-sized cities acquired systems, but more than half were built by the public sector; by 1875 the private share had declined to 46.2 percent. The second wave of private construction occurred between 1875 and 1890, when 877 private and 579 public systems were added and the private share climbed to 57.1 percent of all systems.

Cities were motivated to establish water systems to fight fires as well as to provide clean water for household consumption. Indeed, household consumption was initially modest, since the rates charged by water carts often were not much higher than those charged by the water utility. The most important provisions of early franchise agreements governed the number of fire hydrants the company would provide and the annual fee per hydrant that the city had to pay. Awareness of the health risks of waterborne diseases increased over the nineteenth century, and helped stimulate the second wave of expansion that began in the 1870s. Many of the new private systems of this era were started by private water pump manufacturers, who sought franchises to develop the market for their products.[2]

After 1890 many U.S. cities bought out their private systems and most of

Table 7.1 Private ownership of water utilities in the United States, 1800–1915

Year	Total waterworks	Privately owned waterworks	Municipally owned waterworks	Percentage privately owned
1800	16	15	1	93.7
1825	32	27	5	84.4
1850	83	50	33	60.2
1875	422	195	227	46.2
1890	1,878	1,072	806	57.1
1896	3,179	1,489	1,690	46.8
1915	4,440	1,395	3,045	31.4

Sources: Figures except 1915 from Moses N. Baker, "Water-works," in *Municipal Monopolies,* ed. Edward W. Bemis (New York: Thomas Crowell, 1899), p. 16. The 1915 figures are from Dewey, "Municipal Ownership of Water Utilities," *Public Utilities Fortnightly* 9 (May 26, 1934): 634 as cited in C. Woody Thompson and Wendell R. Smith, *Public Utility Economics* (New York: McGraw-Hill, 1941), p. 603.

the new systems built were public, so that the private share declined to 24 percent by 1915. Most of the remaining private systems were in small communities, moreover, so that the share of the population served by private carriers was far lower.[3] The rise and fall of private water systems was somewhat faster in Canada. Of Canada's two most important cities, Montreal started with a private system in 1801 and bought it out in 1843, while Toronto franchised a private system in 1842 only to buy it out in 1872.[4] By 1897 only 24.8 percent of the water systems in Canada were still privately owned.[5]

Artificial gas was first used for lighting in Britain sometime between 1803 and 1804, and private gas companies appeared as early as 1816 in Baltimore, 1822 in Boston, and 1823 in New York. Improvements in production methods steadily reduced the price and increased the popularity of gas, especially after the Civil War. As a result, the number of cities in the United States served by artificial gas plants increased from 30 in 1850 to 877 in 1900.[6] Natural gas emerged toward the end of the nineteenth century as a by-product of the search for oil, but initially was available only in areas adjacent to gas fields. The development of high-tensile steel and electric arc welding made long-distance, high-pressure pipelines economical in the 1920s, and the companies that had produced and distributed artificial gas shifted to cheaper natural gas. In the United States these companies generally remained in the private sector, although municipal regulation was gradually replaced by state regulation of the distribution companies and federal regulation of interstate gas sales.[7]

Gas was so expensive initially that it was used only to illuminate the streets and the homes of the well-to-do. As a result, the early gas franchises often specified the annual price the city would pay per street lamp, but not the price of gas sold to private customers. Controls on prices charged private customers emerged as private consumption became more common. The pressure to regulate prices was never as intense in gas as in other utilities, however, perhaps because gas suppliers faced more competition. In the early days, the competition often came from other gas suppliers. Cities seemed more willing to grant multiple franchises for gas than for other utilities, although in most cases the competitors eventually consolidated into a monopoly. Over the long term, other energy sources provided more serious competition. Kerosene oil was a competing fuel for illumination in the mid-nineteenth century, and electricity rapidly replaced gas for lighting streets and buildings after the 1880s. The industry maintained the demand for gas by promoting its use for cooking and heating, but even in those applications it faced competition from coal, oil, and electricity.

Constant Renegotiation: Water in San Francisco

The history of nineteenth-century water and gas franchises is replete with stories of contracts that proved to be incomplete, resulting in frequent and controversial renegotiations. The most common problem with water franchises was a failure to anticipate the investments needed to maintain adequate supplies for fire fighting and to serve new neighborhoods. Charles Jacobson's account of the Spring Valley Water Company that supplied San Francisco's water from 1857 to 1930 is in many respects typical.[8] It is unusual only in how long the acrimony lasted, both because of the company's control of the best water sources and because of the city's unwillingness to pay the unpopular company the price it demanded for its assets.

San Francisco realized it needed a water system during the Gold Rush of 1849, when the city's rapid growth caused an increase in the number of fires and cases of dysentery. The Spring Valley Company was given a franchise to serve the city in 1857, after another company franchised in 1851 ran into unexpected problems with its proposed water source.

Spring Valley's franchise had elements of both contract and discretionary regulation. The franchise specified that Spring Valley had to build a system capable of delivering at least 2 million gallons per day and that it provide water for governmental purposes, including fire fighting, for free. Tariffs for domestic and business customers would be determined by a five-member board, however, with two members appointed by the company, two by the city, and the fifth appointed by the other four. The board was to ensure that the company's returns did not exceed 24 percent per year on its investments for the first five years, and 20 percent thereafter. By 1860 the company had laid pipes and begun to serve the city's most densely populated neighborhoods.

The rapid growth of San Francisco soon caused daily consumption to exceed 2 million gallons. The provision of water to households was profitable enough that the company continued to expand its capacity, but so slowly that there were frequent complaints about service. In addition, the company installed mains that were large enough to supply household needs but not large enough to provide the enormous volumes of water needed to fight a fire.

Matters were further complicated in 1865, when Spring Valley took over another water company with a franchise that did not require it to provide water to fight fires for free. The other company had been exempted from that requirement because it owned only a small spring, and thus was expected to supply only its immediate neighborhood. But Spring Valley now claimed that it no longer had to provide free water for public purposes because it had assumed the franchise of the other company.

The dispute resulted in years of litigation, with the courts finally deciding that both franchises had been superseded by an 1858 state water law that required private water companies to provide water free for government purposes. The courts' decision also voided the expiration dates of both franchises, however, making Spring Valley's franchise effectively perpetual. Most important, the decision did nothing to strengthen Spring Valley's incentives to provide adequate fire-fighting capacity.

By the 1870s San Francisco's troubles with Spring Valley stimulated a movement to establish a municipal water system. Spring Valley thwarted the effort, however, by buying the best remaining local reservoir less than two weeks after the city announced its intentions to purchase the site for a municipal system. The city then tried to buy out the company, but they couldn't agree on a price. Expropriating Spring Valley was also ruled out when the city attorney determined that San Francisco had no legal grounds to do so under California law. An 1880 change in the state constitution gave the San Francisco Board of Supervisors the right to set rates for the company, but the company's control of all the key water sources left it in a strong position.

For the next several decades, the city essentially bargained with Spring Valley over tariffs and investments. The city agreed to pay monthly fees per hydrant and to gradually increase tariffs for hydrants and private water in return for improvements. There was little trust between the city and the company, however, and the relationship deteriorated rapidly after 1897, when a series of reform mayors campaigned against the perceived abuses of this private monopoly. The city commissioned an independent valuation of the company's assets and used it to help justify several sharp reductions in tariffs. The company responded by slashing new investment, which provoked the city to pursue the possibility of damming the Hetch Hetchy Valley in Yosemite National Park and building an aqueduct to transport the water 150 miles to San Francisco.

The city's resolve to end its dependence on Spring Valley was strengthened by the fire that followed the 1906 earthquake. The earthquake broke many water mains and those that weren't broken had too little pressure to fight the conflagration. But the company warned that it would take at least ten years to bring water from Hetch Hetchy, and that the rebuilding and growing city would need substantial investments in the meantime. Those investments would not be forthcoming unless the city made commitments to provide an adequate return and to retain the company when the water from Hetch Hetchy finally arrived. The city and the company finally agreed on a price to buy out the private system in 1930, just four years before the Hetch Hetchy supplies arrived in San Francisco. In the interim, inadequate water supplies slowed the development of new neighborhoods and left the city poorly protected against fire.

Controls on Profits instead of Prices: Gas in Toronto

The controversies with gas franchises focused less on the adequacy of capacity than on the fairness of prices. Gas prices dropped dramatically throughout the nineteenth century; in Boston, for example, the price of a thousand cubic feet of gas fell from $5 in 1822, to $2 in 1879, to 80 cents in 1909.[9] City officials usually suspected that prices should fall faster, however, given the cost savings from technological progress and economies of scale. Specifying future prices in a contract was obviously risky given the high rate of technological change in the industry, and threats to franchise a second private company or establish a municipal enterprise did not seem very effective in inducing price reductions. As a result, many cities began to experiment with contracts that set limits on profits instead of on prices. The history of Toronto's private gas company, Consumers' Gas, illustrates the problems encountered.[10]

Gas service began in Toronto in 1842, after the city granted the Toronto Gas, Light and Water Company a perpetual but not exclusive franchise. The franchise did not specify the maximum prices Toronto Gas could charge, an oversight that soon became apparent after the company raised the charge per streetlight from $24 to $28 per year. When the city refused to pay the increase, the company turned off the lights, and the chagrined city began to look for alternative gas suppliers. In 1848 the city franchised a new company, Consumers' Gas Company of Toronto, to provide competing gas service. The owners of Toronto Gas quickly sold out to the newcomers, foiling any attempt to establish competition.[11]

The Consumers' Gas franchise limited profits rather than its prices by capping the company's dividends at 10 percent and diverting any excess to lower tariffs. This arrangement was apparently suggested by the company's founders, who were a group of dissatisfied Toronto Gas customers. Indeed, at the outset Consumers' Gas resembled a cooperative, although it did not have that legal form. In 1850, for example, the company had only 369 customers and over 300 shareholders.

The company gradually lost its cooperative character as capital needs increased and the percentage of customers who were shareholders declined. By the early 1850s, for example, it thwarted the efforts of a competitor to enter the gas business, an action that seemed to champion shareholder over customer interests. To curtail the competitor, Consumers' Gas lobbied the provincial legislature to insert a clause in the new company's charter capping its rates at $2.50 per thousand cubic feet. Consumers' Gas dropped its rates to $2.50 too, but then raised them back to $3.00 a year later, after the efforts to start the competing company faded.

The limit on dividends may have seemed simple and fair, but it encouraged the company to search for loopholes to retain excess earnings for investors. Conflicts over profits were delayed by a severe recession in the late 1850s, which greatly reduced gas consumption and left the company in a weak financial position. As the economy improved in the 1860s, however, the haggling between the city and the company over streetlight and gas prices intensified. In the early 1870s, the city successfully pressed the company to reduce its streetlight prices by threatening to establish a municipal gas company. Soon after, however, the company strengthened its position in future negotiations by convincing the provincial legislature to pass a bill requiring that a municipality starting its own gasworks had to buy out the private works first.

In the second half of the 1870s the profits of Consumers' Gas exceeded 10 percent almost every year, but the company avoided large price reductions by keeping dividends under 10 percent and retaining the excess in a "reserve account."[12] The situation threatened to get worse at the end of the decade, as the company began to adopt the more efficient "carburetted water" technique for producing gas that had been developed in the United States. The city reacted in part by encouraging the development of electricity, which was just beginning to make its appearance in major cities. The city denied the request of Consumers' Gas for an electricity franchise, awarding one instead to a new company, Toronto Electric Light, along with a contract for half of the city's streetlights.

Fearing that the competition from electricity would not be enough, the city also began to press for limits on the size of the gas company's reserve accounts. Consumers' Gas relented only in 1887, when it needed the permission of the provincial legislature to amend its charter so that it could increase its capital stock. The company agreed that any proceeds from selling stock above par would be placed in the reserve fund, and that the fund could never exceed half the amount of paid-up capital without triggering a price reduction. Consumers' Gas soon evaded the new reserve limits by raising capital with debt rather than with equity. Any new stock would have sold well above par given the company's profitability, and quickly filled the reserve fund. By issuing debt instead, the company could expand without adding to reserves or limiting the ability of existing stockholders to protect above-average earnings.

The city's concerns intensified in the late 1880s, when it realized that even effective controls on dividends and reserves would be less meaningful if the company could pad its expenses. Municipal officials were concerned that operating costs were inflated and that new investments were being disguised as maintenance. The company finally agreed to fix reserves at $1 million in 1891, when again it needed the provincial legislature to amend its charter so that it could raise more capital. At the same time, it agreed to put a municipal official on its board of directors. The inside view, perhaps coupled with the growing competition from electricity, helped quiet the city's concerns about Consumers' Gas.

The San Francisco and Toronto cases are typical of nineteenth-century water and gas franchises in that there was almost constant renegotiation—no contract lasted for very long. With little faith in the contract, both parties tried to find other means to protect themselves from opportunism. The municipalities' primary strategy was to threaten to establish a competing private or public company. The firms' strategy was to raise the cost of those threats by buying key assets, convincing new private companies that consolidation was better than competition, or persuading state or provincial legislatures to require cities to buy out private utilities when they established public ones.

Franchise contracts also evolved as the limitations of different approaches became apparent. Perpetual franchises with few requirements, like that of Toronto Gas, soon gave way to twenty- or thirty-year franchises with very specific standards for prices and service quality or adequacy. As the limits of specific service and price standards became apparent, contracts that prescribed profits rather than prices became more common. More sophisticated "sliding-scale" contracts allowed a company to earn profits over certain levels as long as it also reduced prices. In the end, however, the cities usually discovered that they had forgotten to define something important in advance, such as the appropriate level of maintenance and operating expenses. In practice, contract regulation was evolving into cost-of-service regulation, with some of the inevitable ambiguity and discretion that that approach involves.

The Growth of State Involvement

The Street Railway and Electricity Industries

The street railway and electricity industries that developed in the second half of the nineteenth century shared many of the same experiences as the earlier water and gas industries. All four industries experimented with different types of concession contracts, and all four saw state involvement gradually increase. The pressures for state involvement seemed more intense for railways and electricity, however, perhaps because both expanded so rapidly in the late nineteenth century.

Private street railways developed in several phases, the first being from 1832 to 1888, when horses were the railways' primary motive power. Before the street railway, private carriages were beyond the means of most people. The principal alternatives for urban travel were walking, which was slow, and the horse-drawn omnibus, which was expensive and only slightly faster. The introduction of the street railway did not increase speeds much, but it greatly reduced costs and fares by increasing the number of passengers a team of horses could pull. This advantage was such that the number of street railways in the United States grew from 1 in 1832 to 40 in 1860 and almost 600 by 1890, all apparently privately owned.[13]

The industry's second phase began in 1888, with the demonstration of the first practical electric-powered streetcar system in Richmond, Virginia. Electric power revolutionized the industry by reducing costs per passenger mile, increasing speeds, adding capacity on congested downtown tracks, and reducing the challenges posed by hilly terrain. By 1890, only two years after the Richmond system opened, 144 electric street railway systems were in operation in the United States. By 1894 there were 606 electric street railways with roughly double the mileage that the horse-drawn systems had had in their heyday. By 1910 almost every town with a population over 10,000 had electric streetcar service.[14]

In the final phase, which began around World War I, a combination of unrealistically low fares and competition from the automobile gradually drove most systems into bankruptcy and public ownership. Municipal and state regulators weakened the industry by delaying fare increases needed to offset a strong bout of inflation in the years immediately before and during the war. The rapid increase in auto ownership beginning in the 1920s dealt the railways an even more serious blow by stealing their passengers and congesting the streets they used. The industry fought back by eliminating conductors to save costs, designing a modern standard streetcar for all companies to use, and converting lightly used routes to the motor bus. These efforts were not enough to offset the advantages of the automobile, however, and in the two decades after World War II most of the private companies collapsed. Many of the bankrupt systems were taken over by municipal or state authorities, who did not want to see service disappear altogether.

The electricity industry also developed in several phases. In the first phase, from 1882 to roughly 1890, isolated generating stations were built to illuminate the streets, homes, and businesses in their immediate vicinities.[15] The railways and other early businesses that used large amounts of electricity usually had their own private generating plants.

A second phase of plant interconnection occurred roughly between 1890 and 1910. Interconnection was made possible by the development of alternating current and transformers, which made the transmission of electricity over longer distances practical. Interconnection improved service reliability, allowed the use of larger and more efficient generating stations, and increased plant utilization by combining the original evening illuminating loads with daytime streetcar and industrial loads. A single electric company emerged in most cities, often after a brief competition among alternative consolidators.

In later stages, the industry began to build systems that crossed municipal, and often state or provincial, boundaries. Between 1910 and 1925 the companies serving neighboring cities were often consolidated so that the smaller towns could get the benefits of larger generating plants and more reliable supplies. After 1925 the emphasis shifted to interconnecting independent regional systems to allow the sale of wholesale power from large hydroelectric plants or between regions that had different peak demand periods. Through at least the middle of the twentieth century, electricity never faced the problems of rising costs and a strong new competitor that the street railways did. The opportunities for technological improvement were numerous and gradual enough that the cost of electricity declined steadily, which helped to keep much of the industry in private hands.

The State as Mediator: Street Railways in Massachusetts

The states' involvement in regulation began as a mediator of conflicts between the cities and their franchise holders. Cities and private companies frequently renegotiated franchise terms because it was so difficult to draft a complete contract. States would intervene periodically to redress perceived imbalances in the parties' bargaining power by, for example, amending a company charter or the state statute governing municipal expropriation. The street railways of Massachusetts were typical in that the state intervened roughly once a decade from 1853 through 1918, gradually increasing the extent of state involvement.

Massachusetts's policy toward street railways was influenced by its policy toward steam railways, which had appeared in the state two decades earlier, in the 1830s. The state wanted to encourage steam railways both to promote western development and to strengthen the port of Boston against the port of New York and other rivals for hinterland trade. Accordingly, an 1836 law provided that a railroad could set its own fares and that the legislature could order reductions only if they did not bring railway profits below 10 percent per year. The state could buy back the railroad after twenty years, but only if it paid back all the capital invested plus a sum sufficient to make up any deficit on a 10 percent annual return.[16]

When the legislature issued the first street railway charters in 1853, it adopted a similar framework but made the cities the principal regulators, since street railways operated in city streets. A state charter was void unless accepted by the local city council, and the city had the right to specify the streets that could be used and regulate speed and other issues. The city could buy out the railway after ten years if it paid the invested capital plus any amount needed to make up a 10 percent return.[17] Because street railways were seen as an untested technology at the time, however, the legislature also inserted a clause allowing the city to order the company to remove its tracks and restore the streets to their original condition at any time after the first year of operation.

The first two street railways—connecting Boston with Cambridge and Roxbury—opened in 1856 and were such a success that they soon stimulated many other applications for charters. After a period of consolidation in the 1860s, Boston had four major street railways: one each radiating to the southeast, south, west, and north of the city.[18] Although street railways were clearly no longer experimental, the legislature retained the clause allowing the city to order the tracks removed in all subsequent charters. The cities, once accustomed to this leverage over the railways, did not want to lose it.[19]

The effects of giving the cities the power to revoke franchises would be debated off and on for the next sixty years, until the advent of the automobile made the controversy irrelevant. Supporters acknowledged that a perpetual but revocable franchise seemed "absurd" given the substantial investments that street railways required. In practice, however, they argued that the scheme was less disruptive than the franchises with fixed terms used in most other states.[20] The threat of revocation was seldom taken seriously because it would greatly inconvenience the traveling public, but it was useful against an unreasonable concessionaire.[21] Critics responded that the threat of revocation was real enough to force the railways to grant substantial concessions to city governments, sometimes at the risk of their financial health and ability to serve the public.[22]

Whatever the truth of the matter, the controversy induced the legislature to gradually increase the state's role in regulating street railways. The first step occurred in 1864, with a law that established limited state oversight of street railway fares and track usage. The charters of the 1850s had provided that fares within the city of Boston could not exceed 5 cents without permission of the mayor and city council.[23] There was nothing to prevent the cities from forcing fares to below 5 cents, however, presumably backed by the threat of track removal. The 1864 law preempted the cities' power to cut fares, providing instead that a city council or fifty voters could petition the State Supreme Judicial Court for a fare reduction. The court would then appoint a special three-person commission to investigate the new fares, and that commission could order lower fares only if the new fares would not reduce railway profits below 10 percent per year. Perhaps as a consolation to the cities, the new law also provided that a similar special commission could be appointed to force one street railway to allow another access to its tracks if the two railways could not agree to terms.[24]

The 1864 scheme of appeal to ad hoc commissions appointed by the Supreme Judicial Court lasted only five years. The scheme applied to disputes over fares and track access only, and so in 1865 the legislature appointed another special investigative committee to consider whether additional legislation was necessary. That committee reported that the industry was evolving too rapidly to legislate the relationship between the railways and the cities in detail, but that it would be desirable to have a permanent commission to which the parties could appeal in a variety of situations. A permanent commission to supervise the steam railroads was under discussion at the time, and if it was created the committee recommended that its mandate be extended to cover street railways as well.[25]

The legislature finally established the Board of Railroad Commissioners in 1869 with responsibilities for both steam and street railways.[26] The board was not the first state regulatory commission in the United States, nor even the first railroad commission. It was the first railroad commission with a broad mandate, however, and its establishment was widely recognized at the time as a pioneering and influential reform.[27]

Like many later regulatory agencies, the board had three commissioners who were intended to be experts in the industry. Unlike later agencies, however, the board was a "weak" commission whose primary powers were those of information and publicity. It could require railroads to produce accounts and data in the formats it specified, investigate accidents, and issue reports with recommendations. With street railways only, it also inherited the power to compel railroads to share tracks and to lower fares (as long as the new fares did not reduce returns below 10 percent). On other tariff, safety, or service issues, however, the board could not compel the railways to act.[28] The idea was that publicity would force the companies to adopt the board's recommendations. If they did not, there was also the threat that the board's reports would provoke legislative action.

This new balance between the cities and the railway companies seemed to work fairly well for almost two decades, through the end of the horsecar era. During this period, the role of the state in regulating street railways seemed to decline while that of the cities increased. The new Board of Railroad Commissioners was largely preoccupied with steam rather than street railways, and the legislature further reduced its involvement in street railway matters by passing a law granting a standard state charter to any company that secured permission to use the streets from municipal authorities.[29] The cities' leverage over the street railways also increased as they relied less on the threat of revoking franchises and more on the threat of introducing competition by granting new franchises or forcing track to be shared.

Competition had become a more credible threat, because street railway profits were growing as the economy recovered from a recession at the beginning of the 1870s. Applications for new street railway charters increased, and two major new street railways opened in Boston in competition with the four existing lines.[30] The forced use of tracks also spread as weaker street railways convinced city councils that "public convenience and necessity" required that they operate over competitors' tracks. The Metropolitan Railroad in Boston was a particular victim of this strategy, since it had tracks on some of the most important streets in the downtown area. By 1887 one of the Metropolitan's competitors, the South Boston Railway, was running more car miles on the Metropolitan's tracks than it was on its own.[31] The political maneuvering for new franchises and track rights was intense, but the disputes apparently were resolved largely at the local level.[32]

The electrification of the street railways after 1888 seriously upset the balance of power between cities and the railway companies. By the mid-1880s Boston's downtown streets were clogged with slow-moving horsecars, and the presidents of Boston's major railway companies were considering cable cars or electric storage battery systems to increase speeds and capacity. The matter was brought to a head in 1887, when all of Boston's lines were consolidated under a new company: the West End Street Railway. The West End had been formed by a group of entrepreneurs interested in developing suburban Brookline by extending streetcar service to it. Their proposal was impractical unless an alternative to horses was employed, since the cars would have to climb a long grade to reach Brookline. The creation of the West End encouraged two of the incumbent railways to discuss a defensive merger, and the West End responded by buying the other five railways that served Boston at the time. After a practical scheme to deliver overhead electric power was demonstrated in Richmond, Virginia, the next year, the West End rapidly electrified the consolidated streetcar system.

Electrification weakened the cities' position by making the threat of competition less credible. The capital investment per mile was much higher, because electric railways required overhead wires and poles and stronger track to support the larger and heavier cars. As a result, it was less economical to build or maintain competing lines on parallel streets. Electrification also complicated track sharing, which had been difficult enough with the horse-powered cars. The public often complained that horsecars from competing companies raced each other to switches, for example, with the winner then proceeding slowly, knowing that riders would board the first car to arrive at a stop. Electrification would make such practices more dangerous and intensify disputes over how to share the cost of building and maintaining the more expensive infrastructure. Boston officials tolerated the consolidation of the existing local railways under the West End only because they thought it essential to encourage the investments needed to replace their horse-powered system.

But if electrification strengthened the railways' bargaining position by reducing the threat of competition, it also made them more vulnerable by extending streetcar lines across city boundaries. The advantages of electric power stimulated an explosion in streetcar mileage in Massachusetts. While 562 miles of horsecar lines had been built between 1856 and 1888, 2,652 miles of electric-car lines were built between 1888 and 1904.[33] The higher speeds encouraged commuters to live farther from the city center, which the street railways made possible by extending their lines to suburban towns or buying up neighboring systems. By 1896, only nineteen of the seventy-three street railways in Massachusetts still served a single town, while the Lowell street railway passed through ten towns, the West End through twelve towns, and the Boston and Lynn railway through eighteen towns.[34] Matters were made worse because the enthusiasm for electrification among railway promoters and investors raised popular expectations about railway profitability. Cities and towns began to insist that the railways pay higher taxes or fees to maintain or extend their lines, and railway promoters began to complain that small towns in the path of extensions exploited their locations to demand unreasonable terms.

The state could not ignore the changing relationship between the cities and the railways for long. In 1897 a new special investigative committee concluded that the cities deserved compensation for the use of their streets, but within more clearly defined limits. In 1898, following the committee's recommendations, the legislature passed a law that imposed a new state tax on street railway gross receipts whose proceeds were distributed among towns in accordance with their track mileage. In return, the street railways were relieved of any obligation to maintain or widen streets or make other special payments to the towns.[35] The 1898 law also empowered the Board of Railroad Commissioners to review future franchise revocations and to force a town to grant a franchise where it thought the town was imposing unreasonable conditions.[36]

The problems in Boston were more complicated, provoking the state to draft a special concession contract for the city's railways. Electrification had relieved congestion in downtown Boston only temporarily, as the gains in streetcar capacity were soon overwhelmed by increased ridership. Congestion led the city to build a 1.7-mile railway tunnel under the Boston Common, and to rent it for twenty years to the West End Street Railway. The tunnel was not enough, however, and in 1894, the same year the tunnel opened, entrepreneurs secured a franchise to build an elevated electric railway line to Roxbury. The backers of the Boston Elevated Railway soon realized that their proposal would be more workable if they could connect with the West End's lines and use the new tunnel, and in 1897 they sought permission from state and city authorities to amend their franchise so that they could buy out the West End Street Railway.

The resulting statute was drawn as a contract between the Boston Elevated and the state, in effect substituting a purely contractual approach to regulation for the mixed contractual and discretionary system that had been developing. The contract was a version of the "sliding scale" that had become increasingly popular among utility regulators, but with all the downside risks assumed by Boston Elevated. The company promised not to raise the fares above 5 cents for twenty-five years, and the state promised not to order fare reductions that reduced the company's earnings below 8 percent per year. The company promised to pay a franchise tax of $\frac{7}{8}$ percent of its gross receipts to the cities and towns it served, as long as its dividends did not exceed 6 percent per year. When dividends exceeded 6 percent, it would pay an additional tax equal to the excess above 6 percent.[37]

The reforms of 1897 and 1898 worked smoothly for only about a decade. Electrification had weakened the financial strength of the street railways by encouraging overextension and low fares. At the turn of the century, most U.S. and Canadian street railways charged a flat 5-cent fare, regardless of distance traveled. The 5-cent fare was an inheritance from the horsecar era, but it was popular with both the companies and the public alike. The companies thought it stimulated traffic and reduced fare collection costs. Social reformers believed it helped the working class move out of overcrowded city slums.[38]

As the companies extended their lines or absorbed neighboring systems, however, the 5-cent fare meant less revenue per passenger mile, offsetting some, if not all, of the cost savings achieved through electrification. Many of the street railways in smaller towns were already in financial trouble by 1900, and the difficulties spread to the larger properties as inflation heated up in the years immediately before and during World War I. Railway unit costs increased by 14 percent between 1900 and 1910 and then by an astonishing 130 percent between 1910 and 1920, largely as a result of increased wages.[39]

The Massachusetts Board of Railroad Commissioners lacked the power to order the fare increases the street railways needed to remain solvent, but between 1902 and 1912 it persuaded many small towns to increase fares.[40] By 1913, however, the board seemed overwhelmed with street and steam railway problems, and the legislature replaced it with a strong regulatory commission modeled on the public utility commissions that other states had been creating.[41] The new PUC could order fare increases, but it took the position that the companies had to prove that they could not gain the revenue they needed by reducing costs. As a result, the fare proceedings went slowly, and were accelerated only after one major street railway, the Bay State, went bankrupt at the end of 1917.[42] By then the situation seemed hopeless, and matters only got worse as competition from automobiles intensified in the 1920s.

In the Boston metropolitan area, cost inflation had made the Boston Elevated's commitment to a 5-cent fare unworkable. The company appealed to the governor for relief from its concession contract in 1916. In 1918, with the company close to collapse, the legislature finally placed the Boston Elevated under the control of public trustees who were to manage the company for up to ten years and then return it to its private owners.

The trustee scheme restored a measure of local regulation, but at the price of some local financial responsibility. The trustees were to propose fares sufficient to provide stockholders with a 6 percent annual return on their investment, but those fares had to be approved by an advisory board made up of the fourteen cities and towns in the service area. If the advisory board failed to approve the fare increases requested by the trustees, then the fourteen cities and towns had to pay the resulting deficit.

Within a year the trustees had increased fares to 10 cents, but even this was not enough to restore the Boston Elevated to profitability; in 1930 the period of trustee control was extended until 1959. The ridership surge during World War II revived hopes that the company could be returned to private hands, but it was soon evident that there was no politically acceptable fare that would generate enough revenue to make the company profitable. In 1947 the state finally bought out the Boston Elevated Railway's investors, and in the next two decades the state's remaining private street railways also fell into public hands or disappeared.[43]

The Mistrust of Local Politics: Electricity in Chicago

Many states experienced a gradual transition from mediator to regulator, as Massachusetts did with its street railways. But the final step to state regulation was usually marked by a heated debate over charges—brought by a coalition of Progressive reformers and the utilities themselves—that the cities were too incompetent or corrupt to regulate.

One of the organizers of this coalition was Samuel Insull, the head of Chicago's largest electricity company and a leader in the electric industry at the turn of the century.[44] In 1898 Insull gave the presidential address to the annual convention of the National Electric Light Association and surprised the delegates by proposing that the industry acknowledge that electricity was a natural monopoly and support state regulation of electric rates and the quality of service.[45] The association did not adopt Insull's proposal that year, but it would change its mind and join the reform coalition by 1907.

Insull's suggestion was born out of his experience with municipal regulation in Chicago, which was reputed to be one of the most corrupt cities of nineteenth-century America. Insull had worked as Thomas Edison's personal assistant and later as a key executive in General Electric, the equipment manufacturing arm of the Edison empire. In 1892 he was sent to Chicago to head the Chicago Edison Electric Company, one of over twenty electric companies then serving the city. Insull quickly set about acquiring key competitors, and in a decade his company, renamed Commonwealth Electric, became the dominant electricity supplier in Chicago.

Insull developed several strategies to protect his company from municipal corruption. One was to cultivate a reputation for dealing honestly with Chicago's politicians. He acknowledged their needs by contributing openly to their campaigns and by hiring constituents they recommended for jobs in his companies. But he donated to many politicians rather than to a few, and he insisted that his employees be qualified and hard working.

Insull also used his intimate knowledge of electric technology to buy up companies that owned the exclusive rights to use key equipment in Chicago. Thus in 1897, when a group of aldermen asked for a bribe to stop the city council from granting a franchise to a competing company, Insull could safely refuse, knowing that the new company would find it difficult to compete without the needed equipment.[46]

Perhaps most important, Insull lowered electricity tariffs by aggressively adopting new technologies and innovative marketing strategies.[47] Insull believed that larger generating stations would reduce unit costs, and Commonwealth Electric became an industry leader by ordering huge generators and pioneering in the new technology of steam turbines. Insull was also one of the first in the industry to recognize that he could increase the average utilization of his generators and further reduce unit costs by recruiting customers who wanted power during off-peak hours or seasons. Thus Commonwealth Electric moved aggressively to offer very low rates to street railways and other industries, since their daytime loads complemented the evening residential and street lighting loads. Chicago's electricity rates fell far below those in most other comparable cities, as the average tariff for all classes of service declined from 20 cents per kilowatt-hour in 1892 to 10 cents in 1897 and 2.5 cents in 1909.[48] When Chicago politicians moved against Insull's company, they often found that he had undermined their complaints with recent price cuts.

Chicago's other utilities were very unpopular, however, and Commonwealth Electric inevitably absorbed some of the hostility they generated. The main local gas company, Peoples Gas, Light, and Coke, was widely reviled because it constantly opposed the city's requests for price reductions. When the city finally passed an ordinance lowering gas prices, Peoples Gas delayed its implementation for years with lawsuits. The city got its revenge by refusing to change the obsolete technical standards for gas set out in the franchise. The costs of meeting these standards increased over time, driving the company close to bankruptcy before city officials agreed to a compromise.[49]

Chicago's street and elevated railway companies were even less popular than the gas company.[50] In the late nineteenth century, over a dozen nominally independent elevated and street railway companies served Chicago. The elevated railways were legally classified as railroads and regulated by the state, but the street railways were regulated by the city and were a major source of corruption. State law prohibited municipal franchises for longer than twenty years, and bribes were the expected price for renewal. Route extensions or changes also required franchise amendments, providing additional opportunities for extortion. The level of graft was such that one frustrated franchise applicant claimed that he could have reduced fares from 5 cents to 3 cents if he had been able to secure a franchise without bribes.[51] The public was further irritated by the poor quality of street railway service, which the city had limited ability to control. State law allowed the city to specify the location of the lines, the fares, and the railway's obligations to maintain streets. The city could not limit the level of crowding in the cars, however, or reduce transfers by ordering railways to share access to their tracks so as to permit through service.

One railway financier, Charles Tyson Yerkes, soon became the focus of public anger. Yerkes had come to Chicago in 1887, and by 1897 had won control of companies providing roughly two-thirds of the street railway service and one-half the elevated service. Yerkes understood railway economics better than public relations, and he gained notoriety with statements that made him seem indifferent to the welfare of his customers.[52] It was widely assumed that Yerkes had paid bribes to assemble his empire, which further sullied his reputation and increased the demands that corrupt aldermen made on him.

Yerkes eventually tired of paying city graft and, when important franchise renewals were coming due, sought to escape by submitting to state control. In 1897 Yerkes had a state legislator introduce two bills to extend all existing street railway franchises for fifty years and establish a three-person state commission with the power to regulate fares and other matters. The popular outrage over the fifty-year franchises and Yerkes's efforts to bribe the state legislature to approve them provided a turning point for the municipal reform movement in Chicago. Reformers not only defeated the bills but gained control of the city council in 1898, and Yerkes left Chicago for London soon after.

The street railway battle that brought the reformers to power had obvious implications for other utilities. Reform politicians might be more honest than their predecessors, but they were not necessarily more sympathetic to privately owned utilities. The railway battle had focused public attention on municipal corruption from all types of utilities, and left the impression that any alderman who voted for a utility company's proposal must be on the take. In addition, the battle had strengthened popular support for the municipal ownership of street railways, leading to an intense ten-year debate in Chicago over the merits of municipal ownership versus stricter municipal regulation.[53] Although the ownership debate focused on railways, the options and issues were similar in other utilities.

Insull's 1898 proposal to the National Electric Light Association was in many ways similar to Yerkes's proposal of the year before. Both sought to win support by acknowledging that regulation was in the public interest. Yerkes proposed to grant the new state commission the powers to control car frequency, heating, and other dimensions of service quality that city officials had long sought, for example, while Insull conceded that electricity was by nature a monopoly. Insull's reputation for integrity, however, made it easier for him to forge alliances with other reformers who were advocating state regulation.

The Progressive Debate: State versus Municipal Control

The battles in Chicago were part of a larger Progressive movement that swept America in the late nineteenth century. The Progressives were concerned with cleaning up government at all levels, but the cities became a particular focus after the National Conference on Good City Government in 1894. The Progressives' two watchwords were morality and efficiency: corruption was to be eliminated and government was to be operated in a more rational and businesslike manner. With respect to utilities, however, the movement split into two factions, one favoring municipal regulation or municipal ownership and the second favoring state regulation.

In his analysis of the Progressive movement, David Nord argues that the two factions differed fundamentally in their faith in local democracy.[54] The supporters of municipal control believed strongly in the efficacy of local government. Their solution to government corruption and inefficiency was not to remove important public decisions from politics but to educate the electorate so that it would make more sensible choices. They also argued that democratic control ought to be exercised by the level of government whose citizens were most directly affected by and knowledgeable about the problems, which, in the case of most utilities, was the cities.

The advocates of municipal control argued that democracy and efficiency were compatible, but the paramount goal was democracy. As one reformer explained, "Efficiency is a fine thing, but successful self-government is another."[55] Accordingly, a key part of their agenda was a host of reforms—such as at-large elections and the council-manager form of government—intended to improve democracy at the local level. In this vein, many thought that a shift from municipal regulation to municipal ownership would be beneficial, since it would remove the potentially corrupting influence of the private utilities. But the fact that a growing number of utilities favored state control only made the advocates of municipal control more suspicious. "The cry that 'politics' will interfere with municipal regulation," wrote another reformer, "is one of the cleverest pieces of 'politics' in the long history of clever utility corporation tactics."[56]

The advocates of state regulation argued that their proposal was the most efficient. Franchise or contract regulation had proved unworkably rigid, they contended, and needed to be replaced by some form of commission regulation with greater flexibility to adapt to unusual or unforeseen circumstances. A state commission was more practical because the overhead costs of the commission and its expert staff could be spread over a larger number of companies. Local regulation was becoming obsolete, moreover, because utilities were beginning to cross municipal boundaries.

For many advocates of state regulation, however, the efficiency arguments were a convenient cloak for their mistrust of local politics. Pleas for home rule were seen as the ruses of corrupt politicians. Advocates of state regulation recognized that they lived in a democracy, but believed that proceedings before a nonpolitical commission of experts were the best way to "clarify and educate public opinion" and "convince the average citizen of the reasonableness and justice of the decision."[57]

The watershed came in 1907, when three developments shifted the balance toward state regulation. First, the National Civic Federation released a three-volume report on the merits of municipal versus private operation of utilities. The federation was an influential coalition of business, labor, and political leaders that Samuel Insull had helped found in 1900. Its report did not advocate for state regulation specifically, and it even recommended that municipalities have the option of buying and operating utilities, as long as voters approved in a special referendum. But it also recommended that all utilities, whether publicly or privately owned, should be regulated as monopolies and warned that municipal control "depends upon the existence in the city of a high capacity for municipal government."[58] Second, the municipal bond market collapsed during the financial panic of 1907, making it much more difficult for cities to purchase private utilities. The market for bonds issued by the largest cities recovered within a year, but the market for bonds from the smaller cities, where the municipal ownership movement was strongest, would take years to recover.[59] Finally, the states of Wisconsin and New York passed laws establishing the first modern public utility commissions with broad powers. Between 1907 and 1914, twenty-seven states enacted public utility laws, most modeled on the Wisconsin or the New York bills.[60] In 1914 the National Civic Federation issued a new report recommending state regulation.[61]

In the end, both factions of the Progressive movement won partial victories. The advocates of state regulation triumphed, because almost all of the utilities that remained privately owned soon fell under state or provincial regulation. The advocates of municipal control also won in that many utility companies were bought out by cities and became public agencies. However, the system of municipal franchises for private utilities, which some municipal advocates still supported, largely disappeared. Although there were exceptions, the gas and electric companies were much more likely to remain private but state regulated, while water and street railway companies were much more likely to fall under municipal ownership.

The Influence of Technology

Technology did not seem to be a deciding factor in the shift to state regulation. Technological developments might have forced such a shift eventually, especially once it became profitable for gas, electric, and other utility companies to extend their services across municipal boundaries. Even as late as

1907, however, most utilities still served a single city. The main exceptions were the street railways, especially in metropolitan areas, like Boston, where the principal city had been less aggressive in annexing outlying towns. But Chicago had annexed enough territory in the late nineteenth century that its street railways typically did not cross municipal boundaries. And while Insull had acquired the electric companies in Chicago's suburbs, he had been motivated by a desire to protect Commonwealth Electric from encroachments by suburban competitors rather than by a vision of operating all the affiliates as an interconnected or integrated system.[62] Some saw the potential for integrated regional electric systems in the future, but it would be another decade or so before improvements in transmission technology and the correction of the electricity shortages of World War I made such systems economical.[63]

Technology was more influential in determining which types of utilities remained privately owned and which were bought out by the cities. In particular, water and street railway systems were more likely to be bought out, because they generated important benefits for nonusers. These nonuser or external benefits make it difficult to finance the systems needed through the voluntary subscriptions of users.

Water and sewage systems benefit nonusers by reducing the threat of general conflagrations and the spread of disease. For example, fighting fires requires considerably larger mains and higher pressures than are needed for normal household consumption. Nineteenth-century households were not always willing to pay a fee for a domestic connection that was sufficient to finance a system capable of fighting fires.[64] And the household that chose not to connect would still be protected by the fire hydrants in its neighborhood.

The cities might have solved the problem by compelling households to subscribe to the water system or by subsidizing the extra costs of fire fighting out of tax revenues. Compulsory subscription or public subsidies seem to have been politically less acceptable, however, as long as the water company remained in private hands. Piped sewage collection systems didn't become widespread until the late nineteenth century, but the need to compel or subsidize subscriptions to prevent the spread of disease was so obvious that most sewage systems were built by municipalities from the start.

Street railways benefit nonusers by reducing traffic congestion and by maintaining the accessibility of central business districts, concerns that became critical with the advent of the automobile. The automobile seriously increased congestion and the need for public transit, while stealing transit's passengers and profits. As auto ownership grew, it became increasingly clear that the street railways could no longer be financed out of the farebox without cutting back service and raising fares by more than the traveling public and downtown interests were prepared to tolerate. As with water, public subsidies for railways were more palatable when accompanied by public owner-ship. Many big cities temporized for a while, as Boston did with its thirty-year public trusteeship of the Boston Elevated, but eventually most chose to buy out and subsidize their systems.

Gas and electricity, by contrast, generate nonuser benefits in only a few ap-plications, most notably street lighting. The household or business that illu-minates the street in front of its building provides a safety benefit to both neighbors and passersby. Thus it is not surprising that municipalities con-tracted for street lighting, first from oil, then from gas, and finally from elec-tricity suppliers. Street lighting was a key initial market for gas and electricity companies but, unlike firefighting for the water companies, it did not impose unusual technical requirements or costs. And both the gas and the electric companies soon found many other applications and customers besides street lighting.

Municipal ownership of water and street railways may also have been en-couraged by slower rates of technological change and productivity improve-ment. There were significant, even revolutionary, advances in water and rail-ways, such as the development of improved water pumps and pipes in the 1870s and of the electric railway in the 1880s. But the rate of technical im-provement seemed to be steadier in gas and electricity, which may have fore-stalled conflicts by allowing the gas and electric companies to reduce costs and prices more frequently.

Finally, municipal ownership of water companies may have been encour-aged because water systems are relatively capital intensive and simple to oper-ate. The capital intensity of water systems made them especially risky for pri-vate investors, particularly in small cities or when extending service into new suburbs.[65] And the fact that the technology seemed to be relatively simple and standardized reduced the fear of public operation.[66]

The Return of Franchises in the Twentieth Century

Cable TV Franchises

Municipal franchises reemerged in the United States and Canada during the late twentieth century, first in cable TV and later in solid waste disposal, wa-ter, and sewage treatment systems. The cable TV franchises in the United States are by far the best studied of the modern municipal franchises, and their experience seems to be far more favorable than that of their nineteenth-century predecessors.

Cable TV franchises were rare in the United States until the 1970s, when the Federal Communications Commission reversed its policy of discouraging cable in markets served by broadcast TV stations. The FCC had been concerned that competition from cable would hurt the broadcast television stations and make it harder for the agency to require that the broadcast stations provide unprofitable local and community programming.[67]

Once the FCC restrictions were lifted, many cities awarded cable TV franchises to private companies. The typical franchise was for fifteen years, and most franchises were awarded after a competition of some sort. The contract usually specified the deadline for constructing the system; the capacity in number of channels; the price to be charged subscribers for basic (as opposed to premium) services; and often nonprice concessions, such as an annual franchise fee or community studios and programming. Most states allowed municipalities to regulate their cable franchises. Some states made the state PUC or a specialized state cable commission responsible for regulation, however, and a few states prohibited regulation at either the state or the municipal level.

Stories of disputes between cities and their cable TV providers were common, often involving franchise renegotiations that seemed to leave one or both parties vulnerable to opportunism. In Oakland, California, for example, the winner of the cable franchise had proposed a monthly fee for basic service that was half that of the next best bidder.[68] Two years after the award, with the system only half complete and construction behind schedule, the concessionaire approached the city to renegotiate on the grounds that costs were higher and subscriptions lower than expected. The city ultimately decided to renegotiate, believing that it had little chance of enforcing the original contract and that it might not win a much better deal and would suffer long delays if it put the service out to bid again. Oakland was only one example, and its experience might not have been representative. The fact that thousands of municipalities had signed cable TV franchise agreements provided scholars with a unique opportunity for more systematic empirical research on concession contracts.

A series of empirical studies suggested that opportunistic behavior of the kind observed in Oakland was common, but not as widespread or serious as might be feared. One study surveyed municipal officials about disputes and dissatisfaction with their cable TV concessionaires.[69] Of the 221 cities responding, 23.5 percent reported serious disputes, and the patterns were consistent with opportunistic behavior. Disputes were significantly more likely if the franchise had been competitively awarded, for example, which suggested that some concessionaires bid low, expecting to renegotiate later.[70] Municipalities that regulated rates reported more disputes and greater dissatisfaction with quality, both patterns consistent with opportunism.[71] At least some of the disputes seemed to be the result of the inexperience of a new industry rather than opportunism, however. A surprising 87 percent of the municipal officials said they would recommend their concessionaire to another similar city, which implies that almost half of those reporting serious disputes did not blame the company for the conflict.[72]

Another interesting study concluded that incumbents had only modest advantages when cable TV franchises expired and were rebid.[73] The raw statistics suggest otherwise: of the 3,516 franchises that had been renewed by the early 1980s, incumbents had won all but 7. But although incumbents might have advantages relative to other bidders, they did not necessarily have an advantage relative to city governments. Only the city could reuse the incumbent's nonsalvageable investments, which might give the city substantial leverage at the point of franchise renewal. To test this proposition more systematically, the study compared the terms of 59 franchise renewals between 1980 and 1984 with a random sample of 66 contemporary initial franchises. The study found that the terms of the renewals were only slightly more advantageous to the cable companies than the terms of the initial franchises, which implies that the incumbent had only a modest advantage in bargaining with the city at renewal time.[74]

A final focus of empirical research was whether municipal regulation was effective in preventing the concessionaires from overcharging customers. A particular concern was that municipal officials might be using their regulatory powers to capture potential monopoly rents for the city at the expense of consumers. During the late 1970s and early 1980s, cable companies frequently complained that city governments requested expensive "frills" when cable systems were put out to bid. Examples cited included community studios that were seldom used, extensive internal cable systems for city offices and schools, and excess channel capacity.[75] In a survey of 66 systems in 1984, for example, private cable TV managers estimated that nonprice concessions added an average of 26 percent to their system capital costs and 11 percent to system operating costs.[76] Although the managers may have been biased and some of the facilities must have been useful, municipal officials were clearly not passing on as many savings to consumers as they could have.

The frills notwithstanding, there is fairly strong evidence that municipal regulation was effective in reducing the prices consumers were charged, although not necessarily to the levels that would be expected if cable TV were a perfectly competitive industry. Several researchers estimated the effects of municipal regulation by comparing prices and service quality before and after 1984, the year when the federal government severely restricted the powers of municipalities to regulate cable TV rates. Almost all of these studies found that prices increased significantly after cable companies were freed from municipal regulation.[77] But their results have been criticized because the price increases may have been caused by the rapid improvements in cable technology and in the diversity and quality of cable TV programming that occurred during this period.[78]

One study avoided the problems caused by changing technology and programming by comparing prices and service quality across a sample of 1,242 franchises in a single year, 1982.[79] The study examined the effects of different regulatory regimes by comparing franchises in states that allowed municipal regulation with those states that required state regulation or prohibited regulation by either level of government. The authors found that municipal contract regulation resulted in lower prices and higher quality than no regulation at all. Moreover, they concluded that municipal regulation was about as effective as state PUCs or special state cable commissions in controlling price and quality.

The experiment with cable TV franchises ended in 1984, when Congress passed a law severely restricting the powers of local governments to regulate cable TV rates. The 1984 law was a product of intense complaints by cable operators that they were being held up by municipalities at franchise renewal time and that regulation was unnecessary because the operators faced sufficient competition from over-the-air stations, satellite TV, and other forms of entertainment.[80] After the law went into effect, consumers began complaining that the cable companies were raising rates rapidly, and in 1992 Congress responded by imposing federal regulation on cable rates. Federal regulation of thousands of different local systems proved controversial and hard to implement. Moreover, the market power of cable TV companies seemed to be declining with the development of direct satellite TV systems and the threat that telephone companies might soon provide cable TV service.[81] In 1996 Congress reversed itself and mandated the phase-out of federal regulation of cable TV rates by 1999.[82]

Solid Waste, Water, and Sewage

The use of private contractors to dispose of municipal solid waste spread rapidly in the 1970s thanks largely to the promulgation by the U.S. federal government of stricter environmental standards for water and air pollution from landfills and incinerators.[83] The municipally owned landfills and incinerators used by most cities at the time did not comply with the new standards. Modern landfills and incinerators would be larger in scale and much more technically sophisticated than many cities thought they could build or manage, so many cities turned to private companies that had extensive experience in waste disposal for industry. Some of the new private facilities were built under long-term contracts with a city or group of cities, others were "merchant" plants built for the spot market, while many used a combination of the contract and merchant approaches. A half-dozen large firms emerged operating landfills and incinerators throughout the country, presumably because of the economies afforded by experience and by the ability to spread specialized technical and managerial staff over large numbers of facilities. By the late 1990s approximately 58 percent of the tons of solid waste collected by U.S. cities was disposed of in private facilities, while 59 percent of the expenditures on solid waste management by Canadian cities was spent on private contractors.[84]

A similar shift to private provision for water and sewage began in the late 1980s, although it progressed much more slowly.[85] As with solid waste, the impetus was partly stricter environmental standards for sewage effluent and drinking water quality. Cities began to contract with private companies to operate and maintain existing systems and to build and operate new sewage and drinking-water treatment plants. Some of the contractors were drawn from the few large private water utilities that survived the wave of municipal takeovers in the late nineteenth and early twentieth centuries; others were suppliers of chemicals, equipment, or other services to the municipal water utilities. During the 1990s, large private water firms from France and Britain also entered the U.S. and Canadian markets to compete for contracts. Nevertheless, in 1995 only about 12 percent of the U.S. population was served by privately owned community water systems, and many were operated by homeowners' associations rather than by investor-owned utilities.[86] A 1997 survey of city managers revealed that only 5.7 percent were employing private contractors to operate their municipal water distribution systems, 3.7 percent to operate water treatment plants, and 6.2 percent for wastewater collection and treatment.[87] Another survey that year found that 1,200 communities contracted with private firms to operate and maintain their water systems, but many of them were apparently small.[88]

The prospects for water and sewage privatization picked up in the late 1990s, when the federal government reduced two barriers it had created. One barrier involved a program of grants to help cities finance the construction of new water and sewage treatment plants. Funding for the grants was cut back sharply in the early 1980s, but for the next decade the federal government required a city to pay back the grants in full if it sold or leased a grant-financed plant to a private operator. In 1992, the rules were amended to require cities to repay only the undepreciated portion of the grant.

The second barrier stemmed from the fact that the United States is one of the few countries where the interest income from municipal bonds is not subject to personal income tax. This makes it cheaper to finance municipal facilities with municipal rather than private debt, since the interest paid on municipal bonds is lower because it is tax free. Until 1997, the U.S. Treasury held that a municipal facility operated by a private company under a contract for longer than five years was, in effect, a private facility and could not be financed with tax-exempt municipal bonds. In 1997 the U.S. Conference of Mayors got the Treasury to rule that cities could enter into contracts as long as twenty years without losing the ability to use tax-exempt debt. The facilities had to be municipally owned to be eligible for tax-exempt debt, but they could be built, maintained, and operated by private concessionaires under long-term contracts.

These changes contributed to a gradual increase in long-term contracts with private firms. By 2001 several dozen cities had recently entered into contracts to operate and maintain existing water or sewage systems or to build and operate new treatment plants, including Atlanta, Honolulu, Houston, Indianapolis, Milwaukee, Seattle, and Tampa. The typical operating contract was for ten years, while the typical contract to design, build, and operate a new treatment plant was for twenty years.[89]

Concession contracts remain far less common in water and sewage than in solid waste, however, in part because competition is weaker and careful contract design more important with water and sewage. Most cities no longer dispose of their solid waste within the city limits because of the constraints on siting new landfills and incinerators, and as a consequence they usually can choose from among several regional facilities. Cities and facility operators often sign long-term contracts to protect against short-term fluctuations in dumping fees, but there is also a fairly competitive spot market they can use if they need to.

Water and sewage, by contrast, are classic natural monopolies in that economies of scale are such that it is uneconomical to build more than one water distribution or sewage collection system in a community, and systems sited in other communities are not good substitutes. As a result cities and facility operators must protect themselves with concession contracts, because there is no competitive spot market to limit opportunistic behavior. The greater importance of drafting a workable contract has made cities more cautious about water and sewerage privatization.

The cities that have turned to private solid waste disposal, water, or sewerage providers seem to be satisfied, although their contracts have not been studied nearly as intensively as cable TV franchises. In water and wastewater, for example, cities report savings of 15 to 25 percent in construction costs and 20 to 40 percent in operating and maintenance costs from switching from public provision to private concessions or contracts.[90] Competitions for initial operating and maintenance contracts are reportedly fierce, but when the contracts expire many are extended through negotiation rather than re-bidding, which suggests both parties are reasonably well satisfied.

The Nineteenth versus the Twentieth Century

Municipal franchises seemed to be performing better in the United States at the end of the twentieth century than they were at the end of the nineteenth century, notwithstanding the difficulties of such comparisons. The cable TV franchises of the 1970s and 1980s were controversial, much like the franchises of the nineteenth century. When the data are examined closely, however, there is less evidence of opportunistic behavior than one might have expected and municipal franchise regulation seemed to perform as well as state discretionary regulation. There seem to be very few complaints about the solid waste, water, and sewage contracts of the 1980s and 1990s, although the experience in water and sewage is still very limited and none of these industries has been studied as closely as cable TV.

What might account for the apparent difference in the performance of nineteenth- and twentieth-century franchises? One possibility is that many of the problems of the nineteenth century eventually will appear again—they just need more time to develop. Another possibility is that the nineteenth-century experience was more favorable than is generally credited. If scholars had the same detailed data for nineteenth-century franchises that they have for the cable TV franchises, for example, we might find that there was far less opportunism and corruption in the nineteenth century than the citizens of the time suspected. Yet another possibility is that the quality and integrity of municipal government has improved in the last hundred years.

While all of these explanations are probably true to some degree, it is also possible that franchises are performing better because they are being applied in situations that are more favorable to the contractual approach. One difference is that some of the industries where franchises are being used are fairly competitive. This is especially true of solid waste disposal, where there appears to be effective competition not just for long-term contracts but also for the short-term spot market. Even in the 1970s and 1980s, cable TV systems faced competition from broadcast TV, movie rentals, and other forms of entertainment, although these were far from perfect substitutes. The availability of spot markets or substitutes, even if imperfect, limits the degree to which the private company or the city government can behave opportunistically. And this, in turn, should serve to limit contractual disputes and controversies.

Another important difference is that many of the contracts are for relatively short durations. The cable TV franchises were typically for fifteen years, for example, and the operating and maintenance contracts for water and sewage systems are usually for no more than ten years. Shorter contracts are possible because the investments required are smaller or have shorter lives. The cable TV systems were not terribly capital intensive and the equipment probably had a life of only ten or fifteen years, especially given the expectation of technological change. The operating and maintenance contracts anticipate little or no investment, although it is important to provide an incentive for the contractor to do routine or preventative maintenance. The shorter the contract, the easier it is to avoid disputes by anticipating problems and contingencies. And shorter contracts also make a bad contract more tolerable, since both parties know it will be over soon.

When long contracts are used, moreover, they are typically confined to relatively discrete investments rather than to entire infrastructure systems. The longest contracts are for twenty- or twenty-five-year concessions to design, build, and operate new drinking water or wastewater treatment plants. Anticipating the requirements for these plants over twenty-five years is difficult, but it is not as difficult as predicting the requirements of the entire integrated water or wastewater system. The plants are discrete, and their capacity and performance can be fairly easily described and monitored.

In short, the latest round of municipal franchises in the United States and Canada has focused on more limited and realistic applications. Unlike in the nineteenth century, municipal officials are not trying to draft twenty- or thirty-year contracts for complex integrated utility systems. The most complex utilities, such as electricity and telephones, are being regulated at the state or provincial level using a discretionary approach. Concession contracts are being applied where the chances of drafting a complete contract are greatest.

8

The Rediscovery of Private Contracts: U.S. Railroad and Airline Deregulation

with John R. Meyer

Substitutes for Government Control

One of the most intriguing developments in the regulation of monopoly is the expanded use of private long-term contracts to substitute for government control. As explained in Chapter 1, a fundamental cause of natural monopoly is the tendency of infrastructure suppliers and their customers to make durable and immobile investments that leave them vulnerable to opportunism. Yet durable and immobile investments are common throughout the economy, even in industries that are not considered monopolistic. In these other industries, the suppliers and consumers of durable and immobile assets typically protect themselves from opportunism with long-term private contracts. Infrastructure suppliers and customers might be able to use similar long-term contracts for protection, and thereby avoid the need for government regulation.

This chapter explores the circumstances under which private contracts might substitute for government regulation, using the deregulation of the U.S. freight railroad and airline industries as examples. Private contracts were a deliberate strategy during the deregulation of freight railroads in 1980 and emerged spontaneously and to a surprising extent in the passenger airline industry after its deregulation in 1978. Reliance on private negotiated contracts between utilities and their customers has since spread to other countries and other infrastructure industries, and is particularly common for large industrial customers of electricity and water utilities.

Private contracts are important in the U.S. freight railroads and airlines because these industries, though largely competitive, still have significant pockets of potential monopoly power. Railroad deregulation was possible in part because the railroads' monopoly power had eroded long before 1980, particularly with the development of truck and barge competition. Nevertheless, many shippers fear that they are potentially "captive" to the railroad that serves them, particularly if they are moving products unsuitable for trucks or barges and have substantial fixed investments in facilities on the railroad's line. The airlines were never considered by most economists to have strong elements of natural monopoly, and had been regulated largely in the name of protecting and promoting the industry. Nevertheless, many air travelers are concerned that competition is limited at some airports or on some routes because incumbent airlines keep out new entrants by, for example, controlling key gates or landing slots or exploiting the cost and service advantages afforded in operating large hubs. Concern about these pockets of market power increased at the end of the twentieth century, moreover, as mergers significantly reduced the number of major railroads and airlines in the United States.

The experimentation with private contracts as a substitute for government regulation was an innovation born of necessity. The U.S. freight railroad industry had been declining throughout much of the twentieth century, but by the 1970s the situation was critical. There was a growing consensus that regulation was contributing to the railroad industry's problems by preventing it from responding effectively to competition from trucks and barges. Deregulation seemed to be the only alternative to bankruptcy and nationalization, but complete deregulation seemed irresponsible given that some shippers were potentially captive, at least in the short run. The solution adopted was to allow the shippers and the railroads to enter into confidential long-term contracts. The authors of railroad deregulation were unsure how well the contractual solution would work, however, so they also gave the regulatory agency limited powers to set prices in the case of disputes.

Private contracts have proved useful not only in controlling the opportunism associated with monopoly but also in allowing services to be customized to the needs of the infrastructure company and its particular customers. When the government takes responsibility for regulation, it usually encourages the industry to offer a limited menu of standardized service options that is available to all customers at publicly posted prices. Limiting the menu and posting the prices make it easier for the regulator to monitor the performance of the industry and ensure that it is not unduly discriminating against any class of customers. But limited menus make it harder to tailor services in ways that might be advantageous to the industry and its customers alike. Private contracts open up the possibility of negotiating such customized solutions.

Writing a complete contract also seems to be easier with a private contract than with a concession contract, although the evidence on contractual disputes is skimpy. One reason this might be true is that a private contract has to anticipate the service needs of only one customer, while the concession contract must anticipate the needs of a large number of diverse customers. In addition, when a private contract has to be renegotiated, only two parties are involved and they represent their interests directly. When a concession contract has to be renegotiated, one party, the government, represents all the customers, and these customers often have conflicting interests and may not trust the government to negotiate capably on their behalf.

The major limitation on private contracts as a substitute for government regulation is the presence of small customers. The difficulty is not that the small customers have less bargaining power than the utility, although this is sometimes the case. Rather it is that the transaction costs of negotiating contracts with small customers may be high relative to the value of the services involved. For a small company that ships by rail only occasionally, for example, negotiating a long-term contract may simply be more trouble than it is worth to either it or the railroad. The success of private contracting in railroads is due in part to the fact that small shippers account for a very modest proportion of rail traffic. Nevertheless, private contracts seem to have played a surprisingly important role in the airlines as well, even though individual households and small businesses account for a relatively large share of air travel.

The Experience of the U.S. Railroads

The Beginnings of Regulation

The deregulation of the U.S. freight railroads in 1980 represented a reversal of approximately a century of public policy. Railroads were an early target for regulation in part because they were the first nationally prominent big businesses to emerge from the industrial revolution.[1] As such they were almost automatically candidates for envy, suspicion, and government involvement. But the main stimulus for regulation was the concern of many shippers that they were effectively served by only one railroad, which could take advantage of its monopoly position by charging excessive tariffs.

Nineteenth-century railroads fit the description of natural monopoly fairly accurately, despite a fair amount of overbuilding and redundancy. Economies of traffic density were large enough that it was often uneconomical to have more than one railroad serve a community. This was particularly true in thinly populated farm areas, where one single-tracked railroad with a few sidings and primitive signaling might be more than enough to carry the available traffic. And there were few substitutes for rail service, since motor trucks had not been developed and barges and ships were competitive only for shipments that at least roughly paralleled a major river or the coast.

The fact that some railroads charged low rates to highly competitive traffic in the industrial Northeast did little to improve public acceptance. The confidential rebates that the large corporations—such as John D. Rockefeller's Standard Oil or J. P. Morgan's U.S. Steel—negotiated with the railroads were particularly controversial. To farmers and other small shippers, it seemed outrageous that they had to pay more than rich corporations.

The states began to establish commissions to regulate railroad tariffs in the 1870s, particularly in the Midwest, where the pressures from farmers were strongest.[2] Congress debated the merits of federal regulation as early as 1877, when a group of small oil producers proposed federal controls to end what they saw as the unfair competitive advantage Standard Oil had gained by negotiating rebates from the railroads. The final impetus for federal regulation came in 1886, however, when the U.S. Supreme Court ruled that the state commissions could not regulate tariffs for interstate shipments. In 1887 Congress established the first federal regulatory agency, the Interstate Commerce Commission, with the power to prohibit discrimination in railroad rates between persons, localities, and types of traffic.

Although the ICC was initially established to protect small shippers from discrimination, its role gradually changed to emphasize the limitation of competition so as to protect a pattern of cross-subsidies from industrial to agricultural shippers. Some historians argue that the railroads supported tariff regulation as early as the nineteenth century because they realized that regulation could be used to discourage rate wars on trunk routes served by several railroads.[3] It took World War I and the Great Depression, however, before Congress expanded the ICC's authority in ways that allowed it to more effectively limit railroad competition. The railroads emerged from World War I in precarious financial and physical condition, partly from the heavy wartime traffic loads and partly from the allegedly inept government administration of the carriers during the war. To help the railroads recover, Congress passed the Transportation Act of 1920, which authorized the ICC to set minimum as well as maximum tariffs and to control entry, exit, and mergers.[4]

The tendency for detailed government involvement to protect the railroads' economic health was accentuated during the Depression, when the Roosevelt administration and Congress sought to revive the economy by encouraging industry associations to promote cooperation and limit "unfair" competition. The railroads had been particularly hard hit, because the Depression coincided with the emergence of truck and barge competition. In 1935 and 1940, Congress responded by authorizing the ICC to regulate truck and then barge rates for nonagricultural commodities.[5]

The ICC policy that emerged during the 1930s and persisted into the period after World War II might be best described as one of cartelizing the several freight modes so as to stabilize their market shares. In the ICC's parlance, each mode had an "inherent advantage" in the carriage of certain types of commodities over certain distances, and the ICC's job was to make sure that the modes kept to the traffic for which they seemed best suited. This emphasis on stability seemed consistent with the basic economic policy of the period, which was to avoid any repetition of the economic suffering of the Great Depression. A static cartel-like vision of the industry also helped maintain the established pattern of subsidies and redistributions effectuated through transport regulation, which, in turn, greatly simplified the political problems of the regulators.

The Pressures for Deregulation

In the 1950s railroad passenger and freight traffic fell dramatically from the heights reached during World War II, and the railroads' financial situation deteriorated as well. Many factors contributed to the traffic and financial decline, perhaps the most obvious being the steady improvements to the U.S. highway and aviation systems. The railroads increasingly came to view regulation as an important impediment to their efforts to adapt to their new environment. Academic economists also began to argue that the ICC was forcing railroads to charge too much for freight and encouraging excessive diversion of traffic to trucks.[6]

The ICC's resistance to innovation became painfully obvious in 1961, when the Southern Railway attempted to introduce aluminum 100-ton hopper cars in order to cut costs, offer lower rates, and recapture bulk commodity traffic that it had lost to barges and trucks. The ICC disapproved the proposed rates, responding to complaints from barge operators and from other railroads that did not have the new equipment (or the heavier welded rail that made heavier wheel loadings possible). It took a three-year legal battle, including an appeal to the Supreme Court, before Southern Railway finally forced the ICC to relent.[7] The 100-ton hopper car's advantages proved so significant that it soon became the norm for bulk commodity shipments by rail.

Interestingly, informal private contracts developed between some railroads and shippers during the 1960s and 1970s, even though these contracts were illegal and not enforceable in the courts.[8] The Interstate Commerce Act specifically prohibited private contracts on the grounds that they were potentially discriminatory, and the ICC frowned on service guarantees for similar reasons. All traffic had to move at publicly posted rates that were available to all shippers, and railroads could not give priority to particular shippers in the allocation of cars.

The ICC's restrictions on special rates and guarantees posed serious dilemmas in certain industries, such as auto parts and assembly. The railroads were reluctant to invest in special oversized auto-carrying railcars or in enlarged track clearances to accommodate the cars without volume guarantees from the manufacturers. The auto manufacturers, in turn, were unwilling to organize their production and distribution processes around rail delivery without service guarantees from the railroads.

The solution was often an informal handshake agreement between the auto maker's traffic department and the railroad's marketing division, sometimes backed up with a brief memo in the files. Because these agreements, whether oral or written, were illegal, they depended greatly on goodwill and trust. In the words of one researcher, the process placed "a high premium on personnel with long memories, sound hearts, and a penchant for looking both ways before crossing the street."[9]

The case for deregulation finally became dramatic and compelling when major eastern railroads started to go bankrupt. In 1958 the threatened collapse of the New York, New Haven and Hartford Railroad finally convinced Congress to pass legislation stripping state regulatory agencies of their power to force interstate railroads to continue to provide unprofitable commuter services. In 1970 Congress relieved the railroads of their obligation to provide intercity passenger service as well and created a government corporation, Amtrak, to take over that responsibility.

It took the bankruptcy of Penn Central Railroad later in 1970, however, to stimulate a concerted effort to limit the ICC's powers. The Penn Central had been formed only two years earlier when the two largest eastern railroads, the Pennsylvania and the New York Central, merged in the hope that the combined carrier could cut costs by eliminating duplicate facilities. The Penn Central was so important to the economy of the Northeast that the federal government felt compelled to take over the collapsed carrier and keep it operating, at least temporarily, as a public corporation called the Consolidated Rail Corporation (Conrail). Congress was anxious to avoid being forced to take over other carriers as well, and the search for measures that would improve the industry's profitability began in earnest. By that time, both academic studies and practical experience strongly suggested that the industry would have little chance of recovery unless regulatory restraints were loosened.

The Replacement of ICC Regulation with Private Contracts

Congress limited some of the ICC's powers in 1976, but the key reforms were passed in 1980. The central innovation was to make contracts between railroads and shippers legal, exempt from ICC regulation, and confidential. The contracts were motivated partly by the desire to give the railroads more pricing flexibility but primarily to reduce the potential for monopoly abuse and particularly the problem of captive shippers. A shipper is usually considered captive to a railroad if it invests in a valuable and immobile facility served by only that railroad and if there is no competition from other modes of transportation or from other products or locations. Similarly, a railroad can be captive to a shipper if the railroad invests in improving a line that is needed primarily for that shipper's traffic. Before deregulation, the ICC protected the shipper from opportunistic behavior by the railroad and vice versa. After deregulation, long-term contracts would protect them.

ICC review of rates was retained as a safety valve and to aid in the transition to the new contractual system, since initially there would be shippers and railroads with investments that were vulnerable but not protected by contracts. ICC intervention was limited in three ways, however, so as to discourage unnecessary meddling. First, the agency could review a rate only if it exceeded 180 percent of a railroad's variable costs; rates below that threshold were presumed to be reasonable. Second, the ICC had to determine that the shipper was captive to the railroad. Finally, the ICC had to determine each year whether the railroads were making adequate returns and to take their financial needs into consideration. If a railroad's returns were inadequate, the ICC would presumably allow it greater latitude to charge high rates.

In 1995 Congress replaced the ICC with a new Surface Transportation Board (STB), but this was largely a symbolic gesture. The STB was housed administratively in the U.S. Department of Transportation, but otherwise the board members enjoyed the same protections to promote independent decision making that the old ICC commissioners had. The STB also retained the ICC's powers to approve entry, exit, and mergers; to calculate whether railroads were earning an adequate return; and to review tariffs that exceeded the 180 percent threshold.

Changes in Tariffs, Traffic, and Profitability

The railroad industry experienced a dramatic turnaround after deregulation. The timing suggests that deregulation deserves much of the credit, although there has been no careful study to disentangle all the various possible causes. Total ton miles of rail traffic had begun to recover slowly in the two decades before deregulation, largely because U.S agricultural exports grew during this period and coal shipments increased after the oil price run-ups of the early 1970s (see Table 8.1). Average freight rates per ton mile were declining in real terms, however, and profits were at abysmal levels.

Table 8.1 Performance of the U.S. railroad industry, 1947–2001

Year	Ton miles carried (billions)	Containers and trailers carried (thousands)	Freight revenue per ton mile (in 2000 cents)	Average haul length in miles	Miles of right-of-way	Ton miles per employee hour
Before deregulation						
1947	655	N.A.	N.A.	479	214,486	191
1960	572	N.A.	6.56	461	207,334	327
1970	765	2,363	5.26	515	196,479	584
1980	919	3,059	5.38	616	164,822	863
After deregulation						
1981	910	3,151	5.45	626	162,160	906
1982	798	3,397	5.19	629	159,123	927
1983	826	4,090	4.85	641	155,879	1,072
1984	921	4,566	4.63	645	151,998	1,167
1985	877	4,591	4.42	664	145,764	1,196
1986	868	4,997	4.15	664	140,061	1,302
1987	944	5,504	3.77	688	132,220	1,531
1988	996	5,780	3.63	697	127,555	1,683
1989	1,014	5,987	3.43	723	124,236	1,776
1990	1,034	6,207	3.29	726	119,758	1,901
1991	1,039	6,246	3.10	751	116,626	2,020
1992	1,109	6,628	3.02	762	113,056	2,176
1993	1,067	7,157	2.87	794	110,425	2,280
1994	1,201	8,128	2.78	817	109,332	2,509
1995	1,306	7,936	2.62	843	108,264	2,746
1996	1,356	8,143	2.52	842	105,779	2,965
1997	1,349	8,698	2.52	851	102,128	2,973
1998	1,377	8,773	2.43	835	100,570	2,955
1999	1,433	8,908	2.33	835	99,430	3,139
2000	1,466	9,176	2.25	843	99,250	3,293
2001	1,495	8,935	2.19	858	97,817	3,516
Percentage change						
1960–1980	+61%	N.A.	−18%	+27%	−21%	+164%
1980–2001	+63%	+192%	−59%	+39%	−41%	+307%

Source: Association of American Railroads, *Railroad Facts,* various editions. Revenue per ton mile is deflated using the GDP deflator from Council of Economic Advisers, *Economic Report of the President* (Washington, D.C.: U.S. Government Printing Office, 2002), p. 234.

Note: N.A.–Not available. Statistics for class 1 railroads only.

The growth in traffic and the fall in freight rates continued after deregulation, but for the first time in many decades railroad profits approached the levels earned in other industries. Ton miles carried increased by 63 percent between 1980 and 2001, about the same rate as the previous two decades. Freight rates per ton mile declined by 59 percent in real terms, however, three times as fast as before. The falling rates helped the railroads begin to recapture some traffic from trucks, as indicated by the 192 percent increase in containers and trailers loaded. And profits increased despite lower freight rates largely because the railroads managed to increase their average length of haul, cut back on underutilized track, and increase labor productivity. The railroads' average return on equity increased from less than 3 percent in the years 1971–1980, to 5.3 percent in 1980–1989, to 10.7 percent in 1989–1997.[10] The STB viewed the returns as still inadequate to attract capital, but skeptics noted that the railroads were investing and that their share prices were rising faster than many stock market averages.[11]

By the end of the second decade, however, deregulation was being criticized for not providing enough protection to captive shippers. Rates had gone down on average, but not all shippers had benefited equally, and some were pressing Congress to strengthen the STB's powers to control rates, effectively reintroducing regulation. These complaints gained added impetus with the consolidation of the industry into four very large railroads.

Railroad Mergers

From a public policy perspective, mergers involve a balancing of potential costs and benefits. A merger can allow the industry to cut costs and improve service, but it can also reduce competition and allow the industry to charge higher prices. The most desirable mergers are those that offer strong prospects for cost cutting and service improvements and minimal risks of reduced competition. In this regard, transport economists distinguish mergers of carriers whose routes connect end-to-end from mergers of carriers whose routes are parallel to one another.

End-to-end mergers are usually deemed desirable because they reduce costs and improve service without reducing competition. End-to-end mergers do not reduce the number of carriers a shipper can choose from, as long as rail portals (interchange points) remain open. Moreover, end-to-end mergers can produce important cost savings and service improvements if there is a large volume of through traffic. Transferring a car from one railroad to another typically adds a day to the journey and is a major source of unreliability. Railroads that interchange high volumes of traffic can coordinate their schedules and take other steps to make transfers easier, but, as the head of one railroad explained, "There is nothing that is a substitute for one philosophy of management, one agenda, one operating plan, and a single implementation effort."[12]

Parallel mergers, by contrast, are usually more problematic. Parallel mergers can generate substantial savings by eliminating duplicate lines and facilities. For example, the merged railroad can pick the most level and direct route between two points and concentrate enough traffic on it to justify improvements and to exploit economies of traffic density. But parallel mergers also eliminate shipper choices and thus raise competitive concerns.

During the 1960s and 1970s, mergers diminished the number of Class I railroads from around seventy to around forty. Most of these mergers were parallel, like the Penn Central, and motivated primarily by the desire to cut costs. There was relatively little concern about the risk of increased market power at the time, however, because the ICC still tightly controlled railroad tariffs and because policymakers were more preoccupied with preventing bankruptcies than with the risk of monopoly.

After deregulation there were two waves of mergers. Most of these combined end-to-end and parallel elements, with the mixture varying from one merger to the next. The first wave occurred in the early 1980s and, for the most part, was approved enthusiastically by the ICC,[13] although it drew complaints from some shippers and prompted an unsuccessful effort to persuade Congress to reimpose regulation in 1986. The second wave occurred in the 1990s and generated more controversy, because it resulted in the formation of four enormous railroads that together accounted for approximately 90 percent of all rail freight revenues in the United States.[14] Two of the railroads were located west of the Mississippi River and two were to the east. In the West, the Burlington Northern and Santa Fe (BNSF) was created when those two railroads merged in 1995. The Union Pacific (UP) responded in 1996 by absorbing the last remaining large railroad in the West: the Southern Pacific. In the East, there had been three large railroads until 1996, when the Norfolk Southern (NS) and the CSX agreed to divide up Conrail, which by then had become profitable and was once again in private hands. By the end of the twentieth century, the industry seemed to be on the threshold of a third merger wave. Although the STB discouraged an initial proposal in 2000, the expectation was that the western and eastern railroads would eventually try to pair up, leaving the country with two transcontinental railroads.[15]

The Effectiveness of Private Contracts

Contracts seem to have been reasonably effective in protecting captive shippers from monopoly abuse even as the railroad industry became increasingly concentrated. On the basis of a survey conducted in 1998, when there were only four major railroads, Curtis Grimm and Clifford Winston estimate that only about 20 percent of all rail freight traffic met the STB's definition of captivity.[16] Most of the captive traffic was in coal, grains, and chemicals.

The percentage of captive shippers would have been higher had not the STB insisted on track rights as a condition for approving many of the mergers of the 1990s. In the BNSF merger, for example, UP was granted rights to use BNSF track in Kansas and Nebraska so that grain shippers in those states who had been served by both the Burlington Northern and the Santa Fe would still have a choice between two carriers. Similarly, when UP merged with Southern Pacific, the STB required that UP grant BNSF track rights to the many points that had been served by both UP and Southern Pacific.[17] The percentage of shippers served by only one railroad should not be affected significantly if future mergers create two transcontinental railroads, moreover, because any transcontinental mergers would be almost purely end-to-end.[18]

Even where a shipper is served by only one railroad, competition from other modes, locations, or products is reasonably common. Trucks can be an effective alternative for shippers of high-value, time-sensitive goods, and barges can often be used by shippers of bulk commodities. And many shippers, such as coal mines or chemical plants, face such strong competition from other plants and locations that the railroads cannot raise their rates too high without losing the shipment. In the cases of some large shippers, the "competition" may be internal to the company. A large chemical or auto company may have plants in several states and the option of shifting production from one site to another depending upon relative freight rates.

Captive shippers have two routes of relief: one private and contractual and the other public and regulatory. Most captive shippers rely on the contractual approach. In 1998, for example, 94 percent of the traffic classified as captive moved under contracts.[19] The contracts averaged two and one-half years, although some were for as long as ten years. But, surprisingly, much of the traffic that is not captive moves under contract rates as well. Indeed, over 70 percent of all rail traffic in 1998 moved under contract rates.[20]

Contracts were attractive to noncaptive as well as to captive shippers, because they generated new opportunities for cost savings and service improvements. Informal contracts had been used occasionally under regulation, but now that contracts were legal their use exploded.[21] Negotiating the contractual arrangements between themselves, without interference or intervention by regulatory authorities, shippers and their railroads could identify and exploit efficiency opportunities that were not easily achievable within a regulatory system. Shippers and the railroad negotiate trade-offs at many different margins, such as volumes generated, volumes guaranteed, seasonality of shipment, need for and availability of rolling stock, speed of delivery, reliability of delivery, and so on. A power plant might agree to receive a 100-car train of coal every five days and unload it in twenty-four hours, for example, because this commitment allows the railroad to increase crew and equipment productivity and offer significantly lower rates.

Indeed, the individually tailored adjustments and cost savings made possible by contracts probably contributed importantly to the railroads' ability to dramatically cut rates while restoring industry profitability since deregulation. Contracts represented a big change from the old regulatory regime, under which equity considerations often required that roughly similar rates be charged for broad classes of service. The ICC found equity easier to achieve by homogenizing services rather than by allowing individually negotiated adaptations.

For the captive shipper, the alternative to a contract is to appeal to the STB. The STB can decide if a tariff is roughly fair or not, usually compromising between the two final offers made by the parties involved. Clearly the scope, if not the possibility, of negotiating the various marginal valuations and costs of different service characteristics is greatly complicated, perhaps even foreclosed, once the STB intervenes. As a result, a captive shipper may be less interested in using the regulatory option to obtain a rate than to strengthen its negotiating position when the contract comes up for renewal. In effect, the threat to exploit regulatory relief becomes to the captive shipper what competitive relief is to the noncaptive shipper. In the long run, however, the best negotiating threat for the captive shipper is to cease operations at the captive site unless treated fairly enough so that it can be competitive with noncaptive shippers.

Contract disputes seem to be much rarer between railroads and shippers than between cities and concessionaires, although hard data on dispute frequency are lacking. A study by Paul Joskow of similar contracts suggests that disputes between railroads and shippers are probably limited and fairly readily resolved.[22] Joskow examined contracts between coal mines and electric utilities written in the 1970s. These contracts established minimum tonnages that the utilities guaranteed to pay for (regardless of whether they took delivery), the price per ton in the initial year, and a formula for adjusting the price over the life of the contract (typically for ten years or more). The price adjustment formulas were designed to track changes in the various costs of mining coal. These formulas worked well until the early 1980s, when the spot price of coal collapsed because of demand rather than cost factors. Very few utilities reneged on their contracts, even thought they were paying considerably more for coal than the market price. After a number of years many of the contracts that had not expired were voluntarily renegotiated, with the utilities often promising to take more coal in return for a lower price. The lack of acrimony appears to be due to a combination of factors, including the effectiveness of the threat of legal sanctions, the fact that the contracts were relatively short so the situation would not last many years, and the opportunity for the utilities to offer some compensation (in higher volumes) in the event of renegotiation.

As a group, captive shippers appear to be better protected under deregulation than they were before, although perhaps not as well as they would be if they were not captive. On the basis of their 1998 survey, Grimm and Winston estimate that rail rates were 21 percent higher for captive than noncaptive shippers, controlling for such factors as commodity type, length of haul, shipment volume, and corridor.[23] To put this in perspective, average rail rates fell by 47 percent between 1980 and 1999. Even allowing for the fact that the 47 percent figure is not adjusted for commodity mix and length of haul, the typical captive shipper probably paid less in 1998 than he paid under the old system of ICC regulation, although perhaps not as much less as his noncaptive peers.

Despite this favorable overall record, however, some captive shippers remained unhappy. One problem was that small captive shippers seemed less well protected than large captive shippers, largely because the transaction costs of pursuing either contract or regulatory relief are relatively high for them. A second problem was that captive shippers were less and less impressed with comparisons to regulatory regimes of twenty years ago. The fact that captive shippers were paying more than their noncaptive colleagues seemed far more salient than the fact that they were paying less than they might have under the old regulatory regime.

By the end of the 1990s complaints by captive shippers were becoming a rallying cry for efforts to reimpose regulation. Consumers United for Rail Equity (CURE), a group backed by coal and electric utility interests, was lobbying Congress for more protection for captive shippers. The Alliance for Rail Competition (ARC), which represented agricultural, manufacturing, chemical, and other trade associations, was lobbying not just for pricing constraints but also for the more radical idea of forcing the railroads to provide open access to all of their tracks. Open access would likely require some form of regulation, particularly to protect the rights of the remaining small railroads or of shippers who wanted to operate their own trains.[24]

The STB responded to shipper pressure in December 1999 by eliminating the railroad's defense that a shipper should not be considered captive if it faced competition from other products or locations. From then on a shipper would be presumed captive if it did not have a choice of railroads and if there were no barge or truck alternatives. In October 2000, the STB also proposed tougher guidelines for the review of future mergers. In the past, the STB had required merger applicants to "cure" specific reductions in competition that a merger might bring. If the merger reduced the number of railroads serving a point from two to one, for example, the STB would typically expect the applicants to grant track rights to a third railroad, so that shippers at the location would still have a choice of two independent railroads. Under the proposed guidelines, applicants would have to demonstrate that the proposed merger would "enhance" competition, presumably by granting rights to points that were not affected by the merger. Although shippers applauded the proposal, the railroads feared that the effect would be to encourage rent-seeking behavior on the part of the shippers and to reintroduce regulation in the form of controls over the prices that railroads could charge for the access to their tracks.

The Airline Experience

The Rise and Fall of Regulation

Regulation was formally imposed on the airline industry in 1938, when the Congress established the Civil Aeronautics Board (CAB). The CAB was created primarily to nurture the infant airline industry rather than to protect its passengers from monopoly abuse.[25] Nevertheless, the new agency was given wide-ranging authority to intervene in airline decisions, including the authority to set fares; allocate routes; and approve entry, exit, and mergers.

The airline industry never declined under regulation, so most of the early criticism of the CAB came from the academic community rather than from the industry. By the 1960s scholars were arguing that the CAB was excessively concerned with ensuring that the industry was financially strong enough to buy the most modern planes and to extend service to small communities.[26] The CAB often awarded lucrative new routes to the financially weaker carriers, a strategy that was designed to avoid bankruptcies but that also seemed to reward poor management and create inefficient route networks. Fares were thought to be too high, as evidenced by the fact that the intrastate fares in California and Texas, which were not under the CAB's control, were lower.[27] High fares often resulted in wasteful service rather than in large airline profits, moreover, because airlines on routes served by multiple carriers often competed for passengers by offering in-flight amenities—such as fancy meals and even piano bars—that passengers did not value much.[28]

By the 1970s a few airlines began to feel that the CAB's tight controls over routes and fares hampered the industry's ability to respond to economic problems and opportunities.[29] The CAB set fares using a cost-based formula called the "standard industry fare level," or SIFL. Discounts off the SIFL were sometimes allowed, but only with restrictions such as advance purchase and Saturday night stays. The energy crisis of the early 1970s greatly increased airline costs since fuel is a key input, but it also caused a worldwide recession and cut airline traffic. The airlines were left with serious excess capacity, and some companies wished they had more flexibility to respond with pricing and other strategies.

Airline deregulation began informally in 1976, when a forward-looking CAB chairman, John Robson, began to relax controls over fares and routes. The big changes came after 1978, under Chairman Alfred Kahn, when Congress passed a law immediately eliminating most controls and phasing out the CAB. In 1984 the CAB was closed and the U.S. Department of Transportation assumed the CAB's few remaining functions, most notably its authority to review mergers and other interairline agreements and to negotiate international aviation treaties. The regulation of airline safety was not affected by the reforms and remained the responsibility of the Federal Aviation Administration, a separate agency within the U.S. Department of Transportation.

The architects of airline deregulation did not perceive much need for promoting private contracts or providing some residual form of tariff regulation, as in the railroad industry. Most observers thought the airline industry had characteristics that would ensure intense competition. The auto had long been a fairly effective competitor on short distance routes. The economies of flying larger aircraft were not so great that most busy routes couldn't support multiple departures by reasonable size planes. Finally, on routes where autos were not effective competition and which were served by only one airline, the mere threat of entry by another airline might be sufficient to make the incumbent show restraint. Airline routes were often cited as an example of a "contestable" market in that most airline assets were highly mobile and could be redeployed quickly from one market to another.[30] If the sole carrier serving a route raised its fares significantly above costs, it was likely to soon be joined by a competitor.

Improvements in Industry Performance

The overall performance of the airline industry improved significantly with deregulation, although not to the same extent as the performance of the railroad industry. Air fares had fallen and air travel had grown rapidly in the two decades prior to deregulation, in part the result of the widespread introduction of jets in the 1960s and wide-bodied aircraft in the 1970s (see Table 8.2). Fares continued to fall and travel continued to increase rapidly after de-

Table 8.2 Performance of the U.S. airline industry, 1950–2001

Year	Passengers enplaned (millions)	Passenger miles carried (billions)	Revenue per passenger mile (in 2000 cents)	Average trip length (miles)	Load factor (%)	Estimated return on investment (%)
Before deregulation						
1950	19.2	10.2	40.9	431	60.8	N.A.
1960	57.9	38.9	31.6	671	59.3	3.3
1970	169.9	131.7	21.3	775	49.6	1.5
1975	205.1	162.8	20.3	794	53.7	2.5
1978	274.7	226.8	18.4	825	61.5	13.0
After deregulation						
1979	316.7	262.0	17.8	827	63.0	7.0
1980	296.9	255.2	20.6	860	59.0	5.8
1981	286.0	248.9	21.1	870	58.6	5.3
1982	294.1	259.6	19.0	883	59.0	2.7
1983	318.6	281.8	18.0	885	60.6	5.9
1984	344.7	305.1	18.2	885	59.2	10.0
1985	382.0	336.4	16.9	881	61.4	10.0
1986	418.9	366.5	15.5	875	60.3	5.0
1987	447.7	404.5	15.3	903	62.3	7.2
1988	454.6	423.3	15.8	931	63.0	11.0
1989	453.7	432.7	16.0	954	63.2	6.3
1990	465.6	457.9	15.8	984	62.4	−6.0
1991	452.3	448.0	15.2	990	63.0	−0.7
1992	475.1	478.6	14.6	1,007	64.0	−9.0
1993	488.5	489.7	14.9	1,002	64.0	−0.4
1994	528.8	519.2	14.1	982	66.2	5.2
1995	547.8	540.4	14.1	987	67.0	11.9
1996	581.2	578.7	13.9	996	69.3	11.5
1997	599.1	605.6	13.8	1,011	70.3	14.7
1998	612.9	618.1	13.6	1,008	70.7	12.0
1999	636.0	651.6	13.2	1,025	71.0	11.1
2000	666.2	692.8	13.5	1,040	72.4	6.4
2001	622.1	651.7	12.1	1,047	70.0	−6.9
Percentage change						
1960–1978	+374%	+483%	−42%	+24%	+15%	
1978–2000	+143%	+205%	−27%	+26%	+18%	

Source: Air Transport Association, *Air Transport: The Annual Report of the Scheduled U.S. Airline Industry,* various years. Revenue per passenger mile is deflated using the GDP deflator from Council of Economic Advisers, *Economic Report of the President* (Washington, D.C.: U.S. Government Printing Office, 2002), p. 324.

regulation, even though the pace of technological change in the industry seemed to slow somewhat.

It is not obvious how much of the fare decline in the 1980s and 1990s was attributable to deregulation and how much would have occurred anyway with technological and other improvements. The best available estimates are by Steven Morrison and Clifford Winston, who compare the average fares with the likely regulated fares calculated by applying an updated version of the CAB's old SIFL formula. They estimate that the average fare savings climbed from 16 percent in the first year of deregulation to 31 percent in 1982, and then hovered around 25 percent through the 1990s.[31]

Service quality increased as well, though not by all measures. Planes became more crowded as airlines reduced the cost per passenger in part by filling more seats. Load factors (the industry's term for the percentage of seats occupied) increased from the high 50s typical during the years of CAB regulation to the mid 60s and low 70s in the years after (see Table 8.2). Flight times increased slightly, because of growing congestion at the nation's airports and airways. Passengers were also more likely to have to connect flights to complete their trips, as the airlines began to rely on hub-and-spoke route networks. Persons traveling on discount fares often had to put up with the inconvenience of fare restrictions, such as advance purchase, cancellation penalties, or Saturday night stays. And some small communities saw their jet service replaced with smaller, slower, and noisier turboprops.

The decline in some quality measures was offset, at least in part, by increases in others. The frequency of service between city pairs increased significantly, which was of particular benefit to business travelers with busy schedules. Although there were more connections, most of them were on the same airline rather than between airlines, so that the connections were tighter and anxieties about making them lower. Small communities may have lost jet services but their prop replacements flew more often and at more convenient times.

As a whole, travelers appear to be substantially better off. Morrison and Winston estimate that the flying public gained $18.4 billion from airline deregulation in 1993. Of this, $12.4 billion were the savings in lower fares and the remaining $6.0 billion were benefits from higher service quality. In the case of service quality, they argue that the values travelers placed on added frequencies and on-line connections far outweighed the losses suffered from higher load factors, fare restrictions, and added connections.[32]

Whether the airline companies were better off or not is harder to determine. Airline profitability has always been highly cyclical, since both business and pleasure traffic are very sensitive to the ups and downs of the overall economy. Despite persistent concerns that the industry might not be able to attract capital, it has always been able to do so, though not necessarily at the bottom of a business cycle. This situation did not seem to change much after deregulation. Air travel and profits declined precipitously after the attacks on the World Trade Center and the Pentagon in September 2001, but traffic soon recovered and the familiar cycles of profitability seemed likely to resume as long as similar acts of air terrorism could be prevented.[33]

As in the case of the railroads, the generally happy story hid some problems. Although the average traveler was better off, some consumer groups did not feel they had benefited as much—particularly business travelers and travelers who resided in a dozen cities where most air service was provided by a single carrier.[34] As in railroads, these concerns were heightened by increasing concentration in the industry.

Changes in Airline Industry Structure

The airline industry can be divided into two groups: the "old guard" of major carriers that existed before deregulation and the new airlines that have entered the business since deregulation. Immediately after deregulation, in the late 1970s and early 1980s, the old guard carriers were largely preoccupied with developing their hub-and-spoke route networks, with some smaller airlines disappearing quietly in the process.[35] A wave of important mergers also occurred later, in the mid-1980s, heavily motivated by the desire of carriers to develop stronger hubs or a more comprehensive national network.[36] At the end of the decade, other carriers were eliminated by bankruptcy, most notably Eastern and Pan Am (both in 1990).[37] Antitrust authorities discouraged United from buying US Airways in 2001, but American had been allowed to buy the ailing TWA earlier that year, reducing the old guard to six important airlines plus a handful of minor players. Of the six, three (United, American, and Delta) were very large and three (Northwest, Continental, and US Airways) were somewhat smaller but still national in scope and with important international routes.[38] All six were badly hurt by the falloff in airline traffic after the terrorist attacks on New York and Washington in 2001. US Airways and United declared bankruptcy in 2002, although analysts expected both to survive, albeit somewhat scaled down.

While the old guard has consolidated, the new entrants have had mixed success. Only one of the fifty-eight new companies that entered the scheduled airline business between 1978 and 1990 survived into the next millennium.[39] A new crop of start-up carriers appeared during the 1990s, but the pace of new entry slowed after 1996 when a plane of one new airline crashed and all aboard died.[40]

Most of the new entrants compete with the old guard by offering lower fares and no-frills service, but with the exception of Southwest Airlines, this strategy has not been successful in developing a large carrier.[41] Southwest technically should not be considered a new entrant, although it had avoided CAB regulation by operating only intrastate routes in Texas prior to deregulation. Southwest achieves extraordinary productivity from its aircraft and crews by using only one type of aircraft, avoiding congested major airports in favor of secondary airports, and specializing in medium- or short-haul direct flights instead of developing a hub-and-spoke network. By the end of the 1990s, the low-fare, new-entrant airlines accounted for approximately 20 percent of the passengers carried in the United States, and approximately two-thirds of those passengers were carried by Southwest alone.[42]

The consolidation of the industry has meant a decline in direct head-to-head competition between airlines. Table 8.3 combines figures from two studies to show the percentage of city pairs served by three or more carriers from 1979 to 1989 and the percentage of passengers on city pairs with three or more carriers in 1992 and 1997. The percentage of city pairs with three or more carriers increased from 20 percent in 1979 to 53 percent in 1984 but has declined since. By 1997 the percentage of passengers on routes with three or more carriers had fallen to 35 percent, and the percentage of routes had probably fallen even further (since heavily traveled routes are more likely to have three or more carriers). By the end of the 1990s there were a dozen "dominated" hub airports where either a single airline carried over 50 percent of local passengers or two airlines carried over 60 percent, as shown in Table 8.4.

Table 8.3 City pairs by the number of carriers serving them, 1979–1997

Number of carriers	Percentage of city pairs			Percentage of passengers in city pairs	
	1979	1984	1988–1989	1992	1997
One	N.A.	N.A.	N.A.	18	19
Two	N.A.	N.A.	N.A.	43	46
Three or more	20	53	40	39	35

Sources: The data for 1979–1989 are from Transportation Research Board, *Winds of Change: Domestic Air Transport since Deregulation* (Washington, D.C.: National Academy of Sciences Press, 1991) p. 106, and the data for 1992 and 1997 are from Transportation Research Board, *Entry and Competition in the U.S. Airline Industry: Issues and Opportunities* (Washington, D.C.: National Academy of Sciences Press, 1999), pp. 68–71. Used with permission of the Transportation Research Board, National Research Council, Washington, D.C.

Note: Only carriers with at least a 10 percent market share in the city pair are counted, since with a lower share they are unlikely to be effective competitors. N.A.–Not available.

Table 8.4 Hub airports dominated by one or two carriers

Airport	Dominant carrier	Dominant carriers' 1997 percentage share of	
		Enplanements	Flights
Atlanta	Delta	80	61
Charlotte	US Airways	92	89
Chicago O'Hare	United and American	47 and 34	39 and 31
Cincinnati	Delta	94	76
Dallas–Fort Worth	American	66	52
Denver	United	69	57
Detroit	Northwest	78	69
Memphis	Northwest	78	40
Minneapolis–St. Paul	Northwest	80	69
Pittsburgh	US Airways	90	78
St. Louis	TWA	71	54
Salt Lake City	Delta	77	66

Note: Dominance is defined as a single carrier having over 60 percent of emplanements or two carriers having over 80 percent combined.

Sources: Transportation Research Board, *Entry and Competition in the U.S. Airline Industry: Issues and Opportunities* (Washington, D.C.: National Academy of Sciences Press, 1999), p. 74, used with permission of the Transportation Research Board, National Research Council, Washington, D.C.; shares from Federal Aviation Administration data as reported by Don H. Pickrell, "Air Fare Premiums at Hub Airports: A Review of the Evidence," Volpe Center, U.S. Department of Transportation, draft, February 18, 2000, table 1.

The Dispersion of Fares

Considerable attention has been devoted to the question of whether the growing concentration in the airline industry has harmed some groups of passengers. The studies are not conclusive, but they suggest a pattern similar to that in railroads: some passengers enjoy fewer benefits from deregulation than others, but even they are still probably better off than they would have been under the old regime.

One piece of evidence that suggests a possible unequal sharing of the benefits of deregulation is that the dispersion between the lowest and highest fares has grown enormously. Before deregulation discounts rarely exceeded 25 percent off the standard coach fare. By 1992, as Table 8.5 shows, the 10th percentile fare (that is, the fare 10 percent of passengers pay less than) was only half the median fare and one-quarter to one-fifth the 90th and 95th percentile fares. By 1998 the gap had widened further so that the 90th and 95th percentile fares, which are typically paid by business people traveling at the

Table 8.5 Dispersion of airline coach fares, 1992–1998

Year and length of flight	Fares by percentile (median = 100)					
	10th	25th	50th	75th	90th	95th
Short haul (750 miles or less)						
1992	44	68	100	150	200	250
1995	46	71	100	150	250	300
1998	47	67	100	170	270	330
Medium haul (751–1,500 miles)						
1992	50	68	100	150	210	250
1995	65	77	100	150	250	300
1998	60	75	100	140	270	370
Long haul (over 1,500 miles)						
1992	50	67	100	140	210	240
1995	65	80	100	140	260	330
1998	56	77	100	150	290	400

Source: Transportation Research Board, *Entry and Competition in the U.S. Airline Industry: Issues and Opportunities* (Washington, D.C.: National Academy of Sciences Press, 1999), p. 31. Reproduced with permission of the Transportation Research Board, National Research Council, Washington, D.C.

Note: Excludes frequent flyer tickets.

last minute, were three to four times the median fare and six to eight times the 10th percentile fares.

Fare dispersion is often taken as a sign of market power, since charging some customers higher markups is easier if the firm does not have to worry about being undercut by a competitor. But fare dispersion may reflect cost differentials or the presence of joint costs rather than a lack of competition. The higher fares commonly charged for travel during peak periods or for last-minute reservations, for example, are based at least in part on higher costs. It is expensive for airlines to maintain the extra planes and crews needed to serve peak hours of the day or seasons of the year, and to hold some seats empty for last-minute travelers instead of releasing them to passengers searching for discount fares.[43]

Airlines (and railroads) also may be forced to charge some customers higher markups in order to recover joint or fixed costs. Joint costs can occur when a firm uses the same inputs to produce several different types of service. An example might be a flight to an airline's hub carrying travelers bound for many different cities. Much of the flight's costs can be directly attributed to the different destinations served through the hub, since the airline could use a smaller and cheaper plane if any one destination were dropped. But reducing the number of destinations may not affect certain station and overhead costs of the flight, and the costs per seat mile are typically higher on a small plane than on a large one. If such joint or fixed costs exist, the airline must charge travelers to some destinations more than their directly attributable costs if it is to survive. And these differential markups would persist even if the airline industry was competitive.[44]

Empirical studies indicate that airline price dispersion is due to both market power and cost factors. For example, the most careful study to date found higher price dispersion on routes served with two or three carriers rather than with one, which suggests that the introduction of competition forces more cost-based differentials in prices.[45] But that same study also found higher dispersion in fares to airports with severe capacity limitations, which indicates that limitations on competition encourage dispersion as well. In addition, the study used data from 1986, which was close to the high point of competition within the industry when measured by the numbers of routes served by multiple carriers (Table 8.3). But fare dispersion also increased during the 1990s, even as the level of competition seemed to be declining (Table 8.5).[46]

These patterns suggest that price dispersion increased for different reasons at different times. In the 1980s, price dispersion may have increased primarily because the relaxation of CAB fare controls and the introduction of competition forced carriers to introduce more discount fares based on costs. In the 1990s, however, dispersion may have continued to increase because competition subsided a bit and carriers became more sophisticated at exploring differences in passengers' willingness to pay.

Other studies have concluded that passengers traveling to and from dominated hubs pay premium fares. In an early and widely reported study, for example, the General Accounting Office (GAO) estimated that during the 1985–1989 period fares at fifteen dominated hubs averaged 27 percent higher than fares at thirty-eight comparison airports.[47] The airlines argued that the GAO's comparison was unfair, because the cities picked for hubs have a high proportion of short-haul and business traffic that is more expensive per passenger mile to serve. Indeed, later studies showed that if one controlled for trip length the premium was cut in half, to about 15 percent. Statistics on the percentage of business travelers by route are not readily available, but controlling for service qualities normally associated with business travelers cut the premium even further.[48] In addition, if the presence of Southwest at some airports is also controlled for, the hub premium disappears for all but a few airports.[49]

Finally, since the early days of deregulation studies have consistently shown that the number of carriers on a route affects the fares they charge. In other words, the airline market is not perfectly contestable, and the threat of entry is not as powerful as actual competition. Estimates of how much additional carriers reduce fares vary from one study to another, but an increase in the number of carriers from two to three can reduce fares by 4 to 21 percent.[50] By the late 1990s, the presence of Southwest on a route seemed to be particularly important in holding fares down. According to one estimate, entry by Southwest reduced fares on a route by roughly 20 percent and the effects of Southwest accounted for 40 percent of the total fare savings attributable to deregulation in 1998.[51]

Barriers to Entry and Competition

The argument that market power contributes to price dispersion is strengthened by the presence of several barriers that are thought to discourage competitors from entering airline markets and undercutting prices. One suspected barrier is the hub-and-spoke networks that airlines have developed since deregulation. A hub-and-spoke system allows an airline to provide frequent and low-cost service between many city pairs by concentrating traffic bound for many destinations on each spoke. An airline that wishes to serve a city pair served by a hubbing carrier has the unattractive choice of either building its own hub or charging a lower fare. Building a hub is a major investment, but without it the challenger will find it difficult to offer as frequent service at a reasonable cost and may be forced to drop its fares to attract traffic. The fact that hub fare premiums do not appear to be based entirely on costs suggests that hubs may serve as barriers.

A second barrier believed important is constraints on access to airports. For a variety of reasons—congestion, noise, environmental concerns, and so on—the Federal Aviation Administration limits the number of takeoff and landing "slots" per hour at four U.S. airports (Kennedy, LaGuardia, O'Hare, and Reagan National). The large incumbent airlines own the rights to most of these slots, and attempts to force them to transfer the slots to challengers or to create a market in slots have been only partially successful. In April 2000, Congress passed a law calling for the eventual elimination of the slot constraints and exempting, in the interim, flights to small and nonhub airports using aircraft with seventy or fewer seats. By September 2000 the airlines had used the interim exemption to add so many flights at La Guardia that the airport was close to gridlock. The FAA responded by temporarily imposing limits on the exempt flights while it called for public comment on alternative means of dealing with congestion at La Guardia. In the aftermath of the terrorist attack of September 11, 2001, the FAA extended the deadlines for public comment and for the removal of the temporary limits to 2002 and 2004, respectively. In addition, at many airports the major airlines have long-term leases on most of the gates and have resisted efforts to force them to lease gates to challengers at reasonable rates.

A third suspect barrier is airline marketing practices, such as frequent flyer programs and travel agent incentives. Frequent flyer programs give airlines with large networks a competitive advantage, since it is easier to accumulate enough mileage to receive a free flight or special preference at check-in or boarding by traveling on an airline with an extensive route network. An extensive route network also gives the traveler a wider choice of destinations when he redeems his free ticket. And business travelers may be less sensitive to the fares charged if their employer pays for the ticket but the employee retains the frequent flyer benefits.[52]

Predatory behavior by large airlines against small start-up carriers may also create a barrier, although there is controversy about the prevalence and importance of predation. The usual test of predatory behavior is whether an incumbent responds to entry by dropping its prices below short-run marginal cost. Airline costs and pricing strategies are so complex that applying the test is particularly difficult in this industry. Many economists believe, for example, that the short-run costs should include the higher returns that the incumbent forgoes by diverting more aircraft to fly on the contested route. Measuring these forgone returns can be exceedingly difficult, however. By 1999 the Department of Justice's Antitrust Division had become sufficiently concerned to bring a lawsuit against American Airlines for predation against a start-up airline, but the courts ultimately rejected the charges on the grounds that forgone returns should not be included in calculating American's short-run costs.[53]

Finally, international airline alliances may also reduce competition. During the 1990s, the U.S. Department of Transportation approved antitrust exemptions for a number of agreements that allowed U.S. airlines and foreign carriers to share codes for flights and coordinate schedules and capacity.[54] For example, United and Lufthansa concluded an agreement to coordinate and code share both their flights over the North Atlantic and the feeder flights to their various gateways in the United States and Germany. Participating airlines argue that these alliances will improve connections for traffic originating or terminating beyond the gateway airports. But the danger, of course, is that this type of "coordination" will ultimately be used to reduce effective competition on the main gateway-to-gateway routes. If only a few "world alliances" emerge, furthermore, this may limit the number of major U.S. airlines that are able to survive (since a U.S. airline that is not a member of one of the world alliances will not get as much international feeder traffic).

Collectively, the research on fare patterns and entry barriers suggests that there is some truth to the popular impression that passengers on business trips and those who are traveling to and from dominated airports are not benefiting as much as others. Moreover, actual competition matters, so the effects of past and proposed mergers and the survival of low-cost carriers like Southwest should be a matter of public policy concern.

Nevertheless, as in the case of railroads, it is probably true that even the travelers on business and from dominated hubs are better off because of deregulation. Not all of the observed fare differentials are due to limited competition—a good portion are cost based. If only half of the premium paid by travelers from dominated hubs is due to lack of competition, for example, then these travelers are paying perhaps 10 percent more than other flyers, all else being equal. But this may still be less than before deregulation, since deregulation reduced average fares by 25 percent.

The Emergence of Private Contracts

Private contracts have emerged spontaneously, without government encouragement, as practical remedies to some of the airline industry's competitive shortcomings. Many applications involve large corporations with big travel budgets, with the most obvious being negotiated fare discounts. It is apparently common for an air carrier to agree to give a large corporation a discount of 10 percent off all published fares for travel by its employees, and more if the corporation can offer some kind of volume guarantee in return. These negotiated discounts offset, at least in part, any price discrimination that the airlines attempt to practice against business travel by employees of large corporations.

A second form of private contract involving large corporations is agreements to support new airlines. Sometimes these airlines are designed to break existing monopolies. The most prominent example is ProAir, established in 1997 to fly between Detroit and other nearby business centers such as Pittsburgh, Atlanta, and New York. Local businesses had been complaining that Northwest was charging high fares at its Detroit hub and had driven away at least one start-up airline that attempted to offer service out of Detroit. General Motors, Chrysler, and other large Detroit-based corporations backed ProAir with five-year contracts guaranteeing the airline a minimum amount of travel by employees and their families.[55]

In other cases, local companies and governments in communities with little direct air service have contracted with airlines to add flights to key destinations. These contracts establish a monopoly instead of breaking one, so that it is important that the airline guarantee reasonable fares in return for payments or guarantees by local businesses. Local business in Iowa backed the establishment of Access Air in 1998 with these types of contracts, for example.[56] And AirTran, a new entrant with a growing network in the East, extended service in 2001 and 2002 to Biloxi, Pensacola, Grand Bahamas, Rochester, and Wichita under similar contracts.

Employees of small businesses and individual travelers may enjoy some of the advantages of private contracts through the wider menu of fares and quality options that has developed since airline deregulation. Airlines now offer passengers a wide range of service qualities and pricing options in which, for example, travelers willing to book far ahead or to travel in off-peak times are offered cheaper seats. When passengers select from this menu, they enjoy many of the cost savings of customized service that railroad shippers gain through contracts.

Nevertheless, private contracts seem to be emerging for small business and leisure travelers as well, despite the potential for high transaction costs. One traditional form is a ticket broker who buys blocks of tickets in advance and then resells them at prices lower than those available directly from the airline. The ticket broker often receives a low price because he gives the airline a volume guarantee, much like the large company negotiating a corporate rate does. In this case, however, a portion of the discount the airline offers is shared with small business and individual travelers.

Frequent flyer programs can also be viewed as a form of private contract, and as such are much more important to small business and individual travelers than ticket brokers are. Most programs offer different benefit or status levels, depending upon how many miles or flight segments the passenger traveled on the airline in the previous year. Passengers at elite status levels, usually requiring 25,000 miles or more of travel a year, receive additional frequent flyer credits per mile flown, complimentary upgrades, preferential check-in, and other benefits. In essence these passengers are induced to provide something similar to a volume guarantee, since the airline knows that most of them will try hard to retain elite status for the coming year. In return, the airline reduces the cost of travel by giving these passengers more free flights and upgrades and by saving them time at the check-in counters. Seen in this way, frequent flyer programs are analogous to the volume discounts offered to small consumers by other utilities, such as the telephone calling plans that provide a low rate per minute if a caller agrees in advance to buy a minimum number of minutes per month. Such advance commitments are harder for individual air travelers to make, since the frequency of air travel is less predictable and the cost per trip is high.

This is not to deny that frequent flyer programs may also serve to reduce competition by giving incumbent airlines with large networks an advantage over upstarts. Nevertheless, frequent flyer programs seem tailor-made to offset some of the price discrimination that may be practiced against the small business traveler. It is easier for a small business person who lives near a dominated hub to reach elite status, for example, because he or she can use one airline for most trips. And frequent flyer programs cleverly reduce the transaction costs of negotiating and enforcing contracts with many small customers by offering them the option of several benefit levels and by basing status on travel in the previous year.

The Potential for Private Contracts

The experience of the U.S. railroad and airline industries suggests that private contracts can be an effective, even superior, substitute for government regulation in certain circumstances. Monopoly or market power is a problem in both industries, but contracts seem to have alleviated some of the shortcomings in competition. In the railroad industry, captive shippers pay higher tariffs than noncaptive shippers, but the gap is presumably narrowed by the widespread use of contracts. And captive shippers pay less than they did under regulation, which suggests that contracts, whatever their imperfections, are superior to the old regulatory regime. In airlines, the evidence on price discrimination is a little more ambiguous, and the types of contracts more varied. Nevertheless, certain types of travelers—such as those from dominated hubs—seem to pay more than others, although still less than they did under regulation. And private contracts have emerged spontaneously to provide some protection for those travelers, particularly if they are employees of large corporations or frequent flyers.

Contracts are potentially superior to government regulation because they offer the possibility of tailoring tariffs and services more closely to the needs of the companies and their customers. The facts that some railroads and customers had informal contracts even when the industry was regulated and that most noncaptive shippers use contracts since deregulation testify to the powerful advantages that can be gained by tailoring tariff and service offerings. Even when the ICC was protecting them from monopoly abuse, some shippers still found it worthwhile to employ illegal and unenforceable contracts. And even though noncaptive shippers are by definition not vulnerable to monopoly, they choose to move the majority of their traffic under contract.

The interesting question is whether private contracts could be applied more widely to substitute for regulation. The clearest potential is in infrastructure industries where most customers are large corporations buying in volume, so that the transaction costs of negotiating contracts are small relative to the savings received. U.S. railroad deregulation was helped immensely by the fact that the bulk of the rail traffic was generated by large corporations moving high volumes. In essence, the reforms of 1980 turned back the clock one hundred years to the time when Standard Oil and U.S. Steel negotiated private contracts with the railroads. But private contracts were politically more acceptable in the 1980s than they were in the 1880s because small farmers and businesses have long since abandoned the rail industry. Most small shippers either move their products by truck or sell them to large commodity dealers who assume responsibility for transport. Even so, the designers of railroad deregulation felt compelled to retain limited, standby regulation for the few small shippers that remained.

The experience of the airline industry is particularly intriguing, however, because it suggests that private contracts have potential even in industries with many small customers. More elaborate menus of service offerings provide some of the benefits of private contracts. Small customers can also participate in contracts through intermediaries, such as ticket brokers and freight forwarders, who aggregate the demands of many individuals to support volume commitments that allow carriers to reduce their costs and offer lower prices. The Internet may increase the potential for elaborate menus and intermediaries, moreover, by making it easier to disseminate and collect information. And industries with many small customers may also develop novel and more efficient forms of private contracts, such as the airlines' frequent flyer programs.

The experience of the railroad and airline industries also suggests that contracts should be supplemented by government efforts to maintain competition by reviewing mergers and by moving, where appropriate, to reduce barriers to entry. In the railroads, for example, the STB was probably wise to make the last wave of mergers conditional on offers of track rights, so that shippers who could choose between two railroads before the mergers still had a choice after. In airlines, the government might do more to reduce entry barriers by making gates and landing slots more readily available to challengers, particularly at concentrated hub airports; by maintaining an active antitrust policy against predatory behavior by incumbent airlines; and by being more sensitive to the competitive implications of various international alliances that have recently emerged.[57] Private contracts can be effective in overcoming shortcomings in competition, but the task will be easier if the shortcomings are no larger than necessary.

Without vigilance to promote competition, in fact, deregulation through private contracts may turn out to be a relatively short-lived fad. Memories are short, and after twenty years of railroad and airline deregulation the public is more mindful of the problems of the present than the problems of the past. It is well to remember that those seriously complaining about deregulation's adverse effects in the United States seemingly remain a small minority, say 5 to 10 percent, of all shippers or passengers. But an intensely unhappy minority can be very influential.

So far, the experience of other industries in replacing regulation with private contracts appears to be broadly consistent with that of the U.S. railroads and airlines, although most of the other applications have focused mainly on large customers rather than on small ones. Other countries have adopted the U.S. approach when privatizing their freight railroads, particularly in Latin America. Brazil, Chile, and Mexico all assume that most freight will move under private contracts, for example, although they also have regulatory agencies with standby authority to intervene particularly in the cases of small shippers.[58]

The other major application has been privately negotiated agreements for access to the monopoly components of vertically unbundled water, electricity, telephone, and railroad systems. As explained in more detail in Part III, some countries are experimenting with using private negotiations and contracts instead of conventional government regulation to determine the price and terms for access to the monopoly components of the unbundled system.[59] The results are broadly similar to those seen in U.S. railroads and airlines in that negotiation offers the potential for customized solutions, although the transaction costs can be considerable.

In short, the overall record of private contracts has to be regarded as encouraging, despite some limitations and setbacks. Indeed, private contracts may make more of a contribution by preventing the development of government regulation in the first place than by substituting for established regulatory regimes. Very few industries are perfectly competitive—even industries that seem to have a strong potential for competition, like airlines, often harbor pockets of market or monopoly power. Private contracts have long been used to forestall opportunism of all types in markets, including monopoly. If private long-term contracts were abolished, there might be pressures to regulate far more industries than we do today.

9

Price-Cap Regulation:
The British Water Industry

Price-Cap versus Cost-of-Service Regulation

Price-cap regulation, which is often called incentive regulation, had become the dominant form of discretionary regulation by the end of the twentieth century. Price cap was developed by the British when they began privatizing their utilities in the 1980s, although it has its roots in related incentive schemes that regulators have experimented with since the nineteenth century. Many U.S. and European regulatory agencies have adopted some of the elements of price cap, and price cap is the most common alternative to concession contracts in developing countries, particularly for industries such as telecommunications or electricity, where it is difficult to draft a complete contract.[1]

Price cap was designed as an alternative to the cost-of-service approach practiced at the time by most regulatory agencies in the United States. Cost-of-service regulation is often called rate-of-return regulation. Under this approach, the regulator sets prices so that the firm can cover reasonable costs, including a fair rate of return on its investments.

The British academics and officials who designed price cap believed that cost-of-service regulation provided few efficiency incentives, since a company that cut its costs risked seeing its tariffs cut commensurately. Price cap addresses this shortcoming by conducting price reviews at fixed intervals, usually every five years, and by setting a formula to "cap" the annual price increases allowed between reviews. The typical formula is RPI − X, where RPI is the change in the retail price index and X is the expected rate of productivity improvement in the industry. The commitment to a five-year price cap motivates efficiency improvements because a firm can increase its profits by cutting costs between reviews.

In effect, price cap is a hybrid of the discretionary and contractual approaches to regulation, and it is the contractual elements that are central to its efficiency incentives. Price cap is usually thought of as a form of discretionary regulation, since the regulator has substantial latitude to reset initial prices and the X at each periodic review. Price-cap regulators also typically enjoy the protections from political pressure associated with discretionary regulation, such as appointments to fixed terms. But the regulatory statute or the company license usually prohibits the regulator from changing X between reviews. Moreover, there is an implicit understanding that the regulator will not to try to claw back excess profits or restore losses from the previous review period when he sets initial prices and X for the coming period. The regulator considers past profitability only to estimate the prices the industry needs to attract capital in the coming review period. But changing X between reviews, or setting X so as to recoup past profits or losses, would undermine the scheme's incentives.

Price cap is widely credited with strengthening the efficiency incentives of regulation. The incentives are limited to improvements that pay back in a single review period, and review periods longer than five years are rare because of the economic and political risks of committing to an X for distant years. This means that the regulator must encourage long-lived improvements by other means, such as enforcing related quality standards or mandating specific investment programs. Price cap also introduces opportunities for the firm to mislead the regulator by, for example, delaying the implementation of efficiency improvements until just after a price review. Even with these limitations, most observers regard the efficiency features of price cap as a major advance over cost-of-service regulation.

Empirical studies tend to support the argument that price cap should improve efficiency, although so far most of the evidence is restricted to telephone companies in the United States. The United States provides a natural laboratory for comparing regulatory regimes, since some of the fifty state public utility commissions shifted to price-cap regulation during the 1980s and 1990s while others continued to use the cost-of-service approach. Most studies show that telephone companies in states using price-cap regulation charge lower basic rates and install more modern, cost-saving equipment than companies in states with cost-of-service regulation. The reported differences are often modest and may not apply in other industries or contexts, but they are consistent with the efficiency incentives expected from price cap.[2]

Price cap has been less successful, however, in solving other problems associated with cost-of-service regulation. The designers of price cap had hoped that it would reduce the risk of regulatory capture and the heavy procedural burdens often placed on utilities and regulators. Capture would be less likely because the firms would have incentives to reveal their true costs between reviews, so that the regulator would be less dependent on the industry for information. The procedural burdens would be reduced by holding price reviews only every five years (instead of when the industry or customers requested) and by not mandating the extensive public hearings, opportunities for testimony, and the other time-consuming procedures that had developed under U.S. cost-of-service regulation.

In essence, price cap's designers hoped that the prospect of long-term efficiency gains would reduce the need for the time-consuming and intrusive regulatory procedures found in the United States. The genius of price cap was that it didn't matter, at least in theory, that the regulator could never know as much as the industry did as long as the industry was motivated to improve efficiency. The regulator would set X for the coming five years as best he could, and the firms would try their hardest to find efficiency gains. The industry might make excess profits in some review periods and losses in others. But over the long run costs would decline, leaving consumers much better off than they would have been under a stagnant cost-of-service regime.

At least in Britain, however, price cap has evolved to include cumbersome fact-finding and consultative procedures similar to those found in the United States. The basic reason is that while setting X reasonably accurately may not matter much in theory, it matters a lot in politics. If X is set too low and the utilities earn high profits, consumers may not understand that they are still better off in the long run than they would have been with cost-of-service regulation. The price-cap "contract" that the regulator establishes every five years must anticipate what will happen reasonably well, or the political pressure to break the contract will build quickly. Intensive fact-finding and consultation helps both by reducing the likely errors and by making it clear that the errors that do occur were not caused by a lack of concern or effort on the regulator's part. In short, the British found themselves forced to adopt burdensome regulatory procedures in order to maintain political support for the efficiency incentives of price cap.

The experience of the British water industry illustrates the evolution of price-cap regulation. The water regulator was among the first British regulators to recognize the political benefits of the fact-finding and consultative procedures now common in the price-cap approach.

The Privatization of British Utilities and the Origins of Price Cap

Britain's Conservative Party came to power in 1979 with a mandate to revive the British economy by improving the efficiency of public services and reducing the size of the state. Beginning under Margaret Thatcher (prime minister, 1979–1990) and continuing under John Major (prime minister, 1990–1997), the Conservatives privatized many industries that had been nationalized since World War II. The government began with companies that operated in competitive industries, such as Jaguar, British Steel, and British Airways. But it soon tackled infrastructure industries thought to have elements of natural monopoly, beginning with telecommunications in 1984 and going on to airports and gas in 1986, water in 1989, electricity in 1990, and railroads in 1994.[3]

The government's 1982 announcement of its intention to privatize British Telecommunications (BT) triggered a debate about how best to regulate private utilities. It was clear that competition in telephony would be limited for some time. The government had licensed Mercury to compete with BT that same year, but Mercury was obviously handicapped by BT's overwhelming lead in subscribers. And in 1983, in an effort to increase the chances for a successful flotation of BT stock, the government committed to not licensing any more fixed-line providers until the end of the decade.

The Department of Industry officials working on BT's privatization were leaning toward a form of cost-of-service regulation that they called "maximum rate of return" (or MRR). But British academics and government officials were painfully aware of the situation in the United States, where criticism of regulation had recently led to the deregulation of the airline and railroad industries and to calls for the breakup of AT&T.[4] Professor Alan Walters, a senior economic advisor to the prime minister, proposed an alternative scheme, which he called the "output-related profit levy" (OPRL), in which BT's allowed profits would depend upon how much it increased outputs. The Department of Industry hired a second professor, Stephen C. Littlechild, to review the alternatives, and Littlechild came up with the plan for price cap.

There were precedents for many of the elements in Littlechild's proposal.[5] Previous schemes had built in incentives for efficiency improvements, the best-known example being the "sliding-scale" concession contracts popular in Britain and the United States in the late nineteenth and early twentieth centuries. Sliding-scale contracts usually did not limit profits or dividends; instead they required that the firm share a portion of its profits over certain levels with customers in the form of price reductions. The sliding scale established weaker efficiency incentives than price cap, however, since excess profits were effectively taxed by the requirement to share them with customers.[6] A closer precedent for price cap lay in the observation by U.S. scholars that it often took regulators several years to respond to cost reductions by reducing prices, and that this "regulatory lag" provided an incentive for firms to cut costs. In 1967 William Baumol, a well-known U.S. regulatory economist, had proposed mandating a three-year regulatory lag to encourage efficiency improvements.[7]

The idea of regulating the average price of a representative basket of products instead of the prices for individual products also had been proposed earlier. Economists had realized in the 1920s that the pricing strategies of a profit-maximizing monopolist and a social-welfare-maximizing public enterprise were similar when the public enterprise faced a budget constraint that forced it to price above marginal cost.[8] Both the monopolist and the public enterprise would charge the highest markups over cost for products or services with the least elastic demand and the smallest markups for products or services with elastic demand. Thus it was safe to use the average price to control a monopolist's profits, since the monopolist would realize that average through the same pattern of markups as a public enterprise would.

Nevertheless, Littlechild is universally credited with bringing these elements together in a persuasive and comprehensive proposal. Littlechild called his plan the "local tariff reduction" scheme, because it applied only to tariffs for local service, where BT had an effective monopoly, and not to tariffs for long-distance service, where the potential for competition was strong. He compared price cap, as the local tariff reduction scheme was known, and the alternatives (including no regulation) on five criteria: protection against monopoly pricing, incentives for efficiency and innovation, regulatory burden, potential to promote competition, and the ease of selling BT (see Table 9.1). Littlechild argued that the MRR or ORPL schemes might be worse than al-

Table 9.1 Littlechild's ratings for alternative regulatory schemes for telecommunications

Criteria	No explicit controls on prices	MRR (maximum rate of return)	ORPL (output-related profit levy)	Local tariff reduction scheme (price cap)
Protection against monopoly	4	3	2	1
Efficiency and innovation	1 =	3 =	3 =	1 =
Burden of regulation	1	4	3	2
Promotion of competition	1	4	3	2
Prospects for sale of BT	1 =	3	4	1 =

Source: Stephen C. Littlechild, *Regulation of British Telecommunications' Profitability* (London: Department of Industry, 1983), p. 2.

Note: The "=" indicates a rating equivalent to that of another scheme. Littlechild evaluated five schemes in his original report, and ranked the schemes from 1 to 5 with 1 being the best and 5 being the worst. One of the schemes that involved a ceiling on profits has been omitted here because of its similarity to MRR, and the scale of the rankings has been changed to 1 to 4. BT—British Telecommunications, the state-owned telephony company that was to be privatized.

lowing BT to charge whatever it pleased: "with respect to all criteria except the protection against monopoly, both schemes are significantly worse than the absence of constraints. Moreover, [given the potential for capture,] it is not clear that either MRR or ORPL provides adequate protection [against monopoly] in the longer run. In both cases, the 'cure' seems to be worse than the 'disease.' "[9] The local tariff reduction scheme, by contrast, combined strong protection against monopoly with strong incentives for innovation and a modest regulatory burden.

Littlechild devoted little attention in his report to the process by which the X should be set, saying only that the initial X should be negotiated between BT and the Department of Industry.[10] He did not worry much about reset-

Table 9.2 Regulatory agencies and regulators in Britain, 1984–2002

Industry	Year privatized[a]	Regulatory agency	Regulators
Telecoms	1984	Office of Telecommunications (Oftel)	Bryan Carsberg (1984–1992) Bill Wigglesworth (acting, 1992–1993) Don Cruickshank (1993–1998) David Edmonds (1998–)
Gas	1986	Office of Gas Supply (Ofgas) and Ofgem after 1998[b]	James McKinnon (1986–1993) Claire Spottiswoode (1993–1998)
Airports	1986	Civil Aviation Authority (CAA)	Commission[c]
Electricity	1989	Office of Electricity Regulation (Offer) and Ofgem after 1998[b]	Stephen Littlechild (1989–1998)
Water	1990	Office of Water Services (Ofwat)	Ian Byatt (1989–2000) Philip Fletcher (2000–)
Railroads	1995	Office of the Rail Regulator (ORR)	John Swift (1994–1998) Chris Bolt (acting, 1998–1999) Tom Winsor (1999–)
Gas and electricity	—[b]	Office of Gas and Electricity Management (Ofgem)	Callum McCarthy (1999–2000) Commission (after 2000)

a. The year when the first companies were sold to private investors.

b. The gas and electricity industries were privatized in 1986 and 1989, respectively, but the two regulatory agencies were given the same regulator as of January 1, 1999. The agencies were later consolidated into Ofgem, and in 2000 Ofgem was reorganized to be governed by a commission.

c. The Civil Aviation Authority was established in 1986 with a commission rather than a single regulator.

ting X because he hoped that increased competition would soon make regulation unnecessary. As Littlechild explained: "Competition is indisputably the most effective—perhaps ultimately the *only* effective means—of protecting consumers against monopoly power. Regulation is essentially . . . a means of 'holding the fort' until competition arrives."[11] The local tariff reduction scheme would help promote entry and competition, Littlechild argued, since it applied only to the prices of BT's monopoly services.[12]

The British went on to use price cap for all the utilities they privatized in the 1980s and 1990s, adapting it in various ways to the requirements of each industry. For the electricity distribution companies, for example, the formula became known as $RPI - X + Y$, where Y was a measure of the change in wholesale electricity prices. The Y was added to allow the distribution companies to pass on wholesale price increases, on the theory that the companies should not be vulnerable to key input prices they could not control. Littlechild himself was asked to adapt the price cap scheme to the water industry in 1986, and was appointed as the first regulator of the privatized electricity industry in 1990.

Price cap evolved in slightly different ways in each industry, both because of the different economic problems they faced and because of the varying strategies and personalities of their regulators. Britain chose to have a separate regulatory agency for each industry, although the gas and electricity regulatory agencies were combined in 1999 (see Table 9.2). The regulatory agency for the water industry was called the Office of Water Services, or Ofwat for short. Initially, most agencies were headed by a single regulator rather than by a commission and given a relatively small staff, apparently on the theory that price cap required less work. More regulators and staff might encourage unnecessary meddling. The regulators were appointed to fixed terms.[13] Their decisions could be appealed to the antitrust authority, which was called the Monopolies and Mergers Commission until 1998, when it was renamed the Competition Commission.

The Design of Price Cap for the Water Industry

The Industry before Privatization

Water and sewage companies first appeared in Britain during the nineteenth century.[14] Most sewage companies began as municipal enterprises, but the early water companies included private as well as public firms. During the mid-twentieth century, the water companies consolidated to gain the advantages of economies of scale in water collection and treatment, and by the early 1970s there were only 198 water companies, including 101 that were cooperative ventures of two or more local governments and thirty-three private firms. Sewage escaped consolidation, however, so that in the early 1970s there were still over 1,300 different sewage companies with only a few owned jointly by more than one local government.

Growing environmental awareness soon forced a further consolidation of the industry. In 1965 the government created twenty-nine river authorities to be responsible for, among other things, the control of water pollution and extraction in their river basins. The division of responsibility between the water and sewage companies and the river authorities came to be seen as a problem, however, and in 1973 the government established ten regional water authorities in England and Wales to consolidate the control of all water uses for each region in a single body. The new water authorities absorbed both the river authorities and the municipally owned water and sewage companies, but the private water companies remained independent. Three years earlier, the government had created a Department of the Environment to supervise the development and enforcement of environmental policies and standards. Within the department, the Drinking Water Inspectorate (DWI) was responsible for setting and monitoring standards for drinking water.

In 1986 the government decided to privatize the water industry because of the enormous investments needed to bring it up to modern standards. The water authorities had been starved for capital for years in an effort to hold down public sector borrowing. This policy could not be sustained, however, once the European Commission (EC) began to establish strict standards for the quality of drinking water, coastal and bathing waters, and urban waste-water treatment.[15] The government saw privatization as a way to meet the new EC standards without raising public debt and taxes. If the industry were in private hands, the needed investments could be financed by private debt and equity and repaid through a combination of efficiency improvements and higher water prices.

The Privatization Proposal

The government's proposal to privatize water was highly controversial, because water service seemed so basic and so clearly a natural monopoly. Initially, the government proposed to privatize the ten water authorities in their existing form, maintaining their responsibilities for regulating river water quality and water extraction as well as for supplying drinking water and treating sewage.[16] Environmentalists were outraged about the potential conflict between regulatory and commercial responsibilities, while British industry feared that it would be left at the mercy of ten private companies with complete control over all the water sources and sewage disposal options in their territories. In 1987 the government modified its proposal to include a new

National Rivers Authority that would assume the water authorities' regulatory functions when they were privatized. The National Rivers Authority was later absorbed by a new Environment Agency created to consolidate the pollution enforcement functions of the Department of the Environment.

Littlechild's report on how to regulate the water industry was released at the same time as the government's privatization white paper.[17] Littlechild noted that water was more clearly a natural monopoly than any industry the government had privatized to date, and there was little prospect that technological innovation would change that fact.[18] The water privatization forced Littlechild to adapt his price cap scheme so that it would work over a long term.

The key problem for Littlechild was how to reset X at each review without undermining price cap's efficiency incentives. It was clear that the regulator could not consider the regulated firm's past performance directly—he needed an independent yardstick that was outside the direct control of each company but still reflected actual or best practice in the industry. In this respect, Littlechild explained, water enjoyed a key advantage over the previously privatized utilities, because there were ten separate water and sewage authorities instead of just one. X could be based not on each individual firm's performance but on the average for the industry as a whole, so that each firm would always have an incentive to beat the average.

When the government finally privatized the water authorities, it decided it was easier to leave the existing private water companies, whose numbers had dwindled to 29, as separate firms rather than merge them with the ten regional water and sewage authorities. The Water Act of 1989 outlined the basic terms of the privatization, including the system for setting future prices for both the new and the existing private companies.[19] For water the RPI − X formula was changed to RPI + K, where K was expected to be positive to pay for the capital investments needed in water and sewage treatment. The regulator would set K for ten-year periods, although he would have the option of reviewing the K's every five years. The Department of the Environment announced the investment program that would be expected and the price increases that would be allowed for each company over the first ten-year period, from fiscal year 1990/91 through fiscal year 1999/00.

The government was fearful that the water authorities could not be sold, or that, once sold, they might not be able to finance the investments required. To reduce these risks, the government strengthened the authorities' balance sheets by writing off more than £5 billion of their debts and injecting just over £1 billion in cash into the authorities with the biggest investment burdens.[20] Thanks to this so-called green dowry, shares in the ten new private water companies were successfully floated in 1989.

Ian Byatt was appointed the first water industry regulator in 1989 and eventually served two full terms, stepping down in the summer of 2000 and being knighted for his service. Byatt was an economist who had spent most of his career in the government, rising to become the deputy to the Chief Economic Advisor of the Treasury. He had been involved in trying to improve the performance of nationalized industries and later in preparing the plans to privatize them, and he was fascinated by the opportunity to regulate a privatized water industry.

Byatt presided over two reviews of water industry prices. The first, in 1994, demonstrated the political benefits of a more open and consultative regulatory process. The second, in 1999, reinforced the point by demonstrating the difficulty of defending a regulator's decisions on purely technical grounds.

The 1994 Price Review and the Benefits of Consultation

Byatt's Strategy

Byatt adopted a more open and consultative approach than that of other early British utility regulators not just because of his background in government service but also because of the pressure on water prices from stricter environmental standards. In telecoms and gas (and later in electricity and railroads), regulators expected prices to decline in real terms because of the incentives to improve efficiency. But in water, the investment needs were so great that prices were expected to increase rather than decrease.

The price caps set by the Department of the Environment before privatization called for K's averaging over 5 percent per year for the industry as a whole, and much higher for companies with unusual environmental burdens. The coastal and bathing water standards were particularly onerous, especially for a company like South West Water, whose territory had a small year-round population but much of the nation's coastline and many beaches and summer visitors. The government also expected the EC to issue new standards and tighten existing ones in the near future. As a result, the water companies' licenses included provisions to allow the regulator to make "interim determinations" by adjusting the K's between price reviews if either environmental standards or unit construction costs changed from expected levels.

The Department of the Environment had little incentive to resist tighter standards, because the funding no longer came from its budget and the department's primary constituency was environmentalists rather than water consumers. The companies were also enthusiastic about building new water and sewage treatment plants, because they thought they could build the plants for less than the department's estimates and because the new plants would be added to their regulated asset base for the purposes of calculating future prices. The share prices of the water companies had been rising since flotation, moreover, indicating that investors were beginning to think that the government had been too lenient in setting the initial K's.

In this context Byatt believed that his constituency had to be the consumers, since no one else seemed to be looking out for their interests, and that he needed to ensure that they understood the difficult choices he might have to make.[21] Accordingly, Ofwat developed the practice of issuing consultation documents to solicit the views of affected parties in advance of decisions, and policy reports to explain the decisions once made. Moreover, Ofwat made a major effort to improve the quality of its data and analysis and to open both to public comment, so that its decisions would have strong analytic support.

Through this process, Byatt developed a framework for explaining the basic dilemma facing water customers, water companies, and environmental regulators:

> There are in effect two elements in the K factors in the RPI + K formula adopted for water—an X element, relating to usual utility operations, and a Q element, relating to mandatory improvements in quality and the environment (that is, RPI − X + Q). If overall objectives of customers are to be achieved, these elements are not interdependent. The bigger the scale of obligations under the Q element, the more severe the downward pressure must be on the output components of the X element if price increases are to be affordable.[22]

Byatt also argued that customers' bills should list separate charges for water and sewage, with no cross-subsidies between them. Separate charges were necessary because some consumers got their water and sewage services from different companies, but they were also desirable if customers were to understand the causes of the price increases, which were mainly on the sewage side. The strategy was self-consciously political; as Byatt would later explain, "If a regulator expects to be politically independent, then he had better adopt some of the habits of politicians."[23]

The 1994 Price Review

Byatt soon decided that he should exercise his option to review water prices for the second five-year period (from fiscal year 1995/96 through fiscal year 1999/00), because of the continuing rise in water company stock prices and the changes in the environmental standards. The review, announced in August 1991, had to be completed by the end of 1994, since the 1995/96 fiscal year started on April 1, 1995.[24]

To lay the groundwork, Ofwat issued several additional series of consultation documents. One series was addressed primarily to the investment community, and dealt with the cost and value of capital, important issues in setting utility rates.[25] Byatt argued that the 7 percent real post-tax cost of capital the government had assumed in its 1989 price determinations was too high, and that water utilities were an inherently low-risk business that might justify a post-tax return closer to 5 or 6 percent.

Another series of documents was addressed primarily to policymakers at the Department of the Environment. In the initial paper, provocatively titled "The Cost of Quality," Byatt laid out the implications of different environmental standards for customer prices and asked the environmental regulators to make explicit the standards they expected to apply.[26] After the Department of the Environment responded, Byatt released a second report outlining the costs of the new standards and asking the secretary of state for the environment to reconsider.[27]

Other Ofwat reports considered the issue of setting X, the rate of productivity improvement that could be expected in the industry. Littlechild's original idea had been to set X on the basis of the average rate of cost reduction for the industry as a whole. Byatt thought that the target should be tougher than the industry average. If he were to set tougher targets, moreover, then he had to recognize that the cost-saving opportunities might vary among the companies because of local circumstances beyond their control, such as low population density or difficult topography.

The solution was to identify the most efficient water company by using statistical methods to adjust the companies' costs for relevant local circumstances. The efficient firm's performance then could be used as a benchmark for the others. Benchmark analyses would not tell the regulator how much more efficient the best firm could become, but it would tell him how much the other firms could improve just by catching up. The Department of the Environment had done a crude benchmark analysis when setting the water companies' original K factors in 1989. But Ofwat went further by trying to make sure that the data submitted by the companies were comparable, applying more sophisticated statistical techniques, and then circulating the results to the industry for comment.[28]

The desire to maintain benchmark competition also led Ofwat to oppose many mergers in the water industry. The Water Act of 1989 had anticipated the problem by requiring that the Monopolies and Mergers Commission review all mergers involving water companies with assets of over £30 million. In a series of cases beginning in 1990, Ofwat proposed, and the commission agreed, that mergers should be allowed only if the merged firm committed to price reductions that were substantial enough to justify the loss in the number of comparators for the benchmark analyses. In practice this meant that mergers between water and sewage companies were prohibited, since ten was already a very small number of comparators. Fourteen water-only companies were allowed to disappear, however, most through merger with other water-only companies and some through acquisition by a water and sewage company.

The Water Act of 1989 had established ten regional Customer Service Committees, and Ofwat developed them as vehicles for soliciting consumer views. Byatt thought special efforts were necessary, because water consumers had fewer vehicles for expressing their preferences than the customers of other utilities. Water meters were rare in Britain, so the water bill for most households was based on the value of their property. Thus a water customer could not economize by consuming less or choose among different packages of services in the way a telephone or gas customer could. Ofwat and the Customer Service Committees surveyed consumers about their problems, discovering, for example, that avoiding the occasional sewage backup and flooding was a more important priority for consumers than it appeared to be for the companies.

Byatt's goal for the 1994 review had been to reduce the K factor to 0, which would have provided substantial relief after years of real annual price increases averaging over 5 percent for the industry as whole and over 10 percent for some companies. In the end he was able to reduce the average K to +1.5. Although the Department of the Environment had delayed the implementation of some standards, environmental and capacity improvements were expected to add £47 to the average annual household bill of £201 over the next ten years. Greater operating efficiency and reduced capital costs would cut £24 from the average bill, however, so the net increase would be only £23.[29]

Dividends and Drought

In the year that followed, it gradually became clear that Byatt could have set the K's even lower. Only two companies appealed Byatt's decision to the Monopolies and Mergers Commission, and the commission eventually issued rulings essentially upholding Ofwat and even tightening the prices slightly.[30] A clearer sign came in the fall of 1994, when other companies began to announce special dividends for stockholders. Stockholders had been pressing for dividends in part because many water companies had embarked on unsuccessful diversification programs. Those that invested far afield—in electric companies and hotels, for example—had fared badly. But even the companies that had gone into closely related businesses—such as bidding for foreign water concessions—were having trouble with their new investments. In addition, the Labour Party was running strongly in the polls, raising fears that it might win the next general election, which had to be scheduled before the summer of 1997. Labour was making an issue of the high profits in the privatized utilities, and there was talk of a tougher regulatory environment if Labour won. The stockholders wanted some of their earnings returned before they were lost to poor investments or a new government. And the scale of the special dividends—over £500 million between the summers of 1994 and 1995 alone—made it clear how profitable the water companies had become.

As if these difficulties were not enough, Britain suffered from a drought in 1995–1996 that exposed weaknesses in some water companies. The most serious problems were with Yorkshire Water, which had to go to significant lengths—including tankering in water—to maintain essential supplies for some of its customers. But many other companies were forced to impose bans on outside water use, and public outrage grew when critics pointed out that some of the companies lost as much as 40 percent of their water to leaks compared with standards of 15 percent for large cities in the United States. The industry thought the comparison unfair, because losses were primarily a function of the kilometers of mains rather than the amount of water consumed. British water systems were bound to have higher percentage losses, the industry argued, because they were more rural and thus had more kilometers of main per customer or liter consumed. Right or wrong, the popular impression was that the water companies had chosen to pocket big profits instead of making the investments that might have avoided the shortages.

The government also faced growing pressure from large industrial water users who wanted to avoid price increases by contracting with alternative bulk water suppliers. Electricity had been restructured to allow large consumers to buy directly from independent generators, so why not water? The original privatization bills had allowed independent water companies to serve users within an incumbent company's territory if the user was at least 30 meters away from the incumbent's mains or consumed at least 250 megaliters a day.[31] This provision was rarely used, so in 1996 the Department of the Environment and Ofwat reduced the threshold for independent supply to 100 megaliters per day and proposed rules to require that the water companies make their pipes available for transportation of water from independent suppliers to their customers for reasonable fees.[32] The number of industrial consumers purchasing from independent water suppliers increased only slightly over the next several years, but the threat encouraged water companies to offer more discounts for bulk water buyers.[33]

Despite the problems, Ian Byatt was still regarded as one of Britain's best utility regulators. Others had fared worse in recent price reviews, most spectacularly Stephen Littlechild, who was then serving as the electricity regulator. Littlechild had released the results of the first periodic review of electricity prices in August 1994, three weeks after Byatt had announced the new water prices. In the months that followed, two dramatic takeover fights provided graphic proof of the electric companies' large profits. Littlechild had cut tariffs by 11 to 17 percent, but industry insiders claimed that he could have made cuts of up to 25 percent if he had asked the right questions.[34] In March 1995, just before his new tariffs were to go into effect, Littlechild responded by ordering further price reductions. The new price caps earned him cheers from consumers but a storm of criticism from the electricity industry and from academic economists, concerned that he was undermining the incentive system that he had designed.

It is conceivable that Byatt's underestimate of the potential for price cuts was greater than Littlechild's, although comparisons of this type are difficult. Certainly both were surprised by large increases in the value of their companies. Moreover, Byatt had a drought to contend with while Littlechild did not. But Byatt's underestimate seemed to be more quickly forgiven because he had tried so obviously to conduct a comprehensive review.[35] Littlechild, by comparison, had issued only one major consultation paper during the course of his review, and the other regulators had also been relatively secretive up until that point. The lesson of the 1994 reviews was not lost on the other regulators, who adopted a more open and consultative process in the coming years.

In May 1997 Tony Blair led the Labour Party to victory in a general election, ending eighteen years of Conservative Party rule. High utility earnings had been an important theme in the Labour campaign, and in July the new government imposed a onetime £5 billion "windfall" tax on utility profits. The water industry's share was £1.8 billion.

The new government commissioned a review of the system for regulating private utilities that resulted in proposals to keep the system pretty much intact but with an added emphasis on consultation, transparency, and protecting low-income consumers. The most striking change was a proposal to gradually move from individual regulators to small commissions for each sector. The study explained, "there are risks in concentrating too much discretion on an individual," especially those of "unpredictable and unaccountable decision making."[36] In addition, regulators were to establish and publicize their consultation procedures and to explain their decisions in writing, much as Byatt had done.

The government had decided to merge gas and electricity into a single energy regulatory authority, and it took the opportunity to try out a commission in that sector. For water, however, there were few major changes. The Competition Act of 1998 obligated the water regulator to not just "facilitate" but also "promote" competition, a change that stimulated Ofwat to investigate ways to further encourage competition for bulk water customers. And in the Water Industry Act of 1999, the government increased protections for residential customers by requiring that meters be optional, that meter installation be free, that Ofwat develop tariffs to protect "vulnerable groups" of customers that might face hardship from being charged by meter, and that companies not shut off households who had not paid their water bill.

The 1999 Review and the Limits of Technical Analysis

The Methodology for Estimating X

Byatt had been reappointed to a second term in 1995, before the Labour victory, which ensured that he would supervise the second periodic review to be completed in 1999 (in time to apply to prices in fiscal years 2000/01 through 2004/05). Ofwat used the same process as in the 1994 review, releasing a series of consultation papers on the key issues. If anything, however, Byatt wanted to be more thorough, because this time he hoped to give consumers a rate reduction while still funding environmental improvements.

One key battle was over Ofwat's estimate of X, the expected rate of productivity improvement. Other disputes—over the cost of capital or environmental goals, for example—would affect the final tariffs as much or more. But the estimates of X came to illustrate the limits of technical analyses in price reviews. Ofwat's X had a "catch-up" and a "frontier" component.[37] The first was the scope for the less efficient companies to catch up to their most efficient peers; the second was the scope for the most efficient companies to improve their performance further.

The possibilities for catch-up were estimated through benchmark analysis. Ofwat had applied the technique only to operating expenditures in the 1994 review, but in the 1999 review the agency benchmarked capital maintenance and construction activities as well, important additions since those activities accounted for roughly half of water industry costs. Ofwat also adjusted the variables used in its analysis to reflect changes in the industry and improve the accuracy of the cost models. The 1994 analysis had used operating cost per unit of water *supplied* as a key efficiency measure, for example, but the 1999 analysis switched to cost per unit of water *delivered* to reflect the increased attention to leakage since the 1995–1996 drought.

Ofwat's analysis of water operating costs was in many ways typical. Reported operating costs in 1997–1998 varied by a factor of two, from 25 pence per cubic meter at the cheapest firm to 52 pence per cubic meter at the most expensive. Once adjustment was made for local conditions beyond the firms' control, however, the gap between the most efficient and the least efficient firm was reduced to 30 percent. Ofwat made these adjustments by dividing operating costs into four components and estimating a separate equation for each. The equations were fairly simple, using at most two explanatory variables as shown in Table 9.3. For example, water distribution costs per capita were assumed to be a function of only one variable: the proportion of water mains that were over 0.3 meters in diameter. In the case of a few companies, however, Ofwat would make additional adjustments to compensate for variables not included in the equations, such as unusually high wage costs and contaminated water supplies (which affected London area companies) or unusual water softening requirements.[38] Ofwat used the analysis to sort water companies into five "bands," from most efficient (A) to least (E). A company might be classified in band A for one cost category and in band D for another, and its overall catch-up target was based on its weighted average rating.

The equations used in the benchmark analyses were a source of great controversy. The industry complained that the equations were too simplistic and that some made no sense at all. The water distribution equation implied that the companies could cut costs by installing two small mains instead of one large one, for example, while the industry's experience was exactly the opposite.

Ofwat responded that it had to keep the equations simple because the data set was small. The agency had (at the time) only twenty-eight water companies and ten sewage companies to compare.[39] Ofwat also preferred to use data only from the most recent year, because it felt the rapid improvements in the industry made older data misleading. The small number of observations meant that Ofwat could include only a few carefully picked explanatory variables. In the water distribution model, for example, the agency had chosen the percentage of mains over 0.3 meters in diameter as a proxy for the degree of urbanization. Urbanization was the single most important factor affecting water distribution costs, Ofwat argued, and the alternative measures, such as the population density of the service area, disguised important differences among the companies.[40]

Ofwat was reasonably responsive to industry comments about the specifications of the equations and changed the models when it thought the criticisms valid. But in the end it had a fair amount of latitude, because there was little consensus within the industry as to what the best equations might be. Each company wanted to include variables that made it look good, but the variables that favored one company often disadvantaged others.

Estimating the frontier component of X was no easier. Since the basic for-

Table 9.3 Water service operating expenditure equations used in the 1999 review

Dependent variable	Coefficient and (standard error)	Explanatory variable	Number of observations and R^2
Water resources and treatment cost model			
Cost per capita	+0.866 (+1.23)	Constant	Obs = 28 $R^2 = 0.50$
	+17.16 (+3.82)	Number of water sources/total water distribution input	
	+6.72 (+1.43)	Proportion of supplies derived from river sources	
Water distribution cost model			
Natural log of cost per capita	−5.13 (−0.11)	Constant	Obs = 28 $R^2 = 0.39$
	+4.74 (+1.21)	Proportion of mains over 0.3 meters in diameter	
Water service power cost model			
Natural log of costs	−8.97 (−0.25)	Constant	Obs = 28 $R^2 = 0.985$
	+0.94 (+0.02)	Natural log of (total water distribution input × average pumping head)	
Business activities cost model			
Natural log of costs	−4.15 (−0.25)	Constant	Obs = 28 $R^2 = 0.96$
	+0.97 (+0.04)	Natural log of number of billed properties	

Source: Ofwat, "Efficiency Assessments: Econometric Models," directive RD 2/99, Birmingham, January 15, 1999, pp. 2–5.

Note: Based on data from the 1997–98 fiscal year. "Water distribution" is the term Ofwat uses for the amount of water put into the distribution network. The amount of water actually delivered to customers is the water distribution input less leakage, water used to flush mains or for other operational purposes, and water taken illegally.

mula was RPI − X, the key issue was whether the best-performing water companies could improve more rapidly than the best companies in other industries. If they could, the frontier component of X would be negative. If not, it would be zero or positive. The usual approach was to estimate the potential for improvement at the best water companies from trends in real costs per unit of output in other industries thought to be comparable. But there was plenty of scope for disagreement about how real unit costs should be measured, over what periods of time, and for which comparator industries.

In the 1999 review, for example, consultants to Ofwat and the water industry produced conflicting estimates of the frontier component of X. Ofwat's consultants argued the component should be roughly −1.4 percent per year based on analyses of three groups of comparators: private unregulated industries, private regulated utilities, and the water industry itself.[41] For the first analysis, the consultants divided the water industry into nine functional areas and found from one to three comparable private industries for each area. The trends in real unit operating costs in those industries averaged approximately −1 percent per year. The consultants went on to argue that one comparator—the extraction and refining industry—should be thrown out because it was adversely affected by the depletion of natural resources, and with that industry out the trends in unit costs were −1.8 to −2.7 percent per year. The second analysis considered other privatized industries in Britain, where real unit costs had declined by 2.5 to 3 percent per year in many cases, and by as much as 3.9 percent per year in a few industries (electricity distribution and transmission). Finally, Ofwat's consultants estimated that the most efficient water company had reduced its real unit costs by 1.4 percent per year from 1992 to 1998. Assuming that roughly half the decline in unit costs observed in the first two analyses was due to catch up and half to pushing the efficiency frontier, the consultants argued that all three analyses pointed to a frontier cost reduction of 1.4 percent per year.

The largest company in the industry, Thames Water, hired the same consultants that Ofwat had employed to analyze efficiency issues in the earlier 1994 price review, and they estimated that the frontier component of X should be a reduction of only 0.2 percent per year for the coming five-year period.[42] Thames Water's consultants selected a set of comparator industries that had not performed as well as those picked by Ofwat's consultants. They also argued that it was important to decompose the trend in unit cost into the trends of its four components: real wages, labor productivity, real materials prices, and materials productivity. Materials prices paid by the water industry were projected to increase from 2000 to 2005, the consultants argued, offsetting part of the expected gains in materials productivity and reducing the expected savings in unit costs.

Ofwat's Decision and the Appeals

Late in 1999, Ofwat announced that the average K for the next five years would be −2.1 percent per year, which meant that the prices consumers paid would fall for the first time since privatization. Part of the savings came because the Department of the Environment was persuaded to delay some of the more costly quality improvements. The industry still would be required to make £15.6 billion in new investments over the next five years, however, which Ofwat projected would add £30 to the average annual household bill of £248. Price reductions were possible because Ofwat projected that the industry could cut its annual costs by £60 per household over the five-year period, allowing a £30 saving on the average annual bill.[43]

The bulk of the cost savings came from Ofwat's estimates of the catch-up and frontier efficiency gains.[44] In the case of water operating costs, for example, Ofwat stood by its consultants' estimate of a frontier efficiency gain of 1.4 percent per year for all companies and set the average catch-up targets at between 0 and 3.5 percent per year depending on the efficiency of the firm, as shown in Table 9.4. The expected savings in capital maintenance and for sewage operating costs were comparable, and for new capital improvements and their maintenance Ofwat expected an even more aggressive frontier gain of 2.1 percent per year. Instead of spreading the catch-up cost savings over ten years, as he had done in the 1994 review, Byatt took all of them in the first year. Thus while the K's averaged −2.1 over five years, real prices would decline by 12.3 percent in the first year, followed by a further reduction of 0.4 percent in the second year and gradual increases of 0.1, 1.1 and 1.4 percent in the three years that followed (see Table 9.5).

Investors thought that Byatt's targets would be difficult to achieve, and

Table 9.4 Ofwat's operating efficiency targets for 2001–2005

Percentage efficiency gap	Efficiency band	Number of companies in band	Average annual improvement (in percent)		
			Frontier efficiency savings	Catch-up efficiency target	Total efficiency target
<0	A	2	1.4	0.0	1.4
0–5	A/B	7	1.4	0.3	1.7
5–10	B	7	1.4	0.9	2.3
10–15	B/C	3	1.4	1.5	2.9
15–20	C	3	1.4	2.2	3.6
20–25	C/D	2	1.4	2.9	4.3
25–30	D	2	1.4	3.5	4.9
>30	D/E	0	1.4	5.6	7.0

Source: Competition Commission, *Sutton and East Surrey Water plc: A Report on the References under Sections 12 and 14 of the Water Industry Act 1991* (London: Stationery Office, August 2000), p. 265.

Table 9.5 Average K factors set in the 1989, 1994, and 1999 periodic reviews

Periodic review and fiscal year	Water and sewage companies	Water-only companies	Entire water industry
Department of the Environment review, 1989			
1990/91	+5.4	+11.4	+6.3
1991/92	+5.4	+10.2	+6.1
1992/93	+5.4	+6.7	+5.6
1993/94	+5.2	+4.9	+5.1
1994/95	+5.2	+3.3	+4.9
Ofwat review, 1994			
1995/96	+1.5	+0.6	+1.4
1996/97	+1.5	+0.6	+1.4
1997/98	+1.5	+0.6	+1.4
1998/99	+1.5	+0.6	+1.4
1999/00	+1.5	+0.6	+1.4
Ofwat review, 1999			
2000/01	−12.3	−12.4	−12.3
2001/02	−0.4	−0.6	−0.4
2002/03	−0.2	−0.1	−0.1
2003/04	+1.3	0.0	+1.1
2004/05	+1.7	0.0	+1.5

Sources: The figures from the 1989 reviews for the water and sewage and the water-only companies are simple (unweighted) averages from Mark Armstrong, Simon Cowan, and John Vickers, *Regulatory Reform: Economic Analysis and British Experience* (Cambridge: MIT Press, 1994), pp. 337–338. The figures from the 1989 review for the entire industry are from the same source and assume that the water-only companies make up 15 percent of the industry. The 1994 review figures are from Ofwat, *Future Charges for Water and Sewerage Services: The Outcome of the Periodic Review* (Birmingham: Ofwat, July 1994), pp. 5–6. The 1999 review figures are from Ofwat, *Future Water and Sewerage Charges: Final Determinations* (Birmingham: Ofwat, November 1999), pp. 15, 41–66.

water company shares fell by 30 percent relative to the stock market average.[45] Some environmentalists were almost as unhappy as the companies, feeling that Byatt had bullied the Department of the Environment into making too many concessions, and that a minister had aided Byatt by publicly announcing that he expected water rates to decline. During 2000, the Environmental Audit Committee of Parliament held extensive hearings on the 1999 review and issued a report concluding that:

> Ministers should respect the role of the independent regulator, Ofwat, to determine price limits and not influence customer and consumer expectations by publicly announcing its own price expectations. In turn, the Committee recommends that Ofwat seeks to insure that its own statements do not "demonise" environmental and quality investment by

portraying it as the key upward pressure on prices without equally emphasising the customer and public health benefits that it delivers.[46]

But for the first time Ofwat was also criticized on technical grounds by the Competition Commission. Only two small water companies appealed to the commission, reportedly because the other firms did not want to alarm their investors further. The commission explained in its ruling that it approved of Ofwat's basic approach to most issues, but pointed out that there was still substantial room for disagreement about the details, and thus about the results. In particular, where Ofwat had called for price reductions of 21.3 percent over five years for one company and 19.5 percent for the other, the commission ordered reductions of only 13.5 percent and 15.3 percent.[47]

The estimates of X for operating expenses were a central issue in the appeals, and the commission's views were typical of those it held on other issues. On the estimates of the catch-up component, for example, the commission rejected the argument of one company that statistical analyses of comparators should not be considered because the analyses could never fully capture the differences in local conditions. The commission was intrigued, however, when the second company, Mid Kent Water, presented an alternative statistical model that showed that it was far more efficient than Ofwat's models suggested. Mid Kent's model, shown in Table 9.6, explained 99 percent of the variation in operating costs among companies by estimating a single equation for all operating expenses with six years of data (instead of Ofwat's approach of estimating four separate equations with one year of data each). Ofwat's consultants responded that it was easy to explain most of the variance in total operating expenses simply by including a measure of company size as an explanatory variable. To make their point they presented a model, also shown in Table 9.6, which explained 98 percent of the variance in operating expenses by using the number of billed properties as the only explanatory variable.

Instead of discrediting Mid Kent Water's model, the new Ofwat model seemed to cast doubt on the whole science of benchmarking. Almost any statistical model—no matter how simplistic—could explain a good deal of the variance. How then could one choose among models that had plausible specifications but implied very different X's? In the end, the commission decided that both Ofwat's original model and the Mid Kent alternative had merit.[48] The commission concluded, however, that the exercise had demonstrated the need to weigh evidence from many sources since no single statistical model was clearly superior to all others.[49]

The commission reached similar conclusions about the estimates of the frontier component of X. The commission worried that estimates based on

Table 9.6 Water service operating expenditure equations presented to the Competition Commission

Dependent variable	Coefficient and (standard error)	Explanatory variable	Number of observations and R^2
Mid Kent Water's proposed model			
Natural log of costs (£ millions at 1997/98 price levels)	−2.63 (a)	Constant	Obs = 156 $R^2 = 0.99$
	+0.704 (a)	Natural log of total water delivered (millions of liters/day)	
	+0.269 (a)	Natural log of total length of mains (kilometers)	
	−0.982 (a)	Proportion of water delivered to metered nonhouseholds	
	−0.022 (a)	Dummy for observation in 1993/94	
	−0.0685 (a)	Dummy for observation in 1994/95	
	−0.111 (a)	Dummy for observation in 1995/96	
	−0.130 (a)	Dummy for observation in 1996/97	
	−0.137 (a)	Dummy for observation in 1997/98	
Ofwat's example in response to Mid Kent			
Natural log of cost (£ millions)	−2.6279 (−0.0285)	Constant	Obs = 28 $R^2 = 0.98$
	+0.9612 (+0.1764)	Natural log of number of billed properties (thousands)	

Source: Competition Commission, *Mid Kent Water plc: A Report on the References under Sections 12 and 14 of the Water Industry Act 1991* (London: Stationery Office, August 2000), pp. 266–267.

a. The Competition Commission did not report the standard errors on the Mid Kent model, but it did say that the standard errors were small relative to the estimated coefficients for all variables except the dummy for 1993/94 year.

trends in water or other recently privatized industries might be misleading, particularly if productivity had been neglected when the industries were publicly owned. If so, the pace of improvement might slow in the future, becoming more similar to that found in other industries that had always been in the private sector. But the commission also recognized that it was not obvious what alternative private sector comparators to use, so that the range of plausible estimates might be fairly broad.[50]

Ian Byatt finished his second term as the water regulator in July 2000, the month before the Competition Commission's report on the appeals was released. Byatt had not sought reappointment, and the government named Philip Fletcher, another longtime senior civil servant, as his successor.

The controversy over Byatt's last price review waned a bit in Fletcher's first years in office, as the industry seemed to grow a bit more confident about its ability to live within the new price caps and stock prices began to recover. Nevertheless, in 2001 Fletcher approved a novel, and many thought risky, application of one company to shift to nonprofit status and use all-debt financing so as to reduce financing costs and make it easier to live within the price caps.[51] And in 2002 a review of price-cap regulation in gas, water, electricity, and telecoms by Britain's comptroller and auditor general praised Ofwat for its efforts to monitor service quality and to assess shortage risks, but singled out Ofwat's 1999 review as an example of one that might have been too tight.[52]

The Record of Price-Cap Regulation

Strengths

Overall, price cap has to be judged a great success, primarily because of its stronger incentives to improve efficiency. It is difficult to determine how much of the productivity gains achieved by British utilities in the last twenty years were due to price-cap regulation and how much to the fact that the utilities were recently privatized. Nevertheless, the British utilities posted efficiency gains of 3 to 9 percent per year through the 1990s, an impressive record by any standard.[53] Water prices rose but only because of environmental improvements—the increases would have been much larger without the offsetting gains in efficiency. And it is unlikely that the cost savings would have been as great had these industries been privatized with conventional cost-of-service regulation.

The incentives to improve efficiency seem to have survived despite the government's occasional reneging on the explicit and implicit commitments that are central to them. Littlechild's March 1995 lowering of the electricity price caps for 1995–2000 was not illegal, since the price caps were not scheduled to go into effect until April 1.[54] But he had announced the "final" price caps the previous August, so the industry had reason to argue that he had broken faith. The windfall profits tax imposed by the incoming Labour government in 1997 was justified as a onetime event, provoked by the extraordinary circumstances surrounding privatization. But it was clearly the type of regulatory claw back that, if expected, would undermine incentives to reduce costs. In addition, some water company officials argued privately that Byatt had been tough in his 1999 review because he wanted to "get even" for 1994, so that the 1999 review amounted to something of a claw back too. Nevertheless, most utility executives probably believe that events like Littlechild's 1995 reversal or the 1997 windfall profits tax will prove to be relatively rare. And even if they now expect an occasional element of claw back in the periodic reviews, they probably don't expect all the excess profits to be taken so that the efficiency incentives are weakened but not eliminated.

Limitations

Price cap has proved less successful in providing incentives for capital investment, although in this respect cost-of-service regulation has its drawbacks too. With cost-of-service regulation, the traditional concern is that the regulated firm might overinvest. A regulator is likely to err on the side of overestimating the return the firm needs to earn on its invested capital, since an error in the other direction would leave the firm unable to raise money for new investments. But an overly generous return will give the firm incentives to "gold plate" its investments, so as to expand the asset base on which the return applies. As a result, cost-of-service regulators often must review the investments the firm proposes to make sure that they are really needed.[55]

With price-cap regulation, by contrast, the incentives are usually to underinvest. One reason is that price cap does not encourage efficiency improvements that have payback periods longer than the interval between price reviews. Indeed, firms are unlikely even to make improvements with short paybacks as the review date approaches, since by delaying until after the review they will capture the savings as profit longer. Firms will make improvements with long payback periods only if they are convinced that the regulators will recognize them as worthwhile investments and enter them into the regulated asset base to be recovered in future review prices.

A second reason for underinvestment is that price cap gives the firms incentives to cut back on investment programs agreed to with the regulators. The price-cap formula for the coming review period covers the regulator's assessment of investment needs as well as operating costs. But many types of infrastructure are so durable and resilient that underinvestment does not result in a clear or immediate decline in the service quality or performance. In such cases, the firm will be tempted to cut back on the investment program and pocket the savings as profit. Price-cap regulators are usually forced to monitor the firm's current investments to make sure that any underspend is due to efficiencies in investment rather than to a shirking of commitments. Controversies over underspend have been particularly intense in Britain's railways, as discussed in Chapter 11.

It is hard to say whether the risk of overinvesting is worse than the risk of underinvesting. One might argue that price cap is less attractive for developing countries, for example, since their utilities often need substantial investments. But the importance of investment must be balanced against that of increased operating efficiency and of avoiding capture, which makes such generalizations difficult.

Price cap also seems to have failed to significantly reduce the burden of regulatory proceedings. It is true that prices are reviewed only once every five years under price cap, whereas reviews are generally more frequent in cost-of-service regulation. Because the reviews are less frequent, however, the stakes for each review are higher. As a result, most British regulatory agencies follow procedures roughly similar to those used by Byatt in his 1994 and 1999 reviews. The reviews begin three years before the end of the current review period, so that an industry is more often in the midst of a review than not. The regulatory staff develops a series of consultation documents about the overall framework and key issues in the review on which the companies and consumer groups usually feel compelled to comment, often with the aid of consultants. The companies submit business plans that explain their investment programs and their special circumstances, which the regulatory staff scrutinize and discuss with them. The result is reviews that are process-intensive, and intrusive—a far cry from the streamlined approach Littlechild seemed to have in mind in 1983.

These cumbersome procedures have evolved because setting price caps has proved to be both harder and more important than originally expected. Much of the attention has focused on the problems of forecasting X reasonably accurately. Even in the British water industry, with its relatively large number of companies, it is hard to standardize for differences across companies so as to make accurate estimates of catch-up efficiency. And these difficulties are not likely to decline significantly with more sophisticated statistical techniques.[56] There will always be room for argument, given that a variety of very different but plausible cost models can be estimated from the available data. Estimating the frontier efficiency gains is even harder, given the uncertainties about extrapolating from past trends and selecting comparator industries. X is not the only ingredient needed to set price caps, moreover, and there are comparable difficulties with the cost of capital and other elements.[57] In short, the technical analysis is seldom sufficiently precise or certain to provide the agency with adequate political protection.

The hope that efficiency incentives would make it less important to set X reasonably accurately has been disappointed, at least in part. The central insight of price cap was that excess profits or losses were tolerable, and even desirable, in the short run because they encouraged innovation and price reductions in the long run. But five years has proved to be a long time for the public to endure profits that they regard as excessive. And while Britain has not experienced it yet, five years would probably also prove to be a long time for the companies or their consumers to endure returns so low that the industry could not attract capital. Shortening the period between reviews would reduce the political and economic damage from setting price caps that were badly wrong, but a shorter period would also reduce the strength and scope of the efficiency and investment incentives as well. In sum, the fact- and process-intensive regulatory procedures are a compromise that seems to be essential to preserving the popular commitment to a price cap.

One question raised by this compromise, but still unresolved, is whether the evolving procedures will also subject price-cap regulation to greater risks of capture. Littlechild feared that the regulator might be captured by the companies, because the companies had more information. An equally troubling possibility is that the consultation- and fact-intensive process adopted may ultimately make it harder for the regulator to adapt to new challenges or changing circumstances.

Such a preference for the status quo, even at the expense of the long-term health of the industry, has characterized the telephone, railroad, airline, and other regulatory agencies in the United States at various points in their lives, particularly when beset by strong and conflicting pressures. Britain's water industry seems subject to similar risks, for example, inasmuch as the companies, residential consumers, industrial consumers, and environmentalists all have distinct and intensely felt concerns. Factual investigations narrow the scope for debate somewhat, but still leave plenty of room for disagreement. Consultation makes it easier for the varied interests to be heard and, it is hoped, strengthens their understanding and support for the regulatory system. But whether the processes will make it easier or harder for the regulator to make difficult choices remains to be seen.

In the end, the burden of intrusive regulatory procedures and the risk of capture seem unavoidable with discretionary regulation. Discretionary regulators can find some refuge in purely technical analysis but, as the Competition Commission pointed out, the technical analysis is seldom conclusive. In democracies, discretionary regulation seems to require the extensive factual investigations and consultation found in Britain and the United States. And it is arguably better to take the risk of capture with price cap than with cost-of-service regulation, especially where efficiency incentives are important.

III

Vertical Unbundling
and Regulation

10

The Trade-off in Unbundling: Competition versus Coordination

Advantages and Disadvantages

Until recently, most utilities owned, operated, and maintained all the basic facilities needed to serve their customers. Different companies served different geographic areas. An international telephone call required the cooperation of two national telephone companies, for example. But within its service area, each telephone company provided all the telephones and built and maintained both the local and the long-distance lines. Similarly, each railroad owned all or most of the locomotives, tracks, yards, and stations needed for the region it served.[1] Each electricity company generated most of the power it sold in its own plants, transported that power over its own long-distance transmission lines, and then distributed it to retail customers through its own local network. In the parlance of economists, these companies were horizontally separated in that they served different markets or regions, but vertically integrated in that they provided all the key functions needed to serve their regions.

Governments began to vertically separate, or unbundle, their infrastructure companies in the 1980s. In most cases, the restructuring was part of the process of privatizing a government-owned utility. When Britain privatized its national railway in 1994, for example, it sold the railroad off as approximately seventy different companies. The most important company, Railtrack, owned and maintained all the tracks and stations, while twenty-five separate companies operated passenger trains and had to pay Railtrack to use its facilities. In other cases, notably in the United States, the utilities were already in private hands before restructuring. AT&T was private in 1984, for example, when the government ordered it broken up into seven local telephone companies, a long-distance carrier, and an equipment manufacturer.

Vertical unbundling was an outgrowth of the criticism of regulation in the United States in the 1970s and 1980s, and the motive was to reduce the need for regulation by introducing competition wherever technically possible. In the case of railroads, for example, the tracks, signals, and stations are usually considered a natural monopoly, because they are durable and immobile and because the most economical way to serve a rail corridor is with a single rail line (unless the density of traffic is very high). But train operations alone (without the responsibility for infrastructure) are not a natural monopoly, so in theory there should be no cost penalty if several train-operating companies compete with one another in the same corridor. Similarly, local and long-distance electric power lines and local hard-wire telephone networks are thought to be natural monopolies, while the generation of power, the manufacture of telephone equipment, and the provision of long-distance telephone services all are not. If only parts of these industries are natural monopolies, then vertical unbundling can focus regulation on the parts that need it and allow market forces to govern the rest.

This effort to substitute competition for regulation was aided by technological changes that made competition more feasible, particularly in electricity and telephones. Advances in electricity-generating technology in the 1960s and 1970s reduced the minimum efficient-scale generating plant, for example, encouraging competition in generation. Similarly, the spread of microwave technology in the 1970s and of fiber optics in the 1980s made competition more feasible in long-distance telephony. Improvements in cable television and in wireless technologies may soon make effective competition possible for local telephony as well.

But while unbundling reduces the range of activities that have to be regulated, it comes at the cost of making coordination between the different segments of the industry more difficult. A train-operating company cannot offer reliable, high-speed passenger service, for example, unless the rail infrastructure company maintains the tracks to a high standard and makes them available when scheduled. Before restructuring, the coordination of infrastructure and train operations would take place within a single company. Responsibility for track and train operations might have been lodged in separate departments, but the managers were committed to a common enterprise and reported to a common boss. After separation, by contrast, the coordination must be arranged largely through contractual arrangements between separate firms. The firms may have common interests in the success of the passenger service, but they also have conflicting interests regarding who should bear what costs and risks. Although the contracts may be supplemented with informal pressure and understandings, the range and flexibility of the incentives and sanctions are generally more limited. And the failure to carefully coordinate the different levels well may reduce the quality of service and raise prices, thereby offsetting some of the benefits of introducing more competition.

The problem of maintaining coordination is complicated by the pressure for the government to regulate the segments of the industry that still retain elements of monopoly power, such as the rail infrastructure, local telephone, long-distance electricity transmission, and local electricity distribution companies. These firms are sometimes called "bottleneck" companies, since they occupy an essential position or bottleneck in an industry's production chain. After vertical separation, the other firms in the industry must buy critical services, once supplied by a sister division in the old integrated company, from the bottleneck provider. The regulator usually must monitor these transactions, because of the possibility that the bottleneck company will take advantage of its position. But the involvement of the regulator may make drafting these arrangements more difficult than it would be otherwise. In essence, the regulator becomes a third party to an already complicated contractual relationship.

One paradox of vertical unbundling is that the effort to substitute competition for regulation may actually increase the complexity and importance of the regulator's task. That task seems easier in that the regulator can focus his attention on the fraction of the industry's activities that are monopolistic. But the regulator must now supervise complex relationships between the monopolistic and the competitive segments of the industry, and these relationships are critical to the ultimate quality and cost of service for the consumers. As one scholar of reform in telecommunications and financial markets put it, freer markets may require more rules.[2]

Because regulation is so central to unbundling, whether or where unbundling proves to be worthwhile will depend importantly on our ability to solve the special regulatory issues it raises. At its core, unbundling involves a trade-off between the benefits from more competition and the costs from reduced coordination. How favorable that trade-off will be depends on how critical coordination is and how skillfully the regulator can promote it.

This final part of the book considers strategies for encouraging coordination in vertically unbundled and regulated private infrastructure. This chapter provides an overview of the determinants of vertical integration, outlines several complications that unbundling creates for regulation, and then introduces three strategies that regulators often use to maintain coordination in an unbundled industry. Chapters 11 and 12 illustrate these coordination strategies using railroads in Britain and electricity in Argentina as examples. Britain pioneered in railway restructuring and in two coordination strategies: regulated and negotiated access charges. Argentina pioneered in electricity restructuring and in a third coordination strategy: the development of markets for bottleneck capacity. Finally, Chapter 13 presents some speculations about the relative costs and benefits of unbundling in five industries: electricity, railroads, natural gas, water, and telephones.

To foreshadow the results somewhat, the experience in railroads and electricity suggests that we have underestimated the problems of coordination in our enthusiasm to introduce competition. This does not mean that the problems of coordination are so large as to make unbundling undesirable—in most cases, the introduction of competition has brought large benefits that eclipse the problems of coordination. There are some promising solutions to coordination problems in sight, moreover, particularly in the case of electricity. Although we still have much to learn, coordination is likely to prove easier in electricity and gas than in either railroads or telephony.

The Determinants of Vertical Integration

Integration in Private and Unregulated Industries

Private firms constantly face decisions about how vertically integrated they should be.[3] Imagine an automobile manufacturer that assembles chassis, engines, transmissions, body panels, upholstery, and other parts into cars. The firm can produce the parts itself or buy them from independent suppliers. And the firm can sell its cars directly to consumers through its own retail outlets or sell them through independent wholesalers and retailers. The more components the firm produces itself and the more it is involved in the distribution and retailing, the more vertically integrated it is.

As explained in Chapter 2, the firm faces a range of options for its involvement in upstream or downstream activities. At the two extremes are the options of buying the part or service on the spot market and making the part or service internally. In between are options that involve long-term contracts between the firm and independent suppliers or distributors.

Buying on the spot market is often the preferred solution, because competition in spot markets usually ensures lower cost and more reliable supplies. But the spot market discourages buyers and sellers from taking advantage of the potential economies that can be gained from tailoring their facilities, employees, or processes to one another's capabilities and needs. A supplier might be able to make the part the firm desires more cheaply by investing in specialized tools or training, for example, or the firm might reduce the costs of using a particular supplier by locating its plant next door. The party that makes such durable and relationship-specific investments leaves itself vulnerable to opportunism on the part of the other.

Where relationship-specific investments are advantageous, buyers and sellers often try to protect themselves by negotiating a long-term sales contract. If the length of the contract matches the life of the relationship-specific investments, then both parties should be less vulnerable to opportunism. The key limitation of a long-term contract, of course, is that it may prove to be incomplete or obsolete if circumstances change in important and unforeseen ways. Vertical integration can be seen as a last resort, used only when relationship-specific investments are important and it is difficult to draft a complete contract.

It is important to recognize that the difficulty of drafting a complete contract depends not just on the uncertainty of the industry's economic or technological environment but on the complexity and intimacy of the relationship between downstream and upstream activities. The more complex and intimate the relationship, the harder it is to describe in a written contract and the more vulnerable the relationship will be to small changes in the environment. Automobile companies almost always produce their own exterior body panels, for example, in part because a good fit is critical both to customer satisfaction and to the control of assembly costs. Internal production is also encouraged by the desire for speed and secrecy when car models are being redesigned. It is simply easier to produce tight-fitting body panels of changing design by manufacturing the panels internally than by contracting for them through the firm's purchasing office.[4]

Vertical Integration in Infrastructure

One would expect relatively high levels of vertical integration in infrastructure, because infrastructure is characterized by durable and immobile investments that make both suppliers and their customers vulnerable to opportunism. But while some types of infrastructure are highly integrated, others are not. Until recently, for example, railroads, electricity, and telephones were more vertically integrated than highways, airports, and many seaports. If highways were as vertically integrated as most railroads, then highway authorities would own and operate most of the trucks, buses, and automobiles that use the roads.

Two factors tend to reduce opportunism, and the resulting pressures for vertical integration, in some types of infrastructure. The first is that suppliers are less vulnerable to their customers where the infrastructure can be designed for use by many different customers rather than tailored to the needs of a specific one. Each customer depends upon the infrastructure, but the customers' needs are not so distinct or complex that they cannot share the use of a common facility.

The role of customer-specific designs is illustrated by comparing container and bulk materials terminals in seaports. Container terminals are often owned by port authorities and used by many different liner companies, while the major bulk terminals are usually owned and used exclusively by a mining, power, steel, grain, or oil company. The standard container berth, crane, and storage area can readily handle most container vessels, which reduces the advantages that would be gained from tailoring the designs of these facilities to the needs of a particular liner company. With major bulk materials terminals, by contrast, there can be significant savings from closely coordinating the designs of vessels, cargo-handling equipment, and land storage and transfer facilities, particularly if huge volumes are being shipped. An independent port authority would be reluctant to build a custom-designed bulk terminal for a particular customer without the protection of a long-term contract. And if the terminal is intended for a single user, it may be easier for that user to own and operate the terminal than to negotiate a contract for it.[5]

Highways, airports, and some telecommunications facilities are similar to container terminals in that a standard design can often be used by many different customers. Most highways are designed to accommodate a wide variety of motor vehicle types, for example, ranging from small automobiles to heavy trucks. A highway designed for autos only could be built with thinner pavements and narrower lanes than one used by both trucks and autos. But the savings from doing so are often modest,[6] and offset in part by other advantages of joint auto-truck use, such as a larger number of lanes to make it easier to pass slow vehicles or to accommodate surges in demand. Similarly, many airports and long-distance telecommunications lines are designed to be useful for a wide variety of users.

Railroads and long-distance power transmission systems are more like a marine bulk terminal in that they are often tailored to particular users. Branch lines of the railroad or power transmission network are often maintained for specific customers, while trunk lines, though usually shared, are sometimes optimized for specific users. The design of a railroad trunk line varies enormously depending upon whether it is used by passenger or freight trains, for example, and the design of the trunk transmission network can be greatly affected by the location of a new industrial load or generating plant. A private railroad or a high-voltage transmission company would be reluctant to make specialized investments in a branch or main line without the protection of a long-term contract from its customer.

The second factor reducing opportunism and the need for vertical integration is the prevalence of government ownership or regulation to control monopoly. While standard designs reduce the vulnerability of infrastructure suppliers to customers, government ownership or regulation reduces the vulnerability of infrastructure customers to suppliers. Some infrastructure industries might have been organized very differently had it not been for government intervention to control monopoly. In the cases of highways and airports, for example, the combination of durable and immobile investments and economies of scale makes expressways and commercial airports natural monopolies in many markets. Without government ownership or regulation to protect against monopoly power, trucking or airline companies might have been forced to acquire and operate the key highways or airports they used.

Government regulation or ownership is not necessarily a good substitute for vertical integration, particularly where the advantages of close coordination are great. The key problem, as noted earlier, is that the presence of the government may complicate coordination by adding another perspective or party to the negotiations. If the infrastructure firm is privately owned but regulated, then contracts may be harder to negotiate because a third party, the regulator, has to approve each one. And if the infrastructure firm is publicly owned but its customers are private, the contracts may be hard to negotiate because the public and private sectors have different priorities or perspectives.

Government regulation can also distort decisions about vertical integration. Often the government encourages excessive integration in order to protect cross-subsidies for socially or politically desirable services. As explained in Chapter 4, U.S. telephone regulators initially opposed the introduction of competition in long-distance service and customer-premises equipment in part because of fears about maintaining subsidized rates for basic residential service. And sometimes the burden of government-mandated cross-subsidies becomes so heavy that customers vertically integrate simply to avoid it. Some large U.S. corporations built private telephone systems in the 1950s and 1960s specifically to avoid the high markups regulators imposed on business calls and equipment.[7]

Finally, while government regulation may reduce the need for vertical integration, vertical integration usually does not reduce the pressures for regulation. Private long-term contracts, vertical integration, and government regulation are substitutes for one another inasmuch as they are all strategies for limiting the opportunism associated with relationship-specific investments. Vertical integration can be seen as an extreme solution, in which a supplier and customer merge so that their interests coincide and they no longer are tempted to take advantage of one another. But local infrastructure involves relationship-specific investments by both the ultimate retail consumers and the infrastructure suppliers in that both commit themselves to particular locations through durable and immobile investments. Thus a merger between two companies in an infrastructure supply chain may resolve their mutual vulnerability but not the vulnerability between the new integrated company and the final consumer. Only a merger or a long-term contract between the infrastructure supplier and the final infrastructure consumer would eliminate that vulnerability.[8]

Regulatory Complications Caused by Unbundling

Rate Rebalancing and Stranded Assets

Unbundling can complicate regulation in several ways. One is coping with the legacy of unprofitable services and investments from the old, vertically integrated regime. The competition that accompanies unbundling often exposes unprofitable services or investments that had been hidden in the larger integrated firms. This problem is referred to as one of rate rebalancing or of stranded assets. Where vertical unbundling makes old cross-subsidy schemes untenable, rates may have to be rebalanced so that each service is now profitable on its own. If the rates are not rebalanced, or some other source of revenue provided, the assets used to provide the unprofitable services will be stranded in that the owners will never recover their investments.[9]

In some cases, the problem of rebalancing is only transitional. For example, the introduction of competition in electricity generation in the United States left the utilities that owned nuclear power plants in a difficult position, because these plants were unlikely to earn enough in the emerging competitive wholesale power market to repay their construction costs. Few people would advocate building additional nuclear plants knowing that they were unlikely to be cost competitive, so only a one-time solution was needed for the plants that existed. Nevertheless, deciding whether and how the investors in these plants should be compensated proved very controversial. Opponents of compensation argued that it would reward poor management and investment. Proponents of compensation argued that the investments were prudent at the time the plants were started since the demand for electricity was increasing rapidly and many experts were optimistic about the costs of nuclear power. Proponents also claimed that a failure to compensate would increase the perceived risks of investing in regulated utilities and thus the rates of return future investors required. The proponents largely won this argument, as many states imposed special surcharges on electricity prices to pay for the costs of stranded nuclear plants.

In other cases, rate balancing problems are chronic, because there is strong support for continuing the underlying cross-subsidy. In electricity, for example, many environmentalists argue that wind, solar, and other "renewable" energy sources ought to be encouraged on the grounds that they cause less environmental damage than fossil fuel or nuclear alternatives. When the electricity industry was vertically integrated, it was easy for regulators to order utilities to experiment with renewable sources, since their higher costs could be averaged in with cheaper fossil plants in the rates that consumers paid. Once generation is unbundled and made competitive, however, the wind and solar plants are as vulnerable as the nuclear plants, except that there is strong support (at least from environmentalists) for building more of them.

A variety of different solutions have been adopted to maintain cross-subsidies for renewable energy in the United States. Some states require that wholesale electricity buyers show that a specified minimum percentage of the energy they purchase is generated by renewable sources. Other states impose a surcharge on wholesale electricity transactions, and use the proceeds to pay a premium to wind and solar generators. These measures have stimulated debate about whether cross-subsidies for environmentally friendly power are worthwhile. Critics argue that the subsidies required exceed the value of environmental damage avoided, while environmentalists argue that wind and solar costs are declining as we gain more experience with the technologies.

Whatever the merits of the renewable energy cross-subsidy, similar controversies will emerge as other infrastructure industries are unbundled and their cross-subsidies exposed. Vertical unbundling will force regulators to decide whether those cross-subsidies are worthwhile, how to transition out of those that are not, and how to maintain those that are.

Line-of-Business Restrictions and Vertical Foreclosure

Unbundling also involves regulators in policing the separation imposed on the industry. Regulators must decide whether the newly separated segments of the industry should be kept out of each other's line of business and, if not, whether vertical foreclosure is a problem. Vertical foreclosure can occur when one firm is engaged in two stages of production but its competitors are engaged in only one. The fear is that the firm involved in both stages will use its monopoly at the one stage to gain an upper hand over its competitors in the second stage. The essential source of difficulty is the monopoly at the first stage of production, and the problem could be eliminated by effective regulation of that monopoly by public authorities. But the fact that the monopolist is also involved in the second stage gives him added opportunities to evade regulatory constraints, for example, by shifting costs between the two stages.[10]

Concerns about vertical foreclosure often arise in industries where vertical unbundling has been only partial or incomplete. For example, Chile and a number of other countries established competition in electricity generation without completely separating generation from transmission and distribution. In Chile until recently, one company, Enersis, owned the national high-voltage transmission system, the largest distribution company, and 55 percent of the country's generating capacity. Similarly, New Zealand, Britain, and many other countries have introduced competition in long-distance calls while allowing the local telephone companies to continue to offer long-distance service. The concern in these cases is that the operators of the high-voltage transmission system or the local telephone loop may not provide access on fair terms to independent electricity generators or long-distance telephone companies.[11] The problem of regulating transmission and local loop access would have existed anyway, since both are thought to have elements of natural monopoly. But the fact that the monopolists are also in their customers' line of business makes the customers feel much more vulnerable.

Even where separation is initially complete, the firms in the industry may press the regulator to relax restrictions on the businesses they can be in. In the United States, for example, the seven local telephone companies created by the 1984 breakup of AT&T were prohibited from offering long-distance telephone services. Long-distance companies were not prohibited from entering the local telephone business, however, a restriction that seemed increasingly unfair to the ex-AT&T companies, especially after some new long-distance companies began to build competing local telephone networks in the dense central business districts of major cities. The ex-AT&T companies argued that customers wanted the convenience of "one-stop shopping" for local and long-distance telephone service. In addition, these companies claimed that there were economies in offering local and long-distance services together, since many of the assets needed to supply one service were also useful for the other. In 1996 Congress passed a bill that would allow the ex-AT&T local telephone companies to offer long-distance services, but only after their local markets were reasonably competitive. Congress also included elaborate safeguards designed to ensure that the companies would offer connections to competitors in a nondiscriminatory fashion. The regulations developed by the Federal Communications Commission to implement the law have proved to be very complex and highly controversial.[12]

Issues of vertical foreclosure and line-of-business restrictions are not unique to vertically unbundled industries. The fact that these industries were once integrated, however, strengthens the argument that there might be significant advantages to bringing the newly separate activities back together under one firm. As a result, regulators are far more likely to be pressed about line-of-business restrictions and fears of foreclosure in vertically unbundled industries than they would be in industries that were never integrated.

Coordination of Operations and Investment

The final and potentially most important complication caused by vertical unbundling is that regulators may have to be closely involved in the coordination of the operations and investment of the newly separated firms. Before vertical unbundling, most regulated infrastructure companies dealt directly with thousands or millions of retail consumers. The job was made easier by the fact that most of their customers didn't have very specialized needs, so that they could usually make do with one of several standard service packages the firm offered. This simplified regulation as well, since the regulator had to monitor the price, quality, and availability of only a fairly limited set of standardized services.

After vertical unbundling, by contrast, many of the new bottleneck infrastructure suppliers no longer provide services to retail consumers. Instead, the bottleneck firms function more like wholesale or parts suppliers to other new companies that produce and sell retail. In a vertically unbundled railroad system, for example, the infrastructure company supplies track, station, and other services to train-operating companies that, in turn, deal directly with shippers and passengers. Similarly in a vertically unbundled electricity system, the high-voltage transmission company transports electricity between generators and distributors, and the distributors (who are also regulated) deal directly with the public. In a vertically unbundled telephone system, the local telephone companies sell local calling services retail, but they also wholesale access to their local loops to wireless and long-distance telephone companies.

The bottleneck suppliers have many fewer customers than the old integrated companies, but the customers are much more demanding. The services that the bottleneck companies provide are key inputs for their customers, so key that they were once produced internally. And these customers want services tailored exactly to their needs, in part because the stakes of good service are so high. In the case of railroads, for example, the track-infrastructure needs of the train-operating companies are likely to vary considerably among traffic corridors, so that track service standards and charges will vary greatly from one corridor to the next. In addition, where several competing train-operating companies serve the same corridor, they may have conflicting standards for the design of the track and the schedules.

The high stakes and lack of standardization complicate the task of regulation. Because customized services are so important, the regulator may often need to become heavily involved in the details of the design and pricing of services for individual customers. And because the services are key inputs for each customer, the regulator's skill in monitoring individual services may be critical to the performance of the industry.

Three Strategies for Encouraging Coordination

Regulated Access Charges

Policymakers have been experimenting with three strategies for coordinating the activities of newly separated firms. The most common approach has been to authorize an industry regulator to establish the charges that the remaining bottleneck infrastructure companies can charge for access to their facilities or services. In railroads, for example, the regulator would set the charges that train-operating companies pay to use the railroad infrastructure company's track, stations, and yards. In electricity, the regulator would set the charges the generating and distribution companies pay for access to the transmission company's lines. And in telecommunications the regulator would set the charges long-distance and wireless carriers pay the local telephone companies for access to their local loops.

Economists usually argue that the access charges should be set at the incremental or marginal cost, for a reasonably efficient infrastructure firm, of accommodating additional demand. Access charges set at incremental costs will ensure that customers use the services only when they value them at least as much as they cost to produce. Such charges should motivate the firm to control its costs and, one hopes, to provide as much capacity as the customers request.

One problem in setting such charges, noted earlier, is that the customers' service needs are usually more varied and harder to standardize after the industry is unbundled. In practice, regulators don't have the time and resources to determine the incremental costs of many different and specialized services. As a consequence, every access price schedule usually involves some simplifications that result in undercharging for some services and overcharging for others. If unbundling makes customization more important, it will also increase the distortions caused by standardized service offerings and price schedules.

The task of setting charges is also made much harder by the tendency of bottleneck infrastructure facilities to exhibit large sunk costs and economies of scale. Facilities with these characteristics have incremental costs that are lower than average costs, at least as long as the facility is operating with sufficient capacity. This creates two serious pricing problems. First, prices set at incremental costs—the prices that economists tend to recommend—will not generate enough revenue for the firm to be financially self-sufficient over the long run. Some additional source of revenue is needed. Second, incremental costs—and prices based on them—tend to be fairly volatile depending upon whether or not the facility is at capacity or not. When a facility is below capacity, incremental costs are low, because the facility is durable and immobile so that much of its costs appear to be sunk. But when a facility is at capacity, incremental costs are very high, because the facility has to be expanded if it is to accommodate more customers.

Sunk costs and economies of scale are always present in infrastructure industries to some degree, but vertical unbundling intensifies them by separating the portions of the industry where sunk costs and economies of scale are most important from those where they are not. Competition is possible in electricity generation, train operations, and long-distance calling precisely because sunk costs and economies of scale tend to be more modest in these activities. As a result, the separate transmission, track, and local telephone companies have higher proportions of sunk or fixed costs than the old integrated firms did. And this means that the differences between incremental and average costs and the volatility of incremental costs for these bottleneck companies may be enormous.

There are two main solutions to the financial shortfalls caused by pricing at incremental costs, but neither is completely satisfactory.[13] One is to use public subsidies to cover the difference between incremental and average costs. Public subsidies are often unacceptable, however, especially in countries that have turned to private provision of infrastructure because of a shortage of public funds.

The second solution is to charge some customers who are less price sensitive a markup over incremental costs. In theory, this kind of price discrimination, artfully designed, can generate additional revenue but leave demand much the same as it would be if all customers were charged incremental costs. In practice, price discrimination can be difficult to implement because it is often hard to identify the least price sensitive customers and because the customers who pay more have strong incentives to find substitutes in the long run.[14] Price discrimination tends to be politically controversial as well, since the customers singled out to pay more usually complain loudly about the inequity.

The problem of price volatility is equally hard to deal with. Regulators are often tempted to assume, at least initially, that the bottleneck or monopoly portions of the restructured industry have excess capacity. This assumption allows the regulator to keep access prices low, which is both politically popular and reduces the need to search for public subsidies or engage in price discrimination. But the resulting low prices stimulate demand and hasten the day when additional capacity will be needed, without any assurance that the new customers value the added capacity enough to justify it. In addition, the low prices mean the infrastructure firm does not have the resources or incentive to build the added capacity when it becomes necessary.

Once capacity shortages develop, the regulator is usually forced to raise prices to fund the expansions. But the adjustments tend to be ad hoc, in response to problems as they evolve. As a result, the pricing system usually does not anticipate the need for capacity enhancements or build in systematic incentives to provide for them.

Negotiated Access Charges

The second strategy for encouraging coordinating after vertical unbundling is to allow the monopoly or bottleneck infrastructure provider and its customers to negotiate agreements about access charges and related issues. Typically there is some provision to allow the regulator to review the agreement, particularly in the event of an impasse or if the customers complain that the bottleneck infrastructure provider is abusing his monopoly position. If the infrastructure provider and customers agree on a solution, however, the regulator usually will not intervene.

Negotiated agreements are sometimes used to set all access charges. In the United States, for example, the 1996 Telecommunications Act requires that incumbent and new local telephone companies negotiate over all interconnection charges. If they fail to reach an agreement, they submit their dispute to arbitration supervised by the state regulators.[15] More often the regulator will set the basic or standard access charge but then rely on negotiations to establish supplementary access charges for those customers who want special or additional services or capacity improvements. In the British railways, for example, the regulator sets access charges for existing track capacity, but the train-operating companies and the track company negotiate special charges for any capacity enhancements the train-operating companies desire.

Negotiated access agreements got some unintended encouragement from an article written in the 1980s by William Baumol and Robert Willig, two well-known U.S. regulatory economists.[16] At the time the United States was considering deregulating its railroads and unbundling AT&T, and one issue being debated was whether railroad and telephone regulators should intervene in negotiations among railroad and telephone companies about how to share revenues for connecting traffic. Baumol and Willig argued that the firms in a vertically unbundled industry, left on their own and without the supervision of a regulator, had strong incentives to negotiate the least-cost routings for rail cars and telephone calls and to invest in only cost-effective new network links. Their observation became known as the "efficient component pricing rule," because of Baumol and Willig's concern that vertically unbundled industries produce their services using their most efficient components.

Baumol and Willig's argument was initially applied to railroads, although the parallels with telecommunications, electricity, and other infrastructure industries are obvious. Imagine that coal is being shipped from a mine at point A to a power plant at point C, as shown in Figure 10.1. Only one railroad serves the entire route from A to C, but a second railroad serves from an intermediate point B to C. If the first railroad has the lowest incremental cost from B to C, then it will carry the traffic the entire distance from A to C. If the second railroad has the lowest cost from B to C, however, then the first railroad will find it profitable to negotiate to have the second railroad carry the traffic from B to C.

How the two railroads divide the tariffs paid by the coal shipper depends on their relative bargaining skills. The second railroad will insist on recovering at least its own incremental costs for the B-to-C movement, but it may be able to negotiate for more, given that the first railroad's incremental costs for B to C are higher. The important point is that the two railroads will be motivated to use the least-cost route without the intervention of a regulator. Similarly, investors have incentives to build new railroads between A and B or B and C if and only if the new lines have lower incremental costs than the existing ones.

Some policymakers have misinterpreted Baumol and Willig's argument as implying that one can safely allow infrastructure companies and their customers to negotiate access charges on their own, without any form of government regulation.[17] But Baumol and Willig do not argue that regulation is completely unnecessary, only that it is not needed to ensure the use of efficient components. To use the railroad example again, their analysis deals only with the relationship between the two railroads, and not with the relationship between the shipper and the first railroad. Baumol and Willig assumed that the shipper and the first railroad would be protected from opportunism either by private long-term contracts or by government regulation of the railroad's coal tariffs. Similarly, when Baumol and Willig applied their argument to the U.S. telephone system, they focused only on the relationships between local and long-distance companies that wanted access to each other's networks, and assumed that the rates the local telephone companies charged their subscribers were already regulated.[18]

If we set aside the misunderstanding about regulation, Baumol and Willig's observation underlines the principal advantage of negotiated access agreements in allowing firms the flexibility to tailor access arrangements to their particular circumstances. Baumol and Willig point out that the firms

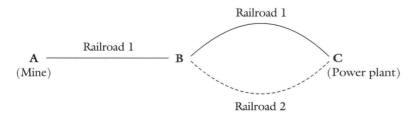

Figure 10.1 Illustration of the Baumol-Willig rule in railroads.

have strong incentives to identify and negotiate agreements that cut their costs. And such cooperative arrangements are particularly important when an industry that was once integrated is unbundled.

The key disadvantage of negotiated access charges is that negotiations can be time consuming and costly. Usually the issues to be negotiated are complex and the stakes high, because the services being purchased are such an integral part of the buyer's production process. Often other users of the bottleneck facility are affected, which complicates negotiations by increasing the number of parties involved. The regulator usually must be involved as well, to ensure that the monopoly or bottleneck supplier is not abusing his position.[19] The transaction costs of negotiations among so many different parties over issues that are so important to them are likely to be high. And the high transaction costs may prevent the parties from reaching an agreement even when the potential gains of a customized solution are high.

Markets for Infrastructure Capacity Rights

A final strategy for coordinating vertically separated industries is to create a market for capacity rights in the monopoly infrastructure system. Such proposals are in their infancy, but have been used with some success in natural gas pipelines and are being discussed in the electricity industry. The basic idea is to establish a competitive market for infrastructure capacity by either auctioning or assigning property rights to existing capacity and allowing those rights to be traded. The resulting market for capacity rights permits users to protect themselves from possible capacity shortfalls by buying the appropriate capacity right. Moreover, the prices at which these rights trade provide a signal as to whether investment is needed. If rights are trading for more than the equivalent annual cost of building additional capacity, for example, then it is economical to expand the system. In some schemes, entrepreneurs are permitted to finance the expansion of the system and, in return, receive (and can sell or rent) the rights to the capacity they create.

Markets for capacity rights have enormous appeal since they promise a relatively decentralized solution to the problem of providing for increased capacity. Capacity rights do not eliminate the need for regulation, since the incumbent infrastructure provider still needs to recover its short-run incremental costs and a regulator needs to determine whether those charges are fair. But the regulator would not need to closely review or supervise negotiations over improvements to capacity. Instead, the market for capacity rights would send the appropriate signals between infrastructure users and suppliers, and independent entrepreneurs could build the capacity if the incumbent was unwilling.

Marketable capacity rights have several practical problems. One is to prevent the market for capacity rights from being monopolized or becoming a source of competitive problems. If one firm bought all the capacity rights, for example, it might exercise substantial monopoly power. The threat of capacity expansion would limit that monopoly power, but that threat may not always be realistic, particularly where environmental or land assembly controversies make it hard to build new facilities. At the very least, one might want to limit the amount of capacity rights that any one firm could acquire and impose restrictions on the circumstances under which an owner could withhold capacity from the market.[20]

A second problem is whether potential investors in infrastructure capacity will be discouraged by the high volatility of the prices for capacity rights. The short-term or rental value of capacity rights will be zero when there is excess capacity, will rise as congestion on the system develops, and then fall back to zero again once new capacity is opened. As a result, investors in new capacity may have to wait a long time before their rights gain any rental value, especially if there are economies of scale in infrastructure capacity so that it is advantageous to build new capacity in large increments. Users may be so desirous of protection from price volatility that they are willing to finance capacity rights in advance of construction or to sign long-term contracts with infrastructure providers. In the absence of such guarantees, investors may be unwilling to build new capacity.

A third practical problem is that it may be hard to define capacity clearly. This problem is most troublesome where the infrastructure system is interdependent in the sense that the flows on one part affect capacity on other parts. The extent of interdependence varies among the different forms of infrastructure—it can be high in electricity transmission networks, for example, but may be low or modest in gas or railway networks. Interdependence means it is difficult to estimate the capacity for any given flow without knowing all the other capacity demands on the system. Some neutral system operator would have to be empowered to define capacity rights and to adjust those rights when users requested changes in the flows.

In sum, vertical unbundling involves a trade-off between the benefits of introducing competition and the costs of increasing coordination. This trade-off is likely to vary from one industry to the next, because the potential gains from competition and the problems of coordination vary across industries. To understand the nature of this trade-off and its implications for regulation, the next two chapters compare the experiences of unbundling in railroads and electricity.

11

Regulating Coordination: British Railroads

Coordination's Importance

The experience of Britain's railroads illustrates how important and difficult it can be to maintain coordination in a vertically unbundled industry. The breakup and privatization of British Rail in the early 1990s is the most ambitious attempt at vertical unbundling in railways to date. The British government divided its national railway into approximately seventy different companies, the most important being a monopoly infrastructure company called Railtrack, twenty-five passenger train–operating companies (nicknamed TOCs), and two freight TOCs. Railtrack owned the track, stations, yards, and other infrastructure used by the TOCs. The twenty-five passenger TOCs specialized in particular travel corridors and service types (commuter, regional, or intercity), while one freight TOC specialized in container traffic and the other in bulk commodities.

Railtrack supported itself from track and station access fees paid by the TOCs, and these fees were set by a government-appointed rail regulator. The rail regulator used a system of preset access charges and performance penalties to manage congestion on the existing track and station network. The regulator relied on supplemental access charges negotiated by Railtrack and the TOCs to fund increases in network capacity.

Initially, the scheme succeeded in improving service and reducing costs. Franchises for the twenty-five passenger TOCs were auctioned off to the bidders who promised to maintain existing services and fares for the least government subsidy. The competition for the franchises was intense, and the winning bids called for substantial reductions in government aid over time. Passenger and freight traffic increased significantly, thanks to improvements in the quantity and quality of train services.

Within a few years, however, performance began to suffer because of poor coordination between Railtrack and the TOCs. The preset schedule of access charges didn't vary much with the number of trains operated, which encouraged the TOCs to congest the tracks with additional trains, reducing system reliability and making track maintenance harder. The negotiations over capacity enhancements proved so difficult, moreover, that Railtrack, the rail regulator, and the TOCs could agree to only one major project to increase track capacity. That agreement—for an upgrade on the West Coast Main Line between London and Glasgow—was reached only by deferring decisions on controversial aspects of the project.

By the end of the 1990s train punctuality and reliability began to deteriorate as the track network became more congested and the upgrade of the West Coast Main Line fell seriously behind schedule and over budget. Public confidence was undermined by three serious accidents in four years, the last caused by the shattering of a section of rail that Railtrack had known was badly worn but had delayed replacing. In 2001 the government finally forced the bankruptcy of Railtrack by refusing to make further payments to help with the costs of the accidents and the overruns on the West Coast Main Line project. In 2002, in a reform critics argued was tantamount to renationalization, the government reorganized Railtrack as a nonprofit company governed by representatives of passenger groups, the TOCs, the rail unions, and the general public.

Railways Separation outside of Britain

Prior to 1988, train operations and infrastructure were separated only in special and limited circumstances. The most notable examples involved Amtrak and private freight railroads in the United States. Amtrak is a government-owned corporation created in 1970 to revive long-distance rail passenger services. Amtrak owns only five hundred miles of its own right of way, primarily in the heavily traveled Washington–Philadelphia–New York–Boston corridor. Elsewhere it uses the tracks of private freight railroads, who have agreed to provide access on reasonable terms in return for being released from their obligations to offer passenger services.[1] Many U.S. freight railroads also have limited rights to operate trains over other railroads' track. In some cases rights have been exchanged in an effort to rationalize operations on parallel lines. In other cases the government has required that merging railroads grant access rights to an independent railroad so that shippers still have a choice of carriers. Although track rights are important to preserve passenger service and maintain competition among freight railroads in the United States, only a modest percentage of trains travel over other railroads' tracks.[2]

During the late 1980s and the 1990s, more than a dozen countries privatized their railways, but only Britain took the opportunity to separate infrastructure from train operations. The far more popular strategy—adopted by

Japan, Argentina, Brazil, Mexico, Chile, and several other countries—was to horizontally restructure by dividing a single national railway into several regional railways. Some countries endowed their new regional railroads with slightly overlapping route networks or limited track rights, so as to provide a degree of interrailway competition. Each regional railroad remained vertically integrated, however, responsible for both infrastructure and train operations.[3]

Sweden made the first systematic effort to separate infrastructure from operations in 1988, when it divided its national railway into two companies: one to own and maintain the infrastructure and the other to operate trains. The Swedes left both companies in public hands, however, and allowed private independent train operators to offer freight and passenger services only under limited circumstances. As a result, there was relatively little private entry into the train-operating business, and the public train-operating company experienced only a modest amount of competition.[4] The rail infrastructure company was heavily subsidized by the government, moreover, and its investments were determined by the Ministry of Transport's plans rather than by their potential to generate revenues from access charges paid by train operators.[5]

Shortly after the Swedish reforms, the European Commission began promoting separate management for track infrastructure and train operations, although not necessarily by creating separate companies. The commission wanted to encourage a more commercial mentality among Europe's railways by requiring them to gradually open access to their railway tracks.[6] In 1991 the commission issued a directive requiring that railways separate the accounts and management for infrastructure and operations. The directive also obligated European railroads to provide track access on a nondiscriminatory basis to any consortia of international railways offering passenger or freight services and to any railway offering international container services. In a 1995 directive, the commission provided more details on how much railroads could charge for track access. For example, the directive prohibited charging more than necessary to recover infrastructure costs over a reasonable period of time.[7]

By the end of the 1990s, the European Commission's directives had not yet stimulated other countries to imitate Britain, although several countries had taken some tentative steps in that direction. Germany was the farthest along toward the British model, having divided its national railway into five companies, one each for long-distance passenger services, short-distance passenger services, freight services, passenger stations, and other infrastructure. These companies were still owned by a single government holding company, although Germany had announced its intention to privatize them as independent companies. Netherlands had also established separate train and infrastructure companies, and Italy was planning to do so. However, most other major European countries, including France, seemed unlikely to follow suit anytime soon.[8] There had been some new entry into domestic train services, particularly in Germany. Only two consortia had taken advantage of the international access rights mandated by the commission.[9]

The Restructuring and Privatization of British Rail

Motives and Constraints

British Rail was created when the government nationalized Britain's private railroads in 1948.[10] British Rail's market share declined fairly steadily from the 1950s through the 1980s, especially on its freight, regional passenger, and intercity passenger services, where it faced the most serious competition from trucks, buses. and private automobiles. Commuter ridership suffered less, particularly in and around London where traffic congestion made auto and bus alternatives less attractive. The government tried to reduce the railroad's need for public subsidies by abandoning services on many unprofitable and lightly used branch lines in the 1960s and then by modernizing the track and rolling stock on many remaining trunk lines in the 1970s. Nevertheless, British Rail remained a substantial drain on the Treasury.

British Rail escaped privatization during the 1980s, when the Conservative Party led by Margaret Thatcher sold off many other utilities. The railroad may have been spared because of the sheer complexity of its services, but as the 1980s ended, the company's performance continued to deteriorate and there was little left to privatize. In 1992 the Conservative Party, then led by John Major, finally announced its intention to sell off British Rail.

The government's decision to separate track infrastructure from train operations was a response in part to criticism that it had failed to exploit similar opportunities to introduce competition in some of its earlier utility privatizations. British Telecom had been sold intact and with protections against new entrants, for example, and British Gas had been sold as a whole instead of separating gas production from transmission or distribution. This had increased the prices the government received for the companies, but it troubled many observers, including the government's own Monopolies and Mergers Commission, which by the early 1990s was considering whether to order the breakup of British Gas.

The privatization of British Rail was challenging, because many of its money-losing passenger services were popular with voters. Moreover, subsidies to rail were thought desirable to reduce auto congestion and air pollution. To avoid controversy, the government promised to maintain or improve the level of passenger services during privatization. The announced goal was to reduce the cost of providing existing services and to provide incentives to create new services.

The Restructuring and Sales

To that end, British Rail was divided into approximately seventy separate companies, the most important being Railtrack. At first the government planned to leave Railtrack in the public sector, but the company's behavior during the transition convinced officials that it would never be innovative and commercially minded unless it was privatized. In May 1996 Railtrack's stock was successfully offered to the public for 390 pence per share, for a total sales price of £1.9 billion.

British Rail's passenger services were divided into twenty-five TOCs, with the government specifying the services to be provided by each TOC, including maximum fares and minimum train frequencies. Most of the TOC franchises were for seven years, but seven franchises where the government desired higher levels of investment were offered for terms of up to fifteen years. The franchises were awarded competitively on the basis of, first, the level of subsidy requested and second, whether the bidder promised to provide additional services or investments beyond the minimum required. The franchise auctions began in December 1995 and were completed in February 1997.

Most winning bidders promised fairly dramatic reductions in subsidy, in some cases actually offering to pay the government during the last years of the franchise (see Table 11.1). The twenty-five franchises were won by thirteen separate companies, all with prior experience in transportation.[11] Private bus companies won fifteen franchises.[12] Richard Branson's Virgin Group—which operated an international airline—bought two franchises, including the intercity service from London to Glasgow that operated on the West Coast Main Line. Sea Containers—which operated the Orient Express passenger train in Europe as well as ocean shipping—bought the intercity service from London to Edinburgh on the East Coast Main Line.

Freight services were initially divided into seven TOCs, but eventually consolidated into two, each specializing in a different line of business.[13] The freight TOCs were declared ineligible for government subsidy, but their track access fees were to be based primarily on Railtrack's variable costs, with only limited responsibility for fixed costs or overhead. The government thought such low access fees would help make freight services profitable; low fees were also thought justified because Britain's track network was maintained largely for passenger service.

Three rolling stock companies (ROSCOs) were established to own and maintain the 11,000 existing passenger cars and locomotives and lease them to the passenger TOCs. The ROSCOs were created to increase the competition for the TOC franchises by eliminating the need for potential TOC bidders to invest in costly fleets. The ROSCOs would inherit leases ranging from four to ten years with the twenty-five TOCs, but the TOCs would be under no obligation to renew the leases when they expired or to use the ROSCOs for any additional equipment the TOCs required. The three ROSCOs were sold in January 1996 for £1.8 billion.

Finally, British Rail's engineering departments were divided into thirteen British Rail infrastructure companies (BRISCOs), of which seven specialized in routine maintenance and six in major reconstruction or renewal. These companies were given initial contracts with Railtrack and sold in 1996, and would have to bid for future Railtrack business.

The Regulatory Framework

The Railway Act of 1993 established two new officials: a rail regulator to oversee Railtrack and a franchising director to award and monitor the passenger TOC franchises. The rail regulator is responsible for promoting the health and growth of the industry, but spends much of his time ensuring that Railtrack does not abuse its position as the sole infrastructure provider. The rail regulator's powers are similar to those of the other utility regulators Britain established in that era. A single regulator is appointed for a five-year term by the secretary of state for transport,[14] and that regulator is free from direction by the secretary and guided mainly by his statutory obligations.[15]

The regulator and his staff in the Office of the Rail Regulator (ORR) have two instruments for controlling the performance of Railtrack and the TOCs. First, the regulator issues each operating company a license that specifies the operator's general obligations. Railtrack's license mandates that it maintain the infrastructure in good condition, for example; the passenger TOC licenses cover such obligations as through ticketing, treatment of passenger grievances, and provisions for the handicapped. Second, the regulator reviews the track access agreements between Railtrack and the freight and passenger TOCs. These agreements specify not only the fee to be paid for access but the specific times the tracks are to be available. The agreements also establish the penalties that Railtrack must pay to a TOC if the tracks are not available when promised and the penalties a TOC must pay to Railtrack if its trains delay those of other operators.

The franchising director was less independent than the rail regulator in that he served at the pleasure of the secretary of state for transport and fol-

Table 11.1 Subsidy requested by winning TOCs, fiscal years 1996/97 to 2002/03

Train-operating company (TOC)	Date sold	Subsidy in millions of pounds (negative figures indicate payment to the government)						
		FY 96/97	FY 97/98	FY 98/99	FY 99/00	FY 00/01	FY 01/02	FY 02/03
Network South East (commuter)								
South West Trains	4 Feb. 96	63.3	63.4	60.8	55.7	50.5	45.2	35.7
LTS	26 May 96	31.1	27.7	25.1	23.4	21.9	20.6	19.3
Connex South Central	26 May 96	92.8	74.7	54.8	46.9	43.4	38.3	35.9
Chiltern	21 July 96	17.4	14.4	12.6	9.9	6.7	4.7	3.3
Connex South Eastern	13 Oct. 96	136.1	114.6	85.1	61.1	49.1	40.4	32.6
Thames	13 Oct. 96	43.7	34.2	24.8	17.0	13.5	7.6	3.8
Island Line	13 Oct. 96	2.3	2.0	1.9	1.8	1.8	1.0	
Anglia	5 Jan. 97	41.0	35.9	26.0	22.1	16.0	13.0	8.6
Great Eastern	5 Jan. 97	41.3	29.0	14.0	8.1	2.8	-0.3	-5.1
West Anglia & Great Northern	5 Jan. 97	72.6	54.9	34.7	25.4	13.1	4.3	-14.6
North London	2 Mar. 97	55.0	48.6	35.5	29.6	26.4	23.0	20.0
Thames Link	2 Mar. 97	18.5	2.5	-6.7	-16.2	-22.5	-23.2	-27.0
Subtotal Commuter		615.1	501.9	352.6	269.3	210.1	168.5	112.5

Regional Railways (medium distance)							
Cardiff	13 Oct. 96	22.5	20.4	18.1	17.1	15.8	15.0	14.3
South Wales & West	13 Oct. 96	84.6	72.9	62.2	57.4	51.4	47.5	44.0
Merseyrail	19 Jan. 97	87.6	80.7	72.8	67.2	64.9	62.0	61.8
North East	2 Mar. 97	231.1	224.5	197.1	175.8	164.3	156.3	150.6
North West	2 Mar. 97	192.9	184.9	184.9	168.9	153.4	140.8	129.7
Central	2 Mar. 97	204.4	187.5	173.4	153.7	145.8	140.9	136.6
Scotrail	1 Apr. 97	297.1	280.1	264.8	250.5	234.9	220.4	209.3
Subtotal Regional		1120.2	1051.0	973.3	890.6	830.5	782.9	746.3
Intercity (long distance)							
Great Western	4 Feb. 96	61.9	58.7	53.9	47.8	42.1	38.7	36.9
Gatwick Express	28 Apr. 96	−4.1	−6.2	−7.9	−9.8	−10.7	−11.5	−12.0
Great Northern Eastern	28 Apr. 96	67.3	55.0	36.3	16.5	6.2	2.0	0.1
Midland Main Line	28 Apr. 96	17.6	8.2	2.4	0.9	−0.6	−2.6	−4.4
Cross Country	5 Jan. 97	130.0	115.9	98.1	82.2	73.9	67.8	50.5
West Coast	9 Mar. 97	94.4	76.8	68.4	56.1	53.7	52.3	−3.9
Subtotal Intercity		367.1	308.4	251.2	193.7	164.6	146.7	67.2
Grand total		2102.4	1861.5	1577.1	1353.6	1205.2	1098.1	926.3

Source: Office of Passenger Rail Franchising, unpublished spreadsheet dated June 24, 1997.
Note: Figures in constant 1996/97 pounds.

lowed his instructions about the level of service desired and the amount of public subsidy available. The franchising director and his staff in the Office of Passenger Rail Franchising (OPRAF) specified the fares, frequencies, and other characteristics of the services required, invited bids, awarded franchises, supervised performance, and assessed penalties for noncompliance. In 1999 the government replaced OPRAF with a new Strategic Rail Authority (SRA), and the SRA chairman assumed the franchising director's duties. The legislation establishing the SRA was not passed until December 2000, but a "shadow" SRA was established in June 1999 in advance of the legislation.

In addition to the rail regulator and the franchising director, the railroad industry was regulated by the Health and Safety Executive (HSE), a government agency responsible for enforcing health and safety standards throughout British industry. The HSE licensed train crews, inspected facilities and equipment, investigated accidents, and ordered improvements where needed.

The First Periodic Review of Access Charges and Competition

The first rail regulator, John Swift, was appointed on December 1, 1993, before the sales of Railtrack and the TOCs had begun.[16] The Department of Transport had already announced an initial schedule of access charges for the first five years that would generate enough revenue to cover its estimates of Railtrack's operating cost plus an 8 percent return on the replacement cost of Railtrack's assets.[17] The new regulator thought that he should review Railtrack's access charges and announce his policy on allowing competition among TOCs before the companies were sold, however, so that potential investors would not be uncertain about his intentions. Swift issued consultation papers and invited comment from interested parties and the public during the summer of 1994, and issued his final decisions on both issues that winter.

Swift concluded that the Department of Transport's access charges were too generous. Eight percent was a higher return than most private companies were earning at the time, Swift argued. In addition, Railtrack did not need to earn a return on the replacement costs of all assets, since some, such as right of way and grading, essentially never depreciated. Railtrack should recover operating costs, depreciation on existing assets, and a return on investments made since privatization. Finally, Swift predicted that Railtrack could reduce its operating expenses by at least 2 percent per year. Swift's new schedule reduced access charges by 8 percent for the next fiscal year, 1995/96. In each of the subsequent five years (through fiscal year 2000/01), Railtrack could increase its charges by the retail price index (RPI) minus 2 percent.[18]

In an arguably more important ruling, Swift decided to significantly limit competition among passenger TOCs until 2002.[19] The government had been more concerned about Swift's competition ruling than about his access charge review. Changes in access charges were unlikely to cause major budgetary problems, because Railtrack and the TOCs had not been sold yet. If the regulator reduced access charges, for example, it would reduce the amount the government received from the sale of Railtrack but it would also reduce the amount of subsidy OPRAF would have to pay to the passenger TOCs. If Swift allowed unrestricted competition among the TOCs, however, the uncertainty might discourage potential bidders for the TOC franchises.

The government privately pressed its competition concerns on Swift, and he agreed. Swift concluded that it was difficult to predict the consequences of unrestricted competition on passenger welfare or the franchising director's subsidy bill, and that this risk should not be run so early in the restructuring process. Some competition would occur because the TOC franchises established by the franchising director inevitably overlapped a bit. But no additional entry would be allowed until April 1, 1999, and then only with severe limitations.[20] The constraints would be in place until March 31, 2002, but would be reviewed in 2001.

Initial Successes and Controversies

Higher Traffic and Lower Subsidies

Rail passenger traffic increased significantly in the years immediately following restructuring and privatization, largely because of improvements in the quality and quantity of train service. Traffic declined in fiscal years 1993/94 and 1994/95, presumably because of the confusion caused by reorganizing British Rail into separate business units in preparation for privatization.[21] Traffic began to pick up when the TOC sales began in 1995/96 and accelerated over the next few years, as shown in Table 11.2. Using fiscal year 1992/93 as the prereform baseline, the number of passenger journeys and passenger kilometers increased by 24 percent by fiscal year 2000/01, with most of the gains occurring in the first three years after privatization. Some of the ridership growth was probably due to the strong British economy in the 1990s, but British Rail's ridership had been relatively stagnant for so many decades that the increase after privatization stands out as a notable exception.[22]

Freight traffic showed a mixed pattern as the number of ton kilometers carried increased by 17 percent while the number of tons lifted declined by 27 percent between fiscal years 1992/93 and 2000/01. Rail freight was heavily

Table 11.2 Trends in rail traffic and revenue support, fiscal years 1986/87 to 2000/01

Fiscal year	Passenger journeys (millions)	Passenger kilometers (billions)	Freight tons (millions)	Freight-ton kilometers (billions)	Passenger revenue (millions of 1999/00 £)	Government revenue support (millions of 1999/00 £)
Prereform						
1986/87	738	30.8	138.4	16.6	2,458	1405
1987/88	798	32.4	144.4	17.5	2,624	1397
1988/89	822	34.3	149.5	18.1	2,733	923
1989/90	812	33.3	143.1	16.7	2,695	783
1990/91	810	33.2	138.2	16.0	2,697	984
1991/92	792	32.5	135.8	15.3	2,614	1,258
1992/93	770	31.7	122.4	15.5	2,575	1,536
Transition						
1993/94	740	30.4	103.2	13.8	2,555	1,252
1994/95	735	28.7	97.3	13.0	2,494	2,444
1995/96	761	30.0	100.7	13.3	2,657	2,284
Postreform						
1996/97	801	32.1	101.8	15.1	2,783	2,246
1997/98	846	34.7	105.4	16.9	2,968	1,881
1998/99	892	36.3	102.1	17.3	3,160	1,566
1999/00	931	38.5	91.6	18.2	3,368	1,343
2000/01	956	39.2	95.3	18.1	3,351	1,109
Percentage change 1992/93 to 2000/01	+24.5%	+23.7%	−27.1%	+16.7%	+30.1%	−27.8%

Sources: Department of the Environment, Transport and the Regions, *Bulletin of Rail Statistics Quarter 2 1999/2000*, publication SB(99) 12, December 1999, pp. 6, 8, 11, 14; and Strategic Rail Authority, *National Rail Trends 2001–02 (Quarter 1)*, September 2001, pp. 3, 4, 10, 23, 25, 28.

Note: Government revenue support includes grants for domestic passenger services by the central government and by Britain's six metropolitan passenger transport executives.

affected by a reduction in coal traffic as the British electric industry shifted to cheaper natural gas after electricity was privatized in 1990. If coal is excluded, the number of tons lifted declined by only 9 percent between 1992/93 and 2000/01, while the number of ton kilometers carried increased by 29 percent during that same period. Among the fastest-growing freight categories were domestic containers and construction materials.[23]

Passenger traffic grew despite modest fare increases. The franchise agreements prohibited the TOCs that provided intercity and regional service from raising average real fares for the first three years, and required them to reduce real fares by 1 percent per year for the following four years. The franchise agreements for the TOCs providing commuter service in the London area called for fare changes that depended on the quality of the service they provided. If a TOC performed well in the previous year, it could increase prices by the retail price index plus 2 percent; but if it performed poorly the increase could be as little as RPI minus 2 percent. The real average fare on all services combined increased by 5 percent between fiscal years 1992/93 and 2000/01.[24]

Government subsidies also declined significantly, although by exactly how much is hard to tell. One source of confusion is that the government's payments to rail doubled between fiscal years 1993/94 and 1994/95 largely because of changes in accounting practices when British Rail was reorganized in April 1994. After the reorganization, British Rail's new train-operating subsidiaries (which were to become the TOCs) began to pay access and rental fees to the new infrastructure and rolling stock subsidiaries (which were to become Railtrack and the ROSCOs). The £1.2 billion paid in 1993/94 was for cash outlays only; the £2.4 billion paid in 1994/95 also included the opportunity cost of invested capital and depreciation, because these costs were built into the access and equipment leasing fees that the new subsidiaries were now charging one another.[25] According to OPRAF, British Rail would have required comparable subsidies in both years if its aid were calculated on a consistent accounting basis.[26]

A second source of confusion is how to treat the proceeds from the sales of Railtrack, the ROSCOs, and various other British Rail subsidiaries. The government netted about £4.5 billion in cash from the sales, receiving approximately £5 billion for the companies but paying approximately £450 million in fees for investment bankers and for other consultants.[27] Just how "profitable" these sales were is difficult to determine, however, since it is hard to place a value on the assets the government transferred to the private sector.

Even ignoring the accounting changes and the sale proceeds, however, the level of government subsidy declined dramatically once the reforms were in place.[28] By fiscal year 2000/01 the level of government support had fallen roughly to £1.1 billion per year, 29 percent less than was paid out in 1992/93 and less than half of the amount paid in 1994/95 (Table 11.2).

The ability of the TOCs to expand service despite rapidly declining subsidies surprised even the advocates of the reforms. The bids for the last franchises auctioned had been substantially more aggressive than those for the first franchises, which led some observers to fear that some bidders had become overly optimistic.[29] Indeed four years later, in 2000, two TOCs gave up their franchises because of losses.[30]

Early Controversies over Profits and Investments

The press and the public paid less attention to the industry's success in attracting traffic and more to charges that the industry was earning excessive profits and reneging on service and investment commitments. Charges that the companies were being sold for too little emerged soon after the sales started. The restructuring received bad publicity when two ROSCOs that had been sold to their managers were quickly resold for much higher prices.[31] In addition, the price of Railtrack's stock doubled within a year of the initial offering and then doubled again in the next six months, a performance that far outpaced that of the British stock market as a whole.[32] The National Audit Office, a nonpartisan watchdog agency that monitors public spending, issued reports critical of both the ROSCO and the Railtrack sales. In Railtrack's case, for example, the agency argued that the government could have realized as much as £1.5 billion more by selling Railtrack's stock in two tranches instead of all at once.[33]

Whether the companies could have been sold for much more remains unclear. Early investors were taking a risk that the privatization scheme would not work out, and were bound to make profits when it seemed that it would. Moreover, some companies had to be sold first if the scheme was to proceed. The Department of Transport argued that it was important to sell Railtrack early, for example, so as to make the government's commitment to restructuring clear to potential investors in the TOCs.[34] The department did not want to hold back a significant block of Railtrack stock for later sale, because doing so would have raised fears among investors that the government might try to influence Railtrack in the interim, or might change its mind and nationalize Railtrack. Such fears were more plausible, the department felt, because the Labour Party was leading in the polls and a general election had to be scheduled by May 1997.

The sense that the managers and investors were benefiting disproportionately was strengthened by subsequent disputes between the companies and their regulators. A rash of well-publicized service problems soon after the TOCs were privatized left the public with the impression that service quality was declining. In the spring of 1997, for example, two important TOC operators could not meet their train schedules because they had underestimated how many employees would respond to an early retirement offer. The franchising director assessed a £900,000 fine on one London commuter operator and threatened to revoke its franchise if the situation did not improve quickly.[35] Service reliability improved overall in 1996/97 and 1997/98 as the TOCs gained more experience, but several companies suffered problems in the fall of 1997 and again in the fall of 1998, leading to widespread complaints and bad publicity.

A more protracted and ultimately more serious dispute also developed over whether Railtrack was living up to its obligations to invest in the rail network. During the regulator's first review of access charges, Railtrack had promised to invest £3.5 billion on renewing worn-out assets during the coming five-year period. Early in 1996 the government agreed to assume approximately £1 billion of Railtrack's past debt to make it more attractive to private investors, and in return Railtrack apparently agreed to increase its investments further, although it was never clear by how much.[36]

The regulator began to complain that Railtrack was investing more slowly than promised soon after Railtrack was sold. Railtrack was keeping the savings as profit, he argued, which was contributing to the run-up in Railtrack's stock price. The regulator's criticisms increased when Railtrack released its first Network Management Statement in 1997. Railtrack was obligated by its license to produce an annual Network Management Statement that described the network's condition and Railtrack's investment plans,[37] but the 1997 statement was vague about when and where the company would invest.[38]

The dispute exposed a weakness in the price-cap approach. The regulator could eventually compensate by reducing Railtrack's access charges, but not until fiscal year 2001/02 when the formula he set in 1995 expired. His only option in the interim was to publicly criticize Railtrack for failing to meet its targets. Moreover, Railtrack offered explanations that were hard for the regulator to counter. The company argued that it had been difficult to increase capital spending, because it took time to prepare construction bidding documents and there was a shortage of qualified contractors. As these problems were solved, the capital program would meet its targets. Railtrack had increased profits by improving performance and becoming more efficient, the company claimed, not by scrimping on investment.[39]

A temporary truce was established in the fall of 1997, when Railtrack promised to increase capital spending and agreed to amend its license to require more details in future Network Management Statements. But the issue of how the regulator could enforce investment obligations in between price-cap reviews would never be resolved. Railtrack's release of its Network Management Statement would become the occasion for an annual ritual in which the regulator would complain that investments and the statement, though improving, were still inadequate and Railtrack would promise to do better next year.

The Labour Government and the Strategic Rail Authority

The Labour Party's landslide victory in the May 1997 parliamentary elections did not result in immediate or dramatic changes to the British approach to regulating private utilities. The Labour Party had campaigned against the utilities' high profits, although other industries had been criticized more sharply than the railroads, particularly electricity and water (see Chapter 9). But it was obvious that the government didn't have the money to buy back Railtrack or any of the other privatized companies. When the Labour government announced a onetime excess profits tax on regulated utilities of £5 billion shortly after the election, Railtrack's share was only £160 million.

Nevertheless, the new secretary of state for transport, John Prescott, was determined to improve the performance of the railroad industry. Prescott, who was a leader of the left wing of the Labour Party and who also served as the deputy prime minister, felt strongly that British Rail should never have been privatized and that rail service had deteriorated since. He commissioned a review of transport policy that recommended in October 1998 the creation of a new Strategic Rail Authority to replace OPRAF.[40] The SRA would assume OPRAF's responsibilities for designing and awarding franchises, but it would be encouraged to take a more strategic and long-term perspective on both passenger and freight service needs and to propose enhancements to Railtrack's infrastructure where needed. Sir Alastair Morton, the former chairman of Eurotunnel, the private company that built the Channel Tunnel, was appointed SRA chairman in 1999. That autumn Morton began to renegotiate the eighteen passenger TOC franchises that were scheduled to expire in 2002.[41]

The rail regulator remained responsible for regulating access charges and agreements.[42] When Prescott announced the new SRA, however, he signaled his desire for a more aggressive regulatory policy by announcing that he would not reappoint John Swift as regulator when his term expired. Tom Winsor was appointed the new rail regulator in July 1999, and he would complete the second periodic review of Railtrack's access charges to apply to the five-year control period beginning in April 1, 2001.[43]

Preset Access Charges and the Development of Congestion

The Structure of Charges

Railtrack's access charges were intended not just to provide sufficient revenue to cover the company's costs but also to encourage the efficient use of its existing track network by the TOCs. When the Department of Transport set the initial schedule of access charges in 1993, it commissioned an accounting firm to study the structure of Railtrack's costs. The accountants concluded that 91 percent of Railtrack's costs were fixed, irrespective of the volume of traffic carried. Of the remaining 9 percent of costs that were variable, 6 percent were for electricity to power trains on electrified lines and 3 percent were additional wear and tear on the infrastructure due to the passage of trains. Accordingly, the department designed a schedule of charges in which, on average, 91 percent of the payment was in the form of a fixed annual fee, 6 percent was in a variable fee for electricity based on ton miles carried with electric locomotives, and 3 percent was in a variable fee for track wear based on vehicle miles operated.[44]

The access charges were supplemented by a system of performance penalties and bonuses designed to encourage the punctuality and reliability of trains. Under the performance system, Railtrack and the TOCs monitored the lateness of the trains against the schedules promised in the access agreements. If a train was late because a track or station was blocked or otherwise not available, Railtrack might have to pay the delayed TOC a penalty. If Railtrack determined that the track was not available because the train of another TOC was blocking it, however, Railtrack could recover the penalty it paid from the TOC at fault. Railtrack was allowed a benchmark number of minutes of train lateness per four-week period for each TOC service group. If delays exceeded the benchmark Railtrack paid the TOC for the excess minutes, but if delays fell below the benchmark the TOC paid Railtrack a bonus for each minute saved. The penalty or bonus per minute was based on estimates of the value that a train's passengers placed on avoiding a minute of travel delay.[45]

In 1995 the rail regulator issued additional rules for the access charges to be applied when a TOC wanted to schedule additional trains. Most TOCs had access agreements that gave them the right to operate 9 percent more trains than the minimum required by the TOC's franchise. In such cases, Railtrack could charge only its variable track wear and tear and (where appropriate) electric power costs. For additional services, the TOC and Railtrack were expected to negotiate a price for the new access rights, although the regulator would review the charge to be sure that Railtrack was not abusing its monopoly position in the negotiations. The regulator expected that the negotiated charges would be at least enough to cover a reasonable estimate of Railtrack's short-run variable costs for the new service. In addition, Railtrack would be entitled to capture a share of the net profits generated by these new rights to the extent that Railtrack assumed a share of the financial risks associated with the new service.[46]

The regulator's rules established a strong presumption that the charge for additional rights to existing network capacity would be extremely low. Railtrack might expect an uphill battle in arguing that its variable costs were higher than the 9 percent originally estimated by the government's consultants, even though the regulator acknowledged that short-run variable costs might be higher in some cases. Moreover, Railtrack normally did not assume the financial risk for a new service, at least directly, so it was presumably not entitled to share in any expected net profits.

There was relatively little controversy about the structure of access charges at first, and most of it focused on the performance regime. The TOCs complained that the regime was too generous to Railtrack, because the benchmarks were based on performance in fiscal year 1994/95, when train punctuality had been at a low.[47] In addition, the TOCs were unhappy that Railtrack was responsible for determining who was at fault for a delay. Railtrack's decision could be appealed to the regulator, but the TOCs felt the burden of an appeal fell on them.

The Development of Congestion

The structure of charges became more of an issue as the network became congested. The high ratio of fixed to variable charges encouraged the TOCs to request additional train paths. Access charges paid to Railtrack accounted for approximately 45 percent of a typical TOC's expenses. Because Railtrack's variable charges were very low, however, a TOC could operate an extra train for only about half the average cost of its existing trains. This often made extra trains profitable even if they attracted only a few extra passengers. And the TOCs were anxious to find additional revenues, given that many had bid aggressively for their franchises.

The high ratio of fixed to variable charges had the opposite effect on Railtrack, discouraging it from making extra capacity available. No one had expected that Railtrack would be willing to invest in creating new capacity in return for such low variable charges. But the variable charges were so low that Railtrack was also reluctant to agree to allow new train paths on the existing system. Railtrack would receive only a pittance in extra access charges for the new paths, while the added congestion might jeopardize Railtrack's ability to meet its performance benchmarks. The rail regulator soon became embroiled in time-consuming disputes between Railtrack and the TOCs as to where and when it was possible to add new paths to the existing schedule. When impasses developed, the regulator often sided with the TOCs and forced Railtrack to add paths.

The access charge structure assumed that Railtrack's facilities were under-utilized, so that Railtrack's variable costs were very low in the short run. Even if Railtrack had extra capacity at the outset, however, the consulting accountants probably underestimated the short-run variable costs. Tracks, signals, power distribution systems, and stations depreciate in large part because of exposure to the elements and technological obsolescence. Nevertheless, it is unlikely that Railtrack's facilities were so durable that the wear and tear from trains accounted for only 3 percent of Railtrack's costs.

Moreover, the accountants' calculations ignored the fact that congestion and delays often increase rapidly as a network approaches capacity. The costs of congestion were reflected in the penalties for delays that were part of the performance regime. In theory, the risk of increased performance penalties should be included in the costs of new access rights, and the regulator had specifically allowed for this possibility.[48] In practice, however, the risk of increased performance penalties seems to have been given little weight in setting the access charges for new paths, or at least less weight than Railtrack thought it deserved.

To the extent that the low variable charges encouraged the TOCs to add trains, they eventually undermined the assumption of excess capacity on which the low charges were based. Railtrack probably did have excess capacity in 1993, when the charges were first established. Between 1992/93 and 2000/01 the TOCs increased the number of train kilometers operated by 22 percent, however, so that the gains in train reliability and punctuality that had been won in the first years after privatization began to erode by 1998/99 (see Table 11.3). By 1999 Railtrack was estimating that each 1 percent increase in train kilometers increased the number of minutes of train delay by 2.5 percent. If train kilometers increased by 40 percent in the coming decade, a figure Railtrack thought plausible, then, absent investments in new capacity, train delays would double.[49]

The Second Periodic Review

By the late 1990s, the inadequacies of the access charge structure had grown so obvious that they became a major topic in the rail regulator's second price review. The review began in 1997 under John Swift, was completed in October 2000 by Tom Winsor, and applied to the five-year period beginning on

Table 11.3 Trends in train kilometers, investment, and passenger service quality, fiscal years 1986/87 to 2000/01

Fiscal year	Train kilometers (millions)	Investment in railways (millions of 1999/00 £)	Percentage of investment in rolling stock	Reliability	Punctuality	Reliability and punctuality combined
Prereform						
1986/87	312	902	15.3	*N.A.*	*N.A.*	*N.A.*
1987/88	325	1,020	16.3	*N.A.*	*N.A.*	*N.A.*
1988/89	339	1,053	29.9	*N.A.*	*N.A.*	*N.A.*
1989/90	344	1,256	26.3	*N.A.*	*N.A.*	*N.A.*
1990/91	355	1,340	32.2	*N.A.*	*N.A.*	*N.A.*
1991/92	354	1,597	35.0	*N.A.*	*N.A.*	*N.A.*
1992/93	349	1,766	36.4	98.7	89.7	*N.A.*
Transition						
1993/94	350	1,380	35.6	98.8	90.3	*N.A.*
1994/95	341	1,436[a]	28.8	98.7	89.6	*N.A.*
1995/96	345	1,228[a]	18.2	98.8	89.5[c]	*N.A.*
Postreform						
1996/97	350	1,325[a]	3.8	99.1	92.5[c]	*N.A.*
1997/98	376	1,625[a]	7.3	98.9	92.5[c]	89.7
1998/99	405	2,045[a,b]	8.8	98.9	91.5[c]	87.9
1999/00	418	2,248[a,b]	10.5	98.8	91.9[c]	87.8
2000/01	427	2,905[a,b]	18.7	*N.A.*	*N.A.*	79.1
Percentage change 1992/93 to 2000/01	+22%	+64.5%				

Sources: Train kilometers to 1996/97 are unpublished figures supplied to the author by the Department of Transport, Local Government and the Regions in 2002. Other data are from the Department of the Environment, Transport and the Regions, *Bulletin of Rail Statistics Quarter 1 2000/01*, publication SB(00) 11, 2000, table 7; and Strategic Rail Authority, *National Rail Trends 2001–02 (Quarter 1)*, September 2001, pp. 13, 16, 29.

Note: Government revenue support includes grants for domestic passenger services by the central government and by Britain's six metropolitan passenger transport executives. *N.A.*–Not available.

a. Figures after the restructuring in April 1994 are not strictly comparable with those before because of accounting changes. For example, certain expenses that British Rail counted as maintenance Railtrack counts as capital.

b. Investment in the Channel Tunnel Rail Link is included from 1998/99 on but excluded from earlier years.

c. In April 1995 the definition of lateness was tightened from 5 minutes 59 seconds to 5 minutes for commuter trains and from 10 minutes 59 seconds to 10 minutes for long-distance trains.

April 1, 2001. Swift appointed a distinguished panel of academic experts to advise on improvements to the structure of charges, and both he and Winsor hired a series of accountants and other consultants to study railway costs and the performance system.[50]

The review resulted in two changes to the structure of access charges. The first was to increase slightly the ratio of variable to fixed costs in the charges for the base set of train paths that the TOCs were entitled to. According to the new calculations, only 82.7 percent of costs were fixed while 9.3 percent varied by the number of train kilometers operated and 8.0 percent by the amount of electricity consumed.[51]

The second, and potentially more significant, change was to replace the system used to determine the access charges for new train paths. Railtrack argued that the old approach of case-by-case negotiations had proved too cumbersome and should be replaced by a predetermined schedule of charges. The rail regulator thought that it had also been a waste of time to consider the profit potential of a new service, since Railtrack seldom assumed any of the demand risk.

Accordingly, the regulator ordered Railtrack to prepare and publish a schedule of charges for new train paths based on estimates of the increase in the congestion costs as well as the wear and tear caused by a new train. The charge per train kilometer would depend on four factors: the geographic route section, thirteen time bands across the week, the speed of the train relative to the average on the line, and the flexibility in the rights given to the TOC. The estimates of congestion costs and the performance benchmarks would be based on the reliability that the regulator expected that Railtrack could deliver, moreover, instead of on the performance with run-down infrastructure prior to privatization.

One danger of the new scheme was that the higher charges for additional trains would force the TOCs to cut back on some of the new services that they had added since privatization. The cutbacks, though arguably economically sensible, would be a political embarrassment to a Labour government committed to encourage the use of trains instead of highways. In a compromise, the regulator decided that only half of Railtrack's estimated congestion costs for a new train would be collected through the access fee. The other half would be added to Railtrack's regulatory asset base, and thus would eventually wind up as part of the fixed component of the TOCs' basic access charges. The compromise meant that the TOCs would still schedule a large number of additional trains (since they would pay only half of Railtrack's congestion costs as a variable fee), but that Railtrack now had a stronger incentive to accommodate the TOCs (since Railtrack eventually would be compensated for its full congestion costs). Given the novelty of the scheme, the regulator decided that the new charges for additional paths would not go into effect until May 2002.

The success of the new scheme would depend upon the accuracy of the estimates of congestion costs by route sections, time periods, and relative train speeds. In addition, Railtrack had to believe that adding half of the congestion costs to the regulatory asset base would provide it with adequate compensation. The regulator estimated that the charges for additional paths would account for only £392 million of the £9,790 million in access charges that Railtrack would collect over the five-year control period, which suggested that Railtrack's congestion costs from added trains would be only £130 million per year.[52] This seemed low given the intense complaints about congestion in 2000 and 2001.

The Hatfield Accident

The debate over the new access charge system was upstaged by a major rail accident at Hatfield on October 17, 2000, just two days before the rail regulator released the conclusions of his second periodic review. Hatfield was the third fatal railway accident since privatization, but it was the first to be blamed immediately on Railtrack and rail restructuring.

In truth, restructuring probably contributed to both of the previous accidents as well, although this was not apparent at the time.[53] The first accident occurred in 1997 at Southall in West London, when an intercity express passed several danger signals and collided with a freight train, killing seven people. Safety investigators blamed the accident on driver inattention, but a back-up warning system on the intercity locomotive was not working because of poor communication between the TOC and the ROSCO that maintained its trains.

The second accident was in 1999 at Ladbroke Grove Junction, near London's Paddington Station, where a commuter train passed a danger signal and collided with an intercity express, killing thirty-one people. The accident was officially attributed to a combination of driver error, a poorly placed signal, and the lack of Automatic Train Protection (ATP) on a congested portion of the system.[54] These conclusions seemed to spread the blame widely, since the Health and Safety Executive had approved the original signal placement and the government and the industry had long been debating when and where to install better train protection systems. Restructuring was also at fault, however, inasmuch as a review of the signal's placement had been recommended before the accident, but was never held because of uncertainty about who in Railtrack or among the TOCs was responsible for follow-up. The main upshot of the Ladbroke Grove accident was a decision to install more advanced train protection and control systems on Britain's railways by 2003, for which the rail regulator allowed an investment of £781 million in the second control period.[55]

The Hatfield accident, in contrast, seemed from the outset to be largely the fault of Railtrack and the restructuring of the rail industry. Four passengers died when an intercity train traveling at 125 mph derailed on a curve after shattering a fifty-meter piece of badly worn rail into three hundred pieces. The rail regulator had been pressing Railtrack to develop effective plans to reverse the decline in track quality since 1998. In August 1999, after the rate of broken rails increased alarmingly, the regulator put Railtrack on notice that it would be in violation of its license if the situation did not improve quickly. And in August 2000, just two months before Hatfield, the regulator had become so frustrated with Railtrack's lack of progress that he hired U.S. railroad engineering consultants to prepare an independent assessment of why rail quality was declining and what Railtrack should do about it.

The access charge and penalty system contributed to the deterioration in rail quality and the Hatfield accident. Railtrack blamed the decline in rail quality in part on the increases in rail traffic that both made the tracks wear faster and made it harder to schedule track maintenance without delaying scheduled trains. And the performance penalty system made it expensive for Railtrack to close track for maintenance. Railtrack had scheduled a brief closure for rail replacement at the Hatfield curve in March 2000, but the new rail could not be unloaded at the site because the crews had brought the wrong kind of equipment. Having paid once to close the track, Railtrack had been reluctant to do so again during the busy summer season; it had rescheduled the replacement for November, a month after the accident.

Other restructuring issues contributed to Hatfield.[56] The BRISCO responsible for maintaining the Hatfield track had recommended the rail replacement originally, but Railtrack may have been skeptical since new rail made the BRISCO's job easier while Railtrack bore all the costs. In addition, some observers suspected that the track was being damaged by train wheels with flat spots in them, and that flat wheels had increased because of poor train maintenance by the ROSCOs. Railtrack's ability to deal with such problems was limited by the size of its engineering staff, which was so small that as early as 1996 the Health and Safety Executive had issued a report questioning whether the company could adequately supervise the work done on its lines. Eight days after the Hatfield crash, the independent consultants that the rail regulator had hired in August reported that Railtrack should inspect and replace its rail more often.

Railtrack responded to the Hatfield accident by immediately imposing speed restrictions on sections of suspect track across the nation. The chairman of Railtrack's board of directors resigned a month later, as Railtrack's responsibility for the accident became clear. The speed limits and delays lasted for the better part of a year, leading to widespread criticism and charges that Railtrack had overreacted. The accident cost the company roughly £600 million: £400 million in penalty payments to the TOCs and £200 million in track repairs.

Negotiated Agreements for Increased Capacity

The Plan for Negotiations

The congestion created by the access charges made it critical to develop a workable scheme for investing in expanded infrastructure capacity. The rail regulator treated investments to renew or maintain existing capacity differently than investments to enhance capacity. Renewal investments were to be recovered through the base access charges, and renewals had been the focus of the dispute, described earlier, over whether Railtrack was living up to its investment commitments. Enhancements were to be financed through special or supplementary access charges.

The government had committed to pay for several significant enhancements to the network when Railtrack was created and the first TOC franchises awarded. The two largest of these investments were Thameslink 2000, a £580 million program of new track, signals, and power distribution systems to increase capacity through central London, and a £160 million upgrading to increase speeds on the West Coast Main Line. The government expected, however, that the TOCs or the franchising director would propose additional improvements, and that it would be up to the regulator to approve the arrangements for allocating the costs and capacity of these improvements through modified access agreements and supplementary access charges.

Early in 1996, the regulator announced that he would rely on negotiations between Railtrack and the TOCs to determine what future enhancements were needed and how to pay for them.[57] The regulator modeled his scheme for negotiating enhancements on his earlier scheme for negotiating additional train paths in the existing network. The regulator mandated that the supplementary access charges be at least sufficient to recover Railtrack's avoidable costs for the enhancement, including the capital invested (with an appropriate return) and added maintenance expenses. Beyond that, the regulator expected Railtrack and the train operator to share the expected benefits from the investment, with each party's share commensurate to the risks it assumed. Mindful that Railtrack might abuse its monopoly position in the negotiations, however, the regulator announced that he would be skeptical of any proposal that gave Railtrack more than half of the expected benefit. Moreover, he would presume that the investments should not be designed to create a monopoly position for any one train operator, and that other train operators should be allowed to use improved facilities upon the payment of an appropriate fee.

The West Coast Main Line Negotiations

Within a year this policy was tested in negotiations over improvements to the West Coast Main Line (WCML), a key route connecting London, Birmingham, Manchester, Liverpool, Glasgow, and, through a spur, Edinburgh (see Figure 11.1). The WCML was used by over two thousand intercity passenger, regional passenger, local commuter, and freight trains per day and had four tracks for the first third of its route and a mixture of two-, three-, and four-track sections thereafter.[58] It had been built in the 1830s and 1840s and had been renewed and electrified in the 1960s and 1970s. The most recent renewal had not straightened the tight curves of the original nineteenth-century alignment, however, and there had been little investment in the line since. For long-distance passenger traffic from London to Scotland, moreover, the WCML competed with the East Main Coast Line, which was much straighter and had been electrified and equipped with modern locomotives and coaches in the early 1980s.

In 1996 the franchising director had offered two options in the competition for West Coast Trains, the TOC that provided long-distance passenger service on the WCML. Under the first, Railtrack would restore the 1960s level of service on the line, with 110 mph maximum speeds. This would require a "Core Investment Program" (CIP) of £1,340 million over five years, all to be financed by the basic access charges paid by West Coast Trains and other users of the WCML. In the second option, Railtrack would invest an additional £160 million, financed through supplementary access charges on West Coast Trains, to bring the maximum speeds up to 125 mph.

Richard Branson's Virgin Rail Group won the West Coast Trains franchise with a bid for the 125-mph option. Virgin's bid was extremely aggressive, however, promising to gradually shift from an annual subsidy of £94.4 million in the first year (fiscal 1996/97) to an annual payment to the government of £220.3 million in the final year (fiscal 2011/12). To achieve this, Virgin would have to significantly increase ridership, and the company immediately wanted to explore the possibility of increasing the speeds to 140 mph. It took two years to negotiate an agreement to further upgrade the WCML.

The WCML experience illustrated many of the difficulties of the negotiation approach. One problem was that Railtrack had incentives to disagree

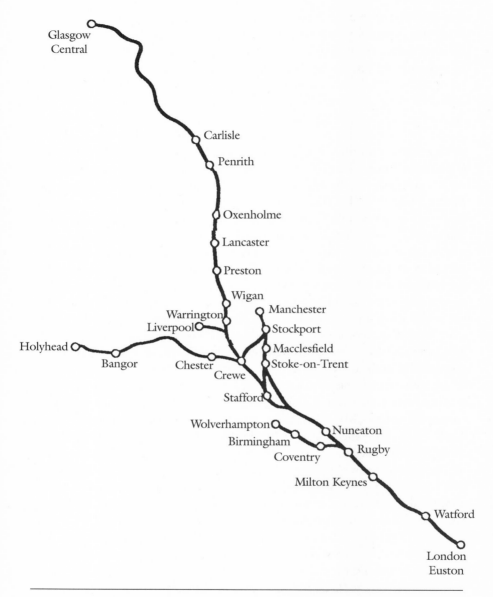

Figure 11.1 The West Coast Trains franchise of Virgin Rail Group, including the West Coast Main Line. (Office of Passenger Rail Franchising.)

with OPRAF and the TOCs about the distinction between renewals and enhancements and about the best way to enhance capacity. In the case of the WCML, Railtrack, OPRAF, and the ORR had fought bitterly over the £160 million price tag for the 125-mph upgrade before the TOC franchises were put out to bid. Some of the old signals and power distribution equipment Railtrack would renew under the CIP were not made anymore, and the modern versions not only performed better but cost less. Railtrack at times held that the better performance of the modern replacement constituted an enhancement, and thus justified raising access charges. Moreover, Railtrack always favored more infrastructure-intensive solutions to problems. OPRAF had wanted to increase speeds with better signals and tilting trains, for example, but at one point Railtrack proposed instead that it should spend over £1 billion to straighten out the curves in the line. As one OPRAF official remembered, "We wanted to do things that maximized the value of the franchise that we were offering. Railtrack wanted to maximize its rate base."[59]

Another difficulty was that the limited duration of the TOC franchises made it harder for Railtrack and the TOCs to reach agreement on how to finance enhancements. The problem was worst when the TOC had one of the shorter franchises or when the investment required was large. The West Coast Trains franchise was for fifteen years instead of the usual seven, for example, because Virgin was going to finance the £160 million in track work and signals needed to increase WCML speeds to 125 mph. But at least £500 million more was needed to increase speeds to 140 mph, and the full improvement was not expected until 2005, only seven years before the franchise was scheduled to expire. At one point, Virgin and Railtrack proposed that the West Coast Train franchise be extended for another fifteen years, to 2027, to give Virgin more time to pay for the 140-mph upgrade. But the franchising director opposed the extension on the grounds that it would postpone for too long his opportunity to redefine service requirements and to solicit competitive offers when the franchise was rebid.

A third problem was that the facilities to be improved were typically used by several TOCs with different interests in the design and success of the project. In the case of the WCML, there were significant disputes between Virgin and the operators of the slower regional passenger, commuter, and freight trains. Where the different operators shared tracks they often preferred different designs. Super-elevating track on curves permitted higher speeds for passenger operations, for example, but it created maintenance problems for freight operations by shifting the weight of the heavy freight axles against the inside wheel and rail. And on some sections of the line, the improvements needed by West Coast Trains created opportunities for other operators that Virgin thought they should help pay for. Operating 140-mph trains would reduce the capacity of the line unless Railtrack upgraded to moving-block signals and built separate slow tracks in some of the sections where they did not already exist.[60] But moving-block signals and separate slow tracks would reduce delays and provide more train paths and scheduling flexibility for the slow trains as well, so Virgin thought they should share the cost. On other sections of the line it would be extremely expensive to make the improvements necessary to accommodate both West Coast Trains and the current slower-speed services, and Virgin wanted some of the slower-speed services canceled.

A related complication was the effects of the enhancement on opportunities for future and current competition. In return for the financial risks it would have to assume, Virgin wanted Railtrack and the regulator to commit to not allowing another TOC or new entrant to offer new competing services on the WCML. Moreover, Virgin wanted permission to serve London-Edinburgh as well as London-Glasgow. Historically, London-Edinburgh service had been provided over the East Coast Main Line, which offered a more direct route. But with the proposed improvements, the WCML would be a competitive route to Edinburgh as well. Virgin's proposal was vehemently opposed by the TOC providing long-distance passenger service on the East Coast Main Line, and stimulated that TOC to begin negotiating with Railtrack for enhancements to its line.

In the summer of 1998 the regulator approved an incomplete agreement for the 140-mph upgrade for fear that further delay would kill the project. Virgin's franchise expired in 2012, so work had to begin soon if it was to begin at all.[61] The upgrade would add £612 million to the £1.5 billion already committed to fund the CIP and the initial upgrade to 125 mph. For this sum, Railtrack agreed to maintain the quantity of passenger and freight services provided on the WCML as of March 1998, upgrade maximum speeds to 140 mph, provide four additional high-speed paths per hour for West Coast Trains, and provide forty-two additional slow paths per day and at least two additional fast paths per hour. The upgrade would be complete in 2005, although significant speed improvements were to be delivered in 2002. Virgin and Railtrack would share the financial risk. Railtrack agreed not to try to recover all the costs from Virgin during its franchise period and Virgin agreed to share some of its revenues with Railtrack. The regulator also approved some of Virgin's requests for protection against new competition, as well as its request to serve Edinburgh.

The 1998 agreement was incomplete because Railtrack still had not reached understandings with some of the other TOCs on how to meet their needs once the high-speed service began. Railtrack had agreed to maintain the total quantity of service as of March 1998, but not specific paths. The forty-two additional slow paths per day and two additional fast paths per hour would help resolve conflicts, but they might not be available for the times and routes that the other TOCs desired. The regulator recognized that some regional services near Birmingham might have to be canceled, for example, although he argued that the public benefit of high-speed service every fifteen minutes between Great Britain's two largest cities was worth the sacrifice. The regulator ordered Railtrack to complete studies of four areas where agreement still had not been reached and promised to work with Railtrack and the TOCs to resolve the outstanding issues.[62]

Second Thoughts on Negotiations

Gradually it became clear that negotiations were not going to work well for enhancement projects of any size. Most of the other agreements negotiated toward the end of the 1990s involved relatively small and simple projects. Even so, the TOCs complained that it was hard to get Railtrack's attention for small schemes. Railtrack became more receptive over time, but it preferred projects that involved only one TOC and where that TOC was willing to pay for all the costs in increased access charges.

Some very large projects, like Thameslink 2000 or WCML, were critical enough that it was worth it for Railtrack, the TOCs, and the government to bear the costs of complex negotiations. Nevertheless, the Thameslink 2000 agreement had been possible only because OPRAF believed the project was so important for London rail services that it was willing to assume all the risks of selling the new train paths to the TOCs. And the WCML negotiations had proved too difficult to complete in a timely fashion.

Most difficult of all were projects of intermediate size. The network seemed to abound with enhancements that cost between a few million and a hundred million pounds. Around London, for example, there were numerous capacity conflicts among the express services to the Heathrow and Gatwick airports, the commuter lines, and the long-distance services. As long as several TOCs were involved or the investment was too large to be recouped during the life of the normal franchise, the difficulties of negotiation discouraged any efforts to deal with them.

The creation of the shadow SRA in June 1999 signaled the beginning of the retreat from relying on negotiations for major enhancements. SRA chairman Alastair Morton interpreted his agency's mandate to take a longer-term perspective as a call for an investment-led strategy. In a key speech soon after the shadow SRA was created, Chairman Morton announced, "It's all about investment, investment, investment."[63] The regulator continued to press for more capacity from the existing network, ordering Railtrack to reduce delays by 12.7 percent by the end of the 1999/00 fiscal year or face substantial fines. But Morton thought the existing network had reached its limit, and publicly disparaged the time the regulator, Railtrack, and the TOCs spent determining the blame for delays as a "sterile activity."[64]

The SRA made its presence felt that fall, when it began to redesign and renegotiate the TOC concessions that were scheduled to expire in 2002/03. The SRA pushed for fewer, larger, and longer concessions with greater investment commitments. To reduce uncertainties for bidders, SRA asked the regulator to extend the restrictions on TOC-on-TOC competition that were scheduled to expire in 2002. In the meantime, the Department of Transport, with Morton's enthusiastic support, developed Britain's first long-term transport plan. *Transport 2010*, released in July 2000, called for a 50 percent increase in rail passenger journeys, to be achieved by doubling the rate of railway investment over the next ten years.[65] Approximately half of the £60 billion to be invested would come from the government and the balance from private investors. The SRA would take the lead in identifying the enhancement projects as it designed the next round of franchises.

The SRA's hand was strengthened first by major cost overruns on the WCML project and then, soon after, by the Hatfield accident. In December 1999, as the Department of Transport was developing its ten-year plan, Railtrack informed the rail regulator that the state-of-the-art moving-block signal system that it had planned to install on the WCML could not be delivered on time. If Railtrack was forced to use conventional fixed-block signals instead, it would need to invest more in track and structures to deliver the capacity it had promised. In January 2000, Railtrack estimated that the signaling change would nearly triple the cost of the renewal and upgrade programs on the WCML from £2.1 billion to £5.8 billion.[66]

Railtrack's new estimate caused consternation in the Office of the Rail Regulator. The second periodic review, which was nearly complete, had to be reopened to consider who should pay for the cost overruns and whether the WCML's planned capacity should be adjusted downward to save money. Moreover, the regulator now noticed that Railtrack had never completed the required studies of the four issues that had been left unresolved in the 1998 upgrade agreement. These problems proved too difficult to resolve by the time the conclusions to the second periodic review were published in October 2000. The regulator announced that Railtrack might not be required to supply the two additional high-speed paths per hour and that most of the cost overrun would be financed by a combination of increases in the base access fees for the WCML and grants from the SRA. The details, he explained, would be worked out in the coming year.[67]

The Hatfield accident was the last straw for negotiated enhancements.

While the WCML cost overruns had raised doubts about Railtrack's ability to manage complex enhancement projects, Hatfield raised doubts about Railtrack's ability to maintain its existing network. In addition, Hatfield further weakened Railtrack's financial position, because the emergency speed restrictions made Railtrack liable for hundreds of millions of pounds in performance penalties.

In the aftermath of the WCML overruns and Hatfield, SRA chairman Morton proposed that Railtrack should focus on operating and maintaining the existing network and leave the business of designing, building, and financing major enhancements to others. The overruns and accident had so undercut Railtrack's confidence and support that it agreed to work with the SRA and the regulator to develop new arrangements for delivering major projects.[68] Instead of Railtrack and the TOCs identifying and negotiating enhancements, the emerging model was that the SRA would identify the projects, assume all or most of the market risk, and contract with Railtrack or other private companies to build them.

The implementation of SRA's new program was soon delayed by disputes with the Treasury over its costs. While not publicly disavowing the goals in the ten-year plan, the Treasury had apparently grown increasingly uncomfortable about the cost of the SRA's program to improve rail service. Treasury's concerns were undoubtedly heightened by its potential liability for WCML cost overruns and for safety improvements once the Hatfield inquiry was complete. When the SRA held a competition for an ambitious twenty-year renewal of the principal intercity franchise on the East Coast Main Line, the Treasury balked at approving the new concession contract and SRA was forced to sign a two-year extension of the existing concession instead.

The Bankruptcy of Railtrack

These disputes were eclipsed when the government forced Railtrack into bankruptcy after losing faith that the company could control the costs stemming from the WCML overruns and the Hatfield crash. In April 2001, the SRA agreed to provide Railtrack with an emergency grant of £1.5 billion to help with both WCML and the consequences of Hatfield. But the next month Railtrack asked for another £2.6 billion, and meanwhile it raised the WCML cost estimates by another £500 million to £6.3 billion. To critics it seemed as if the company thought it had the government over a barrel, with little choice but to supply it with the cash it needed to keep going. By October 2001 the government forced the company into bankruptcy by cutting off further aid.

In 2002 the government reorganized Railtrack as Network Rail, a special type of nonprofit that has no shareholders but is controlled by a board of one hundred "members" representing passenger groups, the TOCs, unions, and the general public.[69] Railtrack's shareholders received the equivalent of approximately 250 pence per share, a bit less than what the company's shares traded for just before bankruptcy but far less than their original sales price of 390 pence or the high of 1,768 pence that they fetched in 1998. The government argued that Network Rail would have lower financing costs and a less adversarial relationship with the rest of industry because the nonprofit had no shareholders pressing for dividends. Critics responded that Network Rail's one hundred members were too diverse to agree on a coherent strategy for the company and that lenders would charge high interest rates for the company's debt to compensate for the lack of an equity cushion. Indeed, the government had to guarantee the initial loans and credit lines the banks provided to Network Rail, which lent credence to the critics' charge that the new nonprofit was essentially a public agency in disguise.[70]

The vertical restructuring of the industry and the strategy of negotiated enhancements almost surely contributed to Railtrack's demise. Railtrack lost some of its capacity to supervise technically complex projects when British Rail's maintenance and construction units were sold off as separate companies. Moreover, Railtrack's incentives to control costs may have been undermined by the regulator's willingness to approve an upgrade agreement that left key issues unresolved. The upgrade was so complex that it proved impossible to reach a complete agreement in a reasonable amount of time. But the approval of an incomplete agreement may have left Railtrack executives with the impression that the government had assumed some obligation to assist with any problems that might arise.

Conclusion

It is striking that the privatized British railways did so well for so long given the complexity of the reforms. In the first five years, passenger and freight traffic increased significantly, fares remained about the same as before, and government subsidies seem to have declined substantially, although subsidy comparisons are difficult. The increase in delays that began in the late 1990s was in part a product of the railways' unexpected success in attracting new passengers. And despite the traffic growth, delays remained below prereform levels until the temporary speed restrictions were imposed in the wake of the Hatfield crash.

The improvement in railway performance was due to privatization rather than to vertical unbundling. The British reforms were implemented in a manner that exposed the industry to the coordination problems of vertical unbundling without any compensating benefit from increased competition. In theory, the gain from unbundling would be competition among TOCs. In practice, the government was too concerned about the effects on government subsidies for unprofitable passenger services to allow significant TOC-on-TOC competition. Restrictions on competition may have been needed to reduce uncertainties in franchise bidding, and competition among TOCs may be less critical given that the railway faces so much competition from other modes. Nevertheless, the restrictions on competition among TOCs eliminated the key advantage claimed for vertical unbundling.

The deterioration of the railway's performance at the end of the 1990s was due largely to the coordination problems created by vertical unbundling. Most observers focus on the safety problems caused by the difficulty of writing and enforcing contracts between Railtrack and the BRISCOs. These concerns were reinforced by a fourth crash in May 2002, after Railtrack was bankrupt. Seven people died when a train derailed after it hit a switch point whose bolts had not been tightened by one of Railtrack's maintenance contractors.

But the capacity and congestion problems caused by poor coordination between Railtrack and the TOCs were arguably even more important and less tractable. The schemes to manage and expand capacity contributed to the safety problems by encouraging higher levels of traffic and discouraging Railtrack from releasing track for maintenance. But these schemes also critically affected the abilities of the passenger TOCs to honor their bids and of the freight TOCs to expand services. The TOCs bid aggressively on the expectation that they could expand services and that marginal access charges would be low. In only a few years, however, the number of trains had increased to the point where Railtrack's capacity was strained. And the system did not provide effective incentives to identify and relieve bottlenecks.

Britain used both preset and negotiated access charges to encourage coordination, and both approaches proved to have serious limitations. In theory, access charges can provide incentives for both the use of existing capacity and the financing of enhancements. In Railtrack's case, however, the charges were initially set on the assumption that there was excess capacity and that 91 percent of Railtrack's costs were fixed. The assumption of excess capacity was probably true at the time, even if the ratio of fixed charges was probably exaggerated. But the assumption was also politically convenient. Excess capacity meant that access charges could be low, since they did not necessarily have to cover the long-run costs of maintaining the network at its current capacity.[71] The low variable charges also made privatization appear more attractive by strengthening the TOCs' incentives to run more trains and by reducing Railtrack's exposure to demand risk so that the company fetched a higher price. But the low charges contained the seeds of their own destruction by encouraging the TOCs to expand services to the point where the excess capacity disappeared.

The congestion might have been moderated had the schemes for negotiating charges for additional paths in the existing network and for network enhancements worked well. Negotiated agreements are attractive because they acknowledge the localized nature of congestion and capacity problems, and provide a safety valve for a system of preset access charges. The opportunity to negotiate supplemental charges compensates for the fact that the basic access charges are usually too simplistic and uniform to provide the proper incentives in every situation. Railtrack would not have offered as many additional paths or agreed to invest in enhanced capacity without the possibility of negotiating supplemental payments.

The drawback of negotiated agreements, however, is the potential for high transaction costs. The negotiations over capacity enhancements seemed particularly burdensome. Even the simplest enhancement projects involved at least three parties—a TOC, Railtrack, and the regulator—and often a fourth —OPRAF or its successor the SRA. And many projects were far more complex because they affected more than one TOC or were too expensive to be recouped during the life of the current TOC's franchise. The costs of negotiation probably discouraged Railtrack and the TOCs from making many modest improvements that might have been quickly undertaken by a vertically integrated firm. And negotiation costs encouraged the regulator to approve an incomplete agreement for the WCML project, which seems to have encouraged the cost overruns that helped to bankrupt Railtrack.

The government abandoned the negotiations approach after only a few years. In 1999 the SRA decided that negotiations were an inadequate method of deciding when to expand capacity. And in 2000 the rail regulator scrapped negotiated charges for additional paths in the existing network in favor of a preset schedule of charges that vary by location and time of day and that include an estimate of the added congestion costs caused by an additional path.

The turmoil created by the reorganization of Railtrack as Network Rail will delay any real test of the new schemes for coordinating infrastructure and train operations. The new preset access charges should provide better incentives for Network Rail and the TOCs to identify and use new paths in the existing network, although how much better will depend on how accurately the new charges reflect the actual congestion costs for specific paths. The new charge structure is unlikely to be sufficient to promote enhancements, however, if only because the new charges are unlikely to be spatially and temporally detailed enough to provide accurate investment signals. Moreover, the government may want to subsidize enhanced capacity on the grounds that promoting rail use generates social benefits in the form of reduced air pollution and highway congestion. It may be unwise, however, to rely primarily on the SRA to identify enhancements, since Network Rail and the TOCs have an intimate knowledge of the network and its limitations.

It is unfortunate that the British government failed to use Railtrack's bankruptcy as an opportunity for a more fundamental rethinking of its railway reforms. If the government was unwilling to permit TOC-on-TOC competition for fear of increasing its subsidy bill, then it should have reconsidered its decision to separate infrastructure from train operations. The coordination problems caused by unbundling have played a major role in the present system's problems, with no compensating benefit in increased competition. The replacement of Railtrack with Network Rail doesn't address the issue of coordination directly, and may make matters worse if governance of the new company by one hundred members proves to be problematic. A more promising alternative is a system of vertically integrated railway concessions organized by corridor or region, perhaps with some limited rights to operate services on connecting railways' tracks.

12

Designing Capacity Markets: Electricity in Argentina

with Martín Rodríguez-Pardina

Coordination through Markets for Capacity

Vertical separation is far more common in electricity than it is in railroads. While Britain provides the only major example of a private and vertically separated railroad industry, by 2002 more than a dozen countries had restructured their integrated electricity industries as separate private generation, transmission, and distribution companies. In electricity, the key bottleneck infrastructure provider is the high-voltage transmission company that delivers power from generators to large industrial customers and to the local distribution companies that serve households and small businesses. Power lines can become congested or overloaded just like railroad lines, and it is important to establish incentives to use scarce transmission capacity wisely and to build new transmission capacity when needed.

A number of countries are attempting to coordinate the use of and investment in transmission facilities by designing markets for transmission capacity. They reject preset transmission access charges, because of the difficulty of forecasting appropriate prices in advance. And they are skeptical of negotiated charges, because the number of transmission system users is typically large enough to make voluntary agreements impractical. Instead they are trying to develop markets for transmission capacity in which the price for transmission will vary according to supply and demand. The hope is that market-determined prices will provide better incentives for transmission users and investors.

Argentina was one of the first countries to restructure its electricity industry and has been among the pioneers in efforts to establish markets for the capacity of bottleneck facilities. Argentina's experience illustrates the way in which introducing competition through restructuring can generate important benefits for consumers. But the most important lessons for our purposes concern the potential for using market mechanisms to alleviate the coordination problems created by restructuring.

Electricity Restructuring in Other Countries

During the 1980s many countries allowed private independent power producers (IPPs) to build generating stations and sell the electricity to integrated electricity companies. The United States pioneered the idea in 1978, when it required its private integrated utilities to buy power at their avoided cost from new independent generators. (Avoided cost is the cost that the integrated utility would have paid to produce the electricity that it now buys from the independent generator.) The U.S. experiment was part of an effort to promote the development of generating technologies that were more energy efficient and less polluting. Private IPPs became popular among developing countries as well, particularly where the publicly owned and integrated electric companies seemed unable to finance and build plants fast enough to prevent electricity shortages. But in the United States and elsewhere, the integrated electric companies usually remained intact, with private IPPs selling electricity wholesale to the integrated companies and to very large industrial customers.

During the 1990s attention shifted to efforts to restructure integrated companies as separate and private generation, transmission, and distribution firms. Often the industry was restructured when it was transferred from government to private ownership. Chile was the first to break up and privatize its integrated electric company beginning in 1978. Britain was the next major example in 1989, Argentina and Norway followed in 1991, New Zealand in the mid-1990s, and Spain and Germany in the late 1990s.[1] By the beginning of the new century, several states and provinces in Australia and Canada and a half-dozen more countries in Latin America had also privatized and restructured their electricity industries.

Other countries kept their major utilities in the public sector while they gradually increased competition between them and the IPPs. In some cases—such as Netherlands, Poland, and Portugal—they broke up their integrated electricity companies but left most of the parts in public hands while they tried to establish reasonably competitive wholesale markets. In other cases—such as Japan—the government initially left the integrated companies intact but expanded the scope of IPP operations by forcing integrated companies to use competitive bidding when securing increased generating capacity.

In the United States, where the integrated electric utilities have long been privately owned, federal and state regulators began to gradually increase the level of competition in wholesale power markets and move toward a vertically separated industry.[2] In 1992 Congress allowed competition in wholesale markets, and in 1996 the Federal Energy Regulatory Commission (FERC) required monopoly utilities to provide "open access" to their transmission grids so as to make sales among independent companies easier. FERC did not define the terms or price for open access, however, and regulators and the industry spent the remainder of the decade debating and refining rules.[3] Approximately two dozen states began the process of restructuring their electricity industries during the 1990s. A number ordered their integrated private utilities to divest themselves of their generating stations so that they would not have a conflict of interest in buying electricity on wholesale markets.

As the decade wore on, some European countries and U.S. states also began to introduce competition in retail electricity markets. Only the local distribution companies and large industrial customers bought enough power to participate directly in the wholesale power markets. But now independent retailers were allowed to buy on the wholesale market and resell the power to households and small business. The independent retailers competed with the local distribution companies for household and small business accounts, and used the wires of the local distribution companies to transport the power from the high-voltage transmission grid to their customers. Regulators determined the fees the local distribution companies could charge the independent retailers to use their wires.

The movement to restructure electricity suffered a temporary setback in 2000, when reforms in California went badly awry. California established a competitive wholesale electricity market, only to see wholesale prices increase tenfold instead of decline. Wholesale prices returned to prereform levels within a year, but in the meantime the state's largest private utility went bankrupt and the state government felt compelled to purchase wholesale power on behalf of its citizens, dominating the wholesale power market.

California was unlucky in that it deregulated wholesale prices at the beginning of an unusually hot summer, when natural gas prices were rising nationwide, and a year before a number of new generating plants were scheduled to go on line. But the authors of the reforms made matters worse by freezing retail electricity prices for four years and by not allowing the old utilities, who were now primarily in the retail distribution business, to protect themselves from price volatility by signing long-term contracts with generators.[4] California had frozen retail prices because it expected wholesale prices to decline, so that the freeze would allow the old utilities four years to recover the costs of assets stranded by the reforms.[5] And the state had discouraged long-term contracts because it believed that declining wholesale prices would make contracts unnecessary, and it wanted to ensure that the spot market was not dominated by a small number of players. It would take California years to dig itself out of the mess it had made, but the experience seemed to make other states more careful about restructuring rather than discouraging them.

Argentina is arguably the most interesting of the several countries that pioneered in the privatization and restructuring of wholesale electricity markets. Argentina avoided some of the problems that tended to limit or complicate competition for other pioneers. Britain created only two large private generation companies, for example, which many observers believe enabled the companies to collude and raise wholesale electricity prices.[6] Until 2000, Chile allowed a company that owned 55 percent of the country's generating capacity to own the transmission system as well, and that company is thought to have used its control of transmission to harm competing generators. In contrast, Argentina tried to enhance competition by having many small generators and to reduce conflicts of interest by prohibiting transmission companies from owning generating or distribution companies and vice versa.

Argentina also faced serious transmission constraints that forced it to confront the problems of coordinating transmission with generation and consumption from the outset. To cope with expected transmission bottlenecks, Argentina adopted a system in which wholesale electricity prices varied by location or node on the transmission network. The bottlenecks also forced Argentina to develop procedures for determining when investments in transmission capacity were needed and who should pay for them. Chile had nodal pricing too, but Britain did not, and neither Chile nor Britain had as well developed or novel a scheme for expanding transmission capacity.[7]

Electricity Transmission, Dispatch, and Spot Markets

To understand the problems of vertically unbundling electricity, it is important to understand the transmission system. Transmission is usually considered a natural monopoly, because average transmission costs fall with the volume of power transmitted. The transmission towers and rights of way account for most of the cost of building a line, and towers that can carry two or more lines are only slightly more expensive than towers that carry only one line. In addition, it is usually cheaper to use one high-voltage line instead of two lower-voltage lines, because the percentage of power lost in transmission declines as the voltage of the line increases.[8]

Transmission also has several characteristics that make it imperative that a central authority control the dispatch of generating plants and, if necessary, the shedding of electricity loads. First, the amount of power generated on the transmission system must match the amount of power consumed from it nearly instantaneously. Otherwise frequencies will be outside tolerances, and system stability will be compromised. Second, the locations at which power can be inserted and withdrawn are often constrained by transmission capacity. Transmission lines that are loaded beyond their capacity will overheat and, ultimately, melt or burn. Finally, in an interconnected transmission system the flows on any one line are often affected by the flows on all parallel or alternative lines. A transmission network is like an aqueduct system in that electricity, like water, takes the route of least resistance, which is not necessarily the geographically most direct route. Like the water in an aqueduct, power is also a homogeneous commodity, so that customers do not care which generator's power they consume. As a result, if loads increase at one point it can be feasible and economical to respond by increasing generation at a distant point because, given the presence of plants and loads at intermediate points, the additional power generated may not have to travel the entire distance to the point at which it is needed.

Some economists argue that transmission interdependencies are the key reason why large vertically integrated companies emerged in electricity.[9] The electricity industry began in most countries as small isolated systems, each with a single generating station connected to nearby customers. These systems saw the advantages of interconnecting to share reserves and increase reliability in the face of occasional surges in demand or failures of key equipment. Once the systems were interconnected, however, it was imperative to coordinate power dispatching and often advantageous (though not essential) to coordinate the locations of new generating stations.

In the jargon of economists, the transmission system creates "externalities"—that is, costs or benefits imposed on other parties. An increase in load by one customer can threaten the reliability of the system for all customers unless more power is dispatched quickly, for example, and changes in flows on one part of the system can threaten the reliability of flows on other parts of the system. Where the interdependencies are modest, they are sometimes resolved by agreements between neighboring electricity companies. But where the interdependencies are strong and complex, they are more easily resolved by merging the companies.

Economies of scale in transmission and generation enhance transmission externalities, but it is the externalities rather than the economies that encourage vertical integration. If there were no economies of scale in transmission, each customer could be connected to a central generating plant by a dedicated line, so that flows on one line would not affect flows on the others. And if there were no economies of scale in generation, each customer could have its own dedicated generator, avoiding the cost and complications of transmission altogether. In the absence of transmission externalities, economies of scale in transmission and generation might have resulted in large transmission and generating companies but not necessarily vertically integrated ones. The externalities created the need for coordinated dispatch and investment, which became the key advantage of vertical integration.

Where several independent electricity companies are interconnected, central dispatch is often managed by an independent system operator, or ISO. ISOs had emerged in the United States decades before restructuring began, in response to the need to manage the regional transmission systems that connected most large, independent vertically integrated utilities. But ISOs are essential once electricity systems are vertically unbundled. The ISO is usually a nonprofit or government agency controlled by representatives of the companies that use the system and relevant government regulatory bodies. The ISO may own the transmission network, but it usually does not.

The ISO's first priority in dispatching electricity is to keep the system stable, but a close second is to minimize the economic cost of generation and transmission. The rules ISOs use for economic dispatch vary in their sophistication. Most ISOs consider the marginal costs of generating power from different plants and dispatch plants with the lowest marginal cost first, transmission constraints permitting. Sometimes the rules also take into account the amount of power lost during transmission because of resistance on the transmission lines. This generally encourages dispatching those plants that cause the smallest increase in the average distance that the power must travel, all else being equal.

Where the electricity industry has been vertically separated, economic dispatch becomes a key element in the design of the competitive wholesale electricity market. In most cases, the generators submit bids to the ISO specifying the amount of electricity they are willing to provide and the prices they will charge for every hour of the coming day. The ISO then dispatches the generators in the order of lowest bids until demand is satisfied. The bid of the final plant dispatched is the spot price for electricity for that hour, and is the price that all dispatched generators receive and that all wholesale customers pay.

Spot prices can be highly volatile, especially when an important piece of generating or transmission equipment fails. To protect against spot market volatility, generators and wholesale customers often sign long-term contracts that obligate the generator to produce and the customer to buy a fixed amount of electricity at a set price. Generators and customers with long-term contracts still participate in the spot market to some degree, since there are inevitably times when the generator cannot produce all the power it promised or when the customer needs less or more power than it contracted for. If the wholesale market is well organized and the spot price is clearly defined, however, contracts for price differences can be used to provide complete protection from price volatility. Under such contracts, the generator sells all its power to and the customer buys all its power from the spot market. Whenever the spot price exceeds the contract price, however, the generator must pay the customer the difference for the amount of power contracted. Similarly, when the spot price falls short of the contract price, the customer must pay the generator the difference. The net result is that the generator always receives and the customer always pays the contract price for the agreed-upon quantity of power, regardless of what happens in the spot market.

The Argentine Electricity Reforms

The privatization and restructuring of Argentina's electricity industry was part of a much larger effort to reduce the role of government in the economy begun by President Carlos Menem in 1989.[10] Argentina's economy had been stagnating for decades, both because of large government deficits and because of government intervention to protect Argentine industry from competition. The Menem government began a radical effort to open the economy to domestic and international competition and to eliminate government deficits, in part by privatizing money-losing public enterprises.

Argentina's electric industry was founded by private entrepreneurs at the end of the nineteenth century, but the companies were expropriated by provincial and national governments beginning in the 1940s. After expropriation, the national government assumed the primary responsibility for developing new generating capacity and a national high-voltage transmission system. The provincial governments assumed responsibility for the local distribution companies, although the national government owned the company that served the greater Buenos Aires metropolitan area where roughly half of Argentina's population lives.[11]

The poor performance of the government-owned electric companies made the industry an early target for Menem's reformers. Under public ownership, electric service had been extended into rural areas and many new generating stations had been built, including major new hydroelectric dams in the west and north as well as two nuclear power plants. But the public companies operated at a deficit and their equipment was poorly maintained. These shortcomings became obvious in the summer of 1988–89, when a combination of low water flows in the hydro systems and poor availability of many thermal and nuclear plants meant that electricity had to be rationed for many months. Initially, the government considered proposals to reform the sector but keep it in public ownership. By 1991, however, key officials became convinced that the industry would improve only through private ownership.

Once Argentina decided to restructure and privatize, it acted quickly. A basic law governing the sector was passed by Congress in December 1991 and went into effect in January 1992. The main thermal plants, distribution, and transmission companies owned by the national government were sold to the private sector through competitive bidding in 1992 and 1993, and most of the national government's hydro plants were sold the following year. The government sold its thermal plants outright, but it sold the hydro plants as concessions of thirty years in order to retain long-term control of the associated water rights. The distribution and transmission companies were also sold as concessions for ninety-five years. The national government retained only two nuclear power plants, the Salto dam that it owned jointly with the government of Uruguay, and the Yacyretá dam that it owned jointly with the government of Paraguay.[12] The provincial governments sold most of their electricity distribution and transmission companies under similar terms.[13]

By 1998, six years after the first company was privatized, there were approximately thirty-seven private generating companies competing to supply power on a wholesale market. The principal buyers were twenty-five distribution companies that had exclusive concessions to retail the electricity to households and other small users in the areas they served. In addition, over a thousand industrial firms that were major electricity users were allowed to buy power directly on the wholesale market, bypassing their local distribution companies.

A not-for-profit company called CAMMESA served as the ISO.[14] CAMMESA dispatched the generators and calculated the market-clearing spot prices. CAMMESA also handled all the financial transactions, paying the generators and collecting from wholesale customers. CAMMESA was governed by a ten-member board of directors that included two members each from the government and from the associations of the generators, distributors, transmission companies, and large users. The subsecretary for energy of the Ministry of Economy and Public Works chaired the CAMMESA board and retained the right to veto board decisions.

The key transmission company was Transener, which maintained and operated the national high-voltage grid. Transener's system included seven thousand kilometers of 500-kilovolt (kV) lines connecting Argentina's major electricity producing and consuming regions. In addition, there were five regional trunk transmission companies that operated lines of 330 kV or less. Their role was to distribute electricity within their regions while Transener distributed electricity among regions.[15] All the transmission companies were required to provide open access to their grids to any generator or buyer, subject only to technical standards and capacity limitations. The transmission companies were excluded from buying or selling electricity so as to avoid conflicts of interest.

A government agency, ENRE, regulated the three distribution companies and six transmission companies that had concessions from the national government.[16] ENRE's main responsibility was to set the tariffs and administer a system of penalties and bonuses designed to control quality. ENRE was governed by five commissioners appointed to five-year terms and removable only for specific and limited causes. ENRE's decisions could be overruled, however, by the minister of the economy and public works. The provinces that had granted concessions to local distribution companies created similar provincial regulatory agencies to control tariffs and service quality.

ENRE was required by law to use a price-cap approach, with tariffs reviewed every five years. In between reviews prices could increase by PI − X, where PI was a weighted average of the consumer and producer price indexes and X was set by ENRE on the basis of expected productivity trends and investment needs. ENRE assessed penalties on distribution and transmission companies if they failed to provide service within acceptable voltage and frequency limits. Penalties were set at the estimated cost to customers of inferior service. The fine for blackouts, for example, was $1,400 per megawatt-hour (MW-hour) for residential customers and $2,700 per MW-hour for industrial customers.

The performance of the Argentine electric industry improved enormously soon after restructuring and privatization. Wholesale prices fell from around $42 per MW-hour in the last months of 1992 to a low of $14 per MW-hour in the last trimester of 1997, and then stabilized at $20 to $22 per MW-hour during 1998. Large industrial consumers who purchased directly from the wholesale market enjoyed price reductions on the order of 40 percent.[17] Most consumers who bought their power from the distribution companies also enjoyed savings, though not as large. As Table 12.1 shows, residential electricity prices in the Buenos Aires metropolitan area fell by about 9.7 percent if taxes are excluded and even more if they are not (taxes on residential

Table 12.1 Electricity tariffs in Buenos Aires, 1970–1997 (in constant 1997 pesos per kilowatt-hour)

Years covered	Residential		Commercial		Small industrial	
	With taxes	Without Taxes	With taxes	Without taxes	With taxes	Without taxes
Average, 1970–1991	0.191	0.104	0.138	0.129	0.059	0.055
Average, 1992–1997	0.115	0.094	0.119	0.118	0.066	0.065
Percentage change	−40.0	−9.7	−13.6	−8.5	+10.4	+18.0

Note: Tariffs for 1970–1990 from SEGBA; tariffs for 1991–1992 from Edenor.

Source: Calculated from Fundación de Investigaciones Económicas Latinoamericas (FIEL), *La Regulación de la Competencia y de los Servicios Públicos: Teoría y Experiencia Argentina Reciente* (Buenos Aires: FIEL, 1999), p. 484.

electricity were cut during the same period). Commercial customers saw a decline of 8.5 percent, while the small industrial customers saw an increase, although from the rates that had been heavily discounted before the reforms. By 1996, the average retail price for electricity was one-third lower in Argentina than in the United States and many European countries.[18]

The fall in prices occurred despite a 67 percent increase in electricity demand during the same period. Electricity consumption grew at an average annual rate of 7.3 percent after the reforms, compared with 2.5 percent in the decade before.[19] The quality of service improved significantly as well. In 1999, Buenos Aires suffered a dramatic blackout because of the failure of equipment owned by the distribution company that served the southern half of the metropolitan area.[20] But blackouts had become the exception rather than the rule; between 1992 and 1997, for example, the annual amount of energy not supplied because of blackouts fell from 125 gigawatt-hours (GW-hours) to 8 GW-hours.[21]

Wholesale prices fell largely because of the dramatic increase in low-cost generating capacity. Installed capacity increased by 37 percent from 1992 to 1997, mostly in the form of new hydro or gas-fired plants located in mountains and gas fields far from Buenos Aires. The average availability of thermal plants also increased from 40 percent to 75 percent, so that the effective increase in generating capacity was an astounding 128 percent.[22] In addition, the efficiency of the older thermal plants improved as old equipment was retired or upgraded. Finally, the expansion of the gas fields and pipelines helped to further reduce wholesale electricity costs by allowing generators to substitute cheaper gas for diesel oil in thermal plants.

Transmission Limitations and Pricing

Transmission Limitations

High-voltage transmission plays a critical role in Argentina's electricity industry, because the cheapest sources of electric power are distant from the main consumption areas. Argentina's electric system is divided into seven regions, as shown in Figure 12.1.[23] In 1997 the Patagonia region was isolated and had to produce all the power it consumed, but the other six regions were connected by Transener's national grid and could share power. Collectively the six regions had 18,052 megawatts of capacity, far in excess of the peak demand of 11,532 megawatts. But three-quarters of the peak demand—8,235 megawatts—were concentrated in the Buenos Aires region. The Buenos Aires region had only 6,559 megawatts of generating capacity and imported

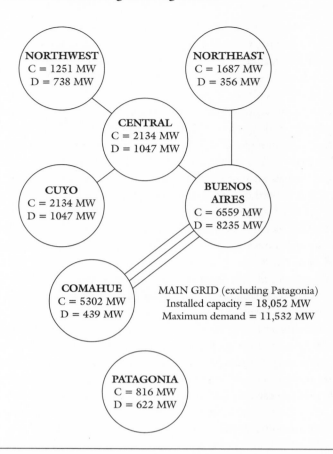

Figure 12.1 The seven regions in Argentina's electric system with installed capacity (C) and maximum demand (D) as of December 31, 1997. (CAMMESA.)

power from other regions. The principal power exporters were the Comahue region, which had abundant hydro resources and natural gas fields, and the Northeast region, which was the site of the Yacyretá and Salto Grande dams.

Nodal Prices

Because transmission constraints were potentially so important, Argentina established one of the first wholesale electricity markets in the world where the price of electricity varied according to the node on the transmission system where the power was input or withdrawn. The idea of nodal pricing was not developed in Argentina, but Argentina was among the first few countries to put it into practice.[24]

Argentina's national grid had approximately two hundred nodes, with about two dozen nodes in each region. The nodes were located where wholesale sellers and buyers connected to the national grid or where lines crossed. For the sake of convenience, nodal prices were expressed as a proportion of the market price at a "market node" located at the approximate geographic center of the demand for electricity in Argentina at Ezeiza, just outside the city of Buenos Aires.

The variation in electricity prices among nodes was designed to reflect the fact that there were constraints and power losses in the transmission system. As much as 5 to 10 percent of the power transported over long distances is lost as heat, because of the resistance of the transmission lines. CAMMESA, the ISO, used a simulation model of how power flowed in the transmission system to estimate the marginal line losses that were incurred when inserting power at one node and withdrawing it from another. An increase in demand at a node in a region that exported electricity, such as Comahue, caused little or no line losses because the power would not be transported far. But an increase in demand at a node in a region that imported electricity, such as Buenos Aires, might cause large line losses because the extra power had to be dispatched from another region, such as Comahue. Given the long distances power was transported in Argentina and the size of the resulting line losses, wholesale prices were often 20 percent higher at importing than at exporting nodes.

One assumption CAMMESA made in its line-loss simulations was not particularly realistic. For simplicity's sake, CAMMESA always assumed that a generator at the market node near Buenos Aires would provide the extra power needed to serve extra demand anywhere in the system.[25] In the parlance of electrical flow modeling, the market node at Buenos Aires served as the "swing bus." In practice, this assumption was seldom true, since usually there was not enough generating capacity in the Buenos Aires region to meet local demand.[26] Nevertheless, the simulations still produced lower prices for nodes in exporting regions, such as Comahue. Even if the extra power needed in Comahue was assumed to be dispatched from Buenos Aires, the model would predict that the extra Buenos Aires production would be consumed locally since electricity flows over the path of least resistance. As a result, the model also would predict a reduction in the amount of power that had to be transported between Comahue and Buenos Aires, and thus a reduction in transmission line losses.

CAMMESA used a variant of this approach to set prices in regions where constraints on transmission capacity limited its ability to dispatch local generators. Such regions were designated as "isolated," and the prices that prevailed in them were the prices that cleared the local power market. Comahue was designated as an isolated region for many hours of the year beginning in 1995, and the Northeast region began to be isolated in 1997. Comahue had 5,302 megawatts of relatively low-cost generating capacity by late 1997, for example, but Transener's three 500-kV lines connecting Comahue and Buenos Aires could safely carry only 2,700 megawatts. When transmission constraints prevented CAMMESA from dispatching as much Comahue power as it wanted, CAMMESA would set the local price in Comahue at the marginal cost of the last Comahue plant that had to be dispatched to satisfy the combination of local demand and 2,700 megawatts of exports. In the hours when an exporting region was designated as isolated, nodal prices in that region were usually much lower than normal.

The nodal pricing system forced generators and consumers to consider transmission losses and constraints when siting new generating stations and loads, notwithstanding the occasional inaccuracies of CAMMESA's simulations. For example, a generator considering whether to build a new station in Comahue or Buenos Aires knew that it would receive a lower price for its power in Comahue, because of the transmission losses between Comahue and the electricity importing regions. If the generator anticipated that Comahue would be isolated many hours of the year, then the expected difference between Comahue and Buenos Aires prices would be even larger. Similarly, a manufacturer could expect to pay less for power if he sited a new plant in Comahue instead of Buenos Aires.

Transmission Access Charges

Transener's transmission access charges played a role in the nodal pricing scheme in that Transener received the line-loss revenues generated by nodal pricing. But Transener's access charges were designed primarily to raise the revenue the company needed to operate and maintain its lines rather than to affect the behavior of generators and wholesale customers that used its system.

Line losses were one of three primary sources of revenue provided to Transener under its concession contract. Line losses meant that CAMMESA had to buy more MW-hours of power on the wholesale market than users consumed.[27] But the nodal pricing system compensated in two ways. First, CAMMESA sold power for a higher average price per MW-hour than it paid simply because CAMMESA sold much of its power in importing regions and bought much of its power in exporting regions. Second, nodal prices were set

Table 12.2 Transener tariffs, selected years

	1994	1997	1999[a]
(1) Line losses	Varies (see text)	Varies (see text)	Varies (see text)
(2) Connection charges			
Per 500 kV connection	$10/hour	$10.849/hour	$22.186/hour
Per 220 kV connection	$9/hour	$9.764/hour	$25.366/hour
Per 132 kV connection	$8/hour	$8.680/hour	$22.549/hour
Per dedicated transformer	$0.05/MVA-hour	$0.054/MVA-hour	$0.141/MVA-hour
(3) Line capacity charges			
Per 100 km of 500 kV line	$50/hour	$52.077/hour	$52.377/hour
Per 100 km of 220 kV line	$40/hour	$43.398/hour[b]	$43.647/hour

Source: CAMMESA.

Note: MVA–megavolt amperes.

a. Note that the first periodic tariff review for Transener occurred in 1998. At that time, ENRE decided to raise connection charges to compensate for the decline in line-loss revenues over the previous five years.

b. This figure is from CAMMESA, but it may be in error. It is not clear why the charge for 220-kV lines increased more rapidly than the charge for 500-kV lines, since both are indexed using the same formula.

on the basis of marginal line losses—that is, the additional line losses caused by an extra megawatt of consumption. Line losses increase as the square of the amount of power carried on a line, so that the marginal line losses are twice as large as the average line losses. As a result, the nodal price system generated more revenue than CAMMESA needed to compensate for actual line losses, and this extra line-loss revenue was given to Transener.

Transener's two other revenue sources were connection and line-capacity charges, as shown in Table 12.2. At the points where wholesale customers connected to the high-voltage system, Transener often supplied and maintained a transformer that converted the high voltage on Transener's lines to the lower voltage of the customer's lines. Each customer paid according the voltage of its connection, the capacity of any dedicated transformers, and the number of hours the connection was maintained. The line-capacity charges varied according to the voltage of the line, the line length, and the number of hours it was used. To apportion the capacity charges for a specific line among different users, CAMMESA employed its simulation model to estimate which generators and buyers used the line during the hours when the loads on the transmission system were highest. The generators using the line were assigned 80 percent of the line-capacity charge and the buyers 20 percent.

Transener's connection and line-capacity charges were not intended to influence generator or distribution behavior. There was no pretense, for example, that they reflected Transener's actual costs of maintaining different types of connections and lines. The primary role of these two charges was to supplement the line-loss revenues so that Transener would have enough income to maintain and operate its system.

The money-raising function of the connection and capacity charges was explicit in the way the two charges varied with line-loss revenues. The authors of the electricity reforms understood that changes in wholesale power consumption or prices would affect the line-loss revenues greatly but would have little effect on Transener's costs. Moreover, they worried that if Transener's revenues depended on line losses the company would have an incentive to oppose new transmission lines in order to keep losses high. To protect Transener from arbitrary revenue fluctuations and perverse incentives, Transener's concession contract set out a target annual level of line-loss revenues for the first five years of the concession. If the line-loss revenues fell short or exceeded the target, ENRE would compensate Transener by increasing or decreasing the capacity charges. The dramatic drop in average wholesale power prices during the 1990s caused line-loss revenues to fall below targets and led to large surcharges on the line-capacity charges. By the mid-1990s line-loss revenues were no longer the single most important source of income for Transener, contrary to the expectations of the framers of the reforms.

Capacity Expansion by a Vote of the Beneficiaries

Voting in Lieu of Negotiations

The 1992 law that restructured Argentina's electricity industry and subsequent regulations provided three different methods for expanding transmission capacity. Two methods were for expansions that were relatively small or that affected only one customer. For improvements costing less than $2 million, ENRE had the discretion to decide whether they were needed, to order Transener to build and maintain them, and to determine which users should pay the cost. For improvements that primarily affected one customer, such as a short extension to connect a new wholesale customer to the high-voltage system, Transener and the customer were expected to negotiate an agreement on how much the customer would pay. ENRE had to approve the agreement to make sure that it served the public interest and that Transener was not abusing its monopoly position in the negotiations.

A third and more novel approach was established for major new lines that would be used by many different parties. Upon the request of a coalition of generators, distributors, and large industrial consumers who were thought to receive at least 30 percent of the benefit from a new line, ENRE would estimate the costs and benefits of the line, identify the beneficiaries more carefully, and hold a public hearing. If parties who stood to gain 30 percent of the expected benefit voted against the project at the public hearing, the project would go no further. If fewer voted against, however, ENRE would conduct a competition for a new concession to construct, operate, and maintain (COM) the new line. The concessionaire would recover its construction costs through an annual fee to be charged for the first fifteen years, and its operating and maintenance costs through a tariff schedule that was the same as Transener's.

The concession would be awarded competitively to the bidder offering the lowest annual construction fee. The users of the line would pay the annual fee, with their individual shares being proportional to the degree to which they were thought to benefit from the line. Transener would remain responsible for the compatibility of the high-voltage transmission system and the technical supervision of the COM contract, and would receive fees from the concessionaire in return.[28] Transener could participate in the competition for the COM contract too, but it would win only if its bid were lowest.

This method had two unusual features. One was to introduce competition in the award for the new line, so as to keep the construction and operating costs low. But the second—and more interesting for our purposes—was to use a vote of the beneficiaries to determine whether the line was needed or not. Voting was less burdensome than a negotiated agreement. But voting also placed a premium on the accuracy of the rules for measuring how much different parties would benefit from the line, and thus how many votes they had.

To identify the beneficiaries of a proposed new line, ENRE relied on the same CAMMESA simulation model that it used to calculate line losses and nodal prices. CAMMESA would add the proposed new line to its model and simulate its operation with a baseline, or typical, geographic pattern of power demand and supply. CAMMESA would then change by 1 megawatt the amount of power inserted or withdrawn at each node to see which nodes affected the flow on the new line. The nodes that affected the flow were said to be in the line's "area of influence," and the users at those nodes were deemed beneficiaries of the line.

To determine the voting shares and financial responsibilities, CAMMESA used a more elaborate series of simulations to estimate how much each node "participated" in the use of the line.[29] The voting share of a beneficiary was the weighted average of its expected participation in the first two years of the line's operation. The share of the annual construction fee that a beneficiary had to pay in any given year during the fifteen-year amortization period was proportional to its estimated participation in the line flow during the year.[30]

The Fourth Comahue Line

The voting procedure was soon tested by a proposal to build a fourth 500-kV line between Comahue and Buenos Aires. The first two lines between Comahue and Buenos Aires had been put in service in the 1970s and the third in 1985. Pressures for a fourth line grew in the early 1990s as President Menem's economic reforms stimulated electricity demand and generators built new plants in Comahue.

The Comahue generators had a strong interest in a fourth line. The line would raise nodal prices at Comahue by reducing line losses and the frequency with which the region was considered isolated. In 1994, the year before the existing three lines began to operate at capacity, a coalition of Comahue generators claiming to represent 30 percent of the beneficiaries of a fourth line successfully petitioned ENRE to open a formal inquiry into the proposal. The generators estimated that the cost of building the line would be around $250 million, and ENRE determined that the benefits in lower electricity prices made the line in the public interest. At the subsequent public hearing in 1995, however, the proposal failed when parties that stood to gain over 30 percent of the estimated benefits voted against it.

The vote revealed several serious difficulties with the procedure for determining who benefited.[31] One was that the distribution companies had few incentives to support increased transmission capacity. The tariff regulations allowed distribution companies to pass on any changes in wholesale prices to consumers. Even if their customers gained from lower prices, the distribution companies would see no direct benefit themselves. The designers of the process had anticipated the distributors' incentives, however, by defining the test for a new line as no more than 30 percent voting against rather than at least 70 percent voting for. The distribution companies had no incentive to vote for added capacity, but they also had no incentive to vote against.

A more serious problem was that CAMMESA's simulation model effectively disenfranchised electricity buyers located in Buenos Aires, including the big industrial and commercial users that bought directly from the wholesale market as well as the distribution companies buying on behalf of their retail customers. These buyers had almost as much stake in the fourth line as the Comahue generators, because the new line would reduce nodal prices in Buenos Aires by increasing access to low-cost Comahue power. But while CAMMESA's swing bus assumption caused only modest distortions in calculating nodal prices, it caused serious problems when identifying the beneficiaries of the fourth line. CAMMESA's simulations suggested that Buenos Aires buyers would not be users of the fourth line, because when loads increased at Buenos Aires, the Buenos Aires swing bus responded rather than generating stations at Comahue. Since the Buenos Aires buyers were not considered users, they were not eligible to vote on the line.

Even if CAMMESA's model had estimated more accurately who would use the new line, use of the line was only a crude proxy for the economic benefits received from it. The benefits to a user depend not just on how many MW-hours of power he inserts or draws from the new line, but also on how much the line changes the price he pays or receives for that power. Some generators who would use the line might see little or no increase in the price they received for their power, for example, and others might even see the price they receive decline.[32] Since use does not correlate well with benefits, voting based on use might not result in sensible decisions about whether a new line is needed.

Finally, the voting rules also provided only limited provisions for representing the interests of future participants in the market. It was probably impractical to identify users beyond the first two years after the line was to open. And the users who were allowed to vote obviously had their future as well as their current interests in mind. But two years was a short time horizon, given the long life of a transmission line and the likelihood that new classes of local users would develop if the price of electric power fell in Buenos Aires.

Changing the Voters' Incentives

The failure of the 1995 vote stimulated both the Comahue generators and the government to find ways around it. The generators hired engineering consultants to look for low-cost ways of improving the effective capacity of the existing three lines. Their consultants developed an innovative program to increase capacity from 2,700 megawatts to 3,300 megawatts with only $12 million in improvements in related lines and equipment.

For its part, the government changed the funding rules to favor a new line. Henceforth, any line-loss revenues that were due to a region's isolation would be placed in a special "surplus" account to be used to help defray the cost of building extra transmission capacity to that region. As funds accumulated in the region's surplus account, support for transmission capacity expansion would grow, because the proportion of the construction cost that beneficiaries would have to pay would fall. To the government, it made sense that these revenues should be used to subsidize capacity expansions, since they reflected the cost of inadequate transmission lines. And Transener would not object to the diversion of a portion of its line-loss revenues, since its total revenues from line losses were guaranteed by the government.[33]

Both strategies paid off in 1996, when the coalition of Comahue generators got ENRE to schedule a public hearing on both the $12 million improvement package and a fourth line. At the hearing, the beneficiaries approved both projects. The approval of the $12 million package was no surprise, since it was such a bargain. In the case of the fourth line, the key difference was the availability of the funds in the special account established for lines that would relieve the isolation of Comahue. The fund balance was accumulating rapidly and was expected to reach $90 million by the time construction began in 1998, which would reduce the amount the beneficiaries had to pay by more than one-third.

After the hearing, the secretary of energy decided that the $12 million package of improvements was small enough that Transener should proceed without competitive bidding and should be reimbursed directly from the surplus account. The improvements were finished by the last months of 1997. ENRE put the concession for the fourth line out to bid in early 1997 and Transener was selected as the lowest bidder. Transener completed construction on schedule and placed the line in service in October 1999.[34]

The Search for New Strategies

Once the fourth line was approved, however, the government began to search for alternative mechanisms for identifying and financing transmission expansion projects. The government and others in the industry believed that there were other worthwhile transmission improvements besides the fourth line. Additional radial lines into the Buenos Aires region would be needed as demand grew, including new links to the Northeast and eventually a fifth line to Comahue.

Equally intriguing was the potential for new ring or circumferential transmission lines to improve the reliability of the electricity system. The biggest need was for a medium- or high-voltage ring line around the Buenos Aires metropolitan area. Such a ring would provide CAMMESA with more options to shift power around the metropolitan area in the event that one of the area's major generating plants or radial transmission lines failed unexpectedly. The ring would also provide tangible financial benefits, since it would allow CAMMESA to reduce the number of old thermal plants it had to keep on standby for metropolitan area emergencies. There were also some advocates in the industry for another high-voltage ring line to connect the outer regions of the country (for example, Comahue–Cuyo–Northwest–Northeast).

Supporters claimed the outer ring would not only increase reliability but also provide additional radial capacity into the Buenos Aires region by allowing more power to flow in along underutilized radial corridors.

The government feared that the combination of voting and the surplus fund accounts might not provide the proper incentives for transmission improvements. On the one hand, the surplus accounts might encourage over-investment in projects that reduced congestion. Just because a region was isolated occasionally didn't mean that a new line was justified. As funds accumulated in the region's surplus account, however, the line eventually would become so cheap that the beneficiaries were bound to vote for it.[35] On the other hand, the accounts might lead to underinvestment in projects that increased reliability. If a line or plant failed, a region might become temporarily isolated and funds would be deposited into its surplus account. Those funds would understate the economic benefits of using transmission to enhance reliability, however, since they wouldn't reflect the potential savings in eliminating local standby generators.

Tradable Transmission Congestion Contracts

The Proposal

In 1998 the secretary of energy proposed an alternative method for selecting and financing new transmission lines that was based on tradable transmission congestion contracts (TCCs).[36] The idea of TCCs had been developed by William Hogan, a respected expert on electricity restructuring at Harvard University, as a complement to contracts for price differences to further protect wholesale market participants against the volatility of nodal prices.[37]

A TCC is the right to the difference in nodal prices due to capacity constraints for a particular flow, and owning a TCC provides a hedge against price volatility caused by transmission constraints. Suppose, for example, a generator wanted to build a 500-megawatt plant in Comahue but was nervous about the effects on local power prices caused by overloads on the lines from Comahue. To protect itself, the generator could buy a TCC for transmitting 500 megawatts of power from Comahue to Buenos Aires. When the lines from Comahue were congested and local prices fell, the generator would receive a lower price for its power but would also get the revenue from the difference between Comahue and Buenos Aires prices to compensate.[38] TCCs were superior to contracts for price differences in that a generator desiring price protection did not have to find a buyer with a corresponding need to contract with.

TCCs appealed to the Argentine government because the market price of a TCC between two points would depend on the severity of transmission constraints, and thus provide a measure of the value of adding transmission capacity between those two points. And if the developers of a new transmission line received the TCCs that the line made possible, then they would have an added financial incentive to build. Ideally, TCCs could help create a market-oriented system where private investors—not the government—decided when and where additional transmission capacity was needed based in part on the values of the TCCs.

TCCs were a relatively new idea, however, and there was relatively little practical experience to guide Argentina. Many transmission systems were seriously considering TCCs, including the national systems of Australia, New Zealand, and Norway and the power pools for the states of New York and California and for the New England region. However, the first transmission system to implement TCCs—the Pennsylvania–New Jersey–Maryland Interconnection (PJM) in the United States—was not scheduled to do so until in April 1999.[39] And even then, no one had fashioned TCCs into a working program of investment incentives.

Argentina's secretary of energy proposed to give TCC owners the rights to differences in nodal prices when regions were isolated, but not to the differences in nodal prices due simply to transmission losses. If the difference between Comahue and Buenos Aires nodal prices was $5 per MW-hour when Comahue was isolated, for example, the owner of 100 megawatts' worth of TCCs from Comahue to Buenos Aires would receive $500 for every hour Comahue remained isolated. The TCCs associated with the existing transmission lines would remain with the government and the revenues from those capacity rights would be deposited into special surplus accounts controlled by the government (just as they were already). The TCCs for new lines would accrue to the investors who financed the construction of the line, although they could subsequently sell or lease the rights.[40]

As part of his scheme, the secretary proposed a new "at-risk" method for building new transmission lines.[41] This method would be initiated when a group of investors who promised to assume responsibility for at least 30 percent of the cost of a new line approached ENRE. ENRE would then conduct two auctions. The first would be to determine which investors would get to finance the line. The investment rights would be awarded to the group of investors that forecast the highest percentage utilization of the line.[42] The second auction would be to award a concession to construct, operate, and maintain the new line. As in the voting method, the construction costs would be amortized over fifteen years and the COM concession would be awarded to the bidder requesting the lowest annual payment.

The at-risk method differed from the voting method in that the investors proposing the line did not have to be generators or other participants in the wholesale power market. Moreover, the investors, rather than the users, would be directly responsible for making the fifteen annual payments to the COM concessionaire. In return, the investors would have the right to charge users a toll equal to the payment due the COM concessionaire times the ratio of the actual to the expected utilization of the line. This scheme forced investors to assume part of the risk of whether the new line was needed. Investors would lose money on the tolls if utilization was lower than they expected and make profits if utilization was higher. In addition, the investors would have the rights to the TCCs from the line.

The secretary's proposal was accepted by much of the industry but strongly opposed by the generators. The generators supported the idea of TCCs and the proposal to assign the TCCs for new lines to the investors that built them. However, they thought the TCCs for existing transmission lines should be assigned to their existing users rather to than the government. In essence, this approach would eliminate the surplus accounts the government had established to encourage the approval of the fourth Comahue line and, in so doing, reduce the total transmission charges the generators paid.[43] It would also, the generators argued, remove the incentive to overinvest in new lines created by the surplus accounts.

The generators also preferred the old voting method for selecting new lines to the new at-risk method. The at-risk method left the generators with substantial obligations for the financing of new capacity (in the form of the tolls the investors could charge) but no say in whether the investment should be undertaken.

Implementation of the proposal was delayed first by the generators' objections and then by a growing economic crisis that resulted in Argentina's defaulting on its debt and devaluing its currency in 2002. The government was likely to be pressed to revisit the issue of transmission investment soon, however, if only because the fourth Comahue line had already reached capacity in 2001, in spite of the weakening economy. If the secretary's proposal was revived, it had two defects that were fairly easily fixed and two that seemed more difficult.

Assigning and Defining TCC Rights

One problem that might be fairly easily overcome is the generators' complaint that they should get the TCCs for existing transmission lines. In theory, the incentives for transmission use and investment are not affected by who gets the rights for the TCCs in the existing transmission system. As long as the TCCs are tradable, they will eventually be transferred to the users who value them the most. In practice, however, the initial allocation creates financial windfalls or losses for some parties. In countries where the transmission company has been saddled with the debt from building the existing system, for example, the revenues from the TCCs may be essential to keep the transmission company solvent. In Argentina, however, the transmission companies were obligated only to maintain existing capacity and had been given revenues sufficient to that task, which meant that the government might have some flexibility in assigning the initial TCCs.

A second problem that probably could have been remedied is the failure to recognize the interdependencies of transmission flows and capacity in defining TCCs. The secretary defined the TCCs in terms of the rated capacities of specific transmission lines or substations. The transmission capacity available between two points does not necessarily correspond to the capacity of the lines directly connecting them, however, because electricity flows through a network by all parallel routes. Parallel flows also mean that the available capacity between two points can be strongly affected by supply and demand at distant points on the network, because the parallel routes can be surprisingly circuitous.

Given the interdependence of power flows, the ownership of particular lines and substations does not imply ownership of particular TCCs or vice versa. Interdependence also makes it impossible to define capacity between two points without making some assumptions about the base flows on the network. Interdependence has advantages in that it makes the definition of a TCC flexible to some degree. Simulations might show, for example, that a TCC to transport 100 megawatts from A to B requires the equivalent capacity as a TCC to transport 80 megawatts from C to D. The ability to redefine a TCC is useful when adapting to changing flows, but it also adds to the complexity of a TCC system.

Proponents of TCCs argue that the problem of defining TCCs can be solved by giving an independent party—most logically the ISO—the responsibility. The ISO would use its simulation model to define an initial set of TCCs that are consistent with the current base flows. As flows change, TCC owners could petition the system operator to redefine their rights, and the operator would use the simulation model to determine whether the proposed new definitions were feasible. The operator would also review proposals by investors for capacity improvements to determine the specific TCCs that the improvements would generate. In Argentina, CAMMESA is the obvious candidate to determine the feasible TCCs. Argentina's high-voltage transmission system is still largely radial rather than a grid, moreover, so flows might not be overly interdependent.

Investments for Congestion Relief

A more serious problem is whether the secretary's at-risk method provides the appropriate incentives to build new transmission capacity. The at-risk method was aimed at encouraging investments to relieve congestion rather than to increase reliability. But even with that limited objective, it is difficult to design a system with appropriate incentives.

Certain provisions of the scheme were clever, notably the use of two separate auctions to keep the transmission tolls at reasonable levels. The competition among concessionaires for the right to build and maintain the new line should ensure that the tolls they request are just enough to recover efficient construction and operating costs.[44] And the competition among investors for the right to finance the new line should mean that the effective tolls are reduced by the expected revenues from the TCC rights.[45]

Nevertheless, Argentina's generators were right in arguing that there is no guarantee that the new line's capacity would be needed, because the users have no direct say in approving a new line but are required to pay the tolls once the line is approved. The users do benefit inasmuch as a new line will reduce differences in nodal prices even in periods when regions are not isolated. And if the tolls exceed the congestion relief afforded to users, the users could respond by shifting the locations of their plants or cutting back electricity production or consumption. This threat is not very credible, however, given the durable, location-specific investments of electricity generators and their industrial customers and the low price elasticity of demand of residential customers. In short, the at-risk method could force users to pay tolls greater than the benefits in congestion relief that they receive from the line.

One way to alleviate this problem is to require that new capacity be financed entirely from TCC revenues, without any supplementary tolls. To do this TCC revenues would have to be expanded to include the nodal price differences at all times, not just when a region was isolated. In that case, the TCC revenues would reflect the costs of transmission constraints to generators and consumers and provide a more appropriate price signal for the need for capacity. If the revenues for a megawatt of TCC between points A and B exceeded the cost of building an extra megawatt of transmission capacity between A and B, then building the extra megawatt of capacity would reduce the total costs of the nation's electricity system.

This approach would discourage the construction of unneeded capacity, but it might not be enough to ensure that all the worthwhile congestion-relieving capacity was built. The problem arises because transmission investments are not just durable and immobile but exhibit economies of scale and are lumpy. Economies of scale are particularly problematic, because they mean that the incremental or marginal cost of transmitting an additional megawatt of power is less than the average cost. Since investors in transmission must recover at least their average costs in order to survive, they will be forced to charge more than their incremental cost and to build less capacity than would be socially worthwhile.[46]

Lumpiness may cause problems because it requires patient investors. Transmission capacity is lumpy in the sense that it is often cheaper to build a large amount of capacity at once than to add to capacity incrementally. When building a new line in a growing corridor, for example, it may be more cost effective to install a large line at the outset than to start with a small line and gradually add more. Lumpiness means that the prices for TCCs will fall immediately after new lines are put in service and that it may take years before congestion develops and investors begin to recover their investment.

It is unclear how important the problems of economies of scale and lumpiness are in practice. It may be that TCC revenues alone will be enough to induce investment levels close to those optimal for relieving transmission congestion. If not, TCCs will have to be supplemented by toll or access charges, and the calculation of the appropriate toll is likely to be technically difficult and controversial.

Investments in Reliability

The at-risk method might have improved reliability simply by encouraging excessive investment in congestion relief. But the method was not designed to encourage reliability, and there is a good chance that facilities needed primarily for reliability, such as the proposed inner and outer high-voltage ring lines, would have been overlooked.

The Argentine system used fines for service interruptions to encourage reliable service from the transmission and distribution companies, but the fines provided little incentive to invest in high-voltage transmission.[47] The transmission companies were fined only if one of their transmission lines or substations was not in service when needed, but not if their facilities were inadequate to meet unexpected surges in loads or shutdowns of generating plants. As a result they had few incentives to build facilities, like the transmission rings, that were designed to protect against those risks.

The distribution companies had more incentive to invest in reliability, since they were fined if service to their customers was interrupted for any reason. A transmission investment often improved reliability for many distribution companies, however, because of the interdependence of the network. As a result, while distribution companies could invest in new lines to reduce their liability to fines, the less vulnerable companies might be tempted to free ride on the investments of the more vulnerable companies.

Conclusion

Argentina's electricity industry demonstrates more clearly than Britain's railroads the potential of unbundling to improve performance by introducing competition. In Britain's railroads that potential is still unrealized, since the government has chosen to limit TOC-on-TOC competition. In Argentina's electricity industry, however, competition among generators encouraged the dramatic improvement in the industry's performance during the 1990s. Some substantial improvement probably would have occurred even if the electricity industry had been privatized as vertically integrated companies. The profit motive would have induced the new owners to seek opportunities to reduce costs, and the regulators would have pressed the industry to pass on some of the savings in lower prices and better service. Nevertheless, vertical unbundling established intense competition in generation that almost certainly contributed to the dramatic increases in generating capacity and the halving of wholesale power prices.

The Argentine electricity and British railroad cases are similar, however, in demonstrating the importance of maintaining coordination while unbundling. In Britain, the ability of the train-operating companies to improve their services or compete with one another depends on the incentives that the monopoly infrastructure company has to create new train paths. In Argentina, the benefits of vertical unbundling depend on the coordination of the plans of the monopoly transmission system with those of the wholesale power generators and buyers.

The need for coordination was not strong when the Argentine electricity industry was first restructured, since the transmission system was not overloaded at the time. But the rapid increases in generating capacity in the Comahue and Northeast regions soon absorbed the excess transmission capacity. As congestion developed, it became important to provide proper signals about where new generating stations and loads should be located and when and where new transmission lines should be built. Without the improvements to the first three Comahue lines in 1997 or the opening of the fourth line in 1999, for example, wholesale power prices almost surely would be higher.

Argentina and Britain used different tools to try to maintain coordination in their electricity and railway industries. The British relied on access charges that were either preset by the rail regulator or negotiated among the infrastructure and the train-operating companies. Argentina used regulated and negotiated access charges as well, but only for the smallest transmission improvements. Instead, it relied primarily on markets or marketlike mechanisms to motivate the industry to use and invest in capacity wisely.

Some of the coordination methods developed in Argentina did not work well, particularly voting by beneficiaries. The great attraction of the voting method is that it gives the beneficiaries a say while avoiding the potential cost and delay of complex negotiations. The great weakness of voting, however, is that the rules for determining who votes and who pays once the project is approved must be carefully thought out if the method is to produce sensible results. Argentina defined voting and financial responsibilities in terms of the degree to which the various parties contributed to the electricity flowing through the new line. CAMMESA complicated matters by estimating inaccurately how much various market participants contributed to the line's flows, although this problem could have been fixed easily by changing CAMMESA's assumption about the swing bus. A more serious problem was that the power flows were only a crude proxy for the financial interests of the various users of the line. In addition, the regulatory system gave the local distribution companies little incentive to try to secure lower wholesale prices by expanding transmission.

Other approaches used by Argentina were more successful, such as the idea of holding an open competition to award the concession to build and operate a new line. The competition did not address the question of whether the new line was needed or who should pay for it. But it meant that Transener was no longer the monopoly provider of new lines, so the regulator, ENRE, did not have to be as concerned that Transener would exaggerate the costs of building new lines.

The most striking feature of the Argentine experience, however, is how much more successful they were in using pricing as a tool of coordination. Nodal pricing in particular seems to provide reasonably sensible incentives for wholesale generators and buyers to consider transmission congestion costs when locating their plants. CAMMESA's line-loss estimates were not completely accurate, but in this case the errors do not seem to have been very serious (and again could have been remedied easily). The key was that the principles used to set nodal prices reflected the real economic costs of congestion or capacity bottlenecks in the existing transmission system. Nodal prices established incentives for the industry to use the existing transmission system wisely, and they were an important step toward establishing the proper incentives to expand the transmission system.

The secretary of energy's proposal for TCCs moved closer to creating a sensible system of incentives for the construction of new lines. TCCs are a derivative of nodal prices, of course, in that they are the rights to the price differences between pairs of nodes. An unresolved problem with TCCs is that TCC rights alone are unlikely to be sufficient to induce investors to build needed new lines, because transmission investments are lumpy and subject to economies of scale. The secretary addressed this concern by allowing the investors to charge a toll in addition to the TCC. But the secretary's proposal ran the risk of creating overly generous incentives to invest in congestion relief while offering no explicit incentives to invest in reliability.

Relying entirely on price incentives to promote transmission investments may prove difficult, however. Workable pricing schemes to encourage investments in congestion-relieving capacity probably will be developed on the basis of TCCs (possibly supplemented with additional revenues). But pricing schemes to promote investments in system reliability may simply prove too difficult. Measuring reliability and apportioning the sources of risk seem more complex than measuring congestion and determining who suffers from it. In the end it may be simpler to grant the regulator or the system operator the authority to identify and mandate the investments needed to increase reliability and to apportion the costs in some reasonable manner.

13

The Prospects for Unbundling

Differences among Industries

The experiences of the British railway and Argentine electricity industries suggest that vertical unbundling is likely to be more attractive in some industries than in others. For a summary of the factors that affect the costs and benefits of vertical unbundling and an impressionistic assessment of their magnitudes in five industries—electricity, natural gas, water, railways, and telecommunications—see Table 13.1.

The benefits of unbundling stem from the introduction of competition into additional activities. The central assumption is that regulation is an imperfect substitute for competition—that regulators can never be as effective in evoking cost and service improvements as the forces of a competitive market. If so, one should introduce competition to those parts of the industry where it can be sustained and restrict regulation to the residual. If we accept this logic, the benefits of unbundling should be roughly proportional to two factors: the share of total industry costs that are in activities where competition can be sustained and the untapped potential for productivity improvements in those potentially competitive activities.

The costs of unbundling stem from the risk of reduced coordination between the newly separated segments of the industry. The industry was vertically integrated presumably because integration once offered important opportunities for coordination that were difficult to achieve through contractual relations between independent firms. The coordination advantages of integration may have diminished with time, perhaps as technology has changed, but they probably have not disappeared altogether. If so, the costs of unbundling are likely to depend on four factors that affect coordination: the share of total industry costs absorbed by the key monopoly or bottleneck infrastructure provider, the degree of heterogeneity in the industry's products or services, the extent to which the flows over the infrastructure network are interdependent, and the prevalence of common functions or assets among vertically separable activities.

The ratings in Table 13.1 suggest that the overall advantages of unbundling vary considerably both among and within industries. The potential is greatest for large consumers of electricity, gas, and water and for telecommunications, and considerably lower for small consumers of electricity, gas, and water and for railways.

Factors That Affect Benefits

Competitive Activity Costs

The share of an industry's costs that are in potentially competitive activities varies depending on local conditions and accounting practices, so the figures in Table 13.1 should be treated with considerable caution. Nevertheless, the range is quite broad, from a low of around 20 percent to a high of around 80 percent.

The main opportunities for competition in electricity and gas are in the production of bulk power supplies.[1] These production activities account for roughly half of electricity and gas industry costs in many countries, although the percentage varies considerably depending upon whether there are abundant local gas, oil, or coal fields or opportunities for hydro power so that fuel or power does not have to be imported long distances. In Argentina, for example, generation accounted for approximately 60 percent of electricity costs in 1992, when the reforms first began, but its share fell to about 33 percent of industry costs by 1997.[2] In Britain, generation accounted for around 40 percent of the electricity costs in the mid-1990s, several years after the privatization of the industry was complete.[3] Similarly, in the United States, the well-head price of gas accounts for roughly half of the total delivered price of gas; in Britain, which has enjoyed plentiful offshore supplies since the early 1970s, the beach price of gas accounts for 43 percent of the average delivered price.[4]

Within the electricity and gas industries, however, there is an important difference between the retail customers served by the local electricity and gas distribution companies and those industrial and commercial consumers large enough to buy wholesale and bypass the local distributors. Retail customers pay substantially higher prices than wholesale customers to cover the added costs of the local network needed to connect them with the long-distance power or gas transmission systems and the expense of servicing and billing small accounts. In the United States, for example, the well-head price of gas

Table 13.1 Comparison of the benefits and costs of unbundling across selected industries

	Electricity		Natural gas		Water		Railways		Telecoms
	Small consumer	Large consumer	Small consumer	Large consumer	Small consumer	Large consumer	Freight only	Passenger or mixed	
Factors that affect benefits									
(1) Competitive activities' share of total costs	20–40%	80–90%	20–40%	60–80%	Variable but low	Variable but high	60–80%	50–60%	50–60%
(2) Opportunities for innovation in the competitive activities	Moderate	Moderate	Moderate	Moderate	Moderate	Moderate	Moderate	Moderate	High
Overall benefit	*Low*	*High*	*Low*	*High*	*Low*	*High*	*High*	*Moderate*	*High*
Factors that affect costs									
(1) Bottleneck infrastructure share of total costs	5–10%	10–20%	20–30%	20–30%	Variable	Variable	20–40%	40–60%	40–50%
(2) Product heterogeneity	Low	Low	Low	Moderate	Low	Moderate	Moderate	High	Moderate
(3) Network interdependence	High	High	Low	Low	Moderate	Moderate	Moderate	Moderate	Moderate
(4) Common functions or assets	Low	Low	Low	Low	Low	Low	Low	Moderate	Moderate
Overall cost	*Low*	*Low*	*Low*	*Low*	*Moderate*	*Moderate*	*Moderate*	*High*	*Low*
Overall advantage	*Low*	*High*	*Low*	*High*	*Low*	*High*	*Low/ moderate*	*Low*	*High*

Sources: Author's subjective assessments and sources cited in the text.

accounts for only 31 percent of the average delivered price paid by customers of local gas distribution companies, but 77 percent of the price paid by electric utilities who buy direct on the wholesale market.[5] Such dramatic differences make vertical unbundling much more important to wholesale than to retail customers.

Water appears to be similar to electricity and gas in that the opportunities for competition are mainly in bulk production and treatment, and there are important differences between customers that must be served by a local distribution company and those large enough to buy directly from bulk suppliers. The experience with vertically unbundled water industries is extremely limited. Wholesale markets for water have been developed in some agricultural areas, such as California, and Britain has had some limited success in encouraging competition among private water companies for large users.[6] Bulk water production and treatment costs are almost certainly a larger percentage of delivered prices for wholesale than for retail buyers, but the percentages probably vary considerably from region to region depending on the quantity and quality of local water supplies and demand.

Water also may be something of a special case in that environmental considerations may limit the opportunity to introduce competition where bulk water accounts for a large portion of the delivered water price. All forms of infrastructure face environmental constraints and objections, but they seem particularly acute in the case of bulk water. Bulk water costs tend to be high where natural or environmental constraints limit supplies. Groundwater aquifers cannot be pumped faster than they are recharged indefinitely, for example, and minimum stream flows may be required to maintain habitats or water quality. Even in such cases there are usually options to increase supplies, such as importing water from distant sources or recycling local wastewater more extensively. But effective competition may be harder to establish in situations where bulk water supplies are expensive and scarce.

In railroads, train operations are potentially competitive; the provision of track and other infrastructure is not. Train operations account for a larger share of total costs for freight than passenger railroads, because the higher speeds of passenger service require a higher standard of track, signals, and power distribution systems. In Britain, for example, approximately 55 percent of the revenues of the passenger TOCs cover the costs of operating the trains, while the balance is used to pay the access fees to Railtrack.[7] On the freight railroads of the United States, by contrast, train operations account for as much as 75 or 80 percent of total costs. The U.S. freight railroads are vertically integrated, however, and their allocation of costs to train operations and infrastructure may not be comparable to that used in Britain. The U.S. railroads include train dispatch and control in operations, for example, when at least some of those functions would have to be assumed by an infrastructure company after unbundling.[8] Nevertheless, the cost differences are large enough to make unbundling much more attractive for freight than for passenger service, all else being equal.

The proportion of telecommunications costs that are in potentially competitive activities depends in part on how the industry is defined, and particularly whether only telephony is considered or whether related services that telephone companies are beginning to provide, such as cable television and Internet services, are also included. If traditional telephone service is considered, then the main opportunities for competition are in long-distance and wireless calling. In the United States and Canada in the early 1990s, for example, long-distance calling accounted for 57 percent and 51 percent, respectively, of telephone revenues while local calls, most of which were hardwire at the time, accounted for the bulk of the rest.[9] The share of competitive activities has been increasing with the growth of wireless services.

Potential for Innovation in Competitive Activities

The potential for innovation has both short- and long-term components. Productivity often increases soon after an industry is vertically unbundled, as the introduction of competition encourages managers to adopt the most obvious and needed improvements. These immediate or short-term gains can be critical in establishing political support for restructuring, but it is hard to forecast or generalize about their size. The gains probably vary considerably from one country to the next, depending upon how poorly the industry was managed or regulated before it was restructured. Moreover, many countries, such as Argentina and Britain, privatized and restructured at the same time, making it difficult to distinguish the short-term improvements that are due to restructuring from those due to privatization.

The potential for long-term productivity gains is no easier to predict, but arguably more important. The presence of competition maintains the pressure on managers to continue to search for productivity over the years, and a modest improvement in the annual rate of productivity growth compounds over time and eventually outstrips the initial gain. The long-term gains are influenced by the quality of a country's regulators, but they also depend on the pace of change in the technologies used by the competitive portions of the industry.

The long-term potential for innovation seems higher in telecommunications than in the other four industries, although any such ranking is bound to be very speculative. The rate of innovation in telecommunications has been incredibly rapid in the last forty or fifty years, even though the industry has not been particularly competitive until fairly recently. Many key technological innovations, such as the transistor, were developed in the labs of integrated monopoly telephone companies. But telecommunications also exploited technologies developed for defense or for other industries that were more competitive, such as electronics and computers. Moreover, the spread of new technologies and services seems to have accelerated in the telecommunications sectors where competition has been introduced, such as long-distance and wireless telephony or the Internet. Whether the pace of innovation can be sustained is anyone's guess. The potential to do so seems strong, however, especially since telecommunications relies heavily on electronics and computing technologies, where progress is continuing at a rapid rate.

The potential for innovation in electric power, railroads, water, and natural gas may still be considerable, even if perhaps not as high as in telecommunications and not from technologies as glamorous as computing or electronics. In the last few decades, for example, the electricity industry has benefited from improvements in gas turbine technology, stimulated in part by the introduction of competition in generation. Similarly, in natural gas there have been steady improvements in well productivity and in the depths at which off-shore drilling is feasible and cost effective. On the more distant horizon, the industry is working to unlock new sources of natural gas, such as those contained in methane hydrates on the deep ocean floors and in the Arctic tundra.[10]

Factors That Affect Costs

Monopoly Infrastructure Costs

In most restructured utilities, coordination depends critically on the performance of a monopoly firm that provides the key or bottleneck infrastructure that connects the industry's various parts. This key infrastructure may be only a subset of the uncompetitive portion of the industry. In a vertically separated electricity, gas, or water industry, for example, the key firm is the company that transports power or water long distance and in bulk from the generating stations, gas fields, or bulk water suppliers to the local distribution companies and large industrial or agricultural users. In a railroad industry the key firm is the one that controls the tracks and stations that all train operators must use. In telecommunications industries it is harder to identify one segment of the industry that plays the coordinating role. The closest analog is the local hard-wire telephone company that still accounts for the majority of subscribers in most countries and whose cooperation is required to complete most calls.

The costs of coordination depend in part on how much of the industry's total costs are absorbed by providing this key piece of infrastructure. The firm providing the key infrastructure often can impose enormous costs on the rest of the industry if its services are inadequate. Where the key infrastructure is relatively inexpensive, however, it may be sensible to ease the industry's coordination problems by encouraging the infrastructure firm to build excess capacity. The cost of this excess capacity should set an upper limit on the other costs of coordination that the industry has to endure. The smaller the key infrastructure's share of total industry costs, the less burdensome excess capacity should be, all else being equal.

The key coordinating infrastructure generally accounts for only 10 to 30 percent of costs in electricity and gas industries compared with 40 to 60 percent of the costs in railroad and telecommunications industries. In electricity, high-voltage transmission often accounts for roughly 20 percent of the total costs of delivered power, although the amount depends on how far the power has to be transported and how regulators treat the long-lived investments in the transmission system.[11] In the U.S. natural gas industry, which has long been vertically separated, pipeline transmission accounts for roughly 25 percent of the delivered cost of natural gas both for customers of the local gas distribution companies and for large industrial and commercial customers that participate directly in the wholesale market.[12] Railroad industries that carry primarily passenger rather than freight traffic are probably similar to Britain's, in which Railtrack accounts for approximately 45 percent of the industry's costs. In railroad industries that carry freight only or predominantly, the proportion of infrastructure costs may be as low as 20 to 40 percent, again using U.S. freight railroads as a guide. Roughly 40 percent of telephone costs are in local hard-wire networks in the United States, although the proportion should be lower in other countries with greater wireless penetration.

Heterogeneous Products

In some industries the customers require distinct products, tailored to their needs. Often these distinct products place different demands on the infrastructure used to supply them. The greater the variety of product and infrastructure types, the more difficult the task of coordinating the different segments of the industry that provide them.

Of the five industries considered, electricity, gas, and water produce the most homogeneous or standardized products, particularly for retail customers. Customers care that power and water are available when and where needed and within acceptable standards for voltage and frequency, moisture and heating content, or purity. Beyond these constraints, however, one kilowatt-hour of electricity or one cubic meter of gas or water is pretty much interchangeable with another. When electricity is dispatched, for example, it is not addressed to a specific customer. A generator does not care which customer consumes its kilowatt and a customer does not care which plant generates the kilowatt it needs—any customer and any kilowatt will do. And because kilowatts and cubic meters are homogeneous, the designs of transmission lines can be highly standardized. Transmission lines vary in location and in the number of kilowatts or cubic meters they can safely carry, of course, but otherwise one transmission line is pretty much like any other.

There is a bit less standardization for wholesale than for retail customers, but seldom enough to create serious complications. Some wholesale water and gas consumers may be able to take advantage of less pure supplies, for example, and some wholesale electricity consumers may agree to power supplies that can be interrupted in the event of constraints in return for a lower price. Different standards of purity require protection against contamination, but this can generally be accommodated without building separate pipelines in the case of gas. And interruptible power may reduce the required capacity of the transmission lines but otherwise does not affect their design.

Railroad service is, by comparison, far more heterogeneous. Railroads often provide both freight and passenger service and may provide different qualities of each. The different types of service place different demands on the railroad's infrastructure. For high-speed passenger trains, for example, it is very important that the track is relatively straight and super-elevated on curves and that there are no or very few grade crossings. For slow-speed freight trains, however, straight tracks and no grade crossings are much less useful and super-elevation is likely to cause maintenance problems because of the weight the heavy freight axles place on the inside wheels and rails. Unlike electricity, gas, or water, moreover, destination and routing is critical to customer satisfaction. Railroad customers care not only that a rail car is available when and where they need it but that it is going to the intended destination. A train's routing is often as important as its origin and destination since trains often serve passengers or cargo bound for intermediate destinations as well.

In terms of product heterogeneity, telecommunications falls somewhere between the extremes of electricity and railroads. Telecommunications is similar to railroads in that it is important to users that their calls go through to specific destinations. But telecommunications is also similar to electricity in that, at least until recently, the design of a transmission line or microwave or satellite system is determined by the volume of calls expected but not tailored to different types of calls. This standardization of infrastructure design may be breaking down to some degree with the growth in importance of high-speed and high-volume data and video transmissions.

Product heterogeneity makes it more difficult to use either negotiated or preset access charges as tools for coordination within the industry. Heterogeneity makes negotiated agreements harder by expanding the range of the issues on which the different parties are likely to disagree. In the case of Argentina's electricity system, for example, the distribution and generation companies battled over whether a fourth line between Comahue and Buenos Aires was really necessary. If they could have agreed on how many kilowatts of additional transmission capacity were needed, however, the design of the new line would have been fairly straightforward and uncontroversial. In the case of Britain's railroads, by contrast, the various TOCs that used the West Coast Main Line had to agree not only on whether the line should be upgraded but on which types of services should be favored in the design. Operators of slower freight and regional passenger services needed different track, signal, and power distribution systems than the operators of the high-speed passenger services. The broad range of issues in dispute made it much harder to develop a consensus on the appropriate design and on how the costs of that design should be apportioned.

Heterogeneity also complicates the use of access charges as a coordinating tool, by making it much more difficult to accurately model infrastructure capacity and congestion costs. With heterogeneous products, infrastructure capacity and performance are harder to define because they have so many more dimensions. And predicting the effects of additional output on infrastructure performance becomes more difficult, because each type of service is likely to have a different effect.

It is telling, for example, that Britain's railroad managers and regulators had no analog to the electricity flow simulation models used by the operators of high-voltage transmission systems in Argentina and elsewhere. Electricity flows are complex, and it is critical that supply and demand be kept in balance instantaneously. But at least the properties of the flows are well understood and the rules that govern them can be described succinctly in mathematical equations. Moreover, there is a clear measure of transmission system performance—line losses—and every kilowatt moving on a line makes the same marginal contribution to line losses as every other.

In railroads, by contrast, the interaction between trains using a single line is usually too complex to be summarized in a few equations, because trains travel in different directions, at different speeds, and make different stops to pick up passengers and freight. Models must be carefully calibrated to local conditions, moreover, since the performance of a line can be strongly affected by details in its design, such as the spacing of passing tracks, stations, and switches. Finally, an appropriate congestion index is harder to develop, because different trains have different tolerances for schedule delays and the cost per minute may vary with the length of the delay.

The ability to model electric power flows and losses makes it possible to develop clear measures of congestion cost on the transmission network and to create nodal prices that reflect that congestion. Argentina's power pool operator made some unrealistic assumptions when calculating nodal prices, but these could have been easily corrected. There is no practical impediment to calculating prices that provide the proper signals to system operators about which plants to dispatch, to generators and consumers about where to locate their plants, and to all parties about the economic value of additional transmission capacity between two points. In theory, one could construct a schedule of congestion prices for a railroad that would provide a similar set of signals to train operators and infrastructure investors. The complexities of accurately modeling rail line performance make calculating the appropriate prices far more difficult, however, especially if the line is used by a variety of different types of trains.

When British Rail was being privatized and restructured, the difficulties of calculating congestion prices on railroads had encouraged some Treasury officials to propose auctioning track and station capacity as an alternative.[13] The idea has much in common with proposals for tradable transmission congestion contracts being proposed in the electricity industry. In this case, train operators would bid for the right to use a section of track or a station at a particular moment in time. The bids would ensure that the capacity was allocated to the train operator that valued it the most, and would reveal to potential investors the value of building additional capacity.

The idea of an auction was abandoned, however, because it proved too difficult to design a scheme that recognized the degree to which different services using a single line impinged on one another. As one British transport economist explained:

> For instance, a wish to run an additional peak hour service on a particular route would require adjustment to the timings of various other trains competing for platforms, slots at junctions as well as space on open track. In a workable system it would scarcely be feasible to auction all these rights separately, since the willingness to pay for each of them depends crucially on obtaining the package as a whole. Thus it would remain necessary to timetable services as a whole and then auction them.[14]

Timetabling, or scheduling, all the services in advance of the auction would not necessarily lead to the best use of the facilities, because the timetable would be constructed by the auction manager rather than by the operators, who presumably know more about their commercial opportunities and costs. The operators might be allowed to negotiate with one another over adjustments to the timetable, with opportunities for side payments and the like. But those negotiations are likely to be complex and time consuming if there are a reasonable number of operators, and might not lead to an efficient solution.

Network Interdependencies

The flows over an electricity transmission network are far more interrelated or interdependent than the comparable flows over railroad, natural gas, or even water and telecommunications networks. Flows on one electric power line often affect flows on other lines in the network, because electricity travels over the paths of least resistance. In railroads, natural gas, and water, by contrast, different rail lines or pipelines may cross or feed one another, but generally the routing options are more limited and the interactions across the network are fewer. Telecommunications may be similar to electricity in that there are more possibilities for rerouting when congestion develops. In telecommunications, however, rerouting usually requires operator intervention and probably does not occur to the degree it does in electricity.[15]

In electricity, the analytical complications created by network interdependence are offset in part by the fact that the product is relatively homogeneous. Network interdependence makes it misleading to analyze capacity and congestion on individual lines in isolation. Capacity problems can only be understood when the entire network is modeled as a whole. But the homogeneity of electricity makes modeling entire networks a fairly manageable proposition. Nodal prices are usually calculated with full network models, for example, and thus reflect the potentially complex interactions of the electric power lines. Network modeling may be reasonably practical in telecommunications as well, because although the products involved are somewhat more heterogeneous than electricity, the networks are also slightly less interdependent.

The most serious problem caused by network interdependence may be that it discourages the creation of markets for infrastructure capacity by making it harder for investors to be sure what they are buying. On an interdependent network, the practical capacity provided by a new line does not necessarily correspond to the rated capacity of the line itself. It also depends on the ratings of other lines and on the pattern of flows on the system. As a result, the effective capacity provided by a line may change over time as other lines are built or the pattern of flows changes. The advocates of tradable capacity or congestion rights for electricity transmission systems argue that the independent system operator can adjudicate changes in rights. The operator would use her simulation model to determine what additional rights a new line made possible, and an owner could petition the operator to see if the rights could be redefined as flow patterns changed. In theory this all seems feasible, but in practice it adds an additional source of risk and uncertainty to the investment.

Common Functions or Assets

Vertical unbundling may also be affected by a final factor, the extent to which different segments of the industry perform common functions or maintain similar assets whose costs might be reduced by consolidating them into a single firm. The most oft-cited example is customer billing and information services in telecommunications. In an unbundled telecommunications industry, long distance, local, and wireless telephone companies, cable TV companies, and Internet access providers all have to bill customers and deal with customer inquiries about services. In the United States, regulators usually require the local telephone company to provide a single consolidated bill for local and long-distance services, even if these services are provided by separate companies. But customers must still call the individual companies if they have questions about their local or long-distance charges, and cable and Internet services are billed separately (unless they are provided by the local telephone company). Some industry observers believe that customer billing and inquiry functions might be both less expensive for the firms and more convenient for customers if they were consolidated.[16]

Passenger railroads offer another example in the form of timetable information and reservations or ticketing for connecting services. Passengers may not know which train companies serve a particular route, so it is convenient if there are sources that maintain up-to-date timetables, accept reservations, and sell tickets for all railroads. In Britain, the rail regulator maintains the timetable and establishes standards and reimbursement systems so that railroads honor tickets issued by others. Nevertheless, the experience of the airline industry shows that competing private firms, left largely on their own, have incentives to develop and support common information and reservation services, so that the desire for such services may not be a significant bar to restructuring.

Conclusion

In sum, the potential for vertical unbundling seems much greater for large electricity, gas, and water customers and telecommunications users than it does for small electricity, gas, and water customers or the users of passenger or freight railroads. Electricity and gas appear very similar in that roughly half of industry costs are in potentially competitive activities, while only 10 to 30 percent of costs are in the long-distance transmission systems that are key to industry coordination. They are also similar in that the share of potentially competitive activity costs is much higher for customers that are large enough to connect directly to the long-distance lines and bypass the local distribution company. It is no surprise that the savings from unbundling have been much greater for large consumers than for small, or that programs to offer small consumers their choice of wholesale suppliers have discovered that most small consumers find the effort of shopping around not worth the small savings they might gain.

Water is similar to electricity and gas, in that large consumers stand to gain much more than small. The potential benefits from restructuring probably vary significantly by region, however, because bulk water costs are much higher in some places than in others. Moreover, environmental constraints may limit the possibility of introducing competition in places where bulk water is costly. These limitations may help explain why there has been much less experience with vertical unbundling in water than in electricity and gas, and why most of that experience has been with water for irrigation or large industrial uses.

Assessing the potential for unbundling in telecommunications is more difficult, because the technological and commercial possibilities are changing so rapidly. Nevertheless, the potential in telecommunications seems close to or greater than that in electricity or gas. The share of telecommunications activities that are potentially competitive is 60 percent and growing, and the potential for innovation seems greater than in electricity or gas. The costs of unbundling may be a little higher than in telecommunications, however, since the services provided are less homogeneous, which may make coordination through negotiation or pricing harder. Moreover, while technology is likely to expand the scope of potentially competitive activities in telecommunications, there will probably always be a need for some degree of coordination within the industry, so that calls can be completed between subscribers of different companies.

Unbundling is least attractive in railroads, particularly for passenger services. The infrastructure critical to coordination accounts for roughly 40 to 50 percent of costs on a rail passenger system, which makes the strategy of easing coordination by building excess infrastructure capacity prohibitively expensive. In addition, the services provided are much less homogeneous or standardized, which makes coordination through negotiations, congestion pricing, or auction regimes more difficult.

Rail freight would seem a more promising candidate for unbundling, since the percentage of potentially competitive activities is much higher. Indeed, in the United States most private freight railroads enjoy limited rights to operate over the tracks of other freight railroads, and these rights seem to increase competition without imposing enormous coordination costs. However, the U.S. system works well in part because the rights are not for access to the entire network, but for access to selected short segments of track over which antitrust authorities thought it important to maintain competition. Moreover, track rights are probably far less critical than competition from other modes and private long-term contracts in keeping the market power of U.S. freight railroads in check. In short, unbundling may be more attractive for freight than for passenger railroads, but it also may be unnecessary if small shippers rely primarily on trucks and large shippers are free to negotiate long-term contracts.

Our assessment of vertical unbundling is likely to change as we gain more experience with the problems and possibilities for maintaining coordination. It seems likely, for example, that tradable transmission capacity rights will be developed to the point where they can encourage appropriate congestion-relieving investments on high-voltage transmission systems. And with time we may learn how to implement a workable system of congestion prices for railroads similar to the nodal pricing scheme used in electricity. But on the whole, unbundling will probably remain more attractive for large customers of electricity, gas, and water and for telecommunications users than for others.

14

The Future of Regulation

The Challenges

Enthusiasm for private utilities waned in the first years of the twenty-first century. The pace of privatization slowed, particularly in the developing and transition economies but also in Europe and North America. It was not so much that the newly privatized utilities were being expropriated by governments, although that happened in a half-dozen highly publicized cases. But many governments faced growing popular resistance—occasionally in the form of violent demonstrations by consumers or workers—to proposals to privatize the utilities that still remained in public hands. And where governments were willing to sell or concession a utility, they sometimes had trouble finding investors.

Among the developing and transition countries, the reputation of private utilities was tarred, arguably unfairly, by the performance of the market-oriented reforms that many governments adopted in the 1980s and 1990s. The experience of Asia's "tigers"—Hong Kong, Korea, Taiwan, and Singapore—in the 1970s and 1980s convinced many development economists that exports and investment were key engines for growth. Meanwhile, the Latin American debt crisis of the early 1980s led many to conclude that fiscal discipline was critical as well. The World Bank, the International Finance Corporation, and many bilateral aid agencies began to press the developing and transition countries to adopt a standard prescription of balanced budgets, low trade barriers, and open capital markets. Privatization was included in the package as a means to reduce the public subsidies required by inefficient state-owned enterprises and to limit public debt by relying on the private sector to finance new infrastructure. When some of the patients taking this medicine faltered—Mexico in 1994, Southeast Asia in 1997, Russia in 1998, and Argentina in 2002—private utilities tended to share the blame, even though other elements of the package were more likely at fault.

But private utilities and their regulators were tarred by their own performance as well. Private management greatly improved the efficiency of many former state-owned utilities, while private concessionaires built many new highways, water treatment plants, and other badly needed infrastructure that the public sector could not finance. Usually consumers benefited from lower tariffs, better service, or both. But sometimes consumers did not, often because the government chose to keep tariffs high in order to increase its proceeds from the sale of the state-owned company or concession. And the fact that literally hundreds of concession contracts had to be renegotiated in the 1990s—usually only a few years after they were signed—undermined public faith in the integrity of the regulatory system.

In the short term, there is little chance that private provision of infrastructure will decline, much less disappear. The memory of the poor performance of the state-owned utilities is already fading in many countries after only a decade or so of private provision. But the same economic forces that encouraged privatization in the first place are still in play, particularly in the developing and transition economies. Government budgets are tight, and the public sector's capacity to issue debt is limited at best. In these circumstances, it would be difficult for government to resume total responsibility for utilities and infrastructure, particularly if some compensation to the private owners was required, if public operation was likely to result in deficits, or if new investments had to be financed. For the moment at least, most governments seem to believe that it is better to try to fix the problems that have arisen within the framework of private provision rather than to abandon that framework altogether.

The long-term prospects for private infrastructure are less clear, however. Continuing frustration over economic reforms associated with privatization, or continuing disputes among consumers, investors, and governments about the fairness of regulated prices, may eventually reduce popular support for private infrastructure to the breaking point. In the words of Raymond Vernon—an astute and longtime observer of the role of private enterprise—we may be currently in the "hurricane's eye," a deceptive and short-lived period of calm before the storm bears down on us again, but this time with winds from the opposite direction.[1]

The premise of this book is that the future of private infrastructure depends importantly on our ability to devise regulatory systems that treat both consumers and investors fairly. The perception of fairness is as important as the reality, moreover, so that regulation is as much a political as a technical act. But how should regulation adapt or evolve in this challenging environment? Part of the answer involves selecting a regulatory strategy to suit the circumstances, and part may involve improving and creating hybrids of the three principal strategies.

Choosing the Strategy for the Circumstances

The Basic Options

A central theme of this volume is that more market-oriented and contractual approaches to regulation are preferable, at least where they are practical. All else being equal, private long-term contracts are better than concession contracts and concession contracts are better than discretionary regulation. An explicit contract provides clearer protection against opportunism, as long as the contract is complete. And the more directly the consumers and investors are involved, the more chance they have to tailor the contract to their mutual advantage and the more likely they are to regard the results as fair.

All else is seldom equal, however, and certain circumstances favor one strategy over others. The contractual approaches work best when the prospects for writing a complete, or relatively complete, contract are strong, and completeness depends, in turn, on our ability to predict or anticipate the needs of consumers and investors relatively accurately. The more stable the economic and technological environment, the more homogeneous the customers, and the shorter the contract, for example, the more likely a complete contract. The contractual approaches also rely on the integrity of the legal system used to enforce commercial contracts. The legal system usually means the courts in the country where the infrastructure is located, although foreign investors often try to shift jurisdiction to foreign courts or arbitration panels. Finally, the private contractual approach is practical only when the transaction costs of negotiating and enforcing contracts with individual customers are reasonable. Transaction costs are typically manageable when there are only a few large consumers, although strategies to contract with large numbers of small consumers have been developed in some circumstances.

The experience of developing countries in the last two decades illustrates both the importance and the difficulty of selecting the appropriate regulatory strategy. The fact that so many concession contracts had to be renegotiated so quickly suggests that the concession approach was overused. In many cases the contracts were signed while the government was implementing other major economic reforms, which added greatly to the uncertainties. And many of the contracts were for twenty or thirty years, which is a long time to predict in any context, let alone in the dynamic world of a developing country. In retrospect, that so many contracts failed is not surprising.

In some cases, some form of discretionary regulation might have performed better. Concession contracts were often used out of concern that many of these countries did not have a tradition of independent regulatory institutions, so that a discretionary regulator was likely to be captured or otherwise abuse its powers. But contract renegotiations are riskier than discretionary regulation in that they involve the exercise of discretion but without many of the procedural and other safeguards that are usually built into a discretionary scheme. If the exercise of discretion is inevitable—because no contract is likely to be complete—then it might be wiser to devise a discretionary approach from the outset.

Discretionary regulation has its shortcomings too, notably the risk of capture and misuse of regulatory powers. While the percentage of concession contracts in developing countries that have been renegotiated is alarming, it is not clear that we have done much better with discretionary regulation. Discretionary regulation regimes tend to deteriorate slowly, rather than in a clear contractual break. It may be years before we know whether the discretionary systems established in the 1980s and 1990s are stable and successful.

Still another possibility in many cases is that the contractual approach was appropriate but the type of contract was not. For example, shorter concessions of ten years or less would have reduced the chance of contractual incompleteness. And shorter contracts would have made it easier to live with an incomplete contract until it expired instead of embarking on the politically perilous task of renegotiation. Private long-term contracts might have substituted for concession contracts in a number of cases, the most obvious being the newly privatized freight railroads in Latin America and Africa. Such contracts not only are more likely to be complete and easier to renegotiate, but usually provide greater opportunities for shared efficiency gains as well.

Weak Institutions and Legitimacy

As important as it is to pick a strategy suitable to the circumstances, there are some circumstances where no strategy is likely to work well. One such case is countries whose economic, legal, and political institutions are weak. In the past two decades a growing body of research has focused on the institutional characteristics that encourage economic growth. The results are still somewhat tentative, but legal systems that protect private property and individuals seem important, as do political systems with checks and balances, such as the separation of executive, legislative, and judicial powers; or a bicameral legislature.[2] The essential idea is that legal constraints and checks and balances limit government opportunism and provide a more stable environment in which economies can grow. It seems logical that many of the factors thought important for economic growth and stability will also prove important to fair and consistent regulation.

Implicit in the institutional research is the idea that the basic political legitimacy of the government matters as well. Checks and balances are important for stability, because they make it more difficult for any one set of interests to gain control of government and change policy. But if it is hard for any one set of interests to gain control that means power is shared, which presumably broadens the base of support for government. A government in which power is too widely dispersed may frustrate efforts to develop policies to solve important problems, and power sharing may not be the only route to legitimacy in some cultures. Nevertheless, legitimacy is fundamental to regulation, no matter how that legitimacy is achieved. Regulation requires some form of commitment by government, whether to an explicit contract or to the fair exercise of discretion. But if the people regard the government as illegitimate or corrupt, it is dangerous to rely on government commitments for long.

We can design regulatory strategies to compensate for weak institutions and political legitimacy, but our ability to do so is probably limited. Concession contracts are popular in many developing countries, for example, largely because they are thought to be less vulnerable to weak institutions than discretionary regulation, although how much this is true is the subject of debate. And to the extent that we cannot compensate fully, then the political and financial risks are likely to reinforce each other in destructive ways. Political risks encourage investors to demand higher returns and to try to get their earnings out quickly, which in turn adds to the chances of political controversy and risk.

There are some countries where institutions and political legitimacy are so weak that regulation will be extremely difficult, if not impossible. Private utilities are being discussed or attempted in many of these countries, and private provision may be preferable to public provision in some cases. If so, it will be only because weak institutions and corruption harm public provision too, and despite the fact that no private arrangement is likely to last long. In such circumstances it would be wise to limit private involvement in infrastructure to conventional construction contracts for new facilities and to relatively short-term management contracts for existing facilities. Any longer-term or more complex involvement is likely to fail, and discredit private utilities for many years in the process.

The Inevitable Economic Crises

A second circumstance that threatens any form of regulation is serious economic crises, such as a severe depression, inflation, or decline in foreign exchange rates. Countries with strong institutions and high levels of political legitimacy presumably tend to avoid crises because their economies are better managed. But our understanding of economics and politics is not sophisticated enough to provide foolproof protection. The crises tend to be much more severe in the developing countries, but even the developed countries suffer periodic recessions. Moreover, some of the developing countries where crises originated in the last decade—such as Mexico, Thailand, or Argentina—had had reputations for reasonably good economic management in the years before. And the crises soon reverberate beyond the countries where they started. The rapid drop in the Thai exchange rate in 1997 caused investors to lose confidence in many of the economies of East Asia, for example, while Argentina's default and devaluation in 2002 undermined confidence in its neighbors as well.

Private infrastructure is seldom the cause of these crises, but it almost always becomes a controversial issue. One might argue that private infrastructure helps avoid inflation and exchange rate crises by improving the efficiency of infrastructure providers, thereby reducing the pressures for government subsidies and unbalanced budgets. But once an inflation or exchange rate crisis starts, it creates pressures for utility regulators to increase tariffs at a time when the public is suffering. And depressions can be difficult too if the public begins to ask why utility prices remain high when household incomes are falling. The Great Depression of the 1930s heightened the controversy about private utilities in many countries, for example, and seemed to lay the groundwork for later public takeovers. The takeovers occurred in the three decades that followed, usually after bouts of wartime and postwar inflation had further weakened the private companies.

It is hard to devise a regulatory strategy—contractual or discretionary—that can fully insulate private infrastructure from economic crises of these magnitudes. Many concession contracts explicitly index tariffs to inflation and exchange rates, for example, and in most discretionary schemes indexation is implicit in the requirement that investors be allowed the opportunity to earn a reasonable rate of return. But explicit or implicit indexation is of little use if many customers are now so poor that they cannot afford to pay the higher rates. An alternative possibility is to restrict the levels of utility investments to those that customers could support even during a severe economic crisis. But that would mean that utility services would be very inadequate in normal years. The essential problem is that providing realistic contingencies against a severe crises is almost always extremely costly. Consumers and investors prefer, perhaps sensibly, to plan for a happier world, hoping that such crises will be relatively rare and brief. The implicit strategy for a crisis is to suspend the regulatory rules and try to survive until the situation is normal enough that the rules can apply again. Specifying how the pain of the crisis should be shared is too difficult to do in advance.

Some of the crises since the latest round of privatization struck countries that still had not privatized many utilities, which made the disputes more limited and easier to manage. In Mexico, for example, the main form of private infrastructure at the time of the 1994 exchange rate crisis was a 5,000-kilometer network of private toll road concessions. The network had been built rapidly and was overextended, and most of the toll road companies were threatened with bankruptcy when the collapse of the economy caused a sharp drop in traffic. Fortunately, the toll road concession contracts did not index tariffs to foreign currencies, because the concessions were largely domestically owned and financed. The government allowed modest toll increases that were enough to save about half of the roads. The others went bankrupt, but the government bailed out the banks that held much of the toll road debt to prevent the collapse of the banking system. The bank bailout was highly controversial, but even most critics acknowledged that bank failures would have harmed Mexico more.[3]

Similarly, the principal form of private infrastructure in the countries affected by the 1997 Asian crisis was independent power plants. Most plants had take-or-pay contracts with state-owned electricity distribution companies that required the companies to pay for a fixed amount of power, whether they took it or not. Many of these plants were also foreign owned and financed, and the contracts indexed prices to foreign currencies. The crises threatened to bankrupt the state-owned electricity companies since they could no longer afford, and no longer needed, the power they had contracted for. Most of the disputes were resolved within five years. The solutions varied from country to country and from plant to plant, and the details of the final settlements were not always public. In some cases the host governments essentially agreed to honor their contractual commitments, and in others a compromise was reached where the private power company did not get all that it was due.

But future crises are likely to be more difficult to resolve, because the private sector is now often involved in a wider variety of sectors. Indeed, the Argentine crisis of 2002 may be more typical of what is to come, since Argentina relies on private providers for a wide range of infrastructure services, including telephones, electricity, water, railways, toll roads, and ports. All of the private infrastructure companies are affected by the onset of high domestic inflation and the collapse of demand, and many are foreign financed and suffering from the devaluation of the peso as well. The government froze tariffs in pesos in January 2002, in violation of all the regulatory contracts, and a year later it was still temporizing, waiting until the economic and political situation stabilized enough to permit renegotiations.

Surviving crises such as these requires extraordinary forbearance on the part of both the governments and the investors. Governments usually don't want to provoke or escalate a conflict with private utilities. Their reputation for managing the economy has already been blackened by the deterioration in foreign exchange rates or the reappearance of hyperinflation. Attacking the companies offers at most a short-term diversion, since utility privatization is rarely the cause of the crisis. And the long-term cost may be high, since most governments understand that they have a long-term interest in maintaining the reputation of their country as a reasonable place to invest.

For their part, investors must appreciate the position of the government and its citizens. Crises such as these impose widespread suffering; often many people lose their jobs, their savings, or both. To assume that utility investors should be treated specially and made whole when everyone else is suffering is unrealistic, and the company that takes that position aggressively is likely to become a target of enormous popular resentment. A more reasonable position might be that utility investors should not be discriminated against, and suffer only as much or as little as other investors in the economy. Even so, determining what constitutes comparable suffering will be difficult, because of the utilities' special characteristics. And some investors are likely to be so short-sighted that they insist on protection, and provoke the opposite reaction instead.

But surviving these crises is important. Most countries turned to private provision because of the poor performance of government-owned utilities. While there have been some notable failures, private provision has generally improved services for consumers and reduced the burden on taxpayers. Making this system work fairly for all parties, even through the inevitable economic crises, is a skill that one hopes will improve with experience.

Refining the Strategies

Private Contracts

Although picking the appropriate strategy for the circumstances is important, opportunities also arise to refine the basic strategies. These opportunities may be greatest with private long-term contracts, because we have only recently come to appreciate that they might substitute for government regulation of monopoly. Contracts are used widely by private companies to protect against opportunism in procurement, and thus have been studied intensively by lawyers and economists. The literature on contracting offers many potential lessons for the use of private contracts in monopolies, particularly with respect to coping with the threat of contractual incompleteness. But there are some special problems with using contracts as a remedy for monopoly.

The most obvious of these special problems is how to reduce the transaction costs of negotiating with large numbers of small customers. The main examples of the successful use of private long-term contracts as a substitute for regulation involve industries dominated by large customers. The success of America's freight railroads in replacing government regulation with private contracts was helped enormously by the fact that most small shippers had switched to trucks long ago. The other recent and oft-cited example is private contracts between wholesale buyers and sellers in unbundled electricity industries. These electricity contracts were not essential for the deregulation of the wholesale market, but they helped by allaying fears about price volatility in the spot market. In electricity too, contracting was made easier by the fact that the parties are large, so that the time and cost of negotiating a contract is small relative to its value.

The small-customer problem may prove tractable in many situations, however. In some cases brokers or other intermediaries might aggregate small accounts and negotiate on their behalf. In other cases, it may be worthwhile for companies to offer a menu of standardized contracts for small customers to choose from. An example might be long-term contracts for lower electricity or gas prices available to homeowners or small businesses considering switching the fuel they use for heating or air conditioning. Standardized contracts may also appear in novel forms, such as the advantages offered to frequent flyers who make an implicit commitment to fly 25,000 or 50,000 miles per year. The possibilities for developing workable contracts for small utility customers seem promising, given that we have only begun to devote effort to the problem.

Concession Contracts

By far the most important drawback of the concession approach is the risk of an incomplete contract. The problem of incompleteness is made worse because consumers are represented by the government instead of directly. The government's involvement solves the problem of negotiating with many small consumers, but raises concerns about whether the government will represent their interests well. These consumer concerns can be reduced by awarding the concession contract competitively, but not if the contract subsequently proves to be incomplete and has to be renegotiated. Indeed, renegotiations are far more difficult for a concession contract than for a private contract, and reducing the risk of incompleteness and renegotiation is the key challenge in concession design.

One promising approach is to design relatively short and simple contracts. Shorter and simpler contracts appear to be a factor behind the successful revival of municipal concessions in North America at the end of the twentieth century, as described in Chapter 7. Sometimes contracts can be simplified by using different contracts for different activities, such as maintenance and investment. Argentina did this with its electricity transmission system, for example, by awarding one concession for the maintenance of its existing high-voltage network and separate concessions, as needed, for the construction of later lines.[4] The Chilean government is contemplating a slightly more complex version for its intercity expressway concessions. The government is often uncertain when traffic volumes will be heavy enough to justify adding lanes to an intercity expressway, and it has been considering offering maintenance concessions for ten or twenty years but asking bidders to supply two sets of prices for each year: one with the existing number of lanes and one with added lanes. The government can then expand when it wants by awarding a separate contract to build the extra lanes and paying the maintenance concessionaire at its higher price. The main limitations of split contracts are that the investments must be in large and discrete increments. In addition, the government must monitor construction quality more carefully, since the firm building the facility may not be the one that maintains it.

Another possibility is to award a single, relatively short contract for both maintenance and investment but use rules for rebidding the contract that maintain the concessionaire's incentives to invest. One of the most interesting examples is the Argentine concessions for the two electricity distribution companies serving Buenos Aires.[5] These concessions are for ninety-five years but are broken into nine "management periods," the first for fifteen years and the remaining eight for ten years each. The concession is put out to bid at the end of each management period, and the incumbent participates in the competition. If the incumbent is not the highest bidder, it loses the concession but receives the amount it bid as compensation.

Because the Argentine concession is rebid every ten or fifteen years, the government never has to wait too long for an opportunity to correct problems in the contract's terms or to get a market test of the concession's profitability. The incumbent has an incentive to bid the true value he places on the concession, since otherwise he may lose the concession and receive less as compensation. The incumbent also has an incentive to continue to invest even as the end of the management period draws near, because he will either keep the concession or receive the value he places on it, including the value of recent investments. This scheme depends in part on the concessionaire's trusting the government not to revise the concession terms too radically at the end of each management period. Unfortunately, Argentina's economic crisis of 2002, which forced the government to break all utility concession contracts before they expired, prevented a practical test of how rebidding might work.

Another promising approach is to develop clauses in the contract that make renegotiation easier and less controversial. These clauses serve like circuit breakers in a fuse box, in that they can be tripped before the relations between the government and the concessionaire overheat. Circuit breaker clauses are essential in long and complex contracts, but are useful in short and simple ones too.

One form of circuit breaker is a clause that provides specific and fair terms for the concessionaire or the government to buy its way out of its responsibilities before the contract ends. One of the most intriguing examples is the "least present value" scheme developed for toll highway concessions in Chile.[6] Under this approach, a concession to improve and maintain a highway is offered to the bidder who requires the lowest present value of toll revenues over the life of the concession. The government specifies the discount rate used to calculate the present value in the bidding documents, and that discount rate is the government's estimate of the long-term weighted average cost of capital for a typical concessionaire. The concession reverts to the government when the concessionaire has received the present value in toll revenues that it bid.

The least present value approach was originally developed as a means of coping with uncertainty about future traffic levels. No matter how slowly or rapidly traffic develops, the concessionaire is guaranteed to receive the present value of its bid (and no more). But a more important advantage of this approach is that it provides a fair price for the government to buy the concessionaire out if the government decides that the concession contract should be revised and rebid. The concessionaire would be due the difference between the present value of the tolls he had already collected and the present value of his original bid. The least present value approach has not been very popular with Chilean concessionaires, in part because it provides the government, but not the concessionaire, with a clear price to buy out its obligations. If the scheme could be redesigned to provide both parties with a way out, then it might be more attractive.[7]

A second classic type of circuit breaker is a clause that provides for the use of arbitration, conciliation, or mediation of disputes between the concessionaire and the government. Almost every concession contract has some form of arbitration clause, but the clauses in some of the early contracts of the 1980s and 1990s were so simplistic and poorly thought out that they were of little practical use. Many contracts called for arbitration panels of three members, for example, with one chosen by each party and the third chosen by the other two. This procedure often seems too risky for high-stakes disputes, however, since so much rides on the choice of the third member. In one early and well-publicized case, a Japanese company with the concession to build and operate an expressway in Bangkok refused to take advantage of three-person arbitration even as its dispute with the Thai government escalated to the point where the Thai government seized the expressway.[8] The Japanese company was eventually compensated, but only after delays and for much less than it thought due. The company presumably believed arbitration would have been even more risky and unsatisfactory than the course it took.

More attention has been devoted to arbitration since, but most of the efforts have been designed to comfort investors more than consumers. Many involve provisions to direct disputes to international arbitration institutions such as the International Chamber of Commerce or the International Center for the Settlement of Investment Disputes. Officials from developing countries traditionally have been skeptical of these institutions, often regarding them as another form of "robbery" imposed on the developing world by the West.[9] Often the arbitrators are restricted to resolving differences in interpretation, which is of little use if the problem is that one of the parties simply cannot comply. Most of the Asian power plant contracts that had to be renegotiated after 1997 had provisions for international arbitration, but these were rarely invoked because the public power companies had no funds to pay judgments entered against them. Supporters of international arbitration argue that attitudes are changing, and that some governments may welcome international intervention to provide the political cover they need to take unpopular actions. Experience with international arbitration of infrastructure disputes is still very limited, however, and it is too early to tell whether it will be accepted in serious disputes.

What may be needed instead are arbitration schemes that seem so obviously fair that they enjoy widespread political legitimacy. Selecting distinguished and independent arbitrators from the host country and in advance of disputes, for example, probably would help reduce fears about various kinds of bias. Another possibility is to restrict the arbitrators to choosing between the parties' "best and final" offers. Professional arbitrators dislike final-offer arbitration, because it prevents them from discovering opportunities for mutual gain and because they fear that it puts the more risk-averse party at a disadvantage.[10] Final-offer arbitration is also harder to apply if more than two parties are involved, a common situation in infrastructure disputes. Nevertheless, the scheme creates obvious incentives for both parties to make reasonable final offers. And the incentives to be reasonable and the chance that the resulting offers will be close may enhance the legitimacy of the effort.

Finally, if renegotiation proves unavoidable, the parties need to learn how to renegotiate in a manner that both the public and the investors will accept. This requires a process that helps consumers and investors to understand the other party's position, so that they can accept the difficult compromises they may have to make. The process is likely to be organized or convened by government or regulatory officials, but it must be done in such a way that consumers and investors do not avoid facing hard choices by making the officials the scapegoats for their frustrations.[11]

Discretionary Regulation

Discretionary regulation avoids the problem of writing a complete contract, but at the price of added technical and political challenges. Most modern discretionary schemes involve some form of price-cap regulation, and one interesting line of research involves the various tradeoffs and options in price cap's design. Jean-Jacques Laffont and Jean Tirole have pointed out that it is possible to vary the strength of the efficiency incentives that price cap provides not just by varying the length of time between price reviews but also by varying the percentage of the firm's costs that are covered by the price cap. Moreover, they argue that the regulator can force firms to reveal information about their costs by offering them a menu of regulatory regimes with incentives of different strength. A firm with very low costs may choose a scheme with strong incentives even if it has a low price cap, for example, while a less efficient firm generally prefers schemes with weaker incentives. In theory, the menu can be designed in such a way that the resulting prices for consumers are lower than they would be if the regulator had to select a single price-cap regime on his own.[12]

In practice, relatively little thought seems to have gone into tailoring the strength of price-cap incentives to different situations and even less to the possibility of offering menus. Most applications of price cap use the original British scheme, with a five-year interval between reviews and almost all costs covered by the cap.[13] A longer interval would motivate improvements with longer payback periods, for example, but at the political and economic cost of tolerating prices that prove to be too high or too low for a longer time. There is no reason to believe that a five-year interval is optimal for every industry or country. A shorter interval might be better, for example, in an industry where improvements have short payback periods or in a country with a more sensitive or volatile political environment. Offering a menu of incentive programs may be advantageous in some circumstances too, although the public may feel uncomfortable with giving the regulated firms a choice.

A more pressing and difficult set of questions involves whether or how discretionary regulation can be applied in governments with limited resources and no tradition of relatively autonomous or technically sophisticated regulatory agencies. Discretionary regulation seems particularly problematic in small developing countries or at the municipal, provincial, or other subnational levels of government. Discretionary regulation may impose disproportionate costs on small countries and subnational governments simply because the complexity of regulatory problems does not decrease proportionately with the size of the industry being regulated. Subnational governments also have more responsibilities than national governments, and are generally less concerned about the effects their regulatory decisions might have on other investments. Municipal and provincial governments were leaders in regulatory disputes in the last era of private infrastructure, from the mid-nineteenth to the mid-twentieth century, and they have been involved in many of the most serious disagreements since the return of private infrastructure at the end of the twentieth century.[14]

One issue being debated is whether, for governments with limited regulatory traditions and resources, price cap is superior to cost-of-service regulation. Proponents of price cap argue that it is more suitable in such environments, because it requires less technical expertise.[15] There is also less opportunity and temptation for political intervention since price reviews can occur only at preset intervals. Proponents of cost-of-service regulation respond that price cap requires as much expertise as cost of service, because the political and economic cost of predicting the firm's costs inaccurately can be very high if one has to wait years for a review. Cost-of-service proponents also argue that the top priority of many of these countries is to increase infrastructure investment rather than to improve efficiency, so that the security that cost-of-service regulation gives investors by providing for tariff reviews when needed is more important than the efficiency incentives that price-cap establishes by limiting tariff reviews to regular intervals. The fact that both sides offer plausible arguments suggests that there is no obvious right choice between the price-cap and cost-of-service approaches for governments with limited resources.

A more promising, but risky, solution is to limit the discretion of the regulator by making the authorizing legislation more specific and prescriptive. This strategy—essentially a hybrid of the discretionary and contractual approaches—was employed in Latin America from the 1930s through the 1960s and revived in the region during the 1980s and 1990s. One of the modern examples is the scheme Chile uses to regulate its private electricity and telephone companies.[16] Chile uses price caps with reviews every four years for electricity and every five for telephones, and the procedures that the regulators employ to calculate the tariffs are set out in detail in the law. The law sets out the usual goal that tariffs should allow an efficient firm to earn a reasonable return on assets. But it goes on to specify how to estimate the operating costs of an efficient firm, the procedure to value assets, and the method of calculating a reasonable rate of return. In the case of electricity, for example, the statute specifies that the tariff should allow an efficient firm to earn a real return of 10 percent and that actual returns should not fall below

6 percent or rise above 14 percent. Amending these statutes is not easy, since Chile has a bicameral legislature and one party seldom has a majority in both chambers.

The detailed statutes have allowed Chile to dispense with most of the trappings of independence usually associated with discretionary regulation. Chile's electricity and telephone regulatory agencies are headed by political appointees, staffed by regular civil servants, and located inside the Ministry of Energy and the Ministry of Transport and Telecommunications, respectively. Moreover, the agencies are only empowered to make public recommendations to the minister of the economy, who has the final say over tariffs and other matters.[17]

Most observers believe that this system has worked reasonably well so far. The minister of the economy is reluctant to overrule the public recommendations of the regulators without good reason. Moreover, the regulators are thought to have used the specifics of the statutes as excuses to resist private ministerial pressures. The statute also seems to be an important source of reassurance for investors. The telephone industry was privatized in 1982, for example, but private investment began in earnest only after 1987, when the regulatory statute was amended to specify the procedure for calculating tariffs in detail.[18]

The drawback of this approach is that the statute must be drafted with just enough detail to protect against incompetence or capture, but not so much that the specifics could prove badly wrong. Chile's statute seems to err on the side of being too generous to investors, which is not surprising given that its drafters wanted to modernize the country's electricity and telephone systems. In 1995, for example, the returns on equity were twice as high in the regulated than in the unregulated sectors of Chile's electricity and telephone industries.[19] These kinds of returns may erode the support for private utilities and encourage tougher amendments in the future.

Moreover, it is important to remember that this strategy of relatively specific statutes was deployed in Latin America and elsewhere in the 1930s and 1940s, but proved insufficient to prevent the gradual erosion of utility profits and the eventual demise of the private companies. It is too risky to write a statute that is so detailed that it attempts to play the role of a complete contract, so that some discretion always remains to be captured by determined political interests. It may be that the relatively specific statute is a useful compromise while a country is establishing a regulatory tradition and resources. It is likely to be relaxed or revised eventually, in the face of unforeseen circumstances and complications. But by then the regulatory tradition may have much stronger roots.

A final set of options worthy of more consideration involves incentives that are extracontractual, in that they lie outside the formal regulatory scheme. The basic idea is to establish or maintain a broader social interest in the private provision of infrastructure that will encourage regulators to behave reasonably toward both consumers and investors. These extracontractual incentives would be helpful for concession as well as discretionary regulation, although they seem more needed with the latter approach.

One tempting but dangerous way to change the political calculus is to expand the availability of political risk insurance for investors. These policies are offered by the governments of the investors' home countries or by international financial institutions (private insurers will write political risk policies for infrastructure investments too, but only if a government or multilateral institution is already insuring part of the risk). The U.S. government will sell U.S. companies investing abroad political risk insurance, for example, and the World Bank has developed a similar product for private investors.[20] Such insurance policies protect primarily against clear breaches of contract or outright expropriation, and are harder to apply to the creeping expropriation that can occur with discretionary regulation.

The concern is that political risk insurance may increase the number and severity of disputes rather than reduce them. Insurance is likely to discourage host countries from taking any action that might provoke a claim, since they know they will earn the enmity not just of the investors but of the U.S. government or the World Bank as well. But insurance will also discourage investors from considering whether a proposed project is an attractive and sustainable deal for the host country as well as for themselves, since they will get some or all of their money back in any event. The U.S. government and the World Bank are unlikely to do a good job of assessing the sustainability of the deal for the host country either, both because they are less expert about the industry than the investors and because they know the country will think twice before provoking a claim. These perverse incentives can be reduced by insuring only a portion of the investment, but they can't be eliminated entirely. The end result is still likely to be more bad contracts rather than fewer, and more aggressive behavior by investors during crises.

A more promising way to change the political calculus is to try to ensure that the stock in private infrastructure companies is held at least in part by many small domestic investors. The history of electric utilities in the Americas described in Chapter 6 suggests that simply replacing foreign investors with domestic is not enough to prevent nationalization, and that spreading the ownership interests widely among the public is helpful but not a panacea. Developing domestic capital markets is also not easy, of course, and widespread stock ownership can be problematic unless the legal system protects the interests of minority shareholders. Nevertheless, efforts to deepen and broaden local capital markets by developing pension funds and other schemes may be extremely important in broadening support for private infrastructure.

The best long-term insurance for a private utility is, of course, that both consumers and investors believe that its service is excellent and its tariffs are fair. Many factors can influence these perceptions, such as the integrity of the process of privatization or the degree to which ordinary people have a stake in the ownership of the companies. But the system of regulation is critical, especially in the long run. We have learned a lot about regulation in the last 150 years, which should make us better at the task. One of the most fundamental lessons is that it is hard to regulate well, so that one should only regulate when it is essential and with the simplest and least intrusive scheme possible. It is this lesson that lies behind this book's basic preference for private contracts over concession contracts and concessions over discretionary regulation. But we still have much to learn about where these different schemes can be applied and how they might be improved.

Notes

Index

Notes

1. Monopoly as a Contracting Problem

1. The view that access to infrastructure is essential to equity is not always accepted, particularly for telecommunications. See Robert W. Crandall and Leonard Waverman, *Who Pays for Universal Service? When Telephone Subsidies Become Transparent* (Washington, D.C.: Brookings Institution, 2000).

2. Alfred E. Kahn, one of the most distinguished scholars of regulation, made this point over thirty years ago in *The Economics of Regulation: Principles and Institutions* (New York: John Wiley & Sons, 1971), p. 123. Kahn's contribution was noted by Milton L. Mueller, Jr., in *Universal Service: Competition, Interconnection, and Monopoly in the Making of the American Telephone System* (Cambridge: MIT Press, 1997), p. 18.

3. Durable and immobile investments reduce the threat of entry by raising the stakes of a battle for market share or control. They increase both the gains from winning (since the victor gets a monopoly) and the costs of losing (since the loser forfeits his investment). The net effect is likely to discourage entry if the challengers are risk averse or if the potential gains from monopoly are small relative to the investment that must be put at risk.

4. Victor P. Goldberg, "Regulation and Administered Contracts," *Bell Journal of Economics* 7, no. 2 (Autumn 1976): 431.

5. The parallels between procurement and the regulation of monopoly have been noted by others, including Jean-Jacques Laffont and Jean Tirole in their classic text *A Theory of Incentives in Procurement and Regulation* (Cambridge: MIT Press, 1993). Laffont and Tirole were more concerned with procurement by government, however, while we are concerned with procurement by private suppliers. For early discussions of the parallels between private contracting and regulation, see Paul L. Joskow, "The Role of Transaction Cost Economics in Antitrust and Public Utility Regulatory Policies," *Journal of Law, Economics and Organization* 7 (special issue, 1991): 51–83; and Keith J. Crocker and Scott E. Master, "Regulation and Administered Contracts Revisited: Lessons from Transaction-Cost Economics for Public Utility Regulation," *Journal of Regulatory Economics* 9 (1996): 24–28.

6. William L. Meggison and Jeffrey M. Netter, "From State to Market: A Survey of

Empirical Studies on Privatization," *Journal of Economic Literature* 39, no. 2 (June 2001): 321–389.

2. The Choice of Regulatory Strategy

1. Mark H. Moore, *Creating Public Value: Strategic Management in Government* (Cambridge: Harvard University Press, 1995).

2. Many scholars credit Ronald H. Coase with originating research into transaction costs in a 1937 article in which he sought to explain the need for firms. For the original article see Ronald H. Coase, "The Nature of the Firm," *Economica*, n.s., 4, no. 16 (November 1937): 386–405. For a review of how Coase's insight was extended by others, see Oliver E. Williamson, "The New Institutional Economics: Taking Stock, Looking Ahead," *Journal of Economic Literature* 38, no. 3 (September 2000): 595–613.

3. Douglass C. North and Robert P. Thomas, *The Rise of the Western World: A New Economic History* (Cambridge: Cambridge University Press, 1973). For further development of these themes, see Douglass C. North, *Institutions, Institutional Change and Economic Performance* (Cambridge: Cambridge University Press, 1990).

4. For a clearly written and stimulating statement of this position, see Richard O. Zerbe, Jr., and Howard E. McCurdy, "The End of Market Failure," *Regulation* 23, no. 2 (2001): 10–14; or Richard O. Zerbe, Jr., and Howard E. McCurdy, "The Failure of Market Failure," *Journal of Policy Analysis and Management* 18, no. 4 (1999): 558–578.

5. Ronald H. Coase, "The Problem of Social Cost," *Journal of Law and Economics* 3 (October 1960): 1–44.

6. Stephen Littlechild applied this phrase to regulation in his influential 1983 report on the options for regulating Britain's telecommunications industry. See Chapter 9 and Stephen C. Littlechild, *Regulation of British Telecommunication's Profitability* (London: Department of Industry, 1983), para. 1.11.

7. Oliver E. Williamson, "The Vertical Integration of Production: Market Failure Considerations," *American Economic Review* 61 (May 1971): 112–123; Oliver E. Williamson, *Markets and Hierarchies: Analysis and Antitrust Implications—A Study in the Economics of Internal Organization* (New York: Free Press, 1975).

8. Oliver E. Williamson, "Transaction Cost Economics: The Governance of Contractual Relations," *Journal of Law and Economics* 22, no. 2 (1979): 233–261.

9. For a review of the empirical literature on the circumstance under which different kinds of contracts are commonly employed, see Keith J. Crocker and Scott E. Master, "Regulation and Administered Contracts Revisited: Lessons from Transaction-Cost Economics for Public Utility Regulation," *Journal of Regulatory Economics* 9 (1996): 24–28.

10. For insightful and extended reviews of the relationship between the transaction cost and regulation literatures see Crocker and Master, "Regulation and Administered Contracts Revisited," pp. 5–39; and Paul L. Joskow, "The Role of Transaction Cost Economics in Antitrust and Public Utility Regulatory Policies," *Journal of Law, Economics and Organization* 7 (special issue, 1991): 51–83. For

a more mathematical treatment of some of these same issues, see Jean-Jacques Laffont and Jean Tirole, *A Theory of Incentives in Procurement and Regulation* (Cambridge: MIT Press, 1993).

11. The differences between these approaches are described in more detail in Chapter 9.

12. The French contracts are called concessions when the private company is expected to build new or improve existing facilities and *affermage* when the private company is to manage an existing facility but not make substantial investments to it. For an excellent description of the French system, see Christopher T. Shugart, "Regulation-by-Contract and Municipal Services: The Problem of Contractual Incompleteness," Ph.D. dissertation, Harvard University, Cambridge, Mass., 1998.

13. For a description of these Latin American systems, see Chapter 14 and David F. Cavers and James R. Nelson, *Electric Power Regulation in Latin America* (Baltimore: Johns Hopkins University Press, 1959), pp. 33–36, 114–116, 118–119.

3. The Behavior of Regulatory Agencies

1. James Landis, one of the most famous architects and defenders of the federal regulatory agencies in the 1930s and 1940s, believed strongly in this public interest perspective. See his biography in Thomas K. McCraw, *Prophets of Regulation: Charles Francis Adams, Louis D. Brandeis, James M. Landis, and Alfred E. Kahn* (Cambridge: Harvard University Press, 1984), pp. 153–209.

2. For reviews of the early and seminal literature on regulatory capture, see Thomas K. McCraw, "Regulation in America: A Review Essay," *Business History Review* 49, no. 2 (Summer 1975); as reprinted in *Managing Big Business: Essays from the Business History Review*, ed. Richard S. Tedlow and Richard R. John, Jr. (Boston: Harvard Business School Press, 1986), pp. 250–274, esp. 253–257; and James Q. Wilson, "The Politics of Regulation," in *The Politics of Regulation*, ed. James Q. Wilson (New York: Basic Books, 1980), pp. 357–447.

3. Richard L. McCormick, "The Discovery That Business Corrupts Politics: A Reappraisal of the Origins of Progressivism," *American Historical Review* 86 (1981): 247–274.

4. Criticism of the public utility commissions began in the 1920s but was fairly limited; see McCraw, "Regulation in America," pp. 253–254.

5. Marver H. Bernstein, *Regulating Business by Independent Commission* (Princeton: Princeton University Press, 1955). An earlier study that made some of the same arguments is Samuel P. Huntington, "The Marasmus of the ICC: The Commission, the Railroads, and the Public Interest," *Yale Law Journal* 6 (April 1952): 467–509.

6. Anthony Downs, *An Economic Theory of Democracy* (New York: Harper, 1957); and Mancur Olson, Jr., *The Logic of Collective Action: Public Goods and the Theory of Groups* (Cambridge: Harvard University Press, 1965).

7. Gabriel Kolko, *Railroads and Regulation, 1877–1916* (Princeton: Princeton University Press, 1965); and Gabriel Kolko, *The Triumph of Conservatism: A*

Reinterpretation of American History, 1900–1916 (New York: Free Press of Glencoe, 1963). Although Kolko's books received wide attention, others had made similar arguments earlier. See especially Forrest McDonald, "Samuel Insull and the Movement for State Utility Regulatory Commissions," *Business History Review* 32, no. 3 (Autumn 1958): 241–254.

8. See Wilson, "The Politics of Regulation," p. 360; and McCraw, "Regulation in America," p. 269. Wilson and McCraw cite Harry S. Kariel, *The Decline of American Pluralism* (Stanford: Stanford University Press, 1961); Murray Edelman, *The Symbolic Uses of Politics* (Urbana: University of Illinois Press, 1964); Grant McConnell, *Private Power and American Democracy* (New York: Knopf, 1966); and Theodore J. Lowi, *The End of Liberalism: Ideology, Policy, and the Crisis of Public Authority* (New York: Norton, 1969).

9. George J. Stigler, "The Theory of Economic Regulation," *Bell Journal of Economics and Management Science* 2 (Spring 1971): 3–21.

10. Richard A. Posner, "Taxation by Regulation," *Bell Journal of Economics and Management Science* 2 (Spring 1971): 22–50.

11. Sam Peltzman, "Toward a More General Theory of Regulation," *Journal of Law and Economics* 19 (August 1976): 211–240.

12. See Theodore E. Keeler, "Theories of Regulation and the Deregulation Movement," *Public Choice* 44 (1984): 103–145; and Sam Peltzman, "The Economic Theory of Regulation after a Decade of Deregulation," *Brookings Papers on Economic Activity, Microeconomics,* vol. 1989 (1989): 1–41.

13. Most scholars agree that the benefits to special interests from regulation had not begun to decline when trucking was deregulated and were threatened but still substantial when the telecommunications industry was deregulated. There is less consensus on how large the benefits to special interests were at the time the airline industry was deregulated. See Keeler, "Theories of Regulation and the Deregulation Movement"; Peltzman, "The Economic Theory of Regulation after a Decade of Deregulation"; and Michael E. Levine and Roger G. Noll, "The Economic Theory of Regulation after a Decade of Deregulation, Comments and Discussion," *Brookings Papers on Economic Activity, Microeconomics,* vol. 1989 (1989): 42–59.

14. Gary S. Becker, "A Theory of Competition among Pressure Groups for Political Influence," *Quarterly Journal of Economics* 98, no. 3 (August 1983): 371–400.

15. Keeler, "Theories of Regulation and the Deregulation Movement."

16. Wilson, "The Politics of Regulation," p. 362.

17. This is a paraphrase of ibid., p. 391.

18. So far, the contribution of the models has been largely to formalize insights that had been developed without their aid. For examples, see Jean-Jacques Laffont, "The New Economics of Regulation Ten Years After," *Econometrica* 62, no. 3 (May 1994): 507–537; and David Martimort, "The Multiprincipal Nature of Government," *European Economic Review* 40 (1996): 673–685. Laffont and Tirole's more important and original contributions are in trade-offs in the design of price-cap and other forms of incentive schemes described in Chapter 14.

19. For reviews of research about capture, see McCraw, "Regulation in America"; Wilson, "The Politics of Regulation"; George L. Priest, "The Origins of Utility Regulation and the 'Theories of Regulation' Debate," *Journal of Law and Eco-*

nomics 36 (April 1993): 289–329; and Paul Eric Teske, *After Divestiture: The Political Economy of State Telecommunications Regulation* (Albany: State University of New York Press, 1990), pp. 17–29.

20. See the review at McCraw, "Regulation in America," pp. 255–260. For typical revisionist articles, see Stanley Crane, "Why Railroads Supported Regulation: The Case of Wisconsin, 1905–1910," *Business History Review* 44 (Summer 1970): 175–189; and William R. Doezema, "Railroad Management and the Interplay of Federal and State Regulation," *Business History Review* 50 (Summer 1976): 153–178.

21. Wilson, "The Politics of Regulation," pp. 366–370.

22. Ibid., pp. 369–370.

23. See, for example, Martha Derthick and Paul J. Quirk, *The Politics of Deregulation* (Washington, D.C.: Brookings Institution, 1985); and Dorothy L. Robyn, *Braking the Special Interests: Trucking Deregulation and the Politics of Policy Reform* (Chicago: University of Chicago Press, 1987).

24. For accounts of the changing interest in institutions among economists, see Malcolm Rutherford, "Institutional Economics: Then and Now," *Journal of Economic Perspectives* 15, no. 3 (Summer 2001): 173–194; and Terry M. Moe, "The New Economics of Organization," *American Journal of Political Science* 28, no. 4 (November 1984): 739–777. For reviews of the current research, see Oliver E. Williamson, "The New Institutional Economics: Taking Stock," *Journal of Economic Literature* 38 (September 2000): 595–613; and Douglass C. North, *Institutions, Institutional Change, and Economic Performance* (Cambridge: Cambridge University Press, 1990).

25. Geoffrey P. Miller, "Comments on Priest, The Origins of Utility Regulation and the 'Theories of Regulation' Debate," *Journal of Law and Economics* 36 (April 1993): 327.

26. For the classic account of the rationale for the act, see Richard B. Stewart, "The Reformation of Administrative Law," *Harvard Law Review* 88 (1975): 1669–1813.

27. Huntington, "The Marasmus of the ICC."

28. For example, see Roger G. Noll, *Reforming Regulation: An Evaluation of the Ash Council's Proposals* (Washington, D.C.: Brookings Institution, 1971). Noll would later argue that regulatory procedures could be used by regulated firms to fight off their competitors; Roger Noll and Bruce Owen, "The Anticompetitive Effects of Regulation: United States vs. AT&T," in *The Antitrust Revolution,* ed. John E. Kwoka, Jr., and Lawrence J. White (Glenview, Ill.: Scott, Foresman, 1989).

29. Mathew D. McCubbins, Roger G. Noll, and Barry R. Weingast, "Administrative Procedures as Instruments of Political Control," *Journal of Law, Economics, and Organization* 3, no. 2 (Fall 1987): 243–277.

30. Douglass C. North and Barry R. Weingast, "Constitutions and Commitment: The Evolution of Institutions Governing Public Choice in Seventeenth-Century England," *Journal of Economic History* 49, no. 4 (December 1989): 803–832.

31. René David and John C. Brierley, *Major Legal Systems of the World Today: An Introduction to the Comparative Study of Law* (New York: Free Press, 1978), p. 11.

32. Other families include socialist and Islamic law.

33. The civil law family is sometimes broken down into three subcategories: French, German, and Scandinavian. The Latin American countries are classified as French civil law; Japan, South Korea, Taiwan, and several other Asian nations are considered to have German civil law systems.

34. Rafael La Porta, Florencio Lopez-de-Silanas, Andrei Shleifer, and Robert W. Vishny, "The Legal Determinants of Finance," *Journal of Finance* 52, no. 3 (July 1997): 1131–1150; Rafael La Porta, Florencio Lopez-de-Silanas, Andrei Shleifer, and Robert W. Vishny, "Law and Finance," *Journal of Political Economy* 106, no. 6 (December 1998): 1113–1155; Rafael La Porta, Florencio Lopez-de-Silanas, and Andrei Shleifer, "Corporate Ownership around the World," *Journal of Finance* 54, no. 2 (April 1999): 471–517.

35. Brian Levy and Pablo T. Spiller, eds., *Regulations, Institutions, and Commitment: Comparative Studies of Telecommunications* (Cambridge: Cambridge University Press, 1996).

36. The other country that enjoyed sustained investment was Chile between 1958 and 1970 and after 1987. Argentina's telephone company was privatized in 1990, and investment in it was strong, but there were only a few years of experience at the time Levy and Spiller's book was written.

37. As explained in Chapter 6, many of the statutes governing the regulation of private electric companies in Latin America during the 1930s and 1940s contained specific statutory constraints on the regulator's behavior. But these constraints often proved not to be in the companies' interests and certainly were not enough to forestall expropriation.

38. For example, a recent study of the effects of institutions on electricity utility investment in seventy-eight countries from 1970 to 1994 did not have enough observations on privately provided utilities to estimate the effects of institutions on their investment. See Bennet A. Zellner and Witold J. Henisz, "Politics and Infrastructure Investment," unpublished paper, Georgetown University and the University of Pennsylvania, September 2000.

4. Capture and Instability

1. Marver H. Bernstein, *Regulating Business by Independent Commission* (Princeton: Princeton University Press, 1955).

2. Gary S. Becker, "A Theory of Competition among Pressure Groups for Political Influence," *Quarterly Journal of Economics* 98, no. 3 (August 1983): 371–400.

3. For a brief overview of the sources of confusion in cost allocation, see José A. Gómez-Ibáñez, "Pricing," pp. 99–136 in *Essays in Transportation Economics and Policy: A Handbook in Honor of John R. Meyer*, ed. José A. Gómez-Ibáñez, William B. Tye, and Clifford Winston (Washington, D.C.: Brookings Institution, 1999), esp. pp. 108–110.

4. There is considerable disagreement as to how important universal service is and how much cross-subsidy is really needed to maintain it. For a critical view in the case of telephones, see Robert W. Crandall and Leonard Waverman, *Who Pays for Universal Service?: When Telephone Subsidies Become Transparent* (Washington, D.C.: Brookings Institution, 2000).

5. Public ownership of bus companies is much more common in Europe and the United States, in part because they can better afford to subsidize inefficient public companies. Not only are per capita incomes higher but the scale of bus operations is relatively much smaller, so bus subsidies do not absorb so much of the government's budget; José A. Gómez-Ibáñez and John R. Meyer, *Going Private: The International Experience with Transport Privatization* (Washington, D.C.: Brookings Institution, 1993), pp. 13–93.

6. This account of the evolution of the Sri Lankan bus industry relies heavily on interviews by the author in Sri Lanka in 1996 and 1997; John Diandas, "Notes for Benefit Comparison of Government Sector and Private Sector Supplied Bus Services" and "The Future of Government Owned Bus Transport in Sri Lanka," pp. 46–84 and 85–120 in *Aspects of Privatization in Sri Lanka* (Colombo: Friedrich-Ebert-Stiftung, 1988); Gabriel Roth, "Improving Bus Service in Sri Lanka: Report to the National Transport Commission," Washington, D.C., July 14, 1995; and Halcrow Fox Ltd., *Appraisal of the Bus Industry,* working paper no. 9 of the Colombo Urban Transport Study, London and Colombo, December 1993. An earlier version of this history appears in José A. Gómez-Ibáñez, *Sri Lanka Transport (A): The Bus Industry,* case no. CR1-97-1377.0, Case Program, Kennedy School of Government, Harvard University, 1997.

7. The private sector's share of passenger traffic was slightly smaller than its share of vehicles, since the private buses were typically smaller than the RTB buses.

8. There was a fare increase in 1997, two fare increases in 2000, and another in 2001. Each time fares were raised by roughly 15 percent, and the cumulative increase was enough to encourage private operators to expand their fleet to 17,250 buses by the end of 2001. The peoplised depots were reorganized into eleven regional public bus companies very similar to old RTBs.

9. According to unpublished figures supplied by the National Transport Commission.

10. For a review of studies of economies of scale in industrialized countries, see Kenneth A. Small, *Urban Transportation Economics,* Fundamentals of Pure and Applied Science, vol. 57 (Chur, Switzerland: Harwood, 1992), pp. 56–57.

11. Daniel B. Klein, Adrian T. Moore, and Binyam Reja, *Curb Rights: A Foundation for Free Enterprise in Urban Transit* (Washington, D.C.: Brookings Institution, 1997).

12. A 1937 commission chaired by Brigadier General E. D. Hammond cited too many buses, not too few, as the key reason to impose regulation and lamented that there were only a "few substantial concerns" providing bus service on the island, while the rest were "fly-by-night" operators. M. C. Premaratne and W. Soysa, "Methods of Managing Routes Served by Multiple Operators," pp. 203–250 in *Background Papers,* vol. 2 of *Sri Lanka Transport Sector Strategy Study,* World Bank Report no. 16269-CE, March 1997, esp. p. 204.

13. These figures are for passenger kilometers traveled in 1995, but had been fairly constant for the last decade or two. In 1982, for example, the shares were 73 percent bus, 8 percent rail, and 19 percent motorcycle, van, or car. Source: National Transport Commission.

14. K. G. D. D. Dehrasinghe (chairman), "Report of the Committee on Transport

Fares," report to the Ministry of Transport, Environment and Women Affairs, Colombo, Sri Lanka, 1995, p. 45.

15. There are many histories of the rise and fall of the Bell System. For a concise account see Richard H. K. Vietor, "AT&T and the Public Good: Regulation and Competition in Telecommunications, 1910–1987," in *Future Competition in Telecommunications,* ed. Stephen P. Bradley and Jerry A. Hausman (Boston: Harvard Business School Press, 1989), pp. 27–103. For longer and very rich accounts it is hard to beat Fred W. Henck and Bernard Strassburg, *A Slippery Slope: The Long Road to the Breakup of AT&T* (Westport, Conn.: Greenwood Press, 1988); Peter Temin with Louis Galambos, *The Fall of the Bell System: A Study in Prices and Politics* (Cambridge: Cambridge University Press, 1987); Gerald W. Brock, *Telecommunication Policy for the Information Age: From Monopoly to Competition* (Cambridge: Harvard University Press, 1994); Gerald Brock, *The Telecommunications Industry: The Dynamics of Market Structure* (Cambridge: Harvard University Press, 1981); or Milton L. Mueller, Jr., *Universal Service: Competition, Interconnection, and Monopoly in the Making of the American Telephone System* (Cambridge: MIT Press, 1997).

16. According to Mueller, AT&T's refusal to interconnect its local exchange subsidiaries with local rivals was not very important in defeating the independent telephone companies. More important was AT&T's policy of aggressively connecting noncompeting independent local exchanges to its long-distance and regional lines. Through this strategy, AT&T subscribers enjoyed superior regional and long-distance calling opportunities. Mueller, *Universal Service.*

17. Vietor, "AT&T and the Public Good," p. 32.

18. Ibid., pp. 33–34.

19. The independents provided only 19 percent of the lines but served 59 percent of the geographic territory; Brock, *Telecommunication Policy,* p. 65.

20. In addition, no more than four commissioners could be from the same political party.

21. Non-traffic-sensitive plant accounted for 51 percent of all investment in the Bell System in 1980; Henck and Strassburg, *A Slippery Slope,* pp. 14, 45–46.

22. The *Smith v. Illinois Bell* case raised extremely sensitive issues about the relationship between state and federal regulation. AT&T was an interstate holding company and interstate calls were subject to FCC regulation, so having state authorities supervise the division of costs between local and interstate calls might be construed as state interference in interstate commerce. The Court finessed this issue by saying that the state authorities had the right to question these divisions but not giving them specific guidance as to how these divisions should be set. See Irston R. Barnes, *The Economics of Public Utility Regulation* (New York: F. S. Crofts, 1947), pp. 630–632.

23. After the state role in railroad regulation declined, NARUC would rename itself the National Association of Regulatory Utility Commissioners.

24. Henck and Strassburg, *A Slippery Slope,* p. 43.

25. Long-distance costs per circuit mile were often higher for intrastate than interstate lines, because interstate lines enjoyed greater economies of distance and traffic density.

26. As quoted in Henck and Strassburg, *A Slippery Slope,* p. 44.

27. The 1947 separations manual also allocated some traffic-insensitive costs on the basis of minutes of relative use, but it apparently applied this approach to a smaller portion of the plant than the Charleston plan did.

28. Vietor, "AT&T and the Public Good," p. 46. As a result, the average monthly local charge fell from $12.14 in 1970 to $8.16 in 1980 in 1980 dollars; Paul Eric Teske, *After Divestiture: The Political Economy of State Telecommunications Regulation* (Albany: State University of New York Press, 1990), p. 4.

29. Brock, *Telecommunication Policy,* p. 70.

30. Henck and Strassburg, *A Slippery Slope,* p. 33.

31. *Hush-A-Phone Corporation v. U.S. and FCC,* 238 F.2d 266 at 269 as quoted in Brock, *Telecommunication Policy,* p. 83.

32. As one commissioner explained in a now-famous quote: "I am not satisfied with the job that the FCC has been doing. And I am still looking, at this juncture, for ways to add a little salt and pepper to the rather tasteless stew of regulatory protection that the Commission and Bell have cooked up." Brock, *Telecommunication Policy,* p. 116.

33. Many of these applications were from MCI for additional links; Henck and Strassburg, *A Slippery Slope,* pp. 144–145.

34. MCI had also filed a separate private antitrust suit in 1973.

35. Paul W. MacAvoy, *The Failure of Antitrust and Regulation to Establish Competition in Long-Distance Telephone Services* (Cambridge: MIT Press, 1996).

36. For more hopeful assessments, see, for example, Robert W. Crandall and Leonard Waverman, *Talk Is Cheap: The Promise of Regulatory Reform in North American Telecommunications* (Washington, D.C.: Brookings Institution, 1995); and Ingo Vogelsang and Bridger M. Mitchell, *Telecommunications Competition: The Last Ten Miles* (Cambridge: MIT Press, 1997).

37. Some states changed their traditional cross-subsidy policies in response to divestiture, but the majority did not. In the nation as a whole, for example, as of 1990 the median business user paid a monthly charge that was 150 percent higher than the median residential customer. Moreover, the residential monthly charge was relatively uniform throughout the nation despite the fact that the incremental monthly costs varied by a factor of four between the 10th and 90th percentile most costly to serve residences. For the 1990 cost and revenue estimates, see Crandall and Waverman, *Talk Is Cheap,* p. 84. For an account of how state regulators' reactions to divestiture varied see Teske, *After Divestiture,* especially chapter 5.

38. The national averages are from 1995–1996 and include the connection charges at either end of the call; see Alfred E. Kahn, *Letting Go: Deregulating the Process of Deregulation* (East Lansing: Michigan State University, Institute of Public Utilities and Network Industries, 1998), p. 105n146. For the variation in intrastate call connection charges by state, see Vogelsang and Mitchell, *Telecommunications Competition,* p. 132.

39. As of 1990, for example, the interstate fee was 1.23 cents per minute at either end, compared with roughly 2.5 cents for the median intrastate fee; see Vogelsang and Mitchell, *Telecommunications Competition,* pp. 115–123 and 132.

5. Incompleteness and Its Consequences

1. Only in France did a form of concession contract regulation survive. France nationalized most of its utilities, including the railroad, telephone, and electric industries. Municipal water supply, waste disposal, and urban public transport often remained in private hands, however, and continued to be regulated by municipal concession contracts. As explained in Chapter 2, the French concession contracts have a strong discretionary element.

2. Harold Demsetz, "Why Regulate Public Utilities?" *Journal of Law and Economics* 11 (April 1968): 55–66.

3. Oliver E. Williamson, "Franchise Bidding for Natural Monopolies—in General and with Respect to CATV," *Bell Journal of Economics* 7, no. 1 (Spring 1976): 73–104; and Victor P. Goldberg, "Regulation and Administered Contracts," *Bell Journal of Economics* 7, no. 2 (Autumn 1976): 426–448.

4. Guasch does not define very clearly what constitutes a renegotiation. José Luis Guasch, "Concessions of Infrastructure Services: Incidence and Determinants of Renegotiations—An Empirical Evaluation and Guidelines for Optimal Concession Design," manuscript, World Bank, Washington, D.C., May 2002.

5. For comprehensive reviews of Argentina's infrastructure privatization programs that focus particularly on regulatory issues, see Fundación de Investigaciones Económicas Latinoamericanas (FIEL), *La Regulación de la Competencia y de los Servicios Públicos: Teoría y Experiencia Argentina Reciente* (Buenos Aires: FIEL, 1999); or Manuel A. Abdala and Pablo T. Spiller, *Instituciónes, Contratos, y Regulación en Argentina* (Buenos Aires: Temas Grupos Editorial, 1999). For a description of the experience with transport concessions in English, see Antonio Estache, José Carbajo, and Ginés de Rus, "Argentina's Transport Privatization and Re-Regulation: Ups and Downs of a Daring Decade-Long Experience," Policy Research Working Paper no. 2249, World Bank, Washington, D.C., November 1999.

6. This account of the Argentine railway concession program is based on interviews of Argentine officials by the author on several visits between 1995 and 2001 as well as on published sources. An early version of this history appeared as José A. Gómez-Ibáñez, *Privatizing Transport in Argentina*, case no. CR1-96-1363.0, Case Program, Kennedy School of Government, Harvard University, 1996.

   For a more complete account of the developments that led to the reforms of 1989, see Gary W. Wynia, *Argentina: Illusions and Realities,* 2d ed. (New York: Holmes and Meier, 1992).

7. The formal name of the Peronist Party is the Justicialista Party.

8. FIEL, *La Regulación,* pp. 177–178.

9. This figure is in 1997 dollars and includes capital as well as operating expenditures; see ibid., p. 237.

10. Subte's official name was Subterráneos de Buenos Aires, Sociedad Estatal (or SABASE).

11. In concession programs where government subsidy was not permitted, such as the metropolitan expressway concessions, the government would typically set

out the minimum services and investments expected and award the concession to the bidder who proposed the lowest toll or tariff.

12. The only notable foreign shareholders were other railways, and their share in the equity was nominal, usually 5 percent. The government had required that each railway concessionaire include an experienced railway operator as part of its team. Bidders were forced to satisfy this requirement by recruiting foreign railways, often from the United States, since there were no experienced railway operators in Argentina besides FA and Subte.

13. Among the urban railway concessionaires, for example, Trenes de Buenos Aires was controlled by a bus company. Among the freight concessions, Ferrosur Roca was owned by a major cement company; Nuevo Central Argentino was owned by grain, cereal, and oil shippers; and Buenos Aires al Pacifico was owned by a construction company.

14. The principal exception was in rail freight, where the concession contracts grant the regulator the right to overturn rail freight rates that are not "fair" as well as broad powers to resolve disputes between the freight concessionaires and provincial authorities who want to run intercity passenger trains over freight tracks.

15. FA required about US$1.47 billion per year in operating and capital subsidies and the municipal subway absorbed about US$40 million per year in operating subsidies. Figures for capital subsidies for the subway are not available. These figures are in 1997 dollars as quoted in FIEL, *La Regulación,* pp. 237, 240.

16. Freight concession fees were scheduled to increase gradually from US$10 million per year in the first year of the concessions to US$17 million in the thirtieth year; data from the Comisión Nacional de Regulación del Transporte.

17. The operating subsidies requested by the winning bidders declined from US$156 million in the first year to US$12 million in year 10, however, while the capital subsidies requested peaked at US$355 million in the fourth year and declined to US$109 million in year 10 and to zero after year 15 (all in 1997 dollars). FIEL, *La Regulación,* pp. 239, 241.

18. For a shipment of 400 kilometers, tariffs fell from 4.4 cents per ton kilometer to 2.9 cents per ton kilometer; FIEL, *La Regulación,* p. 183.

19. The transition began in 1991, when the government split off commuter railways as a separate company (Ferrocarriles Metropolitanos S.A., or FEMESA) and reorganized the freight operations into the separate units that would become the concessions. Subsidies were reduced in anticipation of privatization, and FA employees were understandably apprehensive about their futures.

20. Approximately half of the added rail tonnage was in industrial products, construction materials, and containers, all traffic probably stimulated at least in part by the economic recovery. The other half was in grains and cereals and was presumably less affected by President Menem's economic reforms, since the agricultural sector had always been export oriented. For rail traffic trends by commodity see FIEL, *La Regulación,* p. 182.

21. The share of metropolitan person trips carried by the subway and the commuter railroads increased from 8.5 percent in 1991 to 14.6 percent in 1997. FIEL, *La Regulación,* p. 214.

22. The average laid-off worker had a wage of US$650 per month; data on the severance program are from Jorge H. Kogan, "Experiencias Ferroviarias: Una Revisión del Caso de Buenos Aires," presentation made to the World Bank Seminar on Transport Regulation, Las Palmas, Spain, April 8, 1999.

23. Trucks often compete with railroads in Argentina, even for bulk commodities like grain, because the typical length of haul for a grain shipment is only 500 kilometers.

24. FIEL, *La Regulación,* pp. 188–189.

25. Ibid., pp. 189–190.

26. If one sets aside their unmet commitments, Nuevo Central Argentino (NCA) and Ferrosur Roca were thought to be the most profitable of the freight concessions, Ferroexpresso Pampeano (FEPASA) and Ferrocarril Mesopotamico marginally profitable, while Buenos Aires al Pacifico (BAP) was thought to be losing money.

27. Of the remaining three commuter lines, the Urquiza line had 2 percent less riders than expected while the Roca and Sarmiento lines had 3 and 8 percent more riders than expected, respectively; FIEL, *La Regulación,* pp. 231–232.

28. Between 1993 and 1997, the number of car miles operated increased by 50 percent on the subway and 56 percent on the commuter rail lines. Ridership grew so much faster, however, that the average number of passengers in a car increased by 57 percent; ibid., pp. 232–234.

29. The freight concessionaires had claims against the government in that the provinces were not paying the track access fees they owed for operating passenger trains over freight tracks. The debts the provinces owed the railroads were much smaller, however, than the investments and fees the railroads owed the national government.

30. The government had taken an initial step to renegotiate the freight contracts in 1995, when an executive decree was issued allowing the secretary of transportation to reduce the fees the freight concessionaires had promised to pay the government in return for comparable reductions in the tariffs the concessionaires were charging shippers. This decree proved to be inadequate, however, since the concessionaires' shortfall in fee payments was dwarfed by their shortfall in promised investments.

31. Interview granted on condition of anonymity.

32. In 1998 the Brazilian railway, Ferrovia Sul Atlântico, announced its intention to buy Ferrocarril Mesopotamica, which connects Brazil and Argentina, and Buenos Aires al Pacifico, which extends across Argentina to Chile. The Argentine government did not approve the sale until 1999.

33. Metrovias, Trenes de Buenos Aires, and Ferrovias.

34. Trenes Metropolitano.

35. Metrovias and Trenes de Buenos Aires were approved in March 1999.

36. The Alliance lawyers complained, for example, that the government approved the agreements only twenty-four hours after the hearings.

37. The other two concessions were reported to be earning only 3 and 10 percent per year. "Informe del Jefe de Gabinete Jorge Rodriguez al Congress" as re-

ported in "Sin Barreras: Polémica Renegociación de los Contratos de Trenes," *Clarín,* "Cash" supplement, March 7, 1999, pp. 2–3.

38. In addition, the concession contracts would be extended only fourteen instead of twenty years, so that they would all expire the same year as the subway concession (in 2018). The concessionaires were still arguing for a larger investment program for faster and bigger fare increases; see Antonio Rossi, "Apuran la Renegociación de los Contratos Ferroviarios," *Clarín,* June 4, 2000.

39. In addition, the government owed the concessionaires US$53 million for operating subsidies during the 2001 fiscal year. Figures from "Subsidios," *Clarín,* June 4, 2000. These figures are roughly consistent with the payments required in years 5 and 6 of the contracts as reported in FIEL, *La Regulación,* pp. 239, 241.

40. The typical fare for a 12-kilometer trip rose from US$0.35 to US$0.45. "Autorizarán una Suba Adicional del 10% an el Boleto del Tren," *Clarín,* August 23, 2000.

41. For an account of the revival of the U.S. freight railroads, see Chapter 8.

6. Forestalling Expropriation

1. Particularly helpful histories of electricity companies in Latin American include Duncan McDowall, *The Light: Brazilian Traction, Light and Power Company, 1899–1945* (Toronto: University of Toronto Press, 1988); Judith Tendler, *Electric Power in Brazil: Entrepreneurship in the Public Sector* (Cambridge: Harvard University Press, 1968); Miguel S. Wionczek, "Electric Power: The Uneasy Partnership," in *Public Policy and Private Enterprise in Mexico,* ed. Raymond Vernon (Cambridge: Harvard University Press, 1964), pp. 19–110; Jorge del Río, *Politica Argentina y los Monopolios Eléctricos* (Buenos Aires: Editorial Cátedra Lisandro de la Torre, 1957); Jorge del Río, *Electricidad y Liberación Nacional: El Caso de SEGBA* (Buenos Aires: Colleción la Siringa, 1960); Jorge del Río, *El Porqué de la Crisis* (Buenos Aires: Editorial Cátedra Lisandro de la Torre, 1961); Carlos Sanclemente, *Desarrollo y Crisis del Sector Eléctrico Colombiano 1890–1993* (Bogota: Empresa Editorial Universidad Nacional, 1993); Juan Pablo Pérez Alfonso, *Abusiva Aplicación de Tarifas Eléctricas y Otros Daños Causados a los Intereses Colectivos del Distrito Federal* (Caracas: Contraloria Municipal del Distrito Federal, Imprenta Municipal de Caracas, 1965); Giovanni Bonfiglio Volpe, *Historia de la Electricidad en Lima: Noventa Años de Modernidad* (Lima: Museo de la Electricidad, 1997); Marvin Fink, *Reports on Electric Power Regulation in Brazil, Chile, Colombia, Costa Rica, and Mexico* (Cambridge: Harvard Law School, 1960); and David F. Cavers and James R. Nelson, *Electric Power Regulation in Latin America* (Baltimore: Johns Hopkins University Press, 1959).

There are many histories of individual Canadian companies, but the best overall accounts are Christopher Armstrong and H. V. Nelles, *Monopoly's Moment: The Organization and Regulation of Canadian Utilities, 1830–1930* (Philadelphia: Temple University Press, 1986); John R. Baldwin, *Regulatory Failure and*

Renewal: The Evolution of the Natural Monopoly Contract (Ottawa: Economic Council of Canada, 1989); and Marsha Gordon, *Government in Business* (Montreal: C. D. Howe Institute, 1981).

There are so many histories of the U.S. electricity industry that it is hard to single out a few. Particularly useful for this chapter are the descriptions of the early legal battles over regulation in C. Woody Thompson and Wendell R. Smith, *Public Utility Economics* (New York: McGraw-Hill, 1941); and Irston R. Barnes, *The Economics of Public Utility Regulation* (New York: F. S. Croft, 1947).

2. James S. Carson, "The Power Industry," in *The Industrialization of Latin America,* ed. Lloyd J. Hughlett (New York: McGraw-Hill, 1946), pp. 319–345.

3. For an account of these strategies in Canada, for example, see Armstrong and Nelles, *Monopoly's Moment,* pp. 93–114.

4. Del Río, *Monopolios Eléctricos,* p. 16.

5. The holdout state was Delaware; Barnes, *Public Utility Regulation,* pp. 150–151, 206.

6. Statistics suggest that Roosevelt's threat of competition may have helped reduce electricity rates. See Willis M. Emmons III, "Franklin D. Roosevelt, Electric Utilities, and the Power of Competition," *Journal of Economic History* 54, no. 4 (December 1993): 880–907.

7. On the rise of public power in Ontario, see Baldwin, *Regulatory Failure,* pp. 83–94; Armstrong and Nelles, *Monopoly's Moment,* esp. pp. 154–156, 188–193; H. V. Nelles, *The Politics of Development: Forest Mines and Hydro-Electric Power in Ontario, 1849–1941* (Toronto: Macmillan, 1974); and Neil B. Freeman, *The Politics of Power: Ontario Hydro and Its Government: 1906–1995* (Toronto: University of Toronto Press, 1996).

8. For brief histories of Manitoba, New Brunswick, and Nova Scotia, see Baldwin, *Regulatory Failure,* pp. 73–82; Armstrong and Nelles, *Monopoly's Moment,* pp. 193–200, 300–303; and Gordon, *Government in Business,* pp. 33–35.

9. One exception was the sparsely populated province of Saskatchewan, which was dominated by municipally owned electric companies even before World War I. See Armstrong and Nelles, *Monopoly's Moment,* p. 206; and Clinton O. White, *Power for a Province: A History of Saskatchewan Power* (Regina: University of Regina, 1976).

10. For accounts of Quebec and British Columbia see Baldwin, *Regulatory Failure,* pp. 63–68, 95–102; Armstrong and Nelles, *Monopoly's Moment,* pp. 203–210, 297–300; and Gordon, *Government in Business,* pp. 27–33.

11. Calgary established a city-owned electric utility in 1904, but the province was largely rural and Calgary accounted for only a small portion of its population. See Armstrong and Nelles, *Monopoly's Moment,* pp. 196, 303–304; and Gordon, *Government in Business,* pp. 33–34.

12. Baldwin, *Regulatory Failure,* p. 41; and Armstrong and Nelles, *Monopoly's Moment,* pp. 188–210.

13. Gordon, *Government in Business,* p. 35.

14. See the research by Rafael La Porta, Florencio Lopez-de-Silanas, Andrei Shleifer, Robert W. Vishny, Brian Levy, and Pablo Spiller described in Chapter 3.

15. Thompson and Smith, *Public Utility Economics,* pp. 57–58, 131–132, citing

particularly Hunter, "The Early Regulation of Public Service Corporations," *American Economic Review* 7 (1917): 569–581.

16. Barnes, *Public Utility Regulation,* pp. 197–199; Thompson and Smith, *Public Utility Economics,* pp. 59–65, 133–137.

17. 94 U.S. 133–134 (1877), as cited by Alfred E. Kahn, *The Economics of Regulation: Principles and Institutions,* vol. 1 (New York: John Wiley, 1971), p. 37.

18. The Court set out additional considerations as well. In its words: "We hold . . . that the basis of all calculations as to the reasonableness of rates to be charged . . . must be the fair value of the property being used by it for the convenience of the public. And in order to ascertain that value, the original cost of construction, the amount expended in permanent improvements, the amount and market value of its bonds and stock, the present as compared with the original cost of construction, the probable earning capacity of the property under particular rates prescribed by statute, and the sum required to meet operating expenses, are all maters of consideration and are to be given such weight as may be just and right in each case. We do not say that there may not be other matters to be regarded in measuring the value of the property. What the company is entitled to ask is a fair return upon the value of that which it employs for the public convenience." 169 U.S. (1898) 546–547, as quoted by Barnes, *Public Utility Regulation,* p. 373.

19. Kahn, *The Economics of Regulation,* 1: 38–41; F. M. Scherer, *Industrial Market and Economic Performance* (Chicago: Rand McNally, 1970), pp. 525–527.

20. Christopher Armstrong and H. V. Nelles, "Private Property in Peril: Ontario Businessmen and the Federal System, 1898–1911," *Business History Review* 47, no. 2 (Summer 1973): 158–178; and Baldwin, *Regulatory Failure,* p. 1.

21. This was in a case applying to the expropriation of natural resources rather than utilities; quoted in Armstrong and Nelles, "Private Property in Peril," p. 159.

22. Quoted in ibid., p. 171.

23. It may be that some cases of this type did develop in Canada, but Baldwin, Armstrong, and Nelles do not mention them. See, for example, Armstrong and Nelles's account of the development of early Canadian PUCs in *Monopoly's Moment,* pp. 188–210.

24. Armstrong and Nelles, *Monopoly's Moment,* pp. 188–210; and Patricia E. Roy, "Regulating the British Columbia Electric Railway: The First Public Utilities Commission in British Columbia," *B.C. Studies* 1 (1971): 6.

25. This was not the only example of opportunism by the province during the early years of Ontario Hydro; see Baldwin, *Regulatory Failure,* pp. 88–93; and Armstrong and Nelles, *Monopoly's Moment,* p. 191. Toronto Electric's willingness to sell out was also due to the fact that its franchises were expiring; Freeman, *The Politics of Power,* p. 50.

26. Armstrong and Nelles, "Private Property in Peril," pp. 173–175.

27. This is true, for example, of the 1988 constitution of Brazil.

28. See, for example, Michael Goldberg and John Mercer, *The Myth of the North American City* (Vancouver: University of British Columbia Press, 1986), pp. 12–30.

29. Raymond Vernon made this argument when trying to explain the rise and decline of private foreign investment in developing countries in the twentieth century, and Louis T. Wells, Jr., expanded it to infrastructure investment. See Vernon, *Sovereignty at Bay: The Multinational Spread of U.S. Enterprises* (New York: Basic Books, 1971); and Wells, "Is Foreign Investment in Infrastructure Still Risky," *Harvard Business Review* (August-September, 1995): 44–55.

30. Cavers and Nelson, *Electric Power Regulation,* pp. 11–12; Carson, "The Power Industry," p. 341; and Wionczek, "Electric Power," p. 21–22.

31. McDowall, *The Light;* Tendler, *Electric Power in Brazil,* pp. 30–34; and Carson, "The Power Industry," p. 325.

32. General Electric owned Electric Bond and Share until 1924, when it distributed Electric Bond and Share stock to its stockholders. Electric Bond and Share later changed its name to Ebasco.

33. For accounts of the origins of American and Foreign Power, see Norman Sharp Buchanan, "The Electric Bond and Share Company: A Case Study of a Public Utility Holding Company" (Ph.D. dissertation, Cornell University, 1931), pp. 254–295; and Sidney A. Mitchell, *S. Z. Mitchell and the Electrical Industry* (New York: Farrar, Straus and Cudahy, 1960), pp. 106–112.

34. The eleven Latin American countries were Argentina, Brazil, Chile, Colombia, Costa Rica, Cuba, Ecuador, Guatemala, Mexico, Panama, and Venezuela. Outside of Latin America, American and Foreign Power owned the electric power concessions for the International Settlement in Shanghai and for Bombay and minority interests in utilities in five other countries. Buchanan, "Electric Bond and Share," pp. 256–257.

35. The five Latin American countries were Bolivia, British Guyana, El Salvador, Mexico, and Venezuela. The company's name was changed to International Power Company around 1955, after its founder, Izack W. Killian, died and his shares were bought by U.S. investors. For a brief history, see Jack Sexton, *MONECO: The First 75 Years* (Montreal: Montreal Engineering Company Ltd., 1982), pp. 43–58.

36. Herbert Bratter, "Latin American Utilities' Nationalization Proceeds Inexorably," *Public Utilities Fortnightly* 66, no. 1 (July 7, 1960): 4.

37. Sofina's formal name was Société Financière de Transports et d'Industries Électriques. Although Sofina was based in Brussels, it was founded and owned in large part by Swiss investors. See Luciano Segreto, "Financing the Electric Industry Worldwide: Strategy and Structure of Swiss Electric Holding Companies, 1895–1945," *Business and Economic History* 23, no. 1 (Fall 1994): 162–174, esp. 165.

38. CIADE was a Motor Columbus subsidiary. Del Río suggests that Cia. Suizo-Argentina de Electricidad was as well; see del Río, *Electricidad y Liberación,* p. 27.

39. Bratter, "Nationalization Proceeds Inexorably," p. 11.

40. Sanclemente, *Desarrollo y Crisis,* pp. 7–11.

41. For the São Paulo story, see McDowall, *The Light,* pp. 80–94.

42. McDowall, *The Light,* pp. 110–113, 170–177.

43. Wionczek, "Electric Power," pp. 30, 44–45.

44. Wionczek argues that the utilities were not alarmed; ibid., pp. 48–49. At least

one utility executive, MacKenzie of Light, was pessimistic, however. McDowall quotes MacKenzie in a private communication to a London financier in 1926 as saying, "I regret to say . . . being a foreign company is considered fair game. I even think that a foreign concern exploiting a public utility has had its day and is becoming an anachronism." But McDowall also notes that MacKenzie's fear was very premature; McDowall, *The Light,* p. 273.

45. Wionczek, "Electric Power," p. 54.
46. See, for example, del Río, *Monopolios Eléctricos,* p. 33.
47. Carson, "The Power Industry," pp. 343–345.
48. American and Foreign Power, *Annual Report 1959,* p. 18.
49. American and Foreign Power had been fighting the Colombian government for a promised rate increase for many years, and it was involved in disputes with governments in Argentina and Brazil over compensation for expropriated subsidiaries.
50. This account of the Mexican negotiations is based on Wionczek, "Electric Power," pp. 91–92, 94–99.
51. This history of Bolivian Light and Power is based primarily on telephone interviews with David C. Mitchell, a former president and chairman of the company, on July 10 and 14, 2000; Compañía Boliviana de Energía Eléctrica, "75 Aniversario," pamphlet, 2000; and Sexton, *MONECO,* pp. 47–50.
52. Earlier, Bolivian Power had given up telephone and streetcar services it provided in La Paz. The La Paz telephones were abandoned in the 1940s in the face of competition from a newly established telephone cooperative. The streetcars were abandoned as unprofitable in 1950 when the concession expired.
53. For the government's side, see José Antonio Arze, *La Bolivian Power Co.: Informe Oral del Sr. Ministro de Gobierno en la Camera de Diputados* (La Paz: Editorial del Estado, 1962).
54. The two dictators were General René Barientos Ortuño (1964–1969) and General Hugo Banzar Suárez (1971–1978). Between 1969 and 1971 there were two left-leaning military dictators in two years, and between 1978 and 1982 there were one civilian and seven military governments. Popular disgust with the last brutal and corrupt dictator led to a final coup in 1982 and then to elections.
55. Compañía Boliviana de Energía Eléctrica, or COBEE for short.
56. The Siles administration fought back by passing decrees in 1984 and 1985 requiring Bolivian Power to pay ENDE for wholesale power in U.S. dollars but to charge its retail customers in the national currency. Given the rapid inflation of the time, this scheme would have put Bolivian Power so deeply in debt to ENDE that ENDE could have petitioned the courts to take Bolivian Power's assets in payment. Bolivian Power responded by requesting that ENDE disconnect the high-voltage line between the two companies, explaining that although disconnection risked power failures during peak hours, it would be irresponsible for Bolivian Power to receive power that it could not pay for. This bluff worked, and ENDE continued to supply power without billing Bolivian Power in either currency.
57. President Victor Paz Estenssoro (1985–1989) stopped the efforts to expropriate Bolivian Power, while President Paz Zamora (1989–1993) granted the com-

pany a new concession and studied the possibilities for privatizing the rest of the electric sector. Privatization was done under President Gonzalo Sanchéz de Lozada (1993–1997). Bolivian Power sold off its La Paz and Oruro distribution systems as part of the industry restructuring and survives under the Spanish name it adopted in 1968 as a major generating company.

58. Armstrong and Nelles, *Monopoly's Moment*, pp. 206–210; Baldwin, *Regulatory Failure*, pp. 63–68; Roy, "Regulating the British Columbia Electric Railway."

59. Gordon, *Government in Business*, pp. 31–32.

60. Paul Sauriol, *The Nationalization of Electric Power* (Montreal: Harvest House, 1962), p. 14.

61. In Canada, the popular movement for public ownership of utilities started at the turn of the century as a movement by municipal officials against the permissive charters that provincial and federal authorities were granting to these companies; see Armstrong and Nelles, *Monopoly's Moment*, pp. 141–146.

62. This account of politics in Venezuela and Argentina is based largely on Iêda Siqueria Wiarda, "Venezuela: The Politics of Democratic Developmentalism," in *Latin American Politics and Development*, ed. Howard J. Wiarda and Harvey F. Kline, 2d ed. (Boulder, Colo.: Westview Press, 1985), pp. 293–316; and Gary W. Wynia, *Argentina: Illusions and Realities* (New York: Holmes and Meier, 1992).

63. Harvey F. Kline, "Colombia: Modified Two-Party and Elitist Politics," in *Latin American Politics and Development*, ed. Howard J. Wiarda and Harvey F. Kline, 2d ed. (Boulder, Colo.: Westview Press, 1985), pp. 249–270.

64. These figures are for electricity generated by private or government-owned utilities but exclude self-generation by nonutilities; Joseph W. Mullen, *Energy in Latin America: The Historical Record* (Santiago, Chile: United Nations, CEPAL, 1978), table 35, after p. 54.

65. This was especially true in Brazil; see McDowall, *The Light*, p. 326.

66. The government did not exercise its power before the overthrow of Porfirio Díaz in 1910. See Wionczek, "Electric Power," pp. 26–33.

67. Wionczek, "Electric Power," pp. 41–58. A slightly different account of the key Mexican laws and regulations can be found at Cavers and Nelson, *Electric Power Regulation*, p. 116n10.

68. McDowall, *The Light*, pp. 325–326; and Tendler, *Electric Power in Brazil*, pp. 48–49. A slightly different account of the key Brazilian laws and regulations can be found at Cavers and Nelson, *Electric Power Regulation*, p. 116n6.

69. A specific decree governing the American and Foreign Power subsidiary was issued in 1940. Sanclemente, *Desarrollo y Crisis*, pp. 54, 70; Cavers and Nelson, *Electric Power Regulation*, pp. 116n8, 131.

70. Wionczek, "Electric Power," pp. 63–64.

71. Cavers and Nelson, *Electric Power Regulation*, pp. 110–111.

72. Wionczek, "Electric Power," p. 67 and n. 10.

73. Cecil Ellis, a UN-sponsored advisor to the Colombian government, reported in 1953 that the regulatory authority had been shifted around from ministry to ministry during the 1940s. A "Director of Public Services" within the Ministry of Development had been named only in 1951, but he had no staff. As Ellis put

it, "A condition exists in Colombia compelling electricity enterprises to respect tariff restrictions that appear to have been inexpertly set many years ago, and which often have not been revised to meet the new situation created by large increases in operating costs." Cecil A. Ellis, *Public Utilities in Colombia,* United Nations Technical Assistance Programme, report ST/TAA/K/Colombia/1 (New York: United Nations, 1953), p. 47.

74. The Mexican law required that the rate of return be no lower than the rate on government bonds, but otherwise stated only that the rate be "reasonable," a broad standard more consistent with U.S. practice. The Colombian law required a "reasonable" rate of return as well, although Sanclemente reports that the 1940 decree covering the American and Foreign Power subsidiary ordered a 10 percent return on replacement rather than historical costs; see Sanclemente, *Desarrollo y Crisis,* p. 54. For a summary of regulatory laws in Brazil, Colombia, Mexico, and four other Latin countries, see Cavers and Nelson, *Electric Power Regulation,* p. 131.

75. McDowall, *The Light,* pp. 326–337.

76. Wionczek, "Electric Power," esp. pp. 46, 53, 64–66.

77. The cities included Tucumán, Paraná, Corrientes, Santa Fé, Córdoba, Jujuy, San Luis and several others. Henry Leslie Robinson, "American and Foreign Power in Latin America" (Ph.D. dissertation, Stanford University, 1967), pp. 115–120; and del Río, *El Porqué de la Crisis,* p. 108.

78. This history of conflict between the city of Buenos Aires and its utilities is based largely on three books by Jorge del Río, a lawyer who participated in Argentina's utility disputes from the 1930s through the 1950s. Del Río was an outspoken critic of the private foreign-owned utilities, so his books have a strong point of view, but his accounts are corroborated in their broad outline by other sources. See particularly del Río, *Monopolios Eléctricos,* for a discussion of the 1930s and 1940s, and del Río, *El Porqué de la Crisis,* for accounts of the 1950s.

79. For convenience we use the company's name from 1936. The original company established by German electrical equipment suppliers was called CATE (Compañía Alemana Transatlántico de Electricidad). In 1929 CATE's owners sold out to a combination of Spanish and Sofina interests out of fear that German overseas investments might be seized as payment for war reparations. The company was renamed CHADE (Compañía Hispano-Argentina de Electricidad) and headquartered in Madrid. The Spanish investors sold out to their Sofina partners in 1936 after the outbreak of the Spanish Civil War; the company was then renamed CADE and headquartered in Brussels.

80. Technological improvements that reduced CADE's costs by 20 percent would trigger rate reductions, and half of the cost savings was to be passed on to the customers.

81. The issue arose occasionally, as in the complaint that CADE had increased its residential service from 110 volts to 225 volts in order to save on cable costs, disregarding the increased risk of electrocuting its customers. CADE had made the voltage change without asking municipal permission, the critics noted, and despite the fact that the city of Brussels, where Sofina was headquartered, had prohibited 225 volts in residences as too dangerous.

82. In the United States, for example, electricity prices fell by two-thirds between 1902 and 1930 largely because of economies of scale and technological improvements; Leonard S. Hyman, *America's Electric Utilities: Past, Present, and Future* (Arlington, Va.: Public Utilities Reports, 1983), p. 76.

83. For example, CADE opened a big generating station in the Puerto Nuevo in 1929, and CIADE opened a similar facility on the waterfront in 1933; del Río, *Monopolios Eléctricos*, p. 52.

84. If the city didn't want to pay, then the concession would be extended for a further twenty-five years and the city would be responsible for all investments during the extension. The replacement cost provision could have hurt the companies if the concession ended after a period of low inflation and rapid technological change, but this probably seemed unlikely at the time. Del Río, *Monopolios Eléctricos*, pp. 25–28, 71–72.

85. Del Río says the judge dismissed the allegations on the grounds that the offenses had been committed too long ago; del Rio, *El Porqué de la Crisis*, p. 77. At least one member of the investigative commission appealed to the president publicly to allow the report to be released in 1945; Juan Sabato, *Por una Política Nacional de la Energía Eléctrica* (Buenos Aires: Editorial Nueva Vida, 1945).

86. Del Río, *Monopolios Eléctricos*, pp. 211–212.

87. The original idea in 1958 was that SEGBA would be a mixed public and private company subject to national government regulation. This arrangement broke down when the government would not allow SEGBA to raise prices high enough to earn the 8 percent return on investment allowed under the new regulatory regime. Carlos Manuel Bastos and Manuel Angel Abdala, *Reform of the Electric Power Industry in Argentina* (Buenos Aires, n.p., 1996), pp. 25–26; Carlos José Aga, *La Batalla de la Electricidad* (Buenos Aires: Gabinete Paralelo, n.d.), pp. 23–25.

88. In 1943 the government created a small agency to build hydroelectric facilities, which in 1947 was merged with an irrigation agency to form AEE.

89. These agencies were, respectively, Hidroner (created in 1967), Entidad Binacional Comisión Técnica Mixta de Salto Grande (created in the 1970s and generating power beginning in 1979), Entidad Binacional de Yacyretá (created around 1973 and generating power beginning in 1994), and CNEA (Comisión Nacional de Energía Atómica, created in 1950).

90. On Colombia and Brazil, see Robinson, "American and Foreign Power in Latin America," pp. 120–133; and Sanclemente, *Desarrollo y Crisis*, pp. 51–52.

91. Even in Latin American countries where revaluation was allowed, as in Chile, the regulators were slow to do so; Cavers and Nelson, *Electric Power Regulation*, pp. 114–116.

92. Cavers and Nelson, *Electric Power Regulation*, pp. 118–119.

93. Ibid., pp. 33–36.

94. In 1957 the company's assets were revalued in Brazilian currency, however, which provided them with a one-time increase in the rate base.

95. As quoted in Wionczek, "Electric Power," pp. 68.

96. Wionczek, "Electric Power," pp. 67–69.

97. McDowall, *Light*, pp. 331–337.

98. This began in 1943 with an increase in Light's streetcar fares and was extended to electricity in 1945; McDowall, *Light,* p. 351.

99. Tendler, *Electric Power in Brazil,* p. 64–66.

100. Ibid., p. 53.

101. Wionczek, "Electric Power," pp. 78.

102. American and Foreign Power, *Annual Report, 1952,* p. 16; *Annual Report, 1955,* p. 32; *Annual Report, 1960,* p. 2; *Annual Report, 1962,* p. 14; and McDowall, *Light,* p. 406.

103. Corporación Autónoma Regional del Valle del Cauca (CVC). The aid to municipalities was through the Fondo de Fomento Municipal created in 1940. A second TVA-inspired regional power company was created in the 1960s.

104. In 1952 the state of Minas Gerias created CEMIG to electrify statewide, in 1953 the states of São Paulo and Paraná created USELPA to construct a dam on their state borders, around 1956 the state of São Paulo created CHERP to develop two dams, and in 1957 the federal government created Furnas to build a large dam several hundred kilometers away from São Paulo. An important part of the rationale for the USELPA, CHERP, and Furnas facilities was to sell power to São Paulo. In the early 1960s two more power companies were created: CHEVAP in 1960, by the federal government, to build a dam to supply power to Rio, and CELUSA in 1961, by the states of São Paulo and Mato Grosso, to develop hydro power on a river between the two states. See Tendler, *Electric Power in Brazil,* pp. 25–30, 34–39.

105. International agencies probably financed one-quarter to one-fifth of the cost of the projects they were involved in. Mullen, *Energy in Latin America,* p. 55.

106. Tendler, *Electric Power in Brazil,* pp. 81–106, 175–208.

107. Wionczek, "Electric Power," p. 71.

108. These arguments were made in a 1951 UN technical assistance mission to Colombia, for example, and in a mid-1950s regionwide UN-sponsored study done by Harvard Law School; see Ellis, *Public Utilities in Colombia;* and Cavers and Nelson, *Electric Power Regulation,* pp. 7–8.

109. Wionczek, "Electric Power," pp. 80–81.

110. Ibid., p. 79.

111. Ibid., pp. 103–104.

112. Although the company was transferred almost immediately, disputes about the price dragged on until 1967; Sanclemente, *Desarrollo y Crisis,* pp. 54–59.

113. In 1959 the state of Rio Grande do Sul had taken over the company serving Pôrto Alegre, and in the next few years the state of Espírito Santo took over the company serving Vitória; meanwhile, the state of Pernambuco had persuaded the courts to appoint a receiver to administer the Recife company pending the outcome of a lawsuit. The sale of all the properties was consummated in 1963 but was effective as of the end of 1962. American and Foreign Power, *Annual Report, 1962,* pp. 8–9.

114. McDowall claims that Brazilian Traction, Light and Power was much more aggressive in promoting locals into senior management than American and Foreign Power; McDowall, *The Light,* pp. 336–337, 385–386, and esp. 391.

115. McDowall, *The Light,* pp. 393–398.

116. This account of the history of La Electricidad de Caracas is based heavily on the writings of Dr. Juan Pablo Pérez Alfonso, one of the company's most outspoken critics (particularly his *Abusiva Aplicación de Tarifas*), and on an interview with Dr. Francisco G. Aguerrevere, chief executive officer of La Electricidad de Caracas in Caracas on July 14, 1995.

117. The company's strategy was to develop two small waterfalls near the city and sell the power to small businesses that were then using steam engines to grind grain, run printing presses, and other similar applications. La Electricidad de Caracas, *Setenta Años de una Empresa Venezolana* (Caracas: La Electricidad de Caracas, 1965), pp. 21–27.

118. The contract gave the city a 25 percent discount off the rates charged regular consumers for electricity used for purposes other than streetlighting, but it did not specify what the regular consumers would have to pay.

119. Pérez Alfonso, *Abusiva Aplicación de Tarifas,* pp. 10–11; La Electricidad de Caracas, *Setenta Años,* pp. 118–119.

120. These amendments were in 1926 and 1932. The 1932 amendment also gave the city an additional 10 percent off the regular rates for electricity used for purposes other than streetlights (for a total discount of 32.5 percent).

121. This discussion of the politics of this period is based on Wiarda, "Venezuela," pp. 302–304.

122. Pérez Alfonso is unclear as to whether the lighting contract in dispute in 1938 was with CALEV or La Electricidad de Caracas. The original 1912 lighting contract certainly was with CALEV's predecessor, and the confusion may have come about because, at the time that Pérez Alfonso was writing, La Electricidad de Caracas had just bought out CALEV. See Pérez Alfonso, *Abusiva Aplicación de Tarifas,* pp. 62–63, 80–82.

123. The average reduction was 16 percent; ibid., p. 64.

124. The new technical section was the Sección Técnica de Energía Eléctrica in the Dirección de Industria. The new state-owned electricity company was La Electricidad de Maracay. Ibid., p. 65.

125. Marcos Pérez Jiménez served as head of a provisional government until presidential elections in 1952. When it became clear that he was going to lose those elections, he stopped the counting of ballots and declared himself president.

126. The review was conducted by British consultants in 1955 and resulted in an 8.26 percent reduction in tariffs in 1957; Pérez Alfonso, *Abusiva Aplicación de Tarifas,* pp. 72–76.

127. The U.S. government awarded Pérez Jiménez the Legion of Merit and the resentment was such that when Vice President Richard Nixon visited Caracas shortly after the dictator was overthrown, Nixon's car was stoned and he feared for his life; Wiarda, "Venezuela," p. 305.

128. Pérez Alfonso, *Abusiva Aplicación de Tarifas;* Luis Prieto Oliveira, *Quién Invierte Realmente en las Empresas Eléctricas?* (Caracas: Controlaria Municipal del Distrito Federal, 1964); and Luis Prieto Oliveira, *La Question Eléctrica in la Zona Metropolitana: Pagamos las mas Altas Tarifas de Latinoamerica* (Caracas: Controlaria Municipal del Distrito Federal, 1964).

129. Oscar Machado Zuloaga and Ricardo Zuloaga, *En Defensa de las Empresas de Electricidad: Refutación al Informe del Doctor Luis Prieto Oliveira "Quién Invierte Realmente en las Empresas Eléctricas?"* (Caracas: C.A. La Electricidad de Caracas and C.A. Luz Eléctrica de Venezuela, 1964).

130. La Electricidad de Caracas, *Setenta Años,* p. 86.

131. According to the company's official history, Ricardo Zuloaga told the Americans, "One can't put a price on La Electricidad de Caracas!" La Electricidad de Caracas, *Setenta Años,* p. 119.

132. La Electricidad de Caracas, *Lineas, Año 4 Edición Extraordinaria en Memoria del Doctor Oscar Machado Zuloaga* (Caracas: La Electricidad de Caracas, n.d.), pp. 22–23.

133. Pérez Alfonso, *Abusiva Aplicación de Tarifas,* p. 93.

134. Aguerrevere, interview.

135. The Maracaibo company became ENELVEN; the Valencia company became ENEVAL.

136. One large public company (CADAFE) was created to provide electricity distribution services throughout most of the rest of the country, and a second (ENDELCA) was established to develop the formidable hydro potential of the Guayana region.

137. Aguerrevere, interview.

138. The commission, CREE (Comisión Reguladora de Energía Eléctrica), is composed of four ministers and several consumer representatives. It is staffed by the regulatory agency, Fundalec.

139. Jorgé Pirela, "Marco Regulatorio del Sector Eléctrico: Anarquía e Indefiniciones," in *Servicios Públicos: Clave para el Bienestar,* ed. Janet Kelley (Caracas: Ediciones IESA, 1996), pp. 165–169.

140. In 1953, after five years of effort, American and Foreign Power had sold domestic investors only $20 million in stock in its Brazilian subsidiaries, $4 million in bonds for its Cuban subsidiary, and $1 million in bonds for its Costa Rican subsidiary. After that year the effort to sell shares and bonds to local investors is no longer mentioned in the company's annual reports. American and Foreign Power, *Annual Report, 1953,* p. 3.

7. The Evolution of Concession Contracts

1. George Priest argues that the municipal contracts of the nineteenth century evolved in three distinct phases, as the importance of these utilities and the difficulty of writing complete contracts became clearer. The early contracts were vague, later contracts were very specific, and in the third and final phase the contracts granted substantial discretion to independent boards or commissions. Priest's analysis of the pressures that caused contracts to evolve is compelling, but very few contracts seem to have reached his third stage. See George L. Priest, "The Origins of Utility Regulation and the 'Theories of Regulation' Debate," *Journal of Law and Economics* 36 (April 1993), esp. pp. 301–320.

2. Letty Anderson, "Fire and Disease: The Development of Water Supply Systems

in New England, 1870–1900," in *Technology and the Rise of the Networked City in Europe and America,* ed. Joel A. Tarr and Gabriel Dupuy (Philadelphia: Temple University Press, 1988), p. 143.

3. In 1897 only nine of the fifty largest U.S. cities still had private water systems, while twelve had always had public systems and nineteen had started with private systems that were bought out by the public. Moses N. Baker, "Water-works," in *Municipal Monopolies,* ed. Edward W. Bemis (New York: Thomas Crowell, 1899), pp. 27–28.

4. Christopher Armstrong and H. V. Nelles, *Monopoly's Moment: The Organization and Regulation of Canadian Utilities, 1830–1930* (Philadelphia: Temple University Press, 1986), pp. 12–16.

5. Baker, "Water-works," pp. 24, 28.

6. Delos F. Wilcox, *Municipal Franchises: A Description of the Terms and Conditions upon Which Private Corporations Enjoy Special Privileges in the Streets of American Cities,* 2 vols. (Rochester, N.Y.: Gervaise Press, 1910 and 1911), 1:533–534.

7. For brief accounts of the evolution of the gas industry and regulation in the United States, see C. Woody Thompson and Wendell R. Smith, *Public Utility Economics* (New York: McGraw-Hill, 1941), pp. 15–24; and Richard J. Pierce, "Reconstituting the Natural Gas Industry from Wellhead to Burnertip," *Energy Law Journal* 9 (1988): 1–57.

8. The account of the Spring Valley company that follows is based primarily on Charles D. Jacobson, "Same Game, Different Players: Problems in Urban Public Utility Regulation," *Urban Studies* 26 (1989): 13–31; Charles D. Jacobson, "Water Works, Electric Utilities, and Cable Television: Contrasting Historical Patterns of Ownership and Regulation" (Ph.D. dissertation, Carnegie Mellon University, 1988); and Wilcox, *Municipal Franchises,* 1:423–440.

9. Wilcox, *Municipal Franchises,* 1:534.

10. This history of Toronto's gas franchises is based primarily on Armstrong and Nelles, *Monopoly's Moment,* pp. 13–14, 17–18, 22–30, 81–82, 151–152; and John R. Baldwin, *Regulatory Failure and Renewal: The Evolution of the Natural Monopoly Contract* (Ottawa: Economic Council of Canada, 1989), pp. 56–58.

11. The owner of Toronto Gas, Light and Water was Albert Furniss, who had established Montreal's gas company in 1836. Furniss sold only the gas operations of his company to Consumers' Gas. In the case of water, the city also franchised a second provider in the late 1840s, and Furniss again extinguished any chance for competition by selling his water system to the newcomer. When the newcomer defaulted on its debts in 1853, however, Furniss resumed control of the water system. The city renegotiated hydrant charges and domestic water rates several times during the next two decades, but the acrimony encouraged popular support for a municipal takeover. In 1872, taking advantage of a strong economy and a good market for municipal bonds, Toronto negotiated a buyout price that was acceptable to Furniss's estate.

12. Armstrong and Nelles, *Monopoly's Moment,* p. 29.

13. In 1890 there were 597 street railways not powered by electricity. Most were powered by horses, but a few were run by steam dummy engines. Thompson

and Smith, *Public Utility Economics,* p. 50; and Bemis, *Municipal Monopolies,* p. 505.

14. Thompson and Smith, *Public Utility Economics,* p. 52.

15. These stages are drawn from Thompson and Smith, *Public Utility Economics,* pp. 37–50. See also Thomas Parke Hughes, *Networks of Power: Electrification in Western Society, 1860–1930* (Baltimore: Johns Hopkins University Press, 1983).

16. The following year, the state also began to invest public funds in westward extensions of private railroads. Irston R. Barnes, *Public Utility Control in Massachusetts: A Study in the Commission Regulation of Securities and Rates* (New Haven: Yale University Press, 1930), pp. 87–88.

17. This buyout provision was eliminated in 1874.

18. These were, respectively, the South Boston, Metropolitan, Cambridge, and Middlesex railways. In addition, a fifth major railway, the Lynn and Boston, served communities on the north shore by connecting with the Middlesex railway at Charlestown. For a history of Boston's street railways, see Charles W. Cheape, *Moving the Masses: Urban Public Transit in New York, Boston, and Philadelphia, 1880–1912* (Cambridge: Harvard University Press, 1980), pp. 107–120.

19. Robert Harvey Whitten, *Public Administration in Massachusetts: The Relation of Central to Local Activity* (New York: Columbia University Press, 1898), p. 112.

20. Walter S. Allen, "Street Railway Franchises in Massachusetts," *Annals of the American Academy of Political and Social Science* 27 (January 1906): 109.

21. Whitten, *Public Administration in Massachusetts,* pp. 123–124.

22. See, for example, the story of how Roslindale acquired 5-cent fares to Boston in Louis D. Brandeis, "The Experience of Massachusetts in Street Railways," *Municipal Affairs* 6 (Winter 1902): 721–723.

23. Allen, "Street Railway Franchises in Massachusetts," p. 92.

24. Massachusetts, *Acts,* 1864, 229 as summarized in Whitten, *Public Administration in Massachusetts,* p. 113.

25. The committee also recommended a law that the legislature failed to pass. That law would have required a city to show "extraordinary conditions" and "good and sufficient reasons" before it could revoke a street railway franchise. See Allen, "Street Railway Franchises in Massachusetts," p. 94; and Whitten, *Public Administration in Massachusetts,* p. 113–114.

26. Advocates of the board contended that the legislature was burdened by the large number of individual railway bills, that legislators did not have the time to develop expertise in railway matters, and that powerful railway interests often exercised undue influence. Leonard D. White, "The Origin of Utility Commissions in Massachusetts," *Journal of Political Economy* 29 (March 1921): 177–197, esp. 184–189.

27. On the pioneering and influential nature of the board, see Thomas K. McCraw, *Prophets of Regulation: Charles Francis Adams, Louis D. Brandeis, James M. Landis, and Alfred E. Kahn* (Cambridge: Harvard University Press, 1984), pp. 1–56, esp. 16.

28. The board had some very limited powers to compel tariffs on steam railways, particularly in the case of the transportation of milk.

29. This law was passed in 1874; see Whitten, *Public Administration in Massachusetts*, p. 115.

30. The Highland Street Railway was chartered in 1872 to compete against the Metropolitan Railroad, and the Charles River Street Railway was chartered in 1881 to compete against the Cambridge Railroad.

31. Prentiss Cummings, "The Street Railway System of Boston," in *Professional and Industrial History of Suffolk County, Massachusetts* (Boston: Boston History Company, 1894), p. 291.

32. For a fascinating account of this era by a contemporary railway manager, see Cummings, "The Street Railway System of Boston," pp. 286–302.

33. Allen, "Street Railway Franchises in Massachusetts," p. 98.

34. Whitten, *Public Administration in Massachusetts*, p. 119.

35. For a more complete description of the street railway franchise taxes established in 1898, see Brandeis, "The Experience of Massachusetts in Street Railways," pp. 725–726.

36. Allen, "Street Railway Franchises in Massachusetts," p. 97.

37. The state also guaranteed that it would not impose additional taxes or fees for twenty-five years. For a description of the contract see Allen, "Street Railway Franchises in Massachusetts," p. 106.

38. According to one expert of the time, "the zone fare breeds tenements"; see Paul Barrett, *The Automobile and Urban Transit: The Formation of Public Policy in Chicago, 1900–1930* (Philadelphia: Temple University Press, 1983), p. 24. For a more complete account of the support for the 5-cent fare, see Edward S. Mason, *The Street Railway in Massachusetts: The Rise and Decline of an Industry* (Cambridge: Harvard University Press, 1932), pp. 119–121.

39. Mason, *The Street Railway in Massachusetts*, pp. 12, 15.

40. Ibid., p. 139.

41. The new PUC was called the Public Service Commission and was reorganized as the Department of Public Utilities in 1919; Barnes, *Public Utility Control in Massachusetts*, pp. 16–19.

42. Mason, *The Street Railway in Massachusetts*, pp. 156–159.

43. For an excellent account of the period of trusteeship and the 1947 sale, see Warren H. Deem, *The Problem of Boston's Metropolitan Transit Authority*, publication no. 20 of the Bureau for Research in Municipal Government, Graduate School of Public Administration, Harvard University, 1953, pp. 3–22.

44. This account of Samuel Insull is based primarily on Forrest McDonald, "Samuel Insull and the Movement for State Utility Regulatory Commissions," *Business History Review* 32, no. 3 (Autumn 1958): 241–254; Forrest McDonald, *Insull* (Chicago: University of Chicago Press, 1962), esp. pp. 82–120; and Hughes, *Networks of Power*, esp. pp. 201–226.

45. In his 1898 speech, Insull argued that regulation was needed but recognized the problems and costs of regulatory risk: "In order to protect the public, exclusive franchises should be coupled with the conditions of public control, requiring all charges for services fixed by public bodies to be based on cost plus a reasonable profit. It will be found that this cost will be reduced in direct proportion to the protection afforded the industry. The more certain this protection is made, the

lower the rate of interest and the lower the total cost of operation will be, and, consequently, the lower the price of the service to public and private users." Samuel Insull, "Standardization, Cost System of Rates, and Public Control," in *Central Station Electric Service: Its Commercial Development and Economic Significance as Set Forth in the Public Addresses of Samuel Insull,* ed. William Eugene Kelly (Chicago: privately printed, 1917), p. 45.

46. The aldermen, not understanding the reason for Insull's actions, gave a franchise to the company anyway, only to discover their error. The franchise had a fifty-year life, which was much longer than Insull's other franchises, so Insull bought it out for the relatively small sum of $50,000.

47. Insull's leadership in technology and marketing is described in Hughes, *Networks of Power,* pp. 201–226.

48. Average rates for residential and small commercial accounts fell more slowly, from 20 cents in 1892 to 10 cents in 1908; see McDonald, *Insull,* p. 104. Insull's policy of lower rates for large customers was controversial, and city officials allowed it largely because they had to defer to Insull's superior understanding of the complex economics of electric power; see Harold L. Platt, "The Cost of Energy: Technological Change, Rate Structures, and Public Policy in Chicago, 1880–1920," *Urban Studies* 26 (1989): 32–44, esp. 37–40.

49. The Peoples Gas rate disputes are recounted in Platt, "The Cost of Energy," pp. 36–37; and Werner Troesken, "The Institutional Antecedents of State Utility Regulation: The Chicago Gas Industry," in *The Regulated Economy: A Historical Approach to Political Economy,* ed. Claudia Golden and Gary Libecap (Chicago: University of Chicago Press for the National Bureau of Economic Research, 1994), pp. 55–80, esp. 64–70.

50. This account of street railway policy and politics in Chicago is based primarily on Barrett, *The Automobile and Urban Transit,* pp. 9–45; and Wilcox, *Municipal Franchises,* 2:141–172.

51. See, for example, Bemis, "Street Railways," pp. 529–531.

52. One of Yerkes's most famous misquotes was that "the straphangers pay the dividends," which was popularly interpreted as meaning that the overcrowding of cars was the source of high railway profits. Barrett reports that Yerkes was actually trying to explain that long lines into thinly populated territory are unprofitable. According to Barrett, the original quote was "The short hauls and the people who hang on the straps are the ones we make our money on . . . We make no money on the man who has a seat and rides to the end of the line." Barrett, *The Automobile and Urban Transit,* p. 19.

53. The debate would be resolved in 1907 in favor of more comprehensive municipal regulation, but by 1947 the automobile had weakened the companies so much that they had to be taken over by the city.

54. The description of the debate between the advocates of municipal and state control is drawn primarily from David Nord, "The Experts versus the Experts: Conflicting Philosophies of Municipal Utility Regulation in the Progressive Era," *Wisconsin Magazine of History* 58, no. 3 (Spring 1975): 219–236. For an overview of the origins of the Progressive movement, see Richard L. McCormick, "The Discovery That Business Corrupts Politics: A Reappraisal of

the Origins of Progressivism," *American Historical Review* 86 (1981): 247–274.

55. Stiles P. Jones as quoted in Nord, "The Experts versus the Experts," p. 234.

56. Charles Merriam as quoted in ibid., p. 232.

57. Balthasar Meyer as quoted in ibid., pp. 229–230.

58. The report had compared municipal and private operation in the United States and Britain and explained, "We wish to bring to your consideration the dangers here in the United States of turning over the utilities to the present governments of some of our cities. Some, we know, are well governed, and the situation as a whole seems to be improving, but they are not up to the government of British cities." National Civic Federation, *Municipal and Private Operation of Public Utilities* (New York: National Civic Federation, 1907), 1:25.

59. McDonald, "Samuel Insull and the Movement," p. 248.

60. Gregg A. Jarrell, "The Demand for State Regulation of the Electric Utility Industry," *Journal of Law and Economics* 21 (1978): 270.

61. National Civic Federation, *Draft Bill for the Regulation of Public Utilities, with Documents Relating Thereto* (New York: National Civic Federation, 1914).

62. McDonald, *Insull,* p. 100.

63. Hughes, *Networks of Power,* pp. 285–323.

64. This argument is made by Baldwin, *Regulatory Failure and Renewal,* pp. 55–56; and by Charles David Jacobson, "Private Firms and Public Goods: A Historical Perspective on Contracting Out for Public Services," in *Public Private Partnerships: Privatization in Historical Perspective,* vol. 16 of *Essays in Public Works History* (Washington, D.C.: Public Works Historical Society, 1989), pp. 48–77, esp. 62.

65. Armstrong and Nelles, *Monopoly's Moment,* pp. 30–32.

66. Thompson and Smith, *Public Utility Economics,* p. 603.

67. For a brief history of the origins of the cable TV industry, see Robert W. Crandall and Harold Furchtgott-Roth, *Cable TV: Regulation or Competition?* (Washington, D.C.: Brookings Institution, 1996), pp. 1–4.

68. The Oakland story is well known because Oliver Williamson used it to illustrate his 1976 critique of Harold Demsetz's proposal for contract regulation; see Chapter 5 and Oliver E. Williamson, "Franchise Bidding for Natural Monopolies—in General and with Respect to CATV," *Bell Journal of Economics* 7, no. 1 (Spring 1976): 73–104, esp. 91–101.

69. Robin A. Prager, "Firm Behavior in Franchise Monopoly Markets," *RAND Journal of Economics* 21, no. 2 (Summer 1990): 211–225.

70. Competitive awards increased the share reporting serious disputes by 16 percentage points, a result that was statistically significant at the 10 percent level; ibid., p. 220.

71. Rate regulation also increased the share reporting serious disputes by 16 percent, a difference that was statistically significant at the 5 percent level. Prager expects fewer disputes with rate regulation if concessionaires are opportunistic, but more disputes seem likely, because the control of rates would make it harder to exploit monopoly power without altering the contract; ibid., pp. 223–224.

72. In a related finding, Mark Zupan argues that disputes were most common in big

city systems in the early 1980s because FCC regulations had restricted the development of big city systems more than rural systems. When FCC regulations were relaxed in the late 1970s, the experience in rural systems may have caused bidders to underestimate costs and overestimate penetration in big cities. Zupan also performs a statistical analysis of sixty-eight Massachusetts franchises and finds that the degree to which predicted market penetration fell short of actual penetration is not affected by the number of bidders for the franchise, a finding that is inconsistent with opportunism. See Mark A. Zupan, "The Efficacy of Franchise Bidding Schemes in the Case of Cable Television: Some Systematic Evidence," *Journal of Law and Economics* 32 (October 1989): 401–441.

73. Mark A. Zupan, "Cable Franchise Renewals: Do Incumbent Firms Behave Opportunistically?" *RAND Journal of Economics* 20, no. 4 (Winter 1989): 473–482.

74. Specifically, Zupan found that the renewals promised slightly fewer channels and charged higher rates for premium tier service than the initial franchises. The prices for basic tier service, the franchise fee, and the number of community channels were not discernibly different.

75. For typical complaints, see Pamela Varley, *Cable Wars,* case no. C15-86-716, Case Program, Kennedy School of Government, Harvard University, 1986.

76. Zupan, "The Efficacy of Franchise Bidding Schemes," pp. 404–407.

77. See, for example, T. W. Hazlett, "The Demand to Regulate Franchise Monopoly: Evidence from CATV Rates," *Economic Inquiry* 29 (1991): 275–296; or Robert N. Rubinovitz, "Market Power and Price Increases for Basic Cable Service since Deregulation," *RAND Journal of Economics* 24, no. 1 (Spring 1993): 1–18.

78. Crandall and Furchtgott, *Cable TV,* pp. 25–32; and Yasuji Otsuka, "A Welfare Analysis of Local Franchise and Other Types of Regulation: Evidence from Cable TV," *Journal of Regulatory Economics* 11 (1997): 158–159.

79. John W. Mayo and Yasuji Otsuka, "Demand, Pricing, and Regulation: Evidence from the Cable TV Industry," *RAND Journal of Economics* 22, no. 3 (Autumn 1991): 396–410; and Otsuka, "A Welfare Analysis of Local Franchise," pp. 157–180.

80. Under the terms of the Cable Communications Policy Act of 1984, the FCC ruled that as of 1987 municipalities could not regulate rates of cable systems in communities that had three or more broadcast TV stations, since three stations were enough to provide effective competition.

81. For a strong proponent of this view, see Crandall and Furchtgott-Roth, *Cable TV.*

82. The Cable Television Consumer Protection and Competition Act of 1992 was amended by the Telecommunications Act of 1996.

83. Many municipalities had contracted with private firms for solid waste collection and disposal services in the nineteenth century, but many converted from private to municipal provision, often under the influence of Progressive reformers seeking to reduce corruption. For a history of the industry, see Martin V. Melosi, *Garbage in the Cities: Refuse, Reform, and the Environment, 1880–1980* (College Station: Texas A&M Press, 1981). For an account of the motives behind

the recent private revival, see José A. Gómez-Ibáñez, John R. Meyer, and David Luberoff, "The Prospects for Privatizing Infrastructure: Lessons from the U.S. Roads and Solid Waste," *Journal of Transport Economics and Policy* 25 (September 1991): 259–278.

84. Geoffrey F. Segal and Adrian T. Moore, "Privatizing Landfills: Market Solutions for Solid-Waste Disposal," Policy Study no. 267, Reason Public Policy Institute, Los Angeles, May 2000, part 2.

85. For background on the trend, see Paul Seidenstat, Michael Nadol, and Simon Hakim, eds., *America's Water and Wastewater Industries: Competition and Privatization* (Vienna, Va.: Public Utility Reports, 2000), esp. chap. 1.

86. According to a 1995 survey by the U.S. Environmental Protection Agency, 93 percent of the population was served by community water systems while the balance was served by noncommunity systems, including wells serving a single household or business. Of the population served by community water systems, 13 percent were served by privately owned systems and only half of these were investor owned. If the typical investor- and non-investor-owned private community systems are roughly the same size, this suggests roughly 6 percent of the population was served by investor-owned companies. U.S. Environmental Protection Agency, *Overview*, vol. 1 of *Community Water System Survey*, January 1997, pp. 5, 7.

87. Survey by the International City/County Managers' Association as reported in Robin Johnson and Adrian Moore, "Opening the Floodgates: Why Water Privatization Will Continue," Policy Brief 17, Reason Public Policy Institute, Los Angeles, August 2001, p. 2.

88. Paul Eisenhardt, Andrew Stocking, and William G. Reinhardt, "Gradual Growth and 17 Deals Mark 1997 Waste and Wastewater Contract Operations," *Public Works Financing* (March 1998): 1–10.

89. "Water Privatization Scorecard," *Public Works Financing* 164 (July–August 2002): 8.

90. Seidenstat, Nadol, and Hakim, *America's Water and Wastewater Industries*, p. 13.

8. The Rediscovery of Private Contracts

1. Alfred D. Chandler, Jr., *The Visible Hand: The Managerial Revolution in American Business* (Cambridge: Harvard University Press, 1977), esp. chaps. 3–5.

2. The first state railroad commission with a broad mandate was created by Massachusetts in 1869, but it was advisory only and did not have the power to set tariffs. Other states established railroad commissions with the authority to control tariffs beginning in the 1870s. See George H. Miller, *Railroads and the Granger Laws* (Madison: University of Wisconsin Press, 1971).

3. Gabriel Kolko, *Railroads and Regulation, 1877–1916* (Princeton: Princeton University Press, 1965); Paul MacAvoy, *The Economic Effects of Regulation: The Trunk-Line Railroad Cartels and the Interstate Commerce Commission before 1900* (Cambridge: MIT Press, 1965); Robert M. Spann and Edward W. Erickson, "The Economics of Railroading: The Beginnings of Cartelization and Regulation," *Bell Journal of Economics* 1, no. 2 (1970): 227–244; George W. Hil-

ton, "The Basic Behavior of Regulatory Commissions," *American Economic Review Papers and Proceedings* 62 (1972): 47–54.

4. The act also required the ICC to draft a plan to consolidate parallel railroads into larger and more efficient firms, but the ICC's plan was never implemented because the healthier railroads were reluctant to take over their poorer colleagues.

5. In the case of trucks, rates for shipments of unprocessed agricultural commodities were exempted from regulation, as were rates for carriers that served one firm exclusively. In the case of barges, rates for tows that included five or fewer commodities were exempted, which included most agricultural shipments.

6. The early studies of this type included John R. Meyer, Merton J. Peck, John Stenason, and Charles Zwick, *The Economics of Competition in the Transportation Industries* (Cambridge: Harvard University Press, 1959); and Ann F. Friedlaender, *The Dilemma of Freight Transportation Regulation* (Washington, D.C.: Brookings Institution, 1969).

7. This story is told in Aaron J. Gellman, "Surface Freight Transportation," in *Technological Change in Regulated Industries,* ed. William M. Capron (Washington, D.C.: Brookings Institution, 1971), pp. 166–196; and "Southern Railway System: The Big John Investment," case no. 9-677-244, Harvard Business School, 1977.

8. This account of the informal agreements is based on Thomas M. Palay, "Avoiding Regulatory Constraints: Contracting Safeguards and the Role of Informal Agreements," *Journal of Law, Economics, and Organization* 1, no. 1 (Fall 1985): 155–175.

9. Ibid., p. 165.

10. U.S. General Accounting Office, *Railroad Regulation: Changes in Rates and Service Quality since 1990,* report no. GAO-RECD-99-93, April 1999, p. 40.

11. U.S. General Accounting Office, *Railroad Regulation,* p. 45; John H. Winner, "The Future Structure of the North American Rail Industry," report to the Office of the Secretary, U.S. Department of Transportation, June 1998, p. 11.

12. Burlington Northern and Santa Fe chairman Robert D. Krebs as quoted in Winner, "Future Structure," p. 13. Winner cites as his source Daniel Machalaba, "Railroads Merging to Give Trucks a Run for the Money," *Wall Street Journal,* August 11, 1994.

13. A major exception was the disapproval of a proposed merger of the Southern Pacific and the Santa Fe railroads.

14. The four accounted for 94 percent of all the revenues collected by Class I railroads in the United States in 2001; American Association of Railroads, *Railroad Facts, 2002,* pp. 68–70, 74, 76.

15. In January 2000 the BNSF had expanded the possibilities by announcing its intention to merge with Canadian National (CN), one of Canada's two transcontinental railroads. The BNSF withdrew the proposal after it became clear that the STB was unlikely to approve it without lengthy delays and onerous conditions.

16. The STB considered shippers to be captive if they met three conditions: (1) only one railroad serves either the origin or the destination of their shipment; (2) they have no barge or rail alternative, at least at reasonable cost; and (3) they do

not face significant competition from other products or from companies producing the same product at other locations. If a shipper lacks competition from other products or locations, then the railroad that serves it will not be able to charge a higher price without driving it out of business. See Curtis Grimm and Clifford Winston, "Competition in the Deregulated Railroad Industry: Sources, Effects, and Policy Issues" in *Deregulation of Network Industries: What's Next*, ed. Sam Peltzman and Clifford Winston (Washington, D.C.: Brookings Institution, 2000), pp. 63–64.

17. The division of Conrail between NS and CSX involved extensive track rights as well. For a summary of the track rights, see Paul D. Larson and H. Barry Spraggins, "The American Railroad Industry: Twenty Years after Staggers," *Transportation Quarterly* 54, no. 2 (2000): 35–36.

18. Transcontinental mergers might generate important cost savings and service improvements by eliminating delays at Chicago and the Mississippi River crossings where the eastern and western railroads meet. Winner, "Future Structure," pp. 17, 20.

19. Grimm and Winston, "Competition in the Deregulated Railroad Industry," p. 64.

20. Ibid., p. 56.

21. Information on how frequently contracts were used before deregulation is hard to find, because contracts were illegal at the time. However, the significant increase in unit trains and multiple-car shipments immediately after deregulation suggests a large expansion in contracting. See James M. McDonald, "Railroad Deregulation, Innovation, and Competition: Effects of the Staggers Act on Grain Transportation," *Journal of Law and Economics* 32 (April 1989): 72.

22. Paul L. Joskow, "The Performance of Long-Term Contracts: Further Evidence from Coal Markets," *RAND Journal of Economics* 21, no. 2 (Summer 1990): 251–274.

23. The 21 percent estimate is from Grimm and Winston, "Competition in the Deregulated Railroad Industry," p. 65. Other studies of rail rates since 1980 have shown that rates are lower where shippers are served by more than one railroad or have the option of using barges, a finding that suggests that contracts are not as effective as actual competition. See MacDonald, "Railroad Deregulation, Innovation, and Competition," pp. 63–95, and James M. MacDonald, "Competition and Rail Rates for the Shipment of Corn, Soybeans, and Wheat," *Rand Journal of Economics* 18, no. 1 (Spring 1987): 151–163.

24. Regulation would be needed, since neither group would be able to offer the large railroads the prospect of reciprocal access to their own track.

25. The concerns about monopoly were the result of government action rather than inherent in the technology. Senate investigations in 1934 had revealed that the Postmaster General had reduced competition and divided up markets in its allocation of contracts to carry airmail, which were an important part of airline revenue at the time.

26. Richard E. Caves, *Air Transport and Its Regulators* (Cambridge: Harvard University Press, 1962).

27. Intrastate comparisons were developed by Michael E. Levine, "Is Regulation Necessary? California Air Transportation and National Regulatory Policy," *Yale*

Law Journal 74, no. 8 (July 1965): 1416–1447; William A. Jordan, *Airline Regulation in America: Effects and Imperfections* (Baltimore: Johns Hopkins University Press, 1970); and Theodore Keeler, "Airline Deregulation and Market Performance," *Bell Journal of Economics and Management Science* 3 (August 1972): 399–424.

28. Early and influential discussions of service quality competition include Jordan, *Airline Regulation in America;* George W. Douglas and James C. Miller III, *Economic Regulation and Domestic Air Transport: Theory and Policy* (Washington, D.C.: Brookings Institution, 1974); Arthur S. DeVany, "The Revealed Value of Time in Air Travel," *Review of Economics and Statistics* 56 (1974): 77–82; and George C. Eads, "Competition in the Domestic Trunk Airline Industry: Too Much or Too Little?" in *Promoting Competition in Regulated Markets,* ed. Almarin Phillips (Washington, D.C.: Brookings Institution, 1975), pp. 13–54.

29. See Ivor P. Morgan, "Government and the Industry's Early Development" and "Toward Deregulation," chapters 2 and 3 in John R. Meyer, Clinton V. Oster, Jr., et al., *Airline Deregulation: The Early Experience* (Boston: Auburn House Publishing, 1981).

30. William J. Baumol, John C. Pauzen, and Robert D. Willig, *Contestable Markets and the Theory of Industry Structure* (New York: Harcourt, Brace, Jovanovich, 1982).

31. Steven A. Morrison and Clifford Winston, "The Remaining Role for Government Policy in the Deregulated Airline Industry," in *Deregulation of Network Industries: What's Next?* ed. Sam Peltzman and Clifford Winston (Washington, D.C.: Brookings Institution, 2000), pp. 1–2.

32. All figures in 1993 dollars. Morrison and Winston estimate that the consumer benefits from added frequencies and on-line connections were $10.3 and $0.9 billion, respectively. Consumer losses from higher load factors, fare restrictions, added connections, and slower flight times were $0.6, $1.1, $0.7, and $2.8 billion, respectively. Steven Morrison and Clifford Winston, *The Evolution of the Airline Industry* (Washington, D.C.: Brookings Institution, 1995), p. 82.

33. See, for example, Transportation Research Board, *Entry and Competition in the U.S. Airline Industry: Issues and Opportunities* (Washington, D.C.: National Academy of Sciences Press, 1999); and Transportation Research Board, *Winds of Change: Domestic Air Transport since Deregulation* (Washington, D.C.: National Academy of Sciences Press, 1991), p. 74.

34. Another stakeholder group experiencing mixed results under deregulation was labor. Those working in the industry at the time almost surely lost as competition brought greater efforts to control wages and improve productivity. Labor as a whole may have won, however, since the probability of lower average wages was substantially, and possibly totally, offset by the prospect of greater growth and employment in this traditionally high-wage industry.

35. For example, Southern absorbed North Central (1979) and Hughes Airwest (1980) to become Republic, American took over Air California, Continental absorbed Texas International, and Eastern absorbed the new entrant People's Express.

36. In 1986 Northwest absorbed Republic, Delta took over Western, and TWA ab-

sorbed Ozark, while in 1987 US Air (later renamed US Airways) took over Piedmont.

37. Continental, TWA, and America West were also driven into bankruptcy between 1990 and 1992, although these three carriers emerged from bankruptcy to continue to operate.

38. Of the other surviving old guard carriers, Alaska Airlines also has an important presence, although it is confined mainly to the West Coast.

39. That airline is America West; see Morrison and Winston, "The Remaining Role," p. 9.

40. A plane of Valujet, now known as AirTran, crashed into the Florida Everglades.

41. A few new entrants offered business class or other premium services for somewhat higher fares than a no-frills service. These exceptions included AirTran, Jet Blue, Midway Airlines, and Midwest Express.

42. Transportation Research Board, *Entry and Competition*, p. 5.

43. As a result, a higher proportion of the seats reserved for full or walk-up fares depart empty, while the seats reserved for discount fares are sold out. The airlines attempt to control the costs of walk-up fares by overbooking and then holding auctions to free up seats if too many travelers show up.

44. Michael E. Levine, "Price Discrimination without Market Power," *Yale Journal of Regulation* 19, no. 1 (Winter 2002): 1–36.

45. Severin Borenstein and Nancy Rose, "Competition and Price Dispersion in the U.S. Airline Industry," *Journal of Political Economy* 102, no. 4 (1994): 653–683.

46. Using 1995 data, Joanna Stavins found that the dispersion in posted fares increased as the level of competition increased, suggesting that the high dispersion in the 1990s was still a sign of the presence of competition rather than the lack of it. Stavins's data are for posted fares rather than actual fares paid, however, and thus do not reflect the effect of capacity controls on the availability of deeply discounted fares. This may help explain why she finds that even the discounts for Saturday night stays, which are almost surely not cost based, increase with competition. Joanna Stavins, "Price Discrimination in the Airline Market: The Effect of Market Concentration," *Review of Economics and Statistics* 83, no. 1 (2001): 200–202.

47. General Accounting Office, *Airline Competition: Higher Fares and Reduced Competition at Concentrated Airports*, report GAO/RCED 90–102, July 1990.

48. See Morrison and Winston, *Evolution of the Airline Industry*, pp. 44–49; and the review of other studies at Don H. Pickrell, "Air Fare Premiums at Hub Airports: A Review of the Evidence," Volpe Center, U.S. Department of Transportation, draft, February 18, 2000, pp. 9, 11–13.

49. Pickrell, "Air Fare Premiums," pp. 9, 15; and Morrison and Winston, "The Remaining Role," p. 7.

50. Early studies with these results include Elizabeth Bailey, David R. Graham, and Daniel P. Kaplan, *Deregulating the Airlines* (Cambridge: MIT Press, 1985); and Steven A. Morrison and Clifford Winston, *The Economic Effects of Airline Dereg-*

ulation (Washington, D.C.: Brookings Institution, 1986); and Steven A. Morrison and Clifford Winston, "Evaluating the Performance of the Deregulated Airline Industry," *Brookings Papers on Economic Activities: Microeconomics* (1989): 73–75.

51. Morrison and Winston, "The Role of Government," pp. 33–35 and table 5.

52. The only empirical study of frequent flyer programs dates back to 1990, when American Airlines had the largest and best-developed program. That study estimated that American would have lost 18 percent of its market share if all frequent flyer programs had been eliminated and 50 percent if only American's program had been eliminated. The study probably overestimates the effects because it assumes that American would not lower its fares to compensate for the loss of the program. Morrison and Winston, *The Evolution of the Airline Industry*, pp. 58–59.

53. The Antitrust Division charged that American had driven Vanguard Airlines from American's Dallas–Fort Worth hub. For a fuller discussion of the definition of predation, see Transportation Research Board, *Entry and Competition*, pp. 86, 87.

54. Airline codes are the two-letter identifiers that appear before each flight number (for example, UA for United Airlines and LH for Lufthansa). When two airlines code share, they give certain flights operated by one airline a second flight number with the code of the other airline. Code sharing makes it appear as if each airline operates many more flights than it actually does.

55. Unfortunately, Pro Air was grounded in 2000 by the Federal Aviation Administration for maintenance problems and filed for bankruptcy shortly after. Michelene Maynard, "Big Corporations Combine to Negotiate Airline Fares," *New York Times*, March 12, 2002, p. C2.

56. Transportation Research Board, *Entry and Competition*, p. 61.

57. For a list of recommended actions to reduce barriers to entry in the U.S. airline industry, see ibid., pp. 99–132.

58. Louis S. Thompson, "Private Investment in Railways: Experience from South and North America and New Zealand," World Bank, draft report, 2001; and Javier Campos and Pedro Cantos, "Railways," in *Privatization and Regulation of Transport Infrastructure: Guidelines for Policymakers and Regulators*, ed. Antonio Estache and Ginés de Rus (Washington, D.C.: World Bank, 2000), pp. 171–234.

59. It is important not to confuse these access contracts with other types of contracts common in vertically unbundled industries. All vertically unbundled electricity systems allow very large electricity consumers to enter into direct long-term private contracts with generators, for example, and an increasing number of systems also allow small businesses or individual households to contract either directly with generators or with brokers who serve as intermediaries between the generators and the small consumers. These contracts between generators and consumers are extremely useful to protect both parties from short-term fluctuations in the wholesale prices for power. But they do not address the problem of access by the generators or the consumers to the monopoly transmission and distribution networks.

9. Price-Cap Regulation

1. Some observers argue that the United States has been slow to adopt price cap, and that some of the variants have been poorly thought out. See, for example, Michael A. Crew and Paul R. Kleindorfer, "Incentive Regulation in the United Kingdom and the Unites States: Some Lessons," *Journal of Regulatory Economics* 9, no. 3 (1996): 211–225.

2. One of the most careful telephone studies estimates, for example, that companies charged 3.9 percent less for basic business telephone service and had 5.5 percent more miles of fiber optic cable in states using price-cap regulation than in states using cost-of-service regulation. The companies subject to price-cap regulation also charged less for basic residential service and had more digital lines, but the differences are not statistically significant at the 10 percent level. For that study and a review of other similar studies, see Chunrong Ai and David E. M. Sappington, "The Impact of State Incentive Regulation on the U.S. Telecommunications Industry," *Journal of Regulatory Economics* 22, no. 2 (2002): 133–160. There are few studies of the effects of price-cap on electricity companies in the United States, perhaps because the states have been slower to adopt price-cap regulation for electricity than for telecommunications. One study estimates that price cap resulted in higher costs for electricity generation, but the differences are not statistically significant and the effects on distribution costs are not considered. Christopher R. Knittel, "Alternative Regulatory Methods and Firm Efficiency: Stochastic Frontier Evidence from the U.S. Electricity Industry," *Review of Economics and Statistics* 84, no. 3 (2002): 530–540.

3. These are the dates when the government began to sell companies to the private sector. In the cases of electricity and railroads, it took another year before all of the companies were sold.

4. See Chapters 4 and 8.

5. For a fascinating discussion of the intellectual roots of price cap, see Ingo Vogelsang, "Incentive Regulation and Competition in Public Utility Markets: A 20-year Perspective," *Journal of Regulatory Economics* 22, no. 1 (July 2002): 5–28.

6. The sliding scale also required potentially controversial calculations of past profit rates. Sliding-scale contracts fell out of use in part because the profit-sharing formulas were often made obsolete by changing economic circumstances and in part because by the mid-twentieth century, contract regulation was largely abandoned in favor of state PUC regulation in the United States and nationalization in Britain. Irvin Bussing, *Public Utility Regulation and the So-called Sliding Scale* (New York: Columbia University Press, 1936); Ralph Turvey, "The Sliding Scale: Price and Dividend Regulation in the Nineteenth Century Gas Industry," *Topics* note no. 16, National Economic Research Associates, London, 1995.

7. William J. Baumol, "Reasonable Rules for Rate Regulation: Plausible Policies for an Imperfect World," in *Prices: Issues in Theory Practice and Public Policy,* ed. Almarin Phillips and Oliver E. Williamson (Philadelphia: University of Pennsylvania Press, 1967), pp. 108–123, esp. 114–115. Baumol cited as his inspiration Schumpeter's observation that the prospect of excess profits in the short run is essential to motivate innovation.

8. The seminal contribution on this point was E. P. A. Ramsey, "A Contribution to the Theory of Taxation," *Economic Journal* 37 (March 1927): 47–61.

9. Stephen C. Littlechild, *Regulation of British Telecommunications' Profitability* (London: Department of Industry, 1983), para. 1.11.

10. Ibid., para. 13.11.

11. Ibid., para. 4.11.

12. MRR and ORPL also could be applied to monopoly services only, but only if costs were carefully allocated between monopoly and competitive services to determine the profits on those monopoly services.

13. The agencies governed by commissions of several regulators were the Civil Aviation Authority, which was empowered to regulate private airports in 1986, and Ofgem, a combined gas and electricity regulatory agency created in 1998 and reorganized as a commission in 2000.

14. This description of the industry prior to privatization is drawn primarily from John Vickers and George Yarrow, *Privatization: An Economic Analysis* (Cambridge: MIT Press, 1989), pp. 389–396; and Secretary of State for the Environment, Secretary of State for Wales, and the Minister of Agriculture, Fisheries and Food, *Privatisation of the Water Authorities in England and Wales* (London: Her Majesty's Stationery Office, 1986).

15. In the early 1980s, the European Community issued a Directive on Drinking Water Quality and a Directive on the Quality of Bathing Water which set standards that were to be achieved by 1995. It later issued other directives that affected the water industry, including a Directive on Urban Waste Water Treatment.

16. Secretary of State for the Environment et al., *Privatisation of the Water Authorities.*

17. Stephen C. Littlechild, *Economic Regulation of Privatised Water Authorities* (London: Her Majesty's Stationery Office, 1986). Much of the report is reprinted with some added comments in Stephen C. Littlechild, "Economic Regulation of Privatised Water Authorities and Some Further Reflections," *Oxford Review of Economic Policy* 4, no. 2 (Summer 1988): 40–67.

18. The utilities privatized before water were telecommunications, gas, and airports. In telecommunications, Littlechild noted, there was already competition in long-distance service, customer premises equipment, and the prospect for competition in local calling from wireless phone and cable TV. In gas there was competition from other fuels, while London's airports faced competition from other British and European airports as gateways to Britain or Europe.

19. The existing private companies had been governed by individual acts of Parliament that specified limits on the dividends they could offer their shareholders. The provisions of these individual statutes were replaced in 1990 by the price-cap regulatory scheme.

20. For an account of how the water authorities and private companies were prepared for privatization, see Mark Armstrong, Simon Cowan, and John Vickers, *Regulatory Reform: Economic Analysis and British Experience* (Cambridge: MIT Press, 1994), pp. 345–346.

21. Byatt explains his strategy in Ian Byatt, "Water: The Periodic Review Process,"

in *Utility Regulation: Challenge and Response,* ed. Michael E. Beesley (London: Institute of Economic Affairs, 1995), pp. 21–30.

22. Ofwat, *Setting Price Limits for Water and Sewerage Services: The Framework and Approach to the 1994 Periodic Review* (Birmingham: Ofwat, November 1993), p. 6.

23. Interview with Ian Byatt, London, June 27, 2001.

24. While Byatt was conducting the 1994 price review, he also used the interim determination provisions to adjust the K's several times.

25. Ofwat, *The Cost of Capital* (Birmingham: Ofwat, 1991); and Ofwat, *Assessing Capital Values* (Birmingham: Ofwat, 1992).

26. Ofwat, *The Cost of Quality* (Birmingham: Ofwat, August 1992).

27. Ofwat, *Paying for Quality: A Political Perspective* (Birmingham: Ofwat, July 1993).

28. Ofwat, *Report on the Cost of Water Delivered and Sewage Collected* (Birmingham: Ofwat, December 1994).

29. These figures are in constant 1994–1995 pounds; see Ofwat, *Future Charges for Water and Sewerage Services: The Outcome of the Periodic Review* (Birmingham: Ofwat, July 1994), pp. 7–8.

30. For Portsmouth Water, the commission reduced the K's. For South West Water, the commission left the K's the same but increased the investments required, making the old K's a tighter deal.

31. The early provisions for competitive supply are described in Colin Robinson, "Introducing Competition into Water" in *Regulating Utilities: Broadening the Debate,* ed. Michael E. Beesley (London: Institute of Economic Affairs, 1997), pp. 168–175.

32. The lowering of the threshold from 250 to 100 megaliters increased the number of eligible users from roughly 500 to 1,500 companies. Department of the Environment, *Increasing Consumer Choice: Competition in Water and Sewage Industries, the Government's Proposals* (London: Stationery Office, April 1996); and Ofwat, *The Regulation of Common Carriage Agreements in England and Wales: A Consultation Paper* (Birmingham: Ofwat, April 1996).

33. The number of bulk water buyers had increased from one or two in the mid-1990s to eight in 2000. For an optimistic account of the reforms, see Philip Fletcher, "Regulatory Developments: Moving Forward Towards Total Competition for Utilities?" speech at the Adam Smith Institute's Sixth Annual Conference on the Future of Utilities, London, March 14, 2001, esp. p. 4.

34. "Regulators Need Carrots That Stick," *Mail on Sunday,* April 2, 1995, p. 4.

35. See, for example, the comparison of Byatt and Littlechild's 1994 reviews in Dieter Helm, "Discussants' Comments," in *Utility Regulation,* ed. Beesley, pp. 31–35.

36. Department of Trade and Industry, *A Fair Deal for Consumers: Modernizing the Framework for Utility Regulation* (London: Stationery Office, 1998), para. 7.6, p. 44.

37. In other industries, future investment needs would also be a component of X. In the water industry, however, Byatt treated the investment needs as a separate factor Q in his formula RPI + K = RPI − X + Q.

38. In its final report for the 1999 review, Ofwat says adjustments were made for only "a few" companies, but there appear to have been more. Ofwat, *Final Determination: Future Water and Sewerage Charges 2000–5* (Birmingham: Ofwat, 1999), pp. 91–92.

39. Ofwat could use disaggregated data for company subareas or for individual large treatment plants to get additional observations for some sewage costs.

40. For example, two companies could have the same average population density in their service area, but one might have a mixture of high- and low-density districts while the other served districts that were all moderate density. The first company would have some mains that were larger than 0.3 meters; the second company might not. Competition Commission, *Sutton and East Surrey Water plc: A Report on the References under Sections 12 and 14 of the Water Industry Act 1991* (London: Stationery Office, August 2000), pp. 263–265.

41. The consulting firm was Europe Economics; Competition Commission, *Sutton and East Surrey Water plc,* pp. 256–258.

42. The consultants were Professor Derek Bosworth of University of Manchester and Professor Paul Stoneman of Warwick Business School. Competition Commission, *Sutton and East Surrey Water plc,* pp. 259–261.

43. These figures are in constant 1999–2000 pounds. Ofwat, *Final Determinations,* p. 23.

44. Ofwat also argued that the industry could lower its capital costs by using a higher ratio of debt to equity.

45. This fall occurred in the year between the announcements of the draft and the final price determinations. See Colin Mayer, "Water: The 1999 Price Review," in *Regulating Utilities: New Issues, New Solutions,* ed. Colin Robinson (London: Institute of Economic Affairs, 2001), p. 7.

46. House of Commons, Environmental Audit Committee, *Water Prices and the Environment* (London: Stationery Office, November 2000), vol. 1, summary paragraph (b).

47. Competition Commission, *Sutton and East Surrey Water plc,* p. 4; Competition Commission, *Mid Kent Water plc: A Report on References under Sections 12 and 14 of the Water Industry Act of 1991* (London: Stationery Office, August 2000), p. 4.

48. The commission did express concern that the Mid Kent model had not used the latest statistical techniques for estimating equations using data pooled from several years.

49. In the commission's words, "Ofwat's approach is not necessarily the only valid approach to the econometric analysis of the water service." Competition Commission, *Mid Kent Water,* p. 265.

50. The commission was also concerned that Thames Water's consultants had not controlled for the added cost of quarterly improvements when measuring cost trends in the water industry. Competition Commission, *Sutton and East Surrey Water plc,* p. 261.

51. The company was Welsh Water and the proposal stimulated an intense debate over whether nonprofits have the same incentives to control costs and whether the apparent savings from all-debt finance were real or just represented a transfer

of risk to other parties, primarily customers. José A. Gómez-Ibáñez, *Glas Cymru and the Debate over Non-profits,* teaching case, Infrastructure in a Market Economy Executive Program, Kennedy School of Government, Harvard University, July 2001; and Clive Stones, *Changes in the Pipeline? Economic and Public Policy Implications of Water Industry Restructuring* (London: Social Market Foundation, 2001).

52. Comptroller and Auditor General, *Pipes and Wires* (London: Stationery Office, 2002), pp. 4, 6, 7.

53. Ibid., p. 3.

54. Once Littlechild issued the companies' licenses with the new price caps, he could not change them without the companies' consent.

55. For the seminal article, see Harvey Averch and L. L. Johnson, "Behavior of the Firm under Regulatory Constraint," *American Economic Review* 52 (December 1962): 1052–1069. For a brief overview of the research this article stimulated, see W. Kip Viscusi, John M. Vernon, and Joseph E. Harrington, *Economics of Regulation and Antitrust,* 2d ed. (Cambridge: MIT Press, 1995), pp. 387–391.

56. If anything, some of the more sophisticated techniques, such as data envelope analysis, are probably more sensitive to problems posed by limited data sets and a variety of plausible specifications.

57. See, for example, the critique of Ofwat's estimates of the cost of capital in Ian Cooper and David Cumie, "The Cost of Capital for the U.K. Water Sector," Regulation Initiative Discussion Paper Series no. 28, London Business School, May 1999.

10. The Trade-off in Unbundling

1. Railroad cars were something of an exception, in that railroads would exchange cars so that shipments originating on one railroad and terminating on another did not have to be unloaded and reloaded in transit. In addition, large shippers often owned their own cars, particularly if the cars were dedicated or specialized.

2. Steven K. Vogel, *Freer Markets, More Rules: Regulatory Reform in Advanced Industrialized Countries* (Ithaca, N.Y.: Cornell University Press, 1996).

3. For a seminal and more complete discussion of vertical integration, see Oliver Williamson, *Markets and Hierarchies: Analysis and Antitrust Implications* (New York: Free Press, 1975).

4. This example is drawn from F. M. Scherer, *Industrial Structure, Conduct, and Performance* (Boston: Houghton Mifflin, 1980), p. 87.

5. An added complication in the negotiation is that the port authority is usually from the public sector and the bulk materials shipper from the private sector.

6. There are strong economies of pavement durability, so that the added cost of strengthening the pavement for trucks can be surprisingly modest; see Kenneth A. Small, Clifford Winston, and Carol A. Evans, *Road Work: A New Highway Pricing and Investment Policy* (Washington, D.C.: Brookings Institution, 1989).

7. For example, Sprint, one of the earliest competitors of AT&T's long-distance services, began as a private telephone system of the Southern Pacific Railroad.

8. Consider, as an example, the merger between a local and a long-distance telephone company. The merger would eliminate the potential for opportunism in between the two companies, but it would do nothing to reduce the dependence of retail subscribers on their local telephone company or vice versa. The pressure for regulation would be eliminated only if each local subscriber merged with or created its own local telephone company. This is not an unheard-of option. Large corporations have created private internal telephone systems, for example, particularly where local telephone rates are high or service unreliable. But these systems handle internal communications only. Switching calls between large numbers of private local telephone systems is more practical with a common local telephone company.

9. Rate rebalancing may not be enough to prevent assets from becoming stranded if the customers of the stranded assets are unwilling or unable to pay enough to make those assets profitable.

10. For a further explanation of vertical foreclosure, see an antitrust text such as W. Kip Viscusi, John M. Vernon, and Joseph E. Harrington, *Economics of Regulation and Antitrust*, 2d ed. (Cambridge: MIT Press, 1995), pp. 227–235.

11. In Chile, for example, some independent generators have complained that Enersis's transmission and distribution companies discriminate in favor of Enersis-owned generating companies in the purchase and dispatch of wholesale power. The complaining generators convinced Chile's antitrust agency to order Enersis to sell its high-voltage transmission company in 1999; Pablo Serra, "Regulación del Sector Eléctrico Chileno," *Perspectivas en Política, Economía, y Gestión* 6 (2002), no. 1, pp. 11–43; and Raimundo Sato and Eduardo Saavedra, "Post-Contractual Renegotiation and Disputes in Chile," Graduate Program in Economics, Georgetown University, Washington, D.C., August 1998.

12. Robert G. Harris and C. Jeffery Kraft, "Meddling Through: Regulating Local Telephone Competition in the United States," *Journal of Economic Perspectives* 11, no. 4 (Fall 1997): 102–107.

13. For a review of the choices see pp. 106–108 in *Essays in Transportation Economics and Policy: A Handbook in Honor of John R. Meyer*, ed. José A. Gómez-Ibáñez, William B. Tye, and Clifford Winston (Washington, D.C.: Brookings Institution, 1999).

14. The customers appear to be relatively insensitive to price in the short run, but the high prices provoke them to find alternatives so that in the long run their sensitivity to price is much greater.

15. Harris and Kraft, "Meddling Through," p. 104.

16. This argument was first made in Robert D. Willig, "The Theory of Network Access Pricing," in *Issues in Public Utility Regulation*, ed. Harry M. Trebing (East Lansing: Michigan State University, Public Utility Papers, 1979), pp. 109–152; and William J. Baumol, "Some Subtle Pricing Issues in Railroad Regulation," *Rivista Internazionale di Economia dei Transporti* 10 (1983): 341–355. For later accounts published in more accessible journals, see William J. Baumol, Janusz A. Ordover, and Robert D. Willig, "Parity Pricing and Its Critics: A Necessary Condition for Efficiency in the Provision of Bottleneck Services to Competitors," *Yale Journal of Regulation* 14 (1997): 145–163; and William J.

Baumol and Gregory J. Sidak, "The Pricing of Inputs Sold to Competitors," *Yale Journal of Regulation* 11 (1994): 171–202.

17. One famous such misinterpretation was by the British Privy Council in a ruling on a New Zealand telephone case. See Alan Bollard and Michael Pickford, "Utility Regulation in New Zealand" in *Regulating Utilities: Broadening the Debate,* ed. Michael E. Beesley (London: Institute of Economic Affairs, 1997), pp. 105–111; and Martín M. Calles, *Clear Communications Ltd. vs. Telecom Corporation of New Zealand (A) and (B),* case nos. 9-798-085 and 9-798-091, Case Program, Harvard Business School, 1998.

18. In the telephone context, Baumol and Willig were arguing that incumbent local telephone companies should not be forced to price access to their networks at marginal cost. The local telephone companies were burdened with universal service obligations and other cross-subsidies that new entrants did not have to deal with. To compensate, the local companies had always been allowed to charge some of their customers more than the marginal cost. See William J. Baumol, "Having Your Cake: How to Preserve Universal-Service Cross-Subsidies While Facilitating Competitive Entry," *Yale Journal of Regulation* 16 (1999): 1–17.

19. Regulators are likely to feel compelled to oversee the tariffs charged by the bottleneck supplier in addition to, or instead of, regulating the tariffs charged to the retail customer. In particular, retail price regulation alone is unworkable if the segment of the industry that serves the retail customer is competitive but it relies on key inputs from a bottleneck firm. Such a situation is typical in mobile telephones, for example, where two or more mobile companies often compete with one another but must purchase access to the lines of the local hard-wire telephone monopoly to complete many of their subscribers' calls. Regulating the retail prices charged by the mobile companies would put indirect pressure on the local hard-wire monopoly, but regulating the access charges the hard-wire company charged is a much more direct and reliable solution.

20. For these reasons financial capacity rights may be preferable to physical capacity rights. See James Bushnell, "Transportation Rights and Market Power," working paper PWP-062, Program on Workable Energy Regulation, University of California Energy Institute, Berkeley, April 1999.

11. Regulating Coordination

1. Amtrak's original route network of approximately 25,000 miles has contracted over the years as services have been cut to reduce financial losses. In 1970 the freight railroads granted Amtrak track rights for twenty-five years, and in 1996 those rights had to be renegotiated. See Paul Reistrup, "The United States," in European Conference of Ministers of Transport, *The Separation of Operations from Infrastructure in the Provision of Railway Services* (Paris: Organization for Economic Cooperation and Development, 1997), pp. 131–152, esp. 141.

2. No statistics on the use of track rights are available, but a sense of the scale of the operations can be gleaned from the examples in Reistrup, "The United States."

3. For an overview of these privatization efforts, see Louis S. Thompson and

Karim-Jacques Budin, "Railway Concessions: Progress to Date," *Rail International,* no. 01/02 (1998): 60–73.

4. As of 1996, private operators were operating only a few freight and regional passenger services, although the threat of competition was thought to have reduced the public train–operating company's costs. See Bertil Hylen, "Sweden," in European Conference of Ministers of Transport, *The Separation of Operations from Infrastructure in the Provision of Railway Services,* pp. 91–130, esp. 110–111.

5. Ibid., pp. 102–103, 105–106.

6. The reasoning behind the commission's policy is described at European Conference of Ministers of Transport, *Rail Restructuring in Europe* (Paris: Organization for Economic Cooperation and Development, 1998), pp. 9–12.

7. The commission further directed that public subsidies to infrastructure should be deducted from infrastructure costs when calculating the maximum permissible access charges. European Conference of Ministers of Transport, *Rail Restructuring,* pp. 14, 123–146; and Stuart Holder, "Recent Developments in Rail Infrastructure Charging in the European Union," *Journal of Transport Economics and Policy* 33, no. 1 (January 1999): 111–118.

8. Claude Henry and Emile Quinet, "Which Railways Policy and Organization for France?" *Journal of Transport Economics and Policy* 33, no. 1 (January 1999): 119.

9. Holder, "Recent Developments," p. 112; and European Conference of Ministers of Transport, *Rail Restructuring,* pp. 29–30.

10. For more detailed accounts of the privatization of British Rail, see John Welsby and Alan Nichols, "The Privatization of Britain's Railway: An Insider's View," *Journal of Transport Economics and Policy* 33, no. 1 (January 1999): 55–76; and Christian Wolmar, *Broken Rails: How Privatization Wrecked Britain's Railways* (London: Aurum Press, 2001).

11. For a description of the successful TOC bidders, see Nigel G. Harris and Ernest Goodward, *The Privatization of British Rail* (London: Railway Consultancy Press, 1997), pp. 93–101.

12. National Express, an intercity carrier, bought 5 alone; Prism, 4; Stagecoach, 2; MTL, 2; First Bus, 1; and Go-Ahead, 1.

13. The freight TOC responsible for intermodal containers was bought by its management, but the other six were acquired by Wisconsin Central, a U.S. regional railroad that had bought New Zealand's railway when it was privatized in 1993. Wisconsin Central persuaded the government that there was little to fear from its buying most of the freight TOCs, since they faced such stiff competition from trucks. In addition, major bulk shippers, such as National Power, had the right to (and for a time did) operate their own trains on Railtrack's tracks. Wisconsin Central named its new consolidated freight carrier the English Welsh & Scottish Railway, Ltd. (EWS).

14. Britain's government departments were reorganized several times during the 1990s, so that transport was initially a separate department; was later housed in the Department of the Environment, Transport and the Regions; and finally was placed in the Department of Transport, Local Government and the Regions.

For the sake of simplicity, we will refer to the secretary of state for transport and the Department of Transport.

15. The 1993 Railway Act required the regulator to "take into account guidance given to him from time to time by the Secretary of State" only until December 31, 1996, when the sale of British Rail was expected to be complete.

16. John Swift began work as the prospective rail regulator earlier in 1993, but was not officially appointed until the Railway Act passed.

17. At the time the Ministry of Transport set the initial charges, it expected to keep Railtrack in the public sector. As a result, the ministry used the accounting standards that Her Majesty's Treasury (HMT) had established for public corporations, which included an 8 percent return on the value of Modern Equivalent Assets (MEA). The MEA value was HMT's term for replacement cost.

18. The regulator is under no legal obligation to explain his decisions, and he did not provide any details on his calculations for the new access charges. See Office of the Rail Regulator, *Railtrack's Access Charges for Franchised Passenger Services. The Future Level of Charges: A Policy Statement* (London: ORR, January 1995).

19. Office of the Rail Regulator, *Competition for Railway Passenger Services: A Policy Statement* (London: ORR, December 1994).

20. Beginning on April 1, 1999, each TOC could nominate point-to-point passenger flows that it wanted protected and the regulator would limit entry to a maximum of 20 percent of a TOC's protected flows.

21. Punctuality and ridership fell off in fiscal years 1993/94 and 1994/95; Harris and Goodward, *The Privatization of British Rail,* pp. 114, 117.

22. In an analysis of the effects of real incomes, rail fares, auto use, and other factors on rail ridership since the 1920s, Stephen Glaister concluded that in 1994/95, the fiscal year right before the TOC sales, rail travel was about 7 percent lower than would have been normally expected on the basis of the usual explanatory variables. By fiscal year 1996/97, however, rail travel was 4 percent above expected and in 1997/98 it was 11 percent above expected. Stephen Glaister, "What New Strategy for the Railways?" Imperial College, London, November 24, 1998, pp. 6–7. John Preston uses plausible price and income elasticity estimates to reach similar conclusions; John Preston, "Franchising and Refranchising of Passenger Rail Services in Britain," *Transportation Research Record,* no. 1742 (2001): 3.

23. Strategic Rail Authority, *National Rail Trends 2001–02 (Quarter 1),* September 2001, pp. 23, 25.

24. Calculated from the figures in Table 11.2, the average real fare per passenger journey increased from £3.34 to £3.50 in 1999/00 pounds.

25. The postreform figures also include taxes that Railtrack and other private companies now pay on their profits, while the prereform figures do not. All figures in 1999/00 pounds.

26. On an equivalent accounting basis, for example, OPRAF estimates that in 1996/97 the government would have had to pay British Rail £2,118 million to provide the same services that OPRAF paid the TOCs £2,102 million for.

27. These figures are from Harris and Goodward, *The Privatization of British Rail,* pp. 130–132.

28. Some analysts disagree with this conclusion, most notably Peter White, who argues that even with the promised reductions in TOC subsidies, the privatization was a financial loss for the government. White uses relatively high real discount rates (6 to 8 percent), and his estimates of the profits made under the old British Rail system may not include adequate allowances for capital or depreciation. See Peter R. White, "Impacts of Rail Privatization in Britain," *Transport Reviews* 18, no. 2 (1998): 109–130.

29. Others feared that the TOCs had been encouraged to bid aggressively because they had relatively little money at risk. The TOCs did not have to invest in their own rolling stock and had to post a performance bond amounting to only 15 percent of annual revenues and to demonstrate an equivalent amount in reserve capital. Welsby and Nichols, "The Privatization of Britain's Railways," p. 67.

30. Wolmar, *Broken Rails,* p. 200–201.

31. Porterbrook Leasing had been sold to its management for £527 million in January 1996, and was resold to a large bus company for £825 million only seven months later. Eversholt Leasing was resold at an even larger premium, with one manager making £15.9 million on an investment of only £110,000 and two others making £11.6 million each on investments of £80,000. See Charles Batchelder and George Parker, "Staff Reap £57m Profit in Rail Deal," *Financial Times,* February 20, 1997.

32. National Audit Office, *The Flotation of Railtrack,* report by the Comptroller and Auditor General (London: Stationery Office, December 1998), pp. 2–3.

33. Ibid., p. 8. See also National Audit Office, *Privatization of the Rail Passenger Rolling Stock Leasing Companies,* report by the Comptroller and Auditor General (London: Stationery Office, 1998); and Charles Batchelder, "Watchdog to Review Rail Leasing Sell-off," *Financial Times,* January 7, 1997, p. 7.

34. The department's arguments are summarized in National Audit Office, *The Flotation of Railtrack.*

35. "Stagecoach Prepares for a Bumpy Ride" *Financial Times,* April 4, 1997, pp. 22; "Train Operators Learn the Hard Way," *Financial Times,* March 22, 1997, p. 4.

36. Newspaper accounts mention an understanding about increased investment in return for the write-off, but not a specific amount. The prospectus for Railtrack's stock describes the commitment before the write-off as one for £3,250 million in 1994/95 prices over five years, but later says that Railtrack plans to spend £4,709 million in 1995/96 prices over five years (not counting £3,416 million in routine maintenance). See SBC Warburg, *Railtrack Share Offer Prospectus,* May 1, 1996, pp. 34 and 68; and "Conspiracy Theorists Go to Work on Railtrack: But behind the 15p Share Price Fall Lies a More Complex Reality of Investments," *Financial Times,* January 18, 1997, p. 5.

37. Section 7 of Railtrack's license specified only that the statement describe the network's future capacity needs, the planned modifications, and how they were to

be financed. In September 1996 the ORR and Railtrack had developed a more complete description of what future statements would include and agreed that statements would be issued by March each year. Office of the Rail Regulator, *Railtrack's Network Management Statement: A Consultation Document* (London: ORR, September 1996).

38. The regulator issued a stinging report criticizing the statement; see Office of the Rail Regulator, *Railtrack's Investment Program: Statement by the Rail Regulator* (London: ORR, May 1997).

39. The track access agreements included performance penalties and bonuses for Railtrack. If Railtrack reduced delays or increased safe speeds beyond certain levels, for example, the TOCs would pay it a bonus that had been calculated as a share of the projected operating cost savings that the TOC would gain. Railtrack had been much more successful than anyone had suspected possible, and the TOCs were paying substantially more than they had expected. The regulator doubted this was the whole explanation, and, partly in response to complaints from the TOCs, announced that he intended to accelerate a review of the performance penalties.

40. See Department of the Environment, Transport and the Regions, *A New Deal for Transport: Better for Everyone, The Government's White Paper on the Future of Transport*, Cm 3950 (London: Stationery Office, 1998), pp. 94–100; and Deputy Prime Minister, *The Government's Response to the Environmental, Transport and Regional Affairs Committee's Report on the Proposed Strategic Railway Authority and Railway Regulation: A New Deal for Railways*, Cm 4024 (London: Stationery Office, July 1998).

41. Michael Grant, one of Morton's colleagues from the Eurotunnel, was appointed as the franchising director and the chief executive designate of the SRA.

42. However, the SRA would assume the rail regulator's responsibilities for investigating passenger complaints.

43. Swift resigned in November 1998 and Christopher Bolt, who had been the chief economist for the Office of the Rail Regulator, served as interim regulator until Winsor was appointed.

44. For a more complete description, see Office of Passenger Rail Franchising, *Passenger Rail Industry Overview* (London: OPRAF, June 1996), pp. 119–120.

45. The penalties and bonuses also consider any payments that the TOC must pay to OPRAF for poor punctuality or reliability. For a more complete description, see ibid., pp. 121–125.

46. The policy is summarized in Office of the Rail Regulator, *Criteria for the Approval of Passenger Track Agreements, Second Edition* (London: ORR, March 1995), pp. 23–24; and Office of the Rail Regulator, *New Service Opportunities for Passengers: A Consultation Document* (London: ORR, June 1998), pp. 23–24.

47. For historical data on punctuality, see Harris and Goodward, *The Privatization of British Rail*, p. 114.

48. Office of the Rail Regulator, *Criteria for the Approval of Passenger Track Access Agreements*, p. 23.

49. Unpublished graphs from a presentation by Railtrack chief executive Gerald

Corbett to the Oxford Economic Research Associates (OXERA) seminar on the role of the Strategic Rail Authority, February 2, 1999.

50. Office of the Rail Regulator, *The Periodic Review of Access Charges: A Proposed Framework and Key Issues: A Consultation Document* (London: ORR, December 1997), pp. 31–36; and Office of the Rail Regulator, *The Periodic Review of Access Charges: The Regulator's Conclusions on the Financial Framework, Third Paper* (London: ORR, December 1998), pp. 12–13.

51. The final report estimated that Railtrack would collect £9,398 million in basic access charges plus £392 million in "capacity" charges for additional paths over the five-year control period. Of the £9,398 million, £871 million (9.3 percent) would vary by train kilometers, £751 million (8.0 percent) by electricity consumed, and £7,776 million would be fixed. Office of the Rail Regulator, *The Periodic Review of Railtrack's Access Charges: Final Conclusions* (London: ORR, October 2000), vol. 1, pp. 77–91.

52. Presuming that only half the congestion costs were reflected in the access fee, congestion over the five-year period would be £784 million; ibid., pp. 82, 87, 88, 91.

53. The role that restructuring might have played in all three accidents is analyzed in depth in Wolmar, *Broken Rails,* pp. 1–10, 118–179.

54. U.K., Health and Safety Executive, *Train Accident at Ladbroke Grove Junction, 5 October 1999; Third HSE Interim Report,* April 14, 2000 (at www://www. hse.gov.uk/railway/paddrail/interim3.htm).

55. Office of the Rail Regulator, *The Periodic Review of Railtrack's Access Charges: Final Conclusions,* vol. 1, pp. 54–55.

56. Wolmar, *Broken Rails;* and Ian Jack, "The 12.10 to Leeds," *Granta,* April 2001, pp. 69–105, esp. 94–98.

57. Office of the Rail Regulator, *Investments in the Enhancement of the Rail Network,* March 1996.

58. For a description and history of the WCML, see Office of the Rail Regulator, *The Periodic Review of Railtrack's Access Charges: The West Coast Route Modernisation* (London: ORR, June 2000), pp. 12–15.

59. Interview granted on condition of anonymity.

60. Signal systems warn trains against entering a "block" of track that is occupied by another train. In a fixed-block system, the boundaries of the blocks are fixed and wayside signals tell the operator whether approaching blocks are occupied. In a moving-block system the boundaries of the occupied block move constantly with the moving train, and signals that appear on a screen on the train driver's console warn about the status of the track ahead. Moving-block systems squeeze more capacity out of a given set of tracks.

61. Office of the Rail Regulator, *The Regulator's Conclusions on the Tenth Supplemental Agreement to the Track Access Agreement between Railtrack PLC and West Coast Trains Ltd (the "PUG2" Agreement)* (London: Orr, July 1998).

62. The four areas were freight services, regional services around Birmingham, commuter services in Manchester, and commuter services near London from Euston to Northampton. Office of the Rail Regulator, *The Regulator's Conclusions on the Tenth Supplemental Agreement,* pp. 34–35.

63. Strategic Rail Authority, *A Strategic Agenda,* March 2001, p. 10.
64. Ibid., p. 10.
65. Department of the Environment, Transport and the Regions, *Transport 2010: The 10 Year Plan,* July 2000.
66. Office of the Rail Regulator, *The Periodic Review of Railtrack's Access Charges: West Coast Route Modernisation,* pp. 4, 15.
67. Office of the Rail Regulator, *The Periodic Review of Railtrack's Access Charges: Final Conclusions,* vol. 1, pp. 178–182.
68. Strategic Rail Authority, *A Strategic Agenda,* pp. 22–24, 46–51.
69. Network Rail is a "company limited by guarantee." Britain's water regulator established the precedent for using this form of nonprofit for infrastructure in 2001, when he approved the sale of one of the private water and sewage companies to a company limited by guarantee (see Chapter 9).
70. The guarantees provoked a dispute among government watchdog and auditing agencies as to whether Network Rail should be considered a dependency of government and the debts counted against public borrowings. See David Litterick and Alistair Osborne, "Statistics Head Acts in Rail Row," *Daily Telegraph,* November 19, 2002, p. 31; and Alistair Osborne, "Labour's Third Way on Wheels is Careering Off the Rails," *Daily Telegraph,* December 18, 2002, p. 20.
71. For example, the Regulator's 1995 decision to reduce access charges was justified in part on the grounds that Railtrack did not need to earn a return on the replacement value of its entire network—it needed a return only on the investments in renewals as they became necessary.

12. Designing Capacity Markets

1. New Zealand began to privatize and restructure its electricity industry in 1987, but major reforms were implemented in the mid-1990s.
2. For an overview of U.S. reforms, see William W. Hogan, "Electricity Market Restructuring: Reform of Reforms," *Journal of Regulatory Economics* 21, no. 1 (2002): 103–132.
3. Larry E. Ruff, "Competitive Electricity Markets: Why They Are Working and How to Improve Them," NERA (National Economic Research Associates), May 12, 1999, pp. 9–10.
4. The old integrated utilities had been required to divest themselves of half of their generating capacity, and they had complied by selling most of their fossil fuel plants. For a more complete description of the California reforms and the subsequent crisis, see Paul L. Joskow, "California's Electricity Reforms," Massachusetts Institute of Technology, September 28, 2001.
5. The stranded assets included nuclear power plants and long-term contracts for power generated from environmentally friendly but expensive sources, such as wind farms.
6. See Catherine D. Wolfman, "Measuring Duopoly Power in the British Electricity Spot Market," *American Economic Review* 89 (1999): 805–826; and Catherine D. Wolfman, "Strategic Bidding in a Multiunit Auction: An Empirical

Analysis of Bids to Supply Electricity in England and Wales," *Rand Journal of Economics* 29 (1998): 703–725.

7. For descriptions of the British and Chilean systems, see David M. Newbery, "Privatization and Liberalization of Network Utilities," *European Economic Review* 41 (1997): 357–383; and Hugh Rudnick, Rodrigo Palma, and José E. Fernández, "Marginal Cost Pricing and Supplemental Cost Allocation in Transmission Open Access," *IEEE Transactions on Power Systems* 10, no. 2 (May 1995): 1125–1138.

8. This advantage of high-voltage lines is offset in part by the need for more expensive substations to increase the voltage where power is inserted in the transmission system and to step down the voltage where it is withdrawn.

9. Ruff, "Competitive Electricity Markets," pp. 8–9.

10. For a more extended description of Argentina's electricity reforms and their origins, see Carlos Manuel Bastos and Manuel Angel Abdala, *Reform of the Electric Power Sector in Argentina* (Buenos Aires: n.p., 1996); and Fundación de Investigaciónes Económicas Latinoamericanos (FIEL), "La Regulación del Sector Eléctrico," in *La Regulación de la Competencia y de los Servicios Públicos: Teoría y Experiencia Argentina Reciente* (Buenos Aires: FIEL, 1999), pp. 467–533. Some of the description of the Argentine reforms presented here originally appeared in greater length in a series of teaching cases on Transener, the high-voltage transmission company; see José A. Gómez-Ibáñez and Martín Rodríguez-Pardina, *Transener (A): The Electricity Industry and the Wholesale Power Market; Transener (B): The First Tariff Review; Transener (B): Sequel;* and *Transener (C): Expanding Transmission Capacity,* case nos. 1635, 1636, and 1637, Case Program, Kennedy School of Government, Harvard University, 1999.

11. The division of responsibilities between the provincial and national governments evolved gradually. Many of the less-populated provinces did not assume responsibility for their electricity distribution companies until the early 1980s.

12. These government-owned nuclear power plants and dams collectively supplied about one-third of the power to the wholesale market. For dispatching and other purposes they were treated the same as private generators.

13. By early 1999 eight of the twenty-two provincial distribution companies still remained in public hands; FIEL, "La Regulación del Sector Eléctrico."

14. CAMMESA–Compañia Administradora del Mercado Mayorista Eléctrico Sociedad Anonima.

15. A seventh private transmission company operated a new 800-kilometer 500-kV line connecting the big Yacyretá dam with the Buenos Aires region. In addition, a public company operated transmission lines in the Patagonia network, which was isolated from the national grid.

16. ENRE–Ente Nacional Regulador de la Electricidad.

17. The reductions were generally not as large as those in the spot market, because many of the large industrial customers bought part of their electricity on long-term contracts. See FIEL, "La Regulación del Sector Eléctrico," pp. 482–483.

18. Ibid., p. 482.

19. Ibid., p. 469.

20. The blackout left 150,000 customers without service for eleven days. ENRE required the distribution company to pay US$79 million in fines and compensation to customers.

21. Price and demand data from Federico Mateos, "Análisis de la Evolución del Precio en el Mercado Eléctrico Mayorista de la República Argentina entre 1992 y 1997," Discussion Paper no. 6, Centro de Estudios Económicos de la Regulación, Universidad de Argentina de la Empresa, Buenos Aires, May 1999, pp. 13, 26.

22. Ibid., pp. 8, 26; and FIEL, "La Regulación del Sector Eléctrico," pp. 481–482.

23. The electric system is actually divided into nine regions. For the purposes of this chapter, three regions that are right next to each other—the Greater Buenos Aires metropolitan area, the rest of Buenos Aires Province, and the Litoral region immediately north of Buenos Aires—have been consolidated into a single region which we call Buenos Aires.

24. Nodal pricing to dispatch electricity was developed by F. C. Schweppe, M. C. Caramanis, R. D. Tabors, and R. E. Bohn in *Spot Pricing of Electricity* (Norwell, Mass.: Kluwer, 1988). Of the other early pioneers in electricity restructuring, Chile adopted nodal prices but Britain did not.

25. Another simplifying assumption was that CAMMESA ran the simulations for only a single base pattern of demand. In reality the locations from which power would be dispatched would vary with the system load. For a more complete description of the nodal pricing system, see Gómez-Ibáñez and Rodríguez-Pardina, *Transener (A)*.

26. If Buenos Aires generators were available and not dispatched, it was often because they were very high marginal cost and were serving as standby for emergencies.

27. To simplify the exposition this paragraph is written as if CAMMESA buys and sells wholesale power on behalf of consumers and generators. In fact CAMMESA neither buys nor sells power directly, but it serves as the clearinghouse for the payments from wholesale customers and to generators.

28. The concessionaire would pay Transener a fee equal to 3 percent of total construction costs during the construction period, 4 percent of transmission revenues during the fifteen-year amortization period, and 2.5 percent of transmission revenues thereafter. For more on the division of responsibilities and fees see Bastos and Abdala, *Reform,* pp. 188–189.

29. The process used the same CAMMESA simulation model. For a description, see Omar O. Chisari, Pedro Dal Bó, and Carlos Romero, "High Tension Electricity Network Expansions in Argentina: Decision Mechanisms and Willingness to Pay Revelation," Centro de Estudios Económicos de la Regulación, Universidad Argentina de la Empresa, Buenos Aires, 1998; or see Gómez-Ibáñez and Rodríguez-Pardina, *Transener (C),* p. 7n13.

30. This meant that CAMMESA had to recalculate participation every year, since the users of a line might change.

31. These criticisms are drawn in part from Chisari, Dal Bó, and Romero, "High Tension Electricity Network Expansions in Argentina." See also Kent Anderson, Sally Hunt, Mathie Parmesano, Graham Shuttleworth, and Stephen Powel,

"Analysis of the Reform of the Argentine Power Sector: Final Report," report prepared by National Economic Research Associates (NERA) for the Secretary of Energy of the Argentine Ministry of Economy and Public Works, January 1998, pp. 58–68.

32. An example was the generators along the route between Comahue and Buenos Aires. These generators had higher marginal costs than the Comahue generators. They were often dispatched even when the Comahue–Buenos Aires lines were not operating at capacity, however, because inserting power at intermediate points helps stabilize the flow on long-distance transmission lines. The fourth line might not affect the number of hours these generators were dispatched, but it would decrease their revenues (by reducing the nodal prices outside of Comahue) and increase their costs (since they would be liable for a portion of the fourth line's construction costs).

33. If the diversion caused a shortfall, ENRE was obligated to increase Transener's capacity or connection charges to compensate.

34. ENRE selected Transener as the low bidder on October 27, 1997, and Transener signed the contract with the petitioners (Grupo de Generadores de Energía Eléctrica del Area de Comahue) on November 12, 1997. The contract provided for a twenty-three-month construction period.

35. The surplus fund accounts could be used to fund a maximum of 70 percent of the costs of a new line, so that users would have to pay a minimum of 30 percent.

36. The Secretariat called its proposed TCCs "rights to congestion revenues"; see Subsecretaría de Energía, "Primer Borrador, Ajustes Regulatoros para Incentivar la Eficiencia en el MEM, Transporte y Generación Forzada," October 2, 1998. The proposal was based in part on the earlier study by the consulting firm NERA; see Anderson et al., "Analysis of the Reform of the Argentine Power Sector."

37. For a more detailed description of TCCs by the originator of the concept, see William W. Hogan, "Contract Networks for Electric Power Transmission," *Journal of Regulatory Economics* 4, no. 3 (1992): 211–242; and Hogan, "Transmission Investment and Competitive Electricity Markets," Center for Business and Government, Kennedy School of Government, Harvard University, 1999.

38. Conversely, a Buenos Aires consumer might want to buy a TCC for Comahue to Buenos Aires in order to protect itself from the increase in Buenos Aires prices that would occur when Comahue was isolated.

39. Hogan, "Transmission Investment," p. 34.

40. The proposal provided for a biennial auction of the TCCs in which the incumbent owners would participate. If the incumbents bid the most, they would retain the rights. If the incumbents were outbid, they would lose the rights but receive the proceeds of the auction as compensation.

41. The original three methods could still be used as well.

42. In this first auction the initiating investors and any other interested parties submitted sealed bids for the capacity rights. The bid would specify the proportion of the line's construction cost the bidder wanted to assume and the average percentage of the total capacity of the line the bidder believed would be utilized

during the fifteen-year amortization period. ENRE would rank the bids in descending order of expected capacity utilization and then go down the list until 100 percent of the construction cost was covered. The expected capacity utilization of the last bid accepted would be used later in calculating the remuneration of the investors. The expected utilization had to be at least 70 percent. If the bids received did not cover 100 percent of the construction cost, the government could decide to finance as much as 30 percent using the funds accumulating in its congestion revenue surplus accounts.

43. Before the accounts were established, the users effectively received any surpluses caused by transmission constraints in their corridor in the form of a rebate on their transmission connection or capacity charges.

44. The concessionaire for the new line also would be allowed to recover operating and maintenance costs through line-loss, connection, and line-capacity fees, just as Transener did.

45. If investors believed that their projected TCC revenues and construction tolls would provide a return higher than what was needed to finance construction, then they would be tempted to bid a higher projected line utilization than they actually expected in order to win the investment rights. The higher line utilization would reduce the toll they were allowed to charge, since the toll was the payment the investors owed to the COM concessionaire multiplied by the ratio of actual to expected line use.

46. This assumes that the transmission owners receive only the nodal price differences and cannot price discriminate.

47. For a description of these fines, see Bastos and Abdala, *Reform of the Electric Power Sector*, pp. 187–188, 192–196; and Ente Nacional Regulador de la Electricidad, *El Informe Eléctrico: Cinco Años de la Regulación y Control, 1993—Abril—1998* (Buenos Aires: ENRE, 1999), pp. 17–18, 21–26.

13. The Prospects for Unbundling

1. Long-distance gas transmission may be subject to competition as well in some cases, although normally the strong economies of scale in pipeline construction make transmission a natural monopoly. In some regions such as the northeastern United States, however, the density of demand is high enough to support competition among long-distance pipelines.

2. In 1997 the average residential and industrial tariffs were $89.40 and $55 per megawatt-hour, while the wholesale price of electricity was roughly $20 per megawatt-hour. Given the mix of industrial and residential consumption, these figures imply that wholesale prices received by generators accounted for about 33 percent of delivered electricity costs. In 1992, just when the reforms were beginning, wholesale prices had been about $49 per megawatt-hour, but residential and industrial tariffs were roughly 20 and 10 percent higher than they were in 1997. These figures suggest that generation was approximately 60 percent of delivered prices. Retail prices for 1992 and 1997 are from Ente Nacional Regulador de la Electricidad (ENRE), *El Informe Eléctrico: Cinco Años de la Regulación y Control, 1993—Abril—1998* (Buenos Aires: ENRE, 1999),

pp. 22–23. Wholesale prices are from Fundación de Investigaciones Económicas Latinoamericanos (FIEL), "La Regulación del Sector Eléctrico," in *La Regulación de la Competencia y de los Servicios Publicos: Teoría y Experiencia Argentina Reciente* (Buenos Aires: FIEL, 1999), p. 482.

3. The British electricity regulator capped wholesale power prices at between 2.4 and 2.55 pence per KW-hour in the mid-1990s at a time when the retail prices varied from about 3.5 pence per KW-hour for large manufacturers to 6 pence per KW-hour for small manufacturers; see Colin Robinson, "Profit Discovery and the Role of Entry: The Case of Electricity," in *Regulating Utilities: A Time for Change?* ed. Michael E. Beesley, Readings no. 44 (London: Institute of Economic Affairs, 1996) pp. 127, 129.

4. Stephen Glaister, "Trading and Competition in Gas," in *Regulating Utilities: Broadening the Debate,* ed. Michael E. Beesley, Readings no. 46 (London: Institute of Economic Affairs, 1997), p. 192.

5. From 1995 average prices as reported in U.S. Department of Energy, Energy Information Administration, *Natural Gas 1996: Issues and Trends* (Washington, D.C.: Energy Information Administration, 1996), p. 100.

6. For an account of the British attempt to encourage competition in bulk water supplies, see Colin Robinson, "Introducing Competition into Water," in *Regulating Utilities: Broadening the Debate,* ed. Beesley, pp. 153–187.

7. In fiscal year 1997/98, for example, the TOCs received £4.65 billion in revenues, of which £2.13 billion was paid to Railtrack for access and other charges and the balance was used to cover payments to ROSCOs, the TOCs' direct train operating costs, and profits. Figures from a presentation by Railtrack chief executive Gerald Corbett to the Oxford Economic Research Associates (OXERA) seminar on the role of the Strategic Rail Authority, February 2, 1999.

8. According to unpublished American Association of Railroad figures supplied by Lou Thompson of the World Bank, infrastructure accounts for roughly 20 percent of total expenditures for U.S. freight railroads. Britain's freight TOCs do not provide a very helpful source of data since the rail regulator's policy has been to allocate most of Railtrack's infrastructure costs to the passenger TOCs and charge the freight TOCs only the incremental costs of their use of the track.

9. Figures are for 1992; see Robert W. Crandall and Leonard Waverman, *Talk Is Cheap: The Promise of Regulatory Reform in North American Telecommunications* (Washington, D.C.: Brookings Institution, 1995), p. 28.

10. See, for example, U.S. Department of Energy, Energy Information Administration, *Natural Gas 1998: Issues and Trends* (Washington, D.C.: Energy Information Administration, 1998), esp. chaps. 3 and 4.

11. In Argentina, Transener, the main high-voltage transmission company, has approximately $100 million in annual revenues compared with final electricity sales of roughly $4 billion per year (55 million MW-hours at an average price of roughly $75 per MW-hour). High-voltage transmission may account for an unusually high share of electricity costs in Argentina, because the country's main generating regions are located far from its main consumption centers. However, Transener is not the only transmission company in Argentina: there is another smaller high-voltage transmission company and several smaller medium-voltage

regional transmission companies as well. More important, Argentina's reported transmission expenses probably understate the true long-run costs, because the country's transmission companies have not been allowed to recover the investments made in transmission lines before the privatization of the industry. Argentina's transmission access charges are intended to recover maintenance and operating costs plus the costs of improvements since the industry was restructured. If the costs of building the prereform transmission system were included as well, the access charges might be several times their reported level. In the 1998 tariff review, the industry's regulators placed a value of around $275 million on Transener's asset base for tariff-setting purposes, but the replacement cost of the transmission system was estimated at $2,250 million. For a more complete discussion of the regulator's treatment of Transener's capital costs, see José A. Gómez-Ibáñez and Martín Rodríguez-Pardina, *Transener (B): The First Tariff Review* and *Transener (B): Sequel,* case nos. 1635, 1636, Case Program, Kennedy School of Government, Harvard University, 1999; and ENRE, Staff for Regulatory Analysis and Special Studies, *Expte. ENRE No. 4689/98—Informe Final de Elevación,* report to the Commissioners, November 1998.

12. In the United States in 1995, the average price paid by customers of local distribution companies was $5.06 per thousand cubic feet, the average price paid by electric utilities (who buy almost all their gas wholesale, bypassing the local distribution companies) was $2.02 per thousand cubic feet, the average city gate price at which the local distribution companies buy their gas was $2.78 per thousand cubic feet and the average well head price was $1.55 per thousand cubic feet. This implies that pipeline transportation accounted for roughly $1.23 per thousand cubic feet ($2.78 − $1.55), or 24 percent of the price paid by the customers of local distribution companies, and for roughly $0.47 per thousand cubic feet ($2.02 − $1.55), or 23 percent of the prices paid by electric utilities. Electric utilities pay less per cubic foot for pipeline transportation than local distribution company customers, both because the utilities that burn gas tend to be closer to the well heads and because their gas consumption does not increase as much during the seasonal heating peak so they pay less for basic pipeline capacity. Figures calculated from data in U.S. Department of Energy, Energy Information Administration, *Natural Gas 1996: Issues and Trends* (Washington, D.C.: Energy Information Administration, 1996), p. 100.

13. Christian Wolmar, *Broken Rails: How Privatization Wrecked Britain's Railways* (London: Aurum Press, 2001), p. 61.

14. M. C. A. Nash, "The British Experience," in European Conference of Ministers of Transport, *Separation of Operations and Infrastructure in the Provision of Railway Services* (Paris: Organization for Economic Cooperation and Development, 1997), p. 73.

15. The Internet is an exception, in that routers will automatically choose an alternate route if the connecting router that is their normal first choice is busy or out of service.

16. See, for example, Alfred E. Kahn, *Letting Go: Deregulating the Process of Deregulation* (East Lansing: Michigan State University, Institute of Public Utilities and Network Industries, 1998).

14. The Future of Regulation

1. Ray Vernon made this argument in the context of multinational corporations and their relationship with developing countries, but it applies as well to private utilities. For his original idea of an "obsolescing bargain," see Raymond Vernon, *Sovereignty at Bay: The Multinational Spread of U.S. Enterprises* (New York: Basic Books, 1971). For the extension of the idea to infrastructure, see Louis T. Wells, "Is Private Investment in Infrastructure Risky?" *Harvard Business Review,* August–September 1995, pp. 44–55. Vernon's last book, which updated and developed the theme, was *In the Hurricane's Eye: The Troubled Prospects of Multinational Enterprises* (Cambridge: Harvard University Press, 1998).

2. See the brief summary of institutional research applied to regulation in Chapter 3.

3. For a more detailed account of the Mexican toll road program and the effects of the December 1994 devaluation and the subsequent recession, see José A. Gómez-Ibáñez, *Mexico's Private Toll Road Program,* case no. C15-97-1402, Case Program, Kennedy School of Government, Harvard University, 1997.

4. Another example is the Argentine system of awarding separate concessions for the construction of new high-voltage transmission lines, described in Chapter 12.

5. The Argentine system is described in Fundación de Investigacíones Económicas Latinoamericanas (FIEL), *La Regulación de la Competencia y de los Servicios Públicos: Teoría y Experiencia Argentina Reciente* (Buenos Aires: FIEL, 1999).

6. Eduardo Engle, Ronald Fischer, and Alexander Galetovic, "Highway Franchising: Pitfalls and Opportunities," *American Economic Review* 87, no. 2 (May 1997): 68–72; and Andrés Gómez-Lobo and Sergio Hinojosa, "Broad Roads in a Thin Country: Infrastructure Concessions in Chile," Policy Research Working Paper no. 2279, Institute for Economic Development, World Bank, January 2000.

7. The least present value scheme provides a call option, and what is needed is a put option to match. One possibility is to allow the concessionaire to insist on a buyout for a discount off his least present value bid.

8. José A. Gómez-Ibáñez, *Bangkok's Second Stage Expressway,* case no. C15-97-1401.0, Case Program, Kennedy School of Government, Harvard University, 1997.

9. The characterization of international arbitration as robbery is a quote from an Egyptian official by Eric Schwartz and Jan Paulsson. Schwartz and Paulsson provide an excellent review of the changing attitudes and experience with international arbitration; see Eric Schwartz and Jan Paulsson, "Confronting Political and Regulatory Risks Associated with Private Investment in Infrastructure in Developing Countries: The Role of International Dispute Mechanisms," paper presented at the Conference on Private Infrastructure for Development: Confronting the Political and Regulatory Risks, September 1999, Rome, Italy, esp. pp. 4–5; available at http//www.worldbank.org/html/fpd/risk/papers.htm.

10. For an overview of final-offer arbitration, see Howard Raiffa, *The Art and Science of Negotiation* (Cambridge: Harvard University Press, 1982), pp. 110–118,

217; or Howard Raiffa, with John Richardson and David Metcalfe, *Negotiation Analysis: The Science and Art of Collaborative Decision Making* (Cambridge: Harvard University Press, 2002), pp. 331–333, 342–347.

11. For some interesting observations about the problems of organizing such an effort, see Ronald A. Heifitz, *Leadership without Easy Answers* (Cambridge: Harvard University Press, 1994).

12. For an accessible summary of their ideas, see Jean-Jacques Laffont and Jean Tirole, *Competition in Telecommunications* (Cambridge: MIT Press, 2000), pp. 37–42, 51–60. For a more complete and formal treatment, see Jean-Jacques Laffont and Jean Tirole, *A Theory of Incentives in Regulation and Procurement* (Cambridge: MIT Press, 1993).

13. The main exception is in electricity, where distribution companies are often allowed to pass through their wholesale power costs not subject to the cap.

14. See Chapters 6 and 7 for discussions of municipal leadership in disputes in the late nineteenth century and the first half of the twentieth century. For more recent disputes involving subnational governments, see Louis T. Wells, Jr., "Private Foreign Investment in Infrastructure: Managing Non-commercial Risk," paper presented at the Conference on Private Infrastructure for Development: Confronting the Political and Regulatory Risks, September 1999, Rome, Italy, pp. 6–7; available at http//www.worldbank.org/html/fpd/risk/papers.htm.

15. For example, Ilka Lewington, "Experiences and Trends in Utility Regulation: Developing and Transforming Economies," *Regulatory Review 1997* (London: Center for the Study of Regulated Industries, 1998), pp. 133–158.

16. This account of the Chilean regulatory systems for electricity and telephones is drawn partly from interviews but primarily from Eduardo Bitran, António Esatche, José Luis Guasch, and Pablo Sera, "Privatizing and Regulating Chile's Utilities: Successes, Failures, and Outstanding Challenges," draft, World Bank, December 1997; Ahmed Galal, "Chile: Regulatory Specificity, Credibility of Commitment, and Distributional Demands," in *Regulations, Institutions, and Commitment: Comparative Studies of Telecommunications,* ed. Brian Levy and Pablo T. Spiller (Cambridge: Cambridge University Press, 1996), pp. 121–144; and Eduardo Bitran and Raúl E. Sáez, "Privatization and Regulation in Chile," in *The Chilean Economy: Policy Lessons and Challenges,* ed. Barry P. Bosworth, Rudiger Dornbusch, and Raul Labán (Washington, D.C.: Brookings Institution, 1994), pp. 329–377.

17. The decisions can be appealed to an independent antitrust commission on the grounds that they do not foster competition and to the courts on the grounds that they are inconsistent with the regulatory statute.

18. The first version of the telephone regulatory law, passed in 1982, did not have specific provisions for rate regulation, because its drafters believed that there would be enough competition among the privatized telephone companies to make price regulation unnecessary. The incumbent telephone company recognized that rates were politically sensitive, however, and consulted with the regulator about rate changes anyway. It was not until 1987 that the new law was amended to require rate regulation and specify the procedure in detail. Bitran et al., "Privatizing and Regulating Chile's Utilities," p. 22.

19. Chile's regulated electricity distribution companies were earning returns of 30 percent, for example, while the unregulated electricity generators were earning only 15 percent. Similarly, the regulated local telephone companies were earning 16.9 percent while the unregulated long-distance companies earned 8.4 percent. Bitran et al., "Privatizing and Regulating Chile's Utilities," p. 7.

20. These products and their effects are described in Nina Bubnova, "Guarantees and Insurance for Re-allocating and Mitigating Political and Regulatory Risks in Infrastructure Investment: Market Analysis," paper presented at the Conference on Private Infrastructure for Development: Confronting the Political and Regulatory Risks, September 1999, Rome, Italy, available at http//www.worldbank.org/html/fpd/risk/papers.htm.

Index